CHILDREN
ON
PLAYGROUNDS

SUNY Series, Children's Play in Society

Anthony D. Pellegrini, EDITOR

CHILDREN ON PLAYGROUNDS

Research Perspectives and Applications

Edited by

Craig H. Hart

State University of New York Press

Published by
State University of New York Press, Albany

© 1993 State University of New York

For information, address State University of New York Press,
State University Plaza, Albany, N.Y., 12246

Production by Marilyn Semerad
Marketing by Lynne Lekakis

Library of Congress Cataloging-in-Publication Data

Children on playgrounds : research perspectives and applications /
    edited by Craig H. Hart.
        p.   cm. — (SUNY series, children's play in society)
    Includes bibliographical references and index.
    ISBN 0-7914-1467-1. — ISBN 0-7914-1468-X (pbk.)
    1. Outdoor recreation for children. 2. Playgrounds—Social
aspects. 3. Child development. 4. Social interaction in children.
    I. Hart, Craig H., 1957— . II. Series.
GV191.63.C47   1993
796.5—dc20   92-21057
                                                                   CIP

                          10 9 8 7 6 5 4 3 2 1

*To my colleagues at Louisiana State University
and to my family,
Kerstine, David, Ryan, Sarah, and Kacie*

CONTENTS

FOREWORD
An Inside Look At the Outside

What children do on playgrounds is incredibly understudied. This statement is noted in one form or another in every chapter in this volume. That a phenomenon is understudied is certainly not reason enough to study it but, as most of the authors in this volume note, children's playground behavior has important implications for their development.

First, children spend lots of time on the playground. For example, in most elementary schools in the United States and Britain, children spend as much time, or more, on the playground than they do in instructional groups. The amount of time children spend on the playground at recess is not reflected on coherent school policy towards recess or empirical research on the topic.

Second, and again in school settings, recess time on the playground is one of the few times that children can choose a peer with whom to interact and can interact with him and/or her around a topic of their choice. Most of the school day children are expected to minimally interact with peers and when they are allowed to do so, it is typically around predetermined topics. Current knowledge on the ways children become socially competent suggests that opportunities to interact with peers plays a crucial role.

The information included in this volume will help correct these omissions. Hopefully the interdisciplinary approach to the study of children on playgrounds that has been brought to bare here will be used by researchers, educators, and policymakers to more extensively study children in this setting. The need for systematic study is certainly being expressed by parents of school-age children as well as educators. As an indicator of popular concern, the *New York Times* (January 8, 1989) ran an editorial on the role of recess in elementary school. Many parents and educators are expressing diverse opinions on the place in the school curriculum of recess on the playground.

While the present volume goes a long way towards answering some of these questions, such as the amount of bullying and aggression that occurs, a number of other basic issues still need to be addressed empirically. For example, what are some optimal points during the school day for children of different ages to have playground periods? Relatedly, what are the differential effects on children's behavior and subsequent in-class behavior of different recess configurations? While these questions are beginning to be addressed in the literature (Pellegrini and Huberty, in press; Smith and Hagan, 1980), much more systematic study of this issue is needed. Educators and parents are eager for that sort of information which can be used to help them make informed decisions.

REFERENCES

Pellegrini, A. D., and Huberty, P. D. (in press). Effects on classroom and playground behavior. *British Journal of Educational Psychology.*

Smith, P. K., and Hagan, T. (1980). Effects of deprivation on exercise play in nursery school children. *Animal Behavior, 28,* 922–928.

ACKNOWLEDGMENTS

Appreciation is extended to many who worked behind the scenes to help pull this volume together. The insightful comments of Michele DeWolf, Karen Manuel, and Jeanette Ray were most helpful in the editing process. Their attention to detail and suggestions for improving readability greatly enhanced many of the chapters in this volume. Likewise, suggestions from the blind reviewers selected by SUNY Press were very useful in the editing process. Glenna Simmons also provided much needed technical support in terms of putting several of the chapters on disk for easy editing. Her help was most appreciated. In addition, Janice Robinson spent countless hours pulling the subject and author indexes together. Her competence and familiarity with terminology in the field helped make the subject index most workable for researchers and practitioners who are looking to find information quickly.

Neva Nolen (Director of the School of Human Ecology at Louisiana State University) and Terrance Olson (Chair of the Department of Family Sciences at Brigham Young University) also deserve special recognition for their unwavering support of this project. Without the provision of resources for the countless long distance phone calls, mailings, and other needs, this volume would not have been possible. The photography for the cover and other pages of the volume by Mark Philbrick was also a tremendous contribution.

It was a pleasure to work with Priscilla Ross and Marilyn Semerad at SUNY Press. Their congeniality, encouragement, flexibility, and commitment to this project made it a worthwhile and fulfilling endeavor. Last, but certainly not least, appreciation is extended to each of the authors (and to their research subjects), all of whom gave much to make playground interactions more understandable.

LIST OF CONTRIBUTORS

Steven R. Asher, Professor
Bureau of Educational Research
University of Illinois
1310 South Sixth Street
Champaign, IL 61820

Kathryn M. Borman, Associate Dean
Graduate Education and Research
College of Education
Mail Location #2
University of Cincinnati
Cincinnati, OH 45221

Michael J. Boulton, Senior Lecturer
Psychology Section
School of Health and Community Studies
Sheffield Hallam University
40 Collegiate Crescent
Sheffield S10 2BP
UK

Diane C. Burts, Associate Professor
Family, Child, and Consumer Sciences
School of Human Ecology
Louisiana State University
Baton Rouge, LA 70803

Michele DeWolf, Research Associate
Family, Child, and Consumer Sciences
School of Human Ecology
Louisiana State University
Baton Rouge, LA 70803

Sonda W. Gabriel, Visiting Research Associate
Bureau of Educational Research
University of Illinois
1310 South Sixth Street
Champaign, IL 61820

Amanda W. Harrist, Assistant Professor
Dept. of Educational Psychology
University of Texas
Education Building 504
Austin, TX 78712-1296

Craig H. Hart, Associate Professor
Dept. of Family Sciences
1000 SWKT
Brigham Young University
Provo, Utah 84602

Lynn Hartle, Assistant Professor
College of Education
University of Florida
Dept. of Instruction and Curriculum
258 Norman Hall
Gainesville, FL 32611-2053

Willard W. Hartup, Professor
Institute of Child Development
University of Minnesota
51 E River Road
Minneapolis, MN 55455

Sue Hernandez, Adjunct Professor
College of Education
University of Houston, Clear Lake
2700 Bay Area Blvd.
Houston, TX 77058

James E. Johnson, Associate Professor
157 Chambers Building
The Pennsylvania State University
University Park, State College, PA 16802

Gary W. Ladd, Professor
Children's Research Center
University of Illinois at Urbana-Champaign
51 Gerty Drive
Champaign, IL 61820

Chester H. Laine, Associate Professor
Dept. of Curriculum and Instruction
College of Education
Mail Location #2
University of Cincinnati
Cincinnati, OH 45221

Brett Laursen, Assistant Professor
Dept. of Psychology
Florida Atlantic University
2912 College Avenue
Ft. Lauderdale, FL 33314

Denis S. Lowe, Executive Director
Barbara J. Duncan Family Services Clinic
3212 Woodburn Avenue
Cincinnati, Ohio 45207

Keith Marchessault, Research Associate
Centre for Research in Human Development
Concordia University
1455 de Maisonneuve Blvd., West
Montreal, Quebec, Canada H3G 1M8

Valerie McAffer, Instructor
Douglas College
P. O. Box 2503
New Westminister, British Columbia, Canada V3L 5B2

Lea McGee, Associate Professor
School of Education
Campion Hall
Boston College
Chestnut Hill, MA 02167-3813

Patricia Peters, Doctoral Student
Centre for Research in Human Development
Concordia University
1455 de Maisonneuve Blvd., West
Montreal, Quebec, Canada H3G 1M8

Anthony D. Pellegrini, Professor
425 Aderhold Hall
University of Georgia
Athens, GA 30602

Gregory S. Pettit, Associate Professor
Dept. of Family and Child Development
School of Human Sciences
Auburn University
Auburn, AL 36849-5604

Joseph M. Price, Associate Professor
Dept. of Psychology
6363 Alvarado Court
Suite 103
San Diego State University
San Diego, CA 92120

Dan Olweus, Professor
University of Bergen
Department of Personality Psychology
Oysteinfgate 3
N-5000 Bergen, Norway

Becky L. Reimer
Academic Support Counselor
Rowland Hall-St. Mark's School
843 Lincoln Street
Salt Lake City, UT 84102

Alex E. Schwartzman, Professor
Centre for Research in Human Development
Concordia University
1455 de Maisonneuve Blvd., West
Montreal, Quebec, Canada H3G 1M8

Lisa A. Serbin, Professor
Centre for Research in Human Development
Concordia University
1455 de Maisonneuve Blvd., West
Montreal, Quebec, Canada H3G 1M8

Peter K. Smith, Professor
Department of Psychology
University of Sheffield
Sheffield S10 2TN, England

1

CRAIG H. HART _____

INTRODUCTION:
Toward a Further Understanding of Children's Development on Playgrounds

The purpose of this volume is to provide a collection of research and review papers that shed light on practical and empirical child developmental issues in the context of outdoor play environments.[1] Although there has been a long history of studying children in many different settings (e.g., the home, the classroom), the playground is just beginning to be viewed as an important context for development that warrants further investigation (see Bloch and Pellegrini, 1989; Boulton and Smith, 1989; Frost, 1992; Hart and Sheehan, 1986; Ladd, Price, and Hart, 1990; Pellegrini, 1987; in press; Rubin, Fein, and Vandenberg, 1983). As many authors in this volume suggest, relative to other contexts, playgrounds are outdoor environments where children have more freedom to interact in ways that are largely independent of adult-imposed constraints (see Chapters 3, 5, and 8, this volume). Such environments allow researchers and practitioners the opportunity to explore child behavior and development as it naturally evolves in the context of minimal adult supervision.

This volume should be of particular interest to both researchers and practitioners who work with preschool and school-age children because there is currently no organized body of literature that explores children's behavior and development in outdoor play contexts. Contributors to this volume from Canada, Norway, the United Kingdom, and the United States are researchers and practitioners who share an interest in bringing this literature together and in generating new knowledge. This book represents a beginning to this endeavor.

IMPORTANCE OF PLAYGROUND SETTINGS

Since many advocate the reduction of recess periods and playground time during the school day, it is important to consider the

1

developmental significance that playground experiences may play in children's lives (Pellegrini, 1991, in press). Children spend a substantial portion of their day in outdoor play environments, whether it be in the neighborhood, home, or school. As Pellegrini (1987) points out, in addition to neighborhood and home outdoor play, many children at school spend as much time in specific instructional activities, such as reading, as they do on the playground (35 to 45 minutes per day).

There is a general consensus among many developmentalists and educators that play experiences are influenced by the context in which play occurs (e.g., Christie and Johnsen 1987; Pepler 1987; Smith and Connolly, 1980). From a historical perspective, there has been the continuing debate over which type of play environments are best for children—those that are child-generated and child-controlled versus those that are regulated and supervised by adults (Finkelstein, 1987). Although the answer may lie somewhere in between, there is evidence suggesting that child-generated play serves an important developmental function.

After reviewing several studies focusing on children's play in more and less structured adult-guided situations, King (1987) concluded that the relatively unconstrained environments provided by playgrounds offer children opportunities to create, organize, and control their own play experiences. This allows them to not only learn and practice important social skills but also to exercise decision-making and other practical skills that will be used across the life span. Although adult-directed and/or contrived activities serve many important functions, King argues that child-guided activities are not as readily available in settings that are more tightly regulated by adults, such as the classroom. Indeed, Hartle and Johnson (Chapter 2, this volume) show how varying playground activities can be an important facilitator of learning and development in all of the developmental domains.

Since much of outdoor behavior involves interactions with peers, much of the research and applications presented in this volume is focused on children's social development and peer relationships (e.g., bullies on the playground, conflict, normative playground behaviors, child observational methodologies, play styles of accepted and rejected children). Several chapters are also devoted to discussing ways that outdoor play environments promote cognitive and literacy development in a narrative context.

Specific attention is also given to ways that outdoor play environments are extensions of other developmental settings including the family and classroom. Because the chapters in this volume provide foundational information necessary for discussing what is known about children on playgrounds, the integration of this and other relevant literature will be presented in the concluding chapter of this volume. This will allow the reader to first become familiar with the available information presented in each individual chapter before integrating it with prior relevant work.

OVERVIEW OF THIS VOLUME

Much of what is known about children's behavior and development has been derived from research conducted in classroom, laboratory, and home settings. With the exception of studies that are either reviewed or presented in this volume, investigators have seldom studied children's development in the context of the playground.

Diversity of Chapters

Since playground settings are relatively unexplored contexts for children's development, contributors were allowed to take a variety of creative approaches to begin dealing with issues related to this area. Therefore, this volume was *not* designed to present a systematic set of papers reviewing well-developed lines of research in outdoor play environments. Although contributors shared the common goals of integrating current knowledge, generating new knowledge, and providing a springboard for new questions to be answered in future research and practice, the diversity of approaches is reflected in chapters that vary greatly in content, format, and style.

For instance, Chapter 2 by Lynn Hartle and James Johnson is designed to focus on the history of playgrounds and play equipment and the different theories that have shaped the design of playgrounds. Child behavior is presented as a natural outgrowth of varying playground settings. In contrast, other chapters do not directly address ways that varying types of outdoor environments facilitate development. Rather, reviews of research on aspects of children's behavior and development that have been relatively unexplored in outdoor settings are presented (e.g., peer conflict, victimization, friendship, loneliness, social cognition, etc.). These chapters are written with an eye toward providing conceptual and theoretical backdrops for future research, practice, and intervention in outdoor play settings (Chapters 2, 3, and 13, this volume).

Still other chapters integrate both methodological and conceptual issues that have direct bearing on current research exploring children's behavior in outdoor play settings. These chapters feature different techniques for observing children's behavior on playgrounds and new research questions answered by using these techniques. Some of these questions include: How are children's playground behavior and play patterns linked to acceptance or rejection by peers? Does aggressive behavior in outdoor settings have different developmental significance for boys than for girls? Do children's preferences for play companions and activities vary as a function of both race and sex in less structured outdoor playground settings? How does physical running, screaming, and chasing on the playground translate into classroom reading and writing events? How are parenting styles and other familial background factors related to children's behavior in outdoor play settings?

Two of the chapters focusing on research questions using observational methodologies are presented in more technical journal-like formats (Chapters 6 and 8, this volume). Systematic observational techniques are also presented in several other chapters. Authors of these chapters chose to provide more extensive reviews of prior work and to present new data in more traditional book chapter formats (e.g., Chapters 5, 9, and 10, this volume). Examples of ethnographic research (Chapter 11, this volume) and new approaches for observation with audio and/or video recording (Chapters 6 and 7, this volume) are also featured in this volume. It is hoped that this diversity in approaches by different authors and new findings from original research will provide a smorgasbord from which readers can draw from in developing systematic lines of research and practice in outdoor play settings.

Integration of Chapters

The volume was designed to integrate the diversity of these chapters into conceptually similar areas and is divided into five parts. These include history and theory of outdoor play, conflict on playgrounds, playground behaviors and peer relations, family background influences and children's playground behavior, and playground behavior and literacy development.

In Part I, Chapter 2 is written by Lynn Hartle and James Johnson. This chapter is designed to pull together existing literature concerning the history and theory of outdoor play and the effects of varying outdoor play environments. The authors' aim is to acquaint readers with research and theory that facilitate an applied understanding of unique contributions that outdoor play environments make toward enhancing children's physical, social/emotional, and cognitive development. Results of studies conducted in playground settings are considered and interwoven with theories of development and play to create an applied framework for understanding the developmental significance of outdoor play contexts. In addition, a historical overview of different types of outdoor play environments is presented. This overview leads to a review of literature exploring the effects of developmentally appropriate and inappropriate playground design and equipment features on a variety of developmental outcomes. The chapter culminates in a presentation of specific, practical criteria that should be considered in planning optimal outdoor play settings that are safe and developmentally appropriate.

In Part II, two chapters are presented that deal with conflict on playgrounds. Disagreements among children are common in playground settings. How conflicts occur and how they are managed in the relative absence of adult intervention in outdoor play settings has important implications for the development of young children. Willard Hartup and Brett Laursen consider such implications in Chapter 3.

Although conflict is generally viewed in negative terms, Hartup and Laursen describe ways that experiencing conflict facilitates children's development in a variety of domains. They also provide an extensive review of the conflict literature, describing its nature and significance to development. Issues regarding what conflict is and is not, how conflict is resolved in different contexts, and the contextual determinants of conflict are also discussed. These determinants are presented in the contexts of persons (age and sex differences, social reputation), relationships (friends versus nonfriends, siblings versus peers), group arrangements (space and resources, goal structures, and group relations), and activities (when, where, and why conflicts occur in different types of situations). This literature review culminates in a contexual theory of children's conflicts. The theory takes into account differing dynamics of conflict that occur in open settings, such as the playground where children have considerable freedom to select their playmates and activities, and in closed settings, where such selection is limited (e.g., adult-organized games, activities).

In Chapter 4, Dan Olweus considers bully/victim problems. Situations involving bullies and their victims are prominent in playground environments and in other settings. To assist in dealing with these problems, Olweus provides a wealth of information derived from data collected in two recent large-scale studies that were conducted in Norway and Sweden. In this chapter, Olweus describes what bullying is and is not, how frequently bully/victim problems occur, family background and personality characteristics of bullies and victims, and age and sex differences regarding bully/victim problems. He also presents data suggesting that parents and teachers are generally unaware of bully/victim problems and do relatively little to stop them.

Additional data suggest that most bullying occurs on the school playground and that the size of the class or school has little relation to the relative frequency of bully/victim problems. Readers will be interested in ways that supervision practices during recess promote or discourage bullying behavior. The presentation of an intervention program designed to assist bullies and their victims is also very appealing. Its unusual approach and highly positive effects are rare in the intervention literature. Specific, practical guidelines for helping bullies and victims are also presented at the end of the chapter.

The third part of this volume focuses on playground behaviors and peer relations. This section ties in well with the rapidly emerging literature in the field of peer relations (see Berndt and Ladd, 1989, Asher and Coie, 1990). In Chapter 5, Gary Ladd and Joseph Price explore linkages between children's playground behaviors, play patterns, and acceptance or rejection by peers. Their chapter begins with a discussion of why playgrounds are more conducive to studying children's social behavior and development than are other settings. In this context, results of several recent playground studies conducted by the authors and other colleagues are presented. The longitudinal design employed in one of the studies helped to eliminate confounds inherent in past research and allowed the authors to examine whether preschooler's observed playground behavior patterns were a cause or consequence of their acceptance by peers. In addition, this design provided the opportunity to examine the stability of playground behaviors and play patterns over the course of a school year.

Other work presented in this chapter illuminates playground behaviors and play pattern characteristics of kindergarten and school-age children in existing status groups (e.g., popular, average, and rejected). Outcomes for children found to be more prosocial and cooperative as opposed to those who were more aggressive, disruptive, and argumentative or noninteractive with peers are also presented. The authors make an important contribution by carefully distinguishing between reactive and proactive (bullying, instrumental) aggression in their discussion of findings involving linkages between aggression on the playground and peer status. Finally, the authors present interesting speculations that shed light on ways that interpersonal and setting factors, including the availability of companions that vary in age and social status, presence of adults, and size of the play area, may be related to children's playground behaviors and peer status.

Additional information concerning playground behaviors and peer relations is provided in Chapter 6 by Lisa Serbin, Keith Marchessault, Valerie McAffer, Patricia Peters, and Alex Schwartzman. Their aim was to examine normative playground behaviors of fourth and fifth-grade children. As the authors point out, little is known about unstructured free play in naturalistic settings of children over 7 or 8 years of age. Using a unique videotaping methodology and a normally distributed, nonpreselected group of children, the authors present results of two studies that demonstrate a high level of concurrence between peer ratings of aggression and withdrawal and distinct patterns of playground behavior. Interesting sex differences emerged in these patterns indicating that boys' and girls' aggressive behavior may have very different developmental significance. Additional findings indicated that observations of playground behavior provide more detailed information than do teacher or peer ratings in assessing problem behaviors, particularly in identifying internalizing disorders in girls.

With respect to unique observational methodologies that can be used to investigate playground behaviors and peer relations, in Chapter 7 Steve Asher and Sonda Gabriel discuss the strengths and limitations of various observational methodologies for studying children's conversations in playground settings. These methodologies include field notes, audiotape recordings, and audio-videotape recordings. Particular attention is given to an innovative methodology, a wireless transmission system, that facilitates recording children's conversations at a great distance. Asher and Gabriel have used this methodology, along with simultaneous videotaping, to record nonverbal behavior and context. The inclusion of transcripts in their chapter help illustrate the richness of the conversational material that can be collected.

The final chapter in this section (Chapter 8) is written by Michael Boulton and Peter Smith. These authors investigated race and sex as child characteristics that may influence who children select to interact with during free play periods on the playground. Children who participated in their playground observational study were 8–10 years of age and were in mixed race (white, asian) and in mixed sex settings. Findings indicated that children's preferences for play companions and activities varied as a function of both race and sex. Also of interest was the fact that there was little correspondence between children's stated and observed racial preferences based on their playground interaction patterns. These findings suggest that some aspects of peer relations are more reliably assessed using observational methodologies in relatively unconstrained environments, such as the playground.

The fourth part of this volume is concerned with linkages between family background influences and children's playground behavior. Recently, investigators have become increasingly interested in understanding how families influence children's behavior and competence in the peer group. Many have begun to search for mechanisms that link the family and peer domains (see Parke and Ladd, 1992).

To advance this area of inquiry, Gregory Pettit and Amanda Harrist begin Chapter 9 by reviewing patterns of behavior that are related to children's peer competence. These behaviors are presented in the framework of more and less socially competent children's abilities to read social situations and synchronize their social behavior with ongoing peer group interactions. The authors then review literature documenting family influences on children's social development. In this context, persuasive evidence is presented that shows how family interactional styles involving deficiencies in the use of social-contextual cues and the absence of interactional synchrony may bear close resemblance to social cognitive and behavioral deficits found in less socially competent children. Data are then presented based on naturalistic observations of familial interactions at home and observations of children's playground and classroom interactions with peers several months later in kindergarten. Results of their study largely confirmed that variations in children's social competence was significantly related to expected patterns of family interaction.

Chapter 10 focuses on relations involving maternal and paternal disciplinary strategies; children's prosocial, antisocial, disruptive, and socially withdrawn playground behavior, and peer status. In this chapter, Craig Hart, Michele DeWolf, and Diane Burts review the child-rearing literature and suggest possible linkages between maternal and paternal discipline, child playground behavior, and peer competence. The authors suggest that few, if any, studies have been conducted involving disciplinary strategies as related to child free play behaviors in relatively unconstrained environments such as the playground. Moreover, few studies have explored both individual and interactive influences of both maternal and paternal discipline on child behavior and subsequent peer status. Results of a study conducted by the authors with preschool-age children and their parents indicated that maternal and paternal discipline were both similarly related to some aspects of child playground behavior and peer status and differentially related to others. Overall, findings indicated that children do glean playground behavioral orientations that impact upon their peer status, in part, from both mothers and fathers in disciplinary contexts.

The final section in this volume focuses on ways that playground activities stimulate literacy development. These chapters demonstrate that the playground can be a site for transferring literacy events into the classroom and ties in well with the emerging literature on play and early literacy development (Christie, 1991). In Chapter 11, Becky Reimer details her ethnographic study of 5-year-olds that was conducted over a period of one year. As a participant observer, Reimer collected rich data on the playground that lends itself to understanding ways that children's perceptions of their social world are different from adult perceptions of the child's social world. Reimer found that chase games were the most frequently occurring activity on the playground. These games provided mechanisms for social interaction that crossed gender lines. Through a presentation of representative (and entertaining) narratives, she shows how children naturally transferred these physical running, screaming, and chasing activities from the playground into classroom reading and writing events. Practical implications and questions derived from this study are also presented for researchers and teachers.

Chapter 12, written by Kathryn Borman, Chester Laine, and Denis Lowe, focuses on school and gender differences in ways that adolescent soccer players reflect their knowledge of soccer in written explanations. Soccer is a popular playground sport that involves strategy, competition, and cooperation among peers. Few have considered such sports as contributors to literacy development. Borman, Laine, and Lowe demonstrate that there are connections between the two. Textual features explored in their study of students' writing included rules of the game, object of the game, list of positions, explanatory approach, personal benefits, strategies, cooperation, competition, and number of words. The textual analysis of writing produced interesting findings that facilitate an understanding of connections among sport (soccer), writing, gender, and school-related characteristics.

The next chapter in this section (Chapter 13) is written by Craig Hart, Lea McGee, and Sue Hernandez. The purpose of this chapter was to pull together salient themes in the peer relations research literature and to explore whether these themes are reflected in children's literature that focuses on playground interaction. The first part of the chapter is a literature review pertaining to correlates of peer acceptance (e.g., behavior, social cognition, affect, and nonbehavioral child characteristics) and friendship (e.g., friendship formation processes and skills, friendship selection, friendship interactions and maintenance, and functions of friends). The second part of the chapter demonstrates that many of these themes are indeed reflected in children's literature in humorous, touching, and memorable ways. Such literature can be used not only in teaching young children about peer relations but also to provide further impetus for authors to use playground settings more often in the illustration of these themes. Implications for social skills intervention using children's literature are also elaborated upon.

The final chapter in the volume (Chapter 14), designed to briefly pull together and integrate what has been learned from each of the chapters that are presented, also incorporates relevant research. The chapter concludes with ideas and directions for future research and applications in playground settings.

In sum, this volume describes many advances that are being made in our understanding of children's development by using the playground as a naturalistic setting for inquiry. Advances in our understanding of how children's growth and development are enhanced by outdoor play settings is just beginning. Much more innovative research is needed to further address issues and questions raised by contributors to this book. It is hoped that this volume will provide a springboard for future endeavors in this area.

NOTE

1. Playground environments are broadly defined in this volume (see Chapter 13 this volume).

REFERENCES

Asher, S. R., and Coie, J. D. (1990). *Peer rejection in childhood.* New York: Cambridge.

Berndt, T. J., and Ladd, G. W. (1989). *Contributions of peer relationships to children's development.* New York: Wiley.

Bloch, M. N., and Pellegrini, A. D. (1989). Ways of looking at children, context, and play. In M. N. Bloch and A. D. Pellegrini (Eds.), *The ecological context of children's play* (pp. 1–15). Norwood: Ablex Publishing Corporation.

Boulton, M. J., and Smith, P. K. (1989). Issues in the study of children's rough-and-tumble play. In M. N. Bloch and A. D. Pellegrini (Eds.), *The ecological context of children's play* (pp. 57–83). Norwood: Ablex Publishing Corporation.

Christie, J. F. (1991). *Play and early literacy development.* Albany, NY: State University of New York Press.

Christie, J. F., and Johnsen, E. P. (1987). Preschool play. In J. H. Block and N. R. King (Eds.), *School play: A source book* (pp. 109–42). New York: Garland.

Finkelstein, B. (1987). Historical perspectives on children's play in school. In J. H. Block and N. R. King (Eds.), *School play: A source book* (pp. 17–38). New York: Garland.

Frost, J. L. (1992). *Play and playscapes.* Albany, NY: Delmar Publishers.

Hart, C. H., and Sheehan, R. (1986). Preschoolers' play behavior in outdoor environments: Effects of traditional and contemporary playgrounds. *American Educational Research Journal, 23*(4), 668–678.

King, N. R. (1987). Elementary school play: Theory and research. In J. H. Block and N. R. King (Eds.), *School play: A source book* (pp. 143–166). New York: Garland.

Ladd, G. W., Price, J. M., and Hart, C. H. (1990). Preschoolers' behavioral orientations and patterns of peer contact: Predictive of peer status? In S. R. Asher and J. D. Coie (Eds.), *Peer rejection in childhood* (pp. 90–115). New York: Cambridge.

Parke, R. D., and Ladd, G. W. (Eds.) (1992). *Family-peer relationships: Modes of linkage.* Hillsdale, NJ: Erlbaum.

Pellegrini, A. D. (1987). Children on playgrounds: A review of "What's out there." *Children's Environments Quarterly, 4,* 2–7.

———. (in press). Elementary school children's playground behavior: Implications for social cognitive development. *Children's Environment Quarterly.*

———. (1991). Outdoor recess: Is it really necessary? *Principal, 70,* 40.

Pepler, D. J. (1987). Play in schools and schooled in play: A psychological perspective. In J. H. Block and N. R. King (Eds.), *School play: A source book* (pp. 75–108), New York: Garland.

Rubin, K. H., Fein, G., and Vandenberg, B. (1983). Play. In E. M. Hetherington (Ed.) and P. H. Mussen (Series Ed.), *Handbook of child psychology: Vol. 4. Socialization, personality, and social development* (pp. 698–774) New York: Wiley.

Smith, P. K., and Connolly, K. (1980). *The ecology of preschool behavior.* Cambridge: Cambridge University Press.

PART I

HISTORY AND THEORY
OF
OUTDOOR PLAY

2

LYNN HARTLE AND JAMES E. JOHNSON _____

Historical and Contemporary Influences of Outdoor Play Environments

Play, once thought to be the ludicrous and superfluous behavior of the human species has come to be considered by researchers, child development specialists, and educators as an important medium in learning and development (Bergen, 1987; Kelly-Byrne, 1984). An expanded view of environmental influences on play potential (Smith and Connolly, 1980) has led play enthusiasts to study what children do when they are given space to run, more freedom from adult direction, and a range of features in outdoor play settings. Playground behavior is indeed "a many splendored thing," a multivariate construct with numerous interacting antecedent determinants and behavioral and developmental consequences. Whether or how playground behavior in any significant way also "makes the world go around" for the developing child is, however, another problematic question set forth in these pages.

Are there *unique* contributions that outdoor play environments make towards socializing and educating today's children in our country and abroad? If it proves impossible to answer this difficult question, can we at least learn in what ways and for whom playground behavior is a necessary if not sufficient condition of development and well-being in our youth? Seeking answers to these questions is timely and worthwhile for a variety of reasons, including mounting threats to recess periods and playground time during the school day. Hopefully information on early and contemporary theories of play, a review of research conducted on various outdoor environments, and firmly grounded recommendations will prove useful in such debates.

THEORIES THAT HAVE GUIDED PRACTICE

While the early theorists attempted to explain why children play, the contemporary theorists expanded the study of play to

14

include evidence of how humans play across the life span and why children's play may be important for growth and development across all domains—cognitive, social, physical, emotional (Rubin, Fein, and Vandenberg, 1983). The evolution of outdoor play environments reflects these changing views of play (Frost and Klein, 1983).

Early Theories of Play

Early play theorists left their impressions upon the early playground movement in America. One of those was Spencer (1873) who expressed play as the activity that uses up the surplus energy left over after the life-supporting activities are completed. From this perspective, play was considered an uncontrollable desire during childhood. Early playgrounds and even some playgrounds today are environments lacking creative activities, merely places to run around and "blow off steam."

Not adding much to the creative potential of playgrounds was the much different perspective shared by Lazarus (1883) and Patrick (1916). They suggest that play is either a recreational activity or behavior stemming from the need for relaxation. Play was thought to restore or rejuvenate after mentally stressful work and had no cognitive function or content. Hence, schoolchildren were sent out to the playgrounds by their teachers to rejuvenate. It was believed that the real work of thinking and learning was to happen only in the classroom.

Groos (1901) did see the relationship of play and intelligent behavior. He believed play served an adaptive purpose. Childhood existed so the person could play and develop further. During this play-oriented period of childhood, children practiced skills to take their places as adults. Children played out cooking, cleaning, hoeing, washing, and hunting. Props used during play were the tools of adults or sticks that were transformed in the minds of children.

While Groos saw childhood play as practice for adulthood, Hall (1920) saw childhood play as a period to play out evolutionary development, as the link from animal to human. Children played out the stages of evolutionary development. For example, to play the early stage as primates children engaged in swinging, climbing, and rough and tumble play. The existence of iron and steel ladders, swing sets, and "monkey bars" on school grounds and parks shadow Hall's theory of play.

The nineteenth-century German physical fitness tradition also had a great influence on the design of the first formal playgrounds. Gutsmuth focused upon designing outdoor areas for exercise training and play. Later, his ideas were adapted by the Jahn Gymnastic Association in 1812 and then brought to America influencing outdoor equipment from 1821–1830 (Mero, 1908). The indoor exercise apparatus were taken to out-of-doors.

A few innovative outdoor play environments did emerge in America as early as the last part of the nineteenth century. Characteristics of playgrounds were expanded beyond apparatus that promoted physical exercise and gross motor development to include features that accommodate other types of play such as dramatic, fine motor, and cooperative play. In 1886, a new type of playground, a sandgarten, had been established by Dr. Maria Zakerzewska when she had piles of sand placed in the yards of the Boston Children's Mission (Playground and Recreation Association of America, 1915). Use of this creative medium, sand, led the way for a few other pioneers to expand the selection of materials available to children in outdoor environments.

Patterning the kindergartens established by Friedrich Froebel (1887), others created outdoor environments that facilitated the development of the whole child–physical, cognitive, social, and emotional development. Play for Froebel had a more expanded purpose than only motor development and was considered a significant medium for learning and development. Equipment for these outdoor environments included plant and animal care areas, sand, water, swings, slides, seesaws, and building materials such as nails, hammers, and wood (Osborn, Logue, and Surbeck, 1973; Parker and Temple, 1925).

Unfortunately, in the early 1900s these innovative outdoor play environments were not the norm. The playground movement was not to move forward with these creative outdoor activities until a later time. Commercial playground equipment manufacturers, the advent of public parks, and academically oriented public schools impacted outdoor designs with "sturdy features" that would withstand heavy use by older elementary schoolchildren and exposure to changing weather conditions. Frost and Wortham (1988) have named this period in the early 1900s the Manufactured Appliance era. Iron and steel structures, such as swings, slides, and horizontal bars often located over asphalt or concrete were the common choices of public schools and public parks (Johnson, 1924; Playground and Recreation Association of America, 1910). The developmental value of play reflected the influence of Spencer, Lazarus, Gutsmuth, and Groos with few options for creative involvement with the environment. While these "metal jungles" were of study construction and required little maintenance, cold iron and steel structures mounted over brick or concrete surfaces were not aesthetically pleasing and above all were hazardous. Falls onto these nonresilient surfaces did result in some serious injuries. These dangerous "metal jungles" still haunt us today in some public parks and schools.

Contemporary Theorists' Influences

Fortunately the tide turned again as new light was shed on the study of child development. Although in the early twentieth century play was not viewed as a scientific topic, but rather indirectly through other areas in psychology, later contemporary theorists discussed play as a behavior in its own right. Froebel, Freud, Piaget, Ellis, and others viewed play as an important vehicle in the social, cognitive, and affective development of children (Rubin, Fein, and Vandenberg, 1983). The role of play was emphasized as a necessary and integral part of childhood (Isenberg and Quisenberry, 1988).

One role of childhood play included Freud's (1959) view of play as a safe context for venting socially unacceptable behaviors. Children could act out socially unacceptable activities or pretend to be characters or persons that they admire. To accommodate this context for fantasy play, structures and arrangement of outdoor play yards beyond the "metal jungles" were needed.

In fact, structures were needed that would accommodate all forms of play. The acceptance of Piaget's theory of play into the American culture paved the way for the many stimulating facets of playgrounds today. Piaget (1962) incorporated earlier notions of qualitive differences in play and believed that these reflected stages that parallel cognitive development. The stages or categories of cognitive complexity extend from functional through dramatic play and then to games with rules. Smilansky (1968) in her studies extended Piaget's hierarchy to include constructive play between functional and pretense play. While functional play such as swinging, climbing, and running and games with rules such as football and tag have long been facilitated by outdoor play environments, constructive play and pretense play were more often fostered by indoor settings. Yet, all categories of play have been observed as well as indoor play, when children have been given a wide assortment of materials and equipment (Henninger, 1985).

Materials in physical environments seemed to have direct influences in the play opportunities for children (Bergen, 1987; Phyfe-Perkins, 1980; Wohlwill and Heft, 1987). Playground enthusiasts also recognized the Field Theory proposed by Lewin (1931) as a rationale for the emphasis on features of the physical environment. Although children move in and out of certain fields (or environments), the influence of that environment remains, since children have been affected by interaction with that environment. How the child interacts is greatly affected by situational and environmental factors. Behavior is said to be a function of the interaction between the person and the environment: B = f(PE). He suggests that objects in the environment have certain valences that attract children positively or negatively considering the needs of that child at that moment and the stimulus and context of the environment. Changing developmental levels, age, or psychological state at given times can affect children's play behaviors.

The context of the environment and provision of stimulation, either indoor or outdoor, should be considered along with situational factors within the child (Wohlwill, 1983). On the one hand, Wohlwill refers to "those types of environmental effects derived directly from sheer exposure to stimulation" and, on the other hand, emphasis is placed "on the role of the particular environmental circumstances as modulator of the degree of opportunity afforded the child to engage in the response in question."

Americans came to recognize that the types of materials in certain settings can affect the levels of stimulation and arousal in turn affecting the amount of usage and type of play. The stimulus seeking theory of Ellis (1973) gained popularity in defining how the play of children functions to increase stimulation and increase level of arousal or interest. Creative designs, complex materials that can be used in various ways, and a variety of play materials on outdoor environments would best serve the "stimulus-seeking" player.

The novelty era of the 1950s and 1960s blossomed with imaginative, artistic structures (Frost and Wortham, 1988; National Recreation Association, 1958; Nichols, 1955). Some play environments of the novelty era included structures that resembled some animal or vehicle, such as an elephant or a train. Some had themes such as western or nautical playgrounds (Birkhead, 1959). Landscape architects, artists, recreation specialists, educators, and commercial manufacturers designed play sculptures with the intent of serving the stimulus-seeking child. Yet, observed play behaviors seemed to suggest that the structures provided more aesthetic appeal for adults than play value and stimulation for children (Frost and Klein, 1983).

Americans were also influenced by the Adventure playground from Scandanavia and Europe (Pedersen, 1985). Children on these Adventure playgrounds were given the creative freedom to nail, glue, and build structures with the guidance of a trained play leader. Contemporary child development theories, research of the effects of the physical environment, and the Adventure playgrounds of their European neighbors caught the imagination of American playground designers in the next several decades.

RESEARCHING PLAYGROUND EFFECTS

From the 1970s through the 1990s improvements have been made to the play value for children. Current research on elements of outdoor play environments that stimulate developmentally appropriate play has influenced many contemporary playgrounds (Frost and Sunderlin, 1985; Frost and Wortham, 1988). Research on those optimal play opportunities in outdoor play environments is limited but growing as more is realized about the play out-of-doors. Generally the research falls into two categories: (a) Studies comparing types of play environments to determine resulting play potential, and (b) studies comparing children's play while they're using various equipment and features present on outdoor play environments.

Comparing Types of Playgrounds

The types of playgrounds compared include: traditional, contemporary, adventure, and creative. Frost and Klein (1983) define each according to design and features. The traditional playground is usually located in public parks and schools. The equipment consisting of climbing bars, seesaws, slides, and swings is usually made out of metal, but sometimes is constructed from wood and located over grass or asphalt. Playgrounds that are somewhat sculptured and often based on sand or concrete forms frequently designed by architects are contemporary playgrounds. The emphasis is on novel forms and textures with different heights in aesthetically pleasing arrangements. The raw building materials and tools with which children can build their own structures make each environment of an adventure playground unique. Usually this environment requires the guidance of an adult play supervisor during the construction process. The creative playground, sometimes designed and built through community involvement, varies with equipment and design. Built structures may include reusable discarded materials such as tires. Most often included on a creative playground are loose parts such as sand and sand toys and blocks in storage buildings. Other features may include: a wheel vehicle area; sand and water areas; and complex units for climbing, swinging, and fantasy play. The following five studies compared types of playgrounds and provided insight for future outdoor design.

Hayward, Rothenberg, and Beasley (1974) compared the play activities of persons from preschool age to adult on three of these types of playgrounds in public settings—traditional, contemporary, and adventure. Time children spent on each playground, verbal interactions, type of equipment used, and interactions with the environment and each other were recorded through behavior mapping, behavior setting records, and interviews. Overall observations revealed that children played the longest on the adventure playground, next longest on the contemporary playground, and the shortest length of time on the traditional playground. Perhaps the length of stay at each playground was due to the affordance of certain types of verbal interactions. Use of play equipment and mutual play activities comprised most of the conversation on the traditional and contemporary playgrounds. While on the adventure playground, children discussed a broad spectrum of topics that included their lives outside the playground. The type of available equipment and arrangement on each playground certainly affected conversations, but also length of use and complexity of uses of equipment.

An analysis of equipment usage data suggested some implications with regards to children's preferences of playgrounds and use of particular equipment. On the traditional playground, the most used piece of equipment were the swings, followed by the wading pool and beach areas. The sand areas and mounds and slides were most often used on the contemporary playground with most time spent on multiple equipment. On the adventure playground a clubhouse built by cooperative efforts of children and adults was most often frequented. The researchers suggested that the design of the slides on the contemporary playground seemed to allow for more novelty and variety in play experiences than traditional metal slides since one contemporary slide was built on a cobblestone mountain with tunnels running through it. Children could climb to the top in various ways and slides were in proximity allowing for two children to slide down together. The close proximity of equipment on the contemporary playground allowed for a flow of activity with varied use of equipment. The clubhouse on the adventure playground allowed for fantasy play or a place of retreat and hence a place to have conversations on various topics. This study suggested certain play potential of each type of playground.

Strickland (1979) also compared the play behaviors of children on two types of playgrounds. He observed the cognitive and social play behaviors of third-grade children on a traditional and a creative playground. Generally, the creative playground supported more complex social and cognitive behaviors and was selected more often than the traditional playground.

Similar results were found for second-grade children observed on a creative and traditional playground by Campbell and Frost (1985). On the traditional playground 77.9% of the play of these children was functional with only 2% of the play classified as dramatic. While on the creative playground, 37% of the play was dramatic play. The creative playground also elicited a higher percentage of associative play than the traditional playground. The creative playground was found to have more potential for complex play behaviors.

Brown and Burger (1984) followed with a study comparing six playgrounds rated on a 19-item scale divided into four categories:

social/affective, cognitive, motor, and practical considerations. The researchers suggested that direct relationship of type of playground to play potential seemed too narrow a focus since there were so many variables including materials and specific arrangement. They compared those playgrounds rating higher on the scale (those of more contemporary design) with those rating lower on the scale, but found no significant differences in the amounts of children's social, language, or motor behaviors. In discussing the results, the researchers note that " . . . as a group, playgrounds that reflect contemporary design suggestions do not promote educationally desireable social, language, or motor behaviors to any greater extent than do playgrounds with less contemporary designs." (p. 617). This was not to suggest that children act the same on playgrounds no matter what the design, but rather the researchers noted that three possibilities must be considered.

The first is that the playground may be pleasing to the eye, but only cosmetically different. Beautiful landscaping and natural wood construction of equipment were not considered sufficient features to promote desirable behaviors. The potential of design characteristics to provide for a variety of experiences was available in some cases on the playgrounds (such as the ability to move platforms in a variety of climbing patterns), yet this second possibility was considered underdeveloped. And third, while some potential design qualities existed, some negative characteristics of the environment may have negated those potential qualities. For example, in one playground the sand area was between two highly active zones and so was rarely seen.

One individual playground site in particular did stand out as providing for more desirable behaviors, yet the initial rating was low in contemporary design considering criteria used. Positive possibilities included: more extensive opportunities for physical activity, more encapsulated spaces (enclosures in structures), and more riding vehicles. Researchers concluded that the above-named possibilities along with multifunctional play structures that afford a variety of opportunities for motor development and an increase in adult involvement in play would enhance the desired behaviors of children on playgrounds. The findings seem to suggest that it is the specific features of the playground rather than the type of playground that enhances desired play behaviors of children.

Hart and Sheehan (1986) also expressed concern for playgrounds that are made attractive to adults, but actually hold no more creative play potential for children than traditional playgrounds. The cosmetically changed appearance may be "masking an influence toward passivity or inactivity" (p. 668). These researchers observed 40 children at a university preschool on a playground divided into a contemporary side and a traditional side. Both sides had some of the same equipment such as a slide, swings, and a sandbox. But the traditional side had more open space and moveable equipment (such as wooden crates). The contemporary side had less open space, emphasized sculptured landscape and had relatively few pieces of equipment that could be moved.

Children were observed during their regular outdoor period and were alternated randomly between the two playground environments. Social and cognitive categories of Parten (1932) and Smilansky (1968) respectfully were used to code play behaviors. Analysis of the results indicated no differences in children's cognitive play when using either playground. In fact, there were few observations of constructive play, symbolic play, sociodramatic play, and games with rules on either playground. The researchers suggest that the physical features of outdoor environments may be geared more to functional rather than constructive or dramatic play. Also, involvement in games with rules is generally developmentally beyond the children in their preschool years of development no matter what the environment. Social play behaviors of children on each type of playground differed. Significantly greater incidents of unoccupied behavior, solitary play, sitting behavior, and walking were observed on the contemporary side, as well as less physical activity. There was more active climbing on the traditional side yet there was the same amount of climbing structures on each side. The authors concluded that although there were some significant differences in play behaviors " . . . the findings were not consistent enough or large enough to suggest that either type of playground differentially influences verbal interaction, cognitive play, or social play behaviors to any substantial degree" (p. 676). Findings are consistent with Brown and Burger (1984) that any differences in play behaviors were due not to the type of playground, but rather to the type of equipment and physical arrangement.

Developmental Influences of Well-Designed
Play Environments

A second group of studies took a closer look at specific choices of materials and arrangement on playgrounds. Considering the literature on environmental conditions that would meet children's developmental play needs for safe challenges, Frost and Campbell (1985) designed a study that compared the play behaviors and equipment use of two second-grade classes on traditional and creative playgrounds. As in the Hayward et. al. (1974) study, the swing was the most popular equipment on the traditional playground. On the creative playground, the most used and least used pieces of equipment were the playhouse and slide respectfully. Accounting for one-half of the observations on the creative playground was equipment used for dramatic play, while equipment designed primarily for functional play accounted for only about 20% of the observations. The use of games equipment on the creative playground totaled 4% versus 11% on the traditional playground. The researchers did note that teachers on the traditional playground subtly pushed children into playing games with rules.

Overall, preferences seemed to be for action-oriented and moveable equipment over static equipment. Perhaps for this reason, this particular creative playground did seem to support dramatic play for this group of children, while the traditional did not.

Frost and Strickland (1985) designed three adjacent outdoor environments each with certain equipment and arrangements. They compared the equipment choices of 138 children from kindergarten to second grade. On Play Environment A was a complex unit structure with decks, two tire swings, and various accesses. Play Environment B included 16 different structures (i.e., balance beam, suspension bridge, slide, etc.) that were linked together in close proximity. A mixture of inexpensive commercial equipment and structures built by parents, teachers, and children of the school including a fort, slide, storage shed, and wheel vehicle track made up Play Environment C. All children were given free choice of use of environments during play periods. With 63% of all observations, Play Environment C was the most popular. Play Environment A came in second with 23% of the observations and Play Environment B came in third with 13% of observations. Reasons cited by authors for popularity of Play

Environment C were: wider range of equipment, opportunity to express themselves in a wider variety of play forms, and the availability of action-oriented equipment.

Certain pieces of equipment were reported as more popular overall and among certain grade levels of children. In Environment A swings were the most popular equipment, repeatedly reported as such by other researchers (i.e., Hayward et al, 1974). In Environment B, the climbing structure was most often used. Loose parts available were popular with all grade levels of children, while the kindergarten children used the wheeled toys three times as often as the first and second graders. In Environment A first and second graders played on swings twice as frequently as kindergarteners. The authors concluded that if certain types of materials foster certain types of play, then if adults wish to foster certain types of play they should provide the appropriate props and arrangement.

The linked arrangement of outdoor equipment in the Frost and Campbell study was the least popular of the three environments available, but further study of linked structures by Bruya (1985b) shed more light on the importance of the linked structures as compared to independent free-standing structures. Bruya compared the time 3-, 4-, and 5-year-old children spent off and on linked and nonlinked structures. He observed that peer contacts increased on the linked structures and that there was an increase in time spent on the linked structures as compared to the nonlinked structures. Children would cross their routes of movement on the linked structures and perpetuate their play. Time spent getting on and off the nonlinked structures may have provided interruptions to play. As the greater number of play events were combined, the researchers suggest that the complexity of the linked structure increased. In accordance with Ellis's (1973) stimulus-seeking theory, this increase in complexity increased arousal and hence increased the desire to play for these preschoolers.

The complexity of play, especially imaginative play, was also researched by Barnett and Kruidenier (1981) when they replicated an earlier study of encapsulated spaces (semienclosed or enclosed areas) in outdoor play structures. Children played in areas having three levels of encapsulation: nonencapsulated, semiencapsulated, and highly encapsulated. As predicted by the researchers, the highly encapsulated apparatus elicited the longest duration of total imaginative or dramatic play. More opportunities for imaginative play present themselves in small places to hide or make-believe.

Kindergarten, first-, and second-grade children observed at play indoors with materials that varied in structure exhibited differences in behaviors as related to structure (Pulaski, 1973). Play with moderately structured materials was more varied and inventive as compared with play with highly structured materials that adhered to the content suggested by the materials. Creative designs, complex materials that can be used in various ways, and a variety of play materials on outdoor environments would best serve the stimulus-seeking player.

A study by Gramza (1971) provides support for consideration of both provision of stimulation and context of the environment. Findings revealed that specific pieces of play equipment and specific features of play equipment can be highly variable in their effects on children depending on their context or setting. Even though the authors had intended to isolate a discrete stimulus parameter (i.e., position) affecting play, they concluded that children, in this case, respond to the "total stimulus of a play setting," and their reactions to given play objects can vary significantly depending upon the presentation modality of the play object.

RECOMMENDATIONS FOR OPTIMAL DEVELOPMENT OPPORTUNITIES

Theory and research support PLAE, Inc. (Moore, Goltsman, and Iacafano, 1987) in suggesting that a "well designed, well managed play environment should provide children with [certain] developmental opportunities (pp. 3 and 4). . . ." Some of those opportunities are: (a) opportunities for motor skill development, (b) opportunities for social development, (c) opportunities for learning, (d) opportunities for decision making, (e) opportunities for fantasy play, and (f) opportunities for playing to be fun.

Motor Skill Development Opportunities

Opportunities for all types of motor development for children of various motor skill levels can be supported by a range of outdoor equipment. Certain outdoor play apparatus has been shown to benefit upper body muscular strength and endurance. When

90 children ages 49 to 83 months were given the opportunity to utilize overhead ladder equipment in an outdoor free play situation for 30 minutes per day over a 10-week period, they were found to "increase significantly their upper body muscular endurance as measured by the straight-arm hang" (Gabbard, 1983, p. 538).

Kindergarten children participating in free play periods with various choices of equipment out-of-doors have been observed to display more engagement behaviors, motor behaviors, and locomotor behaviors than during school physical education classes. As predicted, those children with above average motor skills played more actively than those with average or below average skills (Myers, 1985). This seems to suggest that a range of opportunities for active participation should be available to accommodate for the diversity of children's skill and activity level (Moore et. al. 1987). "Playgrounds should provide opportunities that match children's developmental needs" (Guddemi, 1987). During the preschool and elementary years physical fitness and motor development can be facilitated during free play on a comprehensive outdoor play environment with considerations for development opportunities for motor challenge, balancing, eye-hand-foot coordination, and all locomotor skills and nonlocomotor skills (Aronson, 1988; Bennett, 1980; Moore et. al., 1987; Seefeldt, 1984; Staniford, 1979).

Social Development

The social opportunities on an outdoor play environment can also abound. The context provided by play allows for the acquisition of many social skills such as sharing, cooperating, turn taking, and the most fundamental social ability—the ability to understand the rules of play (Garvey, 1974). Children's play in outdoor environments is usually less structured by specific directions from adults and can take advantage of the expanded physical space for more vigorous interactions and social decision making or solitude from activity (Bell and Walker, 1985; Henninger, 1985).

Findings from a review of studies by Ladd and Price (Chapter 5, this volume) suggest that playgrounds "serve as a context for many important social developments during childhood." Children's social reputations have been related to their playground behaviors. Consequences of their reputations suggest possible relationships children form with peers and the types of play opportunities they are afforded in their outdoor play environment. Also, peer status seems to be related to the differential exhibition of proactive and reactive aggression.

While using outdoor play equipment, children can be observed to exhibit the same categories of social play (Parten, 1932) as children do indoors (Henninger, 1985; Vandenberg, 1981). But, as with the indoors, the equipment and physical arrangement affects the level of social behavior (Chapter 5, this volume).

Children should have opportunities for solitary play without the interaction of peers. Younger children may not be developmentally ready for continual interactions with others. Protected spaces such as grassy hills can allow older children to retreat from highly active play for a respite (Moore et. al., 1987).

When two or more children are engaged in the same type of play but little verbal or physical contact is made between those children, they are engaged in parallel play. In their early years, children often participate in parallel play to learn about how others engage in activity, such as making sand castles. Older children may play next to others eventually to gain access to the group activity or game (Bakeman and Brown, 1980).

Finally, group play of children usually involves the sharing of roles and play equipment through verbal and physical interactions. Children are involved in give-and-take situations. Peer interactions through conflict, compromise, and negotiations during the development of indoor games as well as outdoor games contribute to social development (Chapter 3, this volume; Piaget, 1932).

Each of those levels of sociability of children's play are certainly affected by materials and arrangement as the next two studies indicated. Indoors, Weilbacher (1981) simulated two play environments including a trestle and ladder, yet in one environment the equipment could be moved (dynamic), but in the other the equipment was bolted to the floor (static). Thirty-two kindergarten girls were observed playing on and off the equipment in both environments. Girls playing with or on the dynamic equipment exhibited more cooperative behavior. The girls could work together to move the equipment to a variety of positions and uses. Cooperative behaviors off the static equipment were observed more often. Girls played other games or were engaged in social pretend play in the static equipment environment. Both types of environments supported cooperative play, and both were valuable for social play in their own ways. Desired social play can be supported by features in environment, but effects of personal choices also may have factored social interactions.

Vandenberg (1981) observed the behaviors of 28 children (mean age = 55 months) engaged in play in two rooms set up with different equipment. Children had the choice of playing in one room set up with "fine motor" equipment and another with "big muscle" equipment. The play groups in the "big muscle" room were often engaged in a form of group play with a jungle gym, slides or other physical exercise equipment. Those groups in the "small motor" room were involved in parallel play with objects such as paper, pencils, and scissors. Those who were more "cognitively mature and less socially egocentric were more likely to spend time in the environment which 'pulled' for greater social interaction" (p. 173). While the environment had an effect on social behavior, children's cognitive maturity was also a factor in children's level of social interaction.

Social and Cognitive Categories Affected by the Context of Play

Research indicates that it is difficult to separate the social functions of play without associating these with the role of play in cognitive development (Rubin, 1977). Rubin (1977) synthesized several studies which investigated the relationship between cognitive and social categories. Both Parten's social levels of play and cognitive categories of children's play taken originally from Piaget, then elaborated by Smilansky (1968), were coded in observations of children's play. Those cognitive categories included: (a) functional play in which children are exercising their muscles and practicing the components of a skill, (b) constructive play which is the act of constructing something, (c) dramatic play which is directed or spontaneous pretending, and (d) games with rules in which children agree on prearranged rules.

Rubin found that the context of play and the developmental levels of the children affected the social-cognitive play categories. Considering only the social level of play without considering the supplemental cognitive category of play is insufficient to describing the play event and could provide misleading information about play groups or individuals.

When comparing the play of 4-year-old children from low socio-economic status homes with those from middle socio-economic status homes enrolled in the same preschool, Rubin, Maioni, and Hornung (1976) found that lower SES children were less likely to engage in forms of group and constructive play and more likely to engage in functional or parallel play than those of middle SES families. The authors suggest a more global interpretation of the findings. Materials found in this center may be less familiar to the children in the lower SES homes and so they explored the materials first with functional play for longer periods before extending their play to constructive or dramatic play.

Rubin expressed the same caution when interpreting more and less mature forms of social play. Rubin, Watson, and Jambor (1978) compared the cognitive and social play of kindergarten-age children with those of preschool age and found differences in social play, but only for certain forms of social, parallel, and group play combined with cognitive categories. For example, they found differences in play patterns such as the younger age group was more likely to engage in solitary functional play, while the older group was more likely to engage in group-dramatic play. Solitary play was observed to be more cognitively mature as children got older, such as solitary constructive or solitary dramatic play during those times when older children may be developing concentration skills or task persistence.

Learning: Cognitive Developmental Opportunities

Opportunities for learning through functional, constructive, or dramatic play should include children's direct involvement discovering the outdoor environment. When studying innovative problem solving, Smith and Dutton (1979) concluded that the development of solutions requiring innovative play can be of assistance and a source of motivation. Opportunities should be provided in the outdoor environment explore, dig, transform, and observe from various levels and perspective. Play under certain conditions has been associated with improved planning skills (Smilansky, 1968), memory (Saltz, Dixon, and Johnson, 1977), and problem-solving ability (Sylvia, Bruner and Genova, 1976).

Decision Making

Many opportunities in planning and decision making should be included in the design of the total environment. A wide range of choices in a complex environment, such as: what to climb, how high to climb, where to run, and where to hide allows for ongoing decision making. Including children in the initial playground planning may not only be wise but prudent, since children have a better sense of preferred equipment than adults would be able to predict from observations of children's play (Myers, 1985). Some playground planners wouldn't plan without the rich and stimulating ideas of children, since it's to be their space (Eriksen, 1985; Weinstein and David, 1987).

Fantasy Play Opportunities

What better way to allow for decision making than by providing opportunities for fantasy making or pretend play since it has been shown to be essential to divergent problem solving (Li, 1978). Make-believe play is reported to facilitate the shift in thinking from concrete to abstract (Johnson, 1976; Singer and Rummo, 1973). Creative and flexible thinking are considered by-products of pretense play (Lieberman, 1977; Singer, 1973; Smilansky, 1968).

But pretense play cannot be thought of as "appearing in a vacuum." There is no precise correspondence between pretense play and developmental domains since development does not proceed evenly across different task domains (Watson and Fischer, 1977). Rather the context for optimizing pretense play must be considered and, as Schwartzman (1977) suggests, there must be a "sideways glance" of play. Because some studies have conflicting results of correlates of play (Johnson, 1988), "a sideways glance" or more in-depth view of the whole picture surrounding pretense play could provide insight on certain other variables that may have interacted to produce the given effects (i.e., personality, child rearing, variance of play props available, etc.). Hartle (1989) found that sometimes more fantasy play was generated in the absence of any props. Perhaps without props, the four-, five-, and six-year-old children in a preschool's outdoor play environment were forced to use their imaginations. An outdoor environment must have a unique balance between being too literal and too abstract to provide optimal stimulation for imaginative or pretend play.

Those opportunities for fantasy play may also be of great assistance to children as they work through venting socially unacceptable behaviors. Traveling alone across streets or building a fire can be done in the mind and play of children on an outdoor play environment. Children's fantasy may also allow for the expression of imitating those people who have impressed them (Freud, 1959). The roles of mothers, fathers, doctors, and superheros are often developed in the fantasy play of children.

And isn't it most important that the environment provide opportunities for sheer fun? The rejuvenating experience of shouting running in seemingly "nonsense" play also has a vital role in learning impulsivity and impulse control (Sutton-Smith, 1988).

Criteria for Planning the Optimal Outdoor Play Environment

In summarizing the developmental influences and opportunities for outdoor play environments certain criteria should be considered in planning the optimal outdoor site design (Moore, Goltsman, Iacafano, 1987; Bowers, 1988):

1. There should be adequate accessibility for children to be able to use the outdoor environment. The space should provide for the flow of walking, running, and riding vehicle traffic. Children and adults alike should be able to view the environment as attractive and secure, yet easily understandable to those who use it.

2. Challenges should be safe, yet allow for risk taking. Children of various motor development abilities should be able to find areas and equipment in which to experience new challenges in climbing, balancing, or jumping (Jambor, 1986). Children should be able to test new skills and challenge their abilities through a broad range of challenges exhibiting each next greater level of challenge (Moore, Lane, Hill, Cohen, and McGinity, 1979). Each new challenge accomplished can build self-confidence as children discover what their bodies can do. The playground designer in the study by Pinciotti and Weinstein (1986) included a variety of levels and forms in the tire structures to accommodate various graduated challenges.

3. To provide for the diverse interests and abilities of children, a variety of types of materials and landscaping should be available (Frost and Klein, 1983). Children's moods change along with interests so the environment should provide novel materials and arrangement that change regularly (Ellis, 1973). Some features should be complex and usable in a variety of ways to stimulate creative abilities, yet other features should be stable and provide some security in the surroundings.

4. Flexible elements that can be moved or changed provide for more creative play. The "theory of loose parts" espoused by Nicholson (1974) suggests that: "In any environment, both the degree of inventiveness and creativity, and the possibility of discovery, are directly proportional to the number and kind of variables in it" (p. 223). Manipulating loose parts sustain attention and generate the greatest number of responses (Ellis, 1974; Guddemi, 1987).

   R. C. Moore (1973) has suggested that with moveable or loose parts, "kids really know the environment if they can dig it, swat it, lift it, push it, join it." Wise choices of parts by playground planners can allow for optimal play potential.

5. A well-planned outdoor environment can be easily supervised and involve adults. Visibility around structures, visibility into enclosed spaces, tunnels large enough for an adult, and large structures at the back of the site allow for easy supervision of children by adults. The adults' role in children's play out-of-doors can be as vital as it is indoors. Adults can stimulate play, observe play to recognize needs for change, or even get directly involved in children's play (Johnson, Christie, and Yawkey 1987).

6. Multisensory planning includes placing natural and man-made materials that stimulate sight, sound, touch, hearing, and smell. One example is a musical playground with wind chimes, bells, and a suspension bridge that taps as children walk to give enriched experiences with sounds (Booth-Church, 1985).

7. Space needs to vary in texture and purpose with clear zoning that connects and yet separates the zones. Children should be able to crawl into, on top of, and through spaces. In some of these spaces children can gather for large group play, while in others children can retreat by themselves. Each area or zone can provide for a certain kind of play such as ball playing, climbing, care of pets, sliding, swinging, and more if planned with the appropriate play materials and clear definition between areas (such as the use of a fence or line of bushes). Quiet zones for sitting or reading should be away from active zones for running, sliding, active pretending, or rough and tumble play. Care should be taken that clear pathways join these areas so children can easily move to each as desired. Clear distinctions should link settings with graduated challenges so children can progress from the simple to the more complex with relative success (Kritchevsky, Prescott, and Walling, 1977).

8. Safety should be of utmost importance throughout with the playground as safe for the children, but also teaching the children to be safety conscious on the playground (Henninger, Strickland, and Frost, 1985). Surfaces under climbing equipment should be resilient to falls. Decks should be of manageable height for the age of children intending to use the equipment. Stairs and any opening should not allow for entrapment of a child's head. All equipment should be built with high-grade construction materials which are nontoxic and are appropriate to the climatic conditions of the region (Bowers, 1988). A maintenance schedule should be adhered to for proper upkeep and to prevent injuries such as scrapes from loose or exposed bolts (Frost, 1983).

When four top manufacturers of playground equipment were interviewed about major trends in today's market, the concern for safety, colorful equipment, and a modular concept in design came to the top of the list (Parks and Recreation, 1985). Asphalt and concrete surfaces for ball play and riding toys are only part of the comprehensive modern outdoor environment. Now instead of cold iron and steel, climbing, swinging, and sliding structures are being made out of wood, plastic, and powder-coated metal materials by today's manufacturers (Bruya, 1985a; PlayDesigns, 1989). Resilient surfaces such as sand, wood chips, and new manufactured mats are installed below climbing equipment to ensure safety from falls. Many manufacturers offer modular units with low-profile decks (decks close the ground, 2 to 3 feet elevation) and attached features such as ramps, pulleys, swinging bridges, steering wheels, and spiral slides of varying heights. Manufacturers are now considering optimal play opportunities that are developmentally appropriate for children of various ages.

While not all outdoor play environments can provide for all of the above opportunities, adequate planning based on theory and research that considers those who will use the facility can provide for all forms of developmentally appropriate cognitive and social play. It is not always the amount of money that makes the best outdoor play environments, but the quality of time and energy in planning for play opportunities of children of all ages.

REFERENCES

Aronson, S. S. (1988). Safe, fun playgrounds. *Exchange.* 35–40.

Bakeman, R., and Brown, J. V. (1980). Early interaction: Consequences for social and mental development at three years. *Child Development, 51.* 437–447.

Barnett, L. A., and Kruidenier, W. P. (1981). The effects of encapsulation on preschool children's imaginative play. *Journal of Leisure Research, 13*(4), 323–336.

Bell, M. J., and Walker, P. (1985). Interactive patterns in children's play groups. In J. L. Frost and S. Sunderlin (Eds.), *When children play* (pp. 139–144). Wheaton, MD: Association for Childhood Education International.

Bennett, C. (1980). Planning for activity during the important preschool years. *Journal of Physical Education, Recreation and Dance, 15*(7), 30–34.

Bergen, D. (1987). *Play as a medium for learning and development.* Portsmouth, NH: Heinemann.

Birkhead, F. V. (1959). Saddle City. *Recreation, 52,* 132–133.

Booth-Church, E. (1985). The music playground. In J. L. Frost and S. Sunderlin (Eds.), *When children play* (pp. 239–242). Wheaton, MD: Association for Childhood Education International.

Bowers, L. (1988). Playground design: A scientific approach. In L. D. Bruya (Ed.), *Play spaces for children: A new beginning.* Reston, VA: American Alliance for Health, Physical Education, Recreation, and Dance.

Brown, J. G., and Burger, C. (1984). Playground designs and preschool children's behaviors. *Environment and Behavior, 16*(5), 599–626.

Bruya, L. D. (1985a). Design characteristics used in playgrounds for children. In J. L. Frost and S. Sunderlin (Eds.), *When children play* (pp. 215–220). Wheaton, MD: Association for Childhood Education International.

————. (1985b). The effect of play structure format differences on the play behavior of preschool children. In J. L. Frost and S. Sunderlin (Eds.), *When children play* (pp. 115–120). Wheaton, MD: Association for Childhood Education International.

Campbell, S. D., and Frost, J. L. (1985). The effects of playground type on the cognitive and social play behaviors of grade two children. In J. L. Frost and S. Sunderlin (Eds.), *When children play* (pp. 81–89). Wheaton, MD: Association for Childhood Education International.

Ellis, M. J. (1973). *Why people play.* Englewood Cliffs, NJ: Prince Hall

————. (1974). Play: Theory and research. In G. Coates (Ed.), *Alternative learning environments* (pp. 305–310). Stroudsburgh, PA; Dowden, Hutchinson, and Ross.

Eriksen, A. (1985). *Playground design: Outdoor environments for learning and development.* New York: Van Nostrand Reinhold.

Freud, S. (1959). Creative writers and daydreaming. In J. Strackey (Ed.), *The standard edition of the complete psychological works of Sigmund Freud* (Vol. 9). London: Hogarth.

Froebel, F. (1887). *The education of man.* New York: Appleton.

Frost, J. L. (1983). Playground safety checklist. In J. L. Frost and B. Klein, *Children's play and playgrounds.* Austin, TX: Playscapes International.

Frost, J. L., and Campbell, S. D. (1985). Equipment choices of primary-age children on conventional and creative playgrounds. In J.

L. Frost and S. Sunderlin (Eds.), *When children play* (pp. 89–93). Wheaton, MD: Association for Childhood Education International.

Frost, J. L., and Klein, B. (1983). *Children's play and playgrounds.* Austin, TX: Playscapes International.

Frost, J. L., and Strickland, E. (1985). Equipment choices of young children during free play. In J. L. Frost and S. Sunderlin (Eds.), *When children play* (pp. 93–103). Wheaton, MD: Association for Childhood Education International.

Frost, J. L., and Sunderlin, S. (1985). *When children play* Wheaton, MD: Association for Childhood Education International.

Frost, J. L., and Wortham, S. (1988). The evolution of American playgrounds. *Young Children, July,* 19–28.

Gabbard, C. (1983). Muscular endurance and experience with playground apparatus. *Perceptual and Motor Skills, 56,* 538.

Garvey, C. (1974). Some properties of social play. *Merrill-Palmer Quarterly, 20,* 163–180.

Gramza, A. F. (1971). *New directions for sign of play environments.* International report at the Motor Performance and Play Research laboratory, Children's Research Center at the University of Illinois.

Groos, K. (1901). *The play of man.* New York: Appleton.

Guddemi, M. P. (1987, October). Play/playgrounds/safety. *Dimensions,* 15–18.

Hall, G. S. (1920). *Youth* New York: D. Appleton.

Hart, C. H., and Sheehan, R. (1986). Preschoolers' play behavior in outdoor environments: Effects of traditional and contemporary playgrounds. *American Educational Research Journal, 23*(4), 668–678.

Hartle, L. (1989). *Preschool children's play behaviors associated with housekeeping equipment and blocks in an outdoor environment.* Unpublished doctoral dissertation, The Pennsylvania State University.

Hayward, G., Rothenberg, M., and Beasley, R. R. (1974). Children's play and urban playground environments. *Environment and Behavior, 6*(2), 131–168.

Henninger, M. (1985). Preschool children's play behaviors in an indoor and outdoor environment. In J. L. Frost and S. Sunderlin (Eds.),

When children play (pp. 145–149). Wheaton, MD: Association for Childhood Education International.

Henninger, M. L., Strickland, E., Frost, J. L. (1985). X-rated playgrounds: Issues and developments. In J. L. Frost and S. Sunderlin (Eds.), *When children play* (pp. 221–228). Wheaton, MD: Association for Childhood Education International.

Isenberg, J., and Quisenberry, N. L. (1988). Play: A necessity for all children. *Childhood Education, 64*(3), 138–145.

Jambor, T. (1986). Risk-taking needs in children: An accommodating play environment. *Children's Environments Quarterly, 3*(3), 22–25.

Johnson, H. M. (1924). *A nursery school experiment.* New York: Bureau of Educational Experiments.

Johnson, J. (1976). Relations of divergent thinking and intelligence test scores with social and nonsocial make-believe play of preschool children. *Child Development, 47,* 1200–1203.

———. (1988). The role of play in cognitive development. Paper presented at the United States-Israel Binational Science Foundation Summer Workshops: Implications of Children's Sociodramatic Play—Learning and National Policy. Wheelock College, Boston, July.

Johnson, J. E., Christie, J. F., and Yawkey, T. D. (1987). *Play and early childhood development.* Glenview, IL: Scott, Foresman, and Company.

Kelly-Byrne, D. (1984). The meaning of play's triviality. In B. Sutton-Smith and D. Kelly-Byrne (Eds.), *The masks of play* (pp. 165–170). New York: Leisure Press

Kritchevsky, S., Prescott, E., and Walling, L., (1977). *Planning environments for the young children: Physical space* (rev. ed). Washington DC: National Association for the Education of Young Children.

Lazarus, M. (1883). *Die reize desspiels.* Berlin: Fred, Dummlers ver lagsbuchhandlung.

Lewin, K. (1931). Environmental forces in child behavior and development. In C. Murchison (Ed.), *A hand book of child psychology* (pp. 94–127). Worchester, MA: Clark University Press.

Li, A. K. F. (1978). Effects of play on novel responses in kindergarten children. *The Alberta Journal of Educational Research, 23,* 31–36.

Lieberman, J. N. (1977). *Playfulness: Its relationship to imagination and creativity*. New York: Academic Press.

Mero, E. B. (1908). *American playgrounds: Their construction, equipment, maintenance and utility*. Boston: American Gymnasia Co.

Moore, R. (1973). Open space learning place. *New School of Education Journal, 31*(1), 24–53.

Moore, G. T., Lane, C. G., Hill A. W., Cohen, U., and McGinity, T. (1979). *Recommendations for child care centers*. Milwaukee: University of Wisconsin Center for Architecture and Urban Planning Research.

Moore, R. C., Goltsman, S. M., and Iacafano, D. S. (1987). *Play for all guidelines: Planning, design and management of outdoor play settings for all children*. Berkeley, CA: MIG Communications.

Myers, J. (1985). Perceived and actual playground equipment choices of children. In J. L. Frost and S. Sunderlin (Eds.), *When children play* (pp. 157–162). Wheaton, MD: Association for Childhood Education International.

National Recreation Association. (1958). Imagination visits the playground—1958. *Recreation, 51*, 106–108.

Nichols, R. B. (1955). New concepts behind designs for modern playgrounds. *Recreation, 48*, 154–157.

Nicholson, S. (1974). The theory of loose parts. In G. Coates (Ed.), *Alternative learning environments* (pp. 370–381). Stroudsburgh, PA: Dowden, Hutchinson, and Ross.

Osborn, D. K., Logue, C., and Surbeck, E. (1973). *Significant events in early childhood education*. Athens, GA: Early Childhood Education Learning Center, University of Georgia.

Parker, S., and Temple, A. (1925). *Unified kindergarten and first-grade teaching*. New York: Ginn.

Parks and Recreation. (1985). Trends with playground manufacturers. *Parks and Recreation, 20*(8), 60–62.

Parten, M. B. (1932). Social participation among preschool children. *Journal of Abnormal and Social Psychology, 27*, 243–269.

Patrick, G. T. W. (1916). *The psychology of relaxation*. Boston: Houghton-Mifflin.

Pedersen, J. (1985). The adventure playground of Denmark. In J. L. Frost and S. Sunderlin (Eds.), *When children play* (pp. 201–208). Wheaton, MD: Association for Childhood Education International.

Phyfe-Perkins, E. (1980). Children's behavior in preschool settings—A review of research concerning the influence of the physical environment. In L. C. Katz (Ed.), *Current topics in early childhood education (Vol. 3)*. Norwood, NJ: Ablex.

Piaget, J. (1932). *The moral judgment of the child.* New York: Free Press.

———. (1962). *Play, dreams and imitation in childhood.* New York: Norton.

Pinciotti, P., and Weinstein, C. S. (1986). The effects of a tire playground on children's attitude toward play time. *Children's Environment Quarterly, 3* (3), 30–39.

PlayDesigns. (1989). Playground equipment catalog. New Berlin, PA: author.

Playground and Recreation Association of America. (1910). Report of the committee on equipment. *The Playground, 4,* 270–284.

———. (1915). A brief history of the playground movement in America. *The Playground, 9*(1), 2–11, 39–45.

Pulaski, M. A. (1973). Toys and imaginative play. In J. L. Singer (Ed.), *The child's world of make-believe: Experimental studies of imaginative play* (pp. 74–103). New York: Academic Press.

Rubin, K. H. (1977). Play behaviors of young children. *Young Children, 32*(6), 16–24.

Rubin, K. H., Fein, G. G., and Vandenberg, B. (1983). Play. In E. M. Heterington (Ed.) and P. H. Mussen (Series Ed.), *Handbook of child psychology: Vol 4. Socialization, personality, and social development* (pp. 698–774). New York: Wiley.

Rubin, K. H., Maioni, T. L., and Hornung, M. (1976). Free play behaviors in middle and lower class preschoolers: Parten and Piaget revisited. *Child Development, 47,* 414–419.

Rubin, K. H., Watson, K., and Jambor, T. (1978). Free play behaviors in preschool and kindergarten children. *Child development, 49,* 534–536.

Saltz, E., Dixon, D., and Johnson, J. E. (1977). Training disadvantaged preschoolers on various fantasy activities: Effects on cognitive functioning and impulse control. *Child Development, 48,* 367–368.

Schwartzman, H. B. (1977). Children's play: A sideways glance at making-believe. In D. F. Nancy and B. A. Tinal (Eds.), *The study of play: Problems and prospects* (pp. 208–215). West Point, NY: Leisure Press.

Seefeldt, V. (1984). Physical fitness in preschool and elementary school-aged children. *Journal of Physical Education, Recreation and Dance, 55*(9), 33–40.

Singer, J. L. (Ed.). (1973). *The child's world of make-believe: Experimental studies of imaginative play.* New York: Academic Press.

Singer, D. G., and Rummo, J. (1973). Ideational creativity and behavioral style in kindergarten aged children. *Developmental Psychology, 8,* 154–161.

Smilansky, S. (1968). *The effects of sociodramatic play on disadvantaged preschool children.* New York: Wiley.

Smith, P. K., and Connolly, K. (1980). *The ecology of preschool behavior.* Cambridge: Cambridge University Press.

Smith, P. K., and Dutton, S. (1979). Play and training in direct and innovative problem solving. *Child Development, 50,* 830–836.

Spencer, H. (1873). *Principles of psychology* (Vol. 2). New York: Appleton.

Staniford, D. J. (1979). Natural movement for children. *Journal of Physical Education and Recreation, 50*(8), 14–17.

Strickland, E. (1979). Free play behaviors and equipment choices of third grade children in contrasting play environments. Unpublished doctoral dissertation, University of Texas at Austin.

Sutton-Smith, B. (1988). The struggle between sacred play and festive play. In D. Bergen (Ed.), *Play as medium for learning and development.* Portsmouth, NH: Heinemann.

Sylvia, K., Bruner, J. S., and Genova, P. (1976). The role of play in the problem solving of children 3–5 years old. In J. S. Bruner, A. Jolly, and K. Sylva (Eds.), *Play: Its role in development and evolution* (pp. 244–257). New York: Basic Books.

Vandenberg, B. (1981). Environmental and cognitive factors in social play. *Journal of Experimental Child Psychology, 31,* 169–175.

Watson, M. W., and Fischer, K. W. (1977). A developmental sequence of agent use in late infancy. *Child Development, 48,* 828–836.

Weilbacher, R. (1981). The effects of static and dynamic play environments on children's social and motor behaviors. In *Children at Play.* West Penn: Leisure Press.

Weinstein, C. S., and David, T. (1987). *Spaces for children: The built environment and child development.* New York: Plenum Press.

Wohlwill, J. F. (1983). The physical and the social environment as factors in development. In D. Magnusson and V. P. Allen (Eds.), *Human development: An interactional perspective* (pp. 111–129). New York: Academic Press.

Wohlwill, J., and Heft, H. (1987). The physical environment and the development of the child. In D. Stokes and I. Altman (Eds.). *Handbook of Environmental Psychology.* New York: John Wiley and Sons, Inc.

PART II

CONFLICTS ON PLAYGROUNDS

3

WILLARD W. HARTUP AND BRETT LAURSEN_____

Conflict and Context in Peer Relations*

Conflict is an everyday event in children's lives. Disagreements occur between friends and nonfriends alike, and in virtually every situation in which children socialize with one another. Among the most common occurrences on the playground, disagreements are ubiquitous in children's interactions with one another.

Conflicts appear to have both negative and positive implications for the child's development. Disagreements are strong barriers to the establishment of enduring relationships with others and are among the gravest challenges to these relationships once they are established (Selman, 1980; Youniss and Smollar, 1985). At the same time, disagreements illuminate the common ground that exists between individuals, the recognition of which is necessary to their becoming friends (Gottman, 1983). Conflict is also an ingredient in fun, which children consider an important element in their relations with one another (Goodnow and Burns, 1988), and conflicts are known to be mechanisms through which children arrive at a mature understanding of social rules, including their origins, workings, and changeability (Piaget, 1932; Sullivan, 1953).

Disagreements vary in their manifestations according to the settings in which they occur. Conflict management differs according to whether children are the same or opposite sex, friends or nonfriends, whether the disagreement concerns their relationship with one another or an extrinsic matter, and whether alternatives to disagreement are readily available. We examine these varia-

---

*Support in the completion of this chapter was provided by Grant No. R01-42888, National Institute of Mental Health, a grant from the Netherlands Organization for Scientific Research, and a Fulbright Research Scholarship to the first author. The authors would also like to acknowledge the generous support of the Psychologisch Laboratorium, University of Nijmegen.

tions and their implications in this chapter, but we consider first the nature of conflict and the nature of context. We argue that relationships themselves are contextual elements that constrain children's disagreements, and that social reputations as well as age and sex also affect them. Group arrangements, space, and resources are considered, too, along with constraints deriving from the activities in which children engage and the importance of these activities to them. Playground conflicts will be discussed, taking into account the fact that many relevant studies have been conducted indoors.

CONFLICT: ITS NATURE AND SIGNIFICANCE

What Are Conflicts?

Conflicts are social events involving *opposition* or *disagreement* between individuals. Words like "opposing," "refusing," "denying," and "objecting" anchor the construct for most observers, along with words like "protesting" and "resisting" (Shantz, 1987). Both children and adults tend to think about conflicts, however, in terms of fighting and quarreling, that is, episodes of protracted and aggressive opposition rather than fleeting disagreements (Selman, 1980). These differences are important, since recent studies show that simple, two-turn disagreements resemble compliance episodes and differ markedly from longer ones. Two-turn disagreements among nursery school children, for example, occur most commonly between children in ongoing interaction, are not very intense, are resolved mainly by "insistence" rather than negotiation, and typically end with the children remaining together. Longer disagreements, on the other hand, are more variable both in terms of the situations in which they arise and the way they are resolved (Laursen and Hartup, 1989). Conflict, viewed as opposition or disagreement, thus shares aspects of meaning with constructs like noncompliance, aggression, fighting, and quarreling.

Conflict has been difficult to distinguish from aggression. To the extent that conflict involves interference or competition for resources, it always carries injurious or harmful potential. And, indeed, many conflicts are noxious and many are viewed as synonymous with fighting and quarreling (see above). Nevertheless, other conflicts are not resolved aggressively; some disagreements are actually humorous (e.g., Abbott and Costello), even to the opposing individuals themselves. Clearly, then, conflict and aggression are different constructs.

Distinguishing conflict from competition has also been difficult. At various times, conflict has been considered as synonymous with competition, as one subtype of competition, and as a class of events that actually subsumes competition (Peterson, 1983). Competition, of course, refers to situations in which the interdependencies existing between two individuals constrain their access to rewards (e.g., the zero-sum or winner/loser situation). In this sense, it is difficult to argue that every conflict represents an instance of competition. But when issues like "who's right" are regarded as competitive, as well as issues like "who wins the tricycle," it is easier to claim that conflict and competition are one and the same.

Conflict is thus difficult to differentiate in structural terms from noncompliance, aggression, competition, fighting, and quarreling. It may be that the only meaningful way to classify oppositional events is in functional terms, for example, whether oppositions lead to constructive or destructive ends. Many writers have suggested this course of action (Coser, 1967; Shantz and Hobart, 1989), although it is widely disregarded in contemporary research with children.

The lack of a uniform definition of conflict may not be a major failing. Many social and psychological constructs are used elastically, including ones like cooperation and sympathy as well as aggression and frustration. The issue, rather, is *specification:* the requirement that an investigator must say what is meant and mean what is said about one's terminology. In this sense, then, we propose that *opposition* be considered the sine qua non of social conflict, a view with which many investigators agree (Shantz, 1987).

The Conflict Episode

Conflicts can be viewed as "time-distributed social episodes" encompassing *issues* (what the disagreement is about), *instigating tactics, oppositional tactics, resolution strategies,* and *outcomes* (Shantz, 1987). The interrelations among these elements have not been studied in very many situations, but attention to these dynamics is crucial in both normative studies and investigations examining the role of conflict in childhood socialization and relationships.

Most studies show that children's conflicts in naturalistic situations are usually brief and do not involve aggression. Surprisingly, they also do not involve negotiation or bargaining to any great extent. Conflicts are resolved without adult intervention and most often by insistence; most eventuate in winner/loser outcomes even though the children remain together after the conflict (Green, 1933; Hay, 1984; Laursen and Hartup, 1989).

One of the clearer predictors of children's activities after the conflict is whether or not the children are interacting before the conflict starts. When conflict arises within ongoing interaction rather than from outside intervention, the disagreement is less likely to involve aggression and to be shorter as well as to involve continued interaction after it is over. Indeed, what occurs after a disagreement is determined more extensively by predisagreement conditions than by the conflict behaviors that actually occur (Laursen and Hartup, 1989).

The tactics that children use to resist the demands of others nevertheless determine a great deal about the episode. Insistence, used to resist the demands of another child, results mainly in reactive insistence as well as reduced likelihood that the conflict will end in compromise (Eisenberg and Garvey, 1981; Laursen and Hartup, 1989). In addition, when disagreements are not marked by aggression, when affective intensity is relatively low, and when conciliation rather than dominance behaviors are employed, interaction between the children tends to continue after the conflict whether or not interaction was occurring beforehand (Sackin and Thelen, 1984; Laursen and Hartup, 1989). Stated in the reverse, conflict episodes that encompass strong affect and aggression, "standing firm" as an oppositional tactic, and inequitable outcomes, tend to be followed by discontinuation rather than continuation of interaction.

These conflict dynamics, observed among children in playrooms and on playgrounds, suggest a close connection between conflict management on the one hand, and continuities in social interaction on the other. What is usually called "productive" or "effective" conflict management (i.e., controlled emotions, cooperation, and equitable demands) is associated with ongoing and continuing social interaction whereas "ineffective," inequitable conflict resolution is associated with discontinued interaction and social avoidance. Current evidence does not otherwise differentiate conflict dynamics associated with constructive outcomes from those associated with destructive ones. Nor does current evidence differentiate conflict dynamics according to situational context. Nevertheless, the evidence supports the general hypothesis that the maintenance of social interaction is closely associated with the manner in which the time-distributed elements of the conflict episode are configured.

Conflict: Developmental Significance

Most theories of child development consider conflicts (i.e., opposing beliefs, motives, emotions, and objectives) to contribute importantly to socialization. Different writers consider different conflicts to be developmentally significant, but nearly every major theorist has argued that developmental change emerges mainly from oppositions between the individual and society (i.e., other individuals).[1]

This dialectic between the individual and society bears simultaneously on two developmental tasks (Shantz and Hobart, 1989): *individuation* (becoming an independent "self") and *connectedness* (becoming attached or related to others). From earliest infancy, children are occupied simultaneously with becoming a "me" and a "we" and, in one sense, the various developmental "stages" or "eras" simply involve different manifestations of this dualism. In infancy, for example, becoming an independent causal agent (and understanding what that means) is a major developmental task; forming an attachment to a primary caretaker is another. Similarly, in adolescence, one major developmental task is the elaboration of a distinctive self-system (especially as related to sex and work), but another is the elaboration of one's social network through alterations of old relationships (e.g., relationships with parents) and the construction of new ones (e.g., relationships with romantic partners).

Long-standing views (e.g., Baldwin, 1897; Cooley, 1909; Freud, 1930; Mead, 1934; Piaget, 1932; Lewin, 1935; Dollard and Miller, 1950; Sullivan, 1953; Erikson, 1950; Bowlby, 1969) suggest that both one's sense of self and one's interpersonal relationships emerge mainly from two kinds of social transactions—*affirmations* and *conflict*. Affirmations provide the individual with a sense of what is correct and workable as well as with secure bases from which new ideas and new challenges can be undertaken. Self-worth also derives from "consensual validation" (Sullivan, 1953) and much evidence shows that close relationships are founded on personal similarities, affirmation, and common cause (Kelley, et al., 1983).

Disagreements, on the other hand, create doubt about what has been assumed to be "correct and workable," thereby motivating change in habitual modes of thinking and acting. But disagreements also "affirm oneself through the negation of others" (Simmel, 1955) and affirm one's connectedness to others. Negation (opposition), like affirmation, is a relational construct: " . . . to argue necessitates taking the attitude of the other at the same time as one contradicts it" (Maynard, 1986, p. 252) and " . . . when children are at odds, they are tacitly affirming that one another's behavior is of significance" (Shantz and Hobart, 1989, p. 88). Conflicts also contribute to the construction of social relationships by illuminating the "fit" between individuals, that is, by demonstrating when the skills, interests, and goals of two individuals mesh and when they don't. Indeed, many conflicts between children and their friends concern their relationships with one another and the rules that govern them (Corsaro, 1981; Laursen, 1989). Conflicts assist children in recognizing just when common ground exists between them, as when two children first disagree about whether to play indoors or outdoors and then agree to play outside. Also, certain kinds of disagreements are humorous, eliciting the glee that friends relish and that enhances their intimacy with one another (Foot, Chapman, and Smith, 1977).

Social development thus involves a continuous dialectic between social affirmation and social conflict. Both agreement and disagreement are believed to contribute to the individual's self-regard as well as the individual's sense of connectedness to others. Children themselves recognize the delicate balance that exists between agreement and disagreement in interpersonal relations: "A friend is someone you fight with, but not forever," says one youngster (Goodnow and Burns, 1988); "sometimes when you have a real fight and find out you're still friends, then you've got something that is stronger," says another (Selman, 1980).

THE PEER CONTEXT: ITS NATURE AND SIGNIFICANCE

What Is the Peer Context?

A social context is " . . . a pattern of activities, roles, and interpersonal relations experienced over time by the developing person in a given setting with particular physical and material characteristics" (Bronfenbrenner, 1979). These elements can be arranged in a two-dimensional matrix according to the *interpersonal units* and *setting components* involved (see Figure 3.1).

Setting Components

Interpersonal Units

	Persons	Setting	Activity
Interactions			
Relationships			
Groups			
Structures			

Figure 3.1.   The peer context (after Hartup, 1984).

The vertical axis of the matrix consists of a hierarchical arrangement of the units into which interpersonal relations can be divided (Hinde, 1976). The most basic of these are *interactions*, which consist of meaningful encounters between individuals. *Relationships* are a series of interactions occurring over time between two individuals, each interaction being relatively limited in duration but affected by past interactions and affecting future ones. Relationships are more or less enduring ties or connections between individuals. *Groups* subsume both interactions and relationships and consist of the collectives to which one belongs either by virtue of personal characteristics (i.e., membership groups) or one's identification with group norms and objectives (i.e., reference groups). *Structures* refer to higher-order contexts that we commonly call institutions or societies and that encompass constituent interactions, relationships, and groups.

Social contexts also consist of specific objects and events occurring at specific times and locations. The horizontal axis of the matrix thus consists of three major classes of setting components: *persons,* that is, the actors with whom the target individual interacts or relates; *situations,* that is, the geographical surround or milieu in which the subjects interact; and *activities,* that is, the "problems" or "challenges" that activate or energize the subjects.

Using this matrix we can describe the structure, content, expectations, affects, and diversity of children's behavior with other children, thus delineating what can be called the *peer context.* This matrix is not a dynamic model of peer relations; it refers neither to mechanisms of developmental change or mechanisms of interpersonal influence. Rather, it simply schematizes the situations in which children interact with one another in terms of the environmental elements known to constrain that interaction. Generally speaking, the peer context includes children who are more or less equivalent in chronological age and social skill. As will be seen, however, the peer culture is actually demographically heterogeneous.

Persons and Relationships as Contextual Determinants

When two children interact, the exchange reflects *subject effects, partner effects,* and *relationship effects* (Hinde, 1979; Kenney and La Voie, 1984), that is, contributions from both individuals separately as well as a contribution emanating from their relationship with one another. Children differ from one another in myriad ways (e.g., age, sex, and race) and some of these are sources of both subject and partner variance. For example, when same- and mixed-age dyads of 3- and 5-year-old children (strangers) are observed, social interaction is: (a) least frequent between two 3-year-olds, (b) moderately frequent between a 3-year-old and a 5-year-old, and (c) most frequent between two 5-year-olds (Lougee, Grueneich, and Hartup, 1977). The difference between "a" and "c" can be attributed to subject effects in these data, that is, to the subjects' ages. The "a/b" and "b/c" differences, however, are more difficult to allocate. Since *both* the 3-year-olds and the 5-year-olds in mixed-age dyads behaved differently from their counterparts in same-age dyads, it is difficult to attribute the difference between mixed-age and same-age interaction entirely to partner effects or relationship effects, that is, to one or the other. Clearly, though, children do not simply behave according to their own and their partners' ages: Relationships between children of different ages are themselves different from relationships between children of the same age and this is reflected in their interaction.

Differences between children in social skill are reflected similarly in the interaction between them. Thus, when two toddlers were brought together in one investigation (Pastor, 1981), both with histories of "secure" attachments to their mothers, their interactions with one another were relatively harmonious and reciprocal. When a securely attached toddler was brought together with another toddler with a history of "anxious-resistant" attachment, conflicts were also infrequent. But interaction between secure toddlers and toddlers who were "avoidantly resistant" to their mothers was punctuated by relatively frequent disagreements—instigated by *both* children. In this case, then, the children were clearly responding differently according to their own relationship histories and those of their partners, and these emerging relationships also varied according to their earlier attachments.

Other demonstrations that persons and relationships are significant contextual determinants of children's social interaction are legion: For example, sex differences in social interaction are ubiquitous and same-sex interaction differs from cross-sex interaction (see Hartup, 1983). Friends interact more cooperatively with one another than nonfriends (Berndt, 1986; Hartup, 1989), and it is also the case that "unilateral friendships" (unreciprocated friendship choices) resemble mutual friendships in some ways and "neutral" associations in others (Hartup, Laursen, Stewart, and Eastenson, 1988). Several reviews showing that persons and relationships are significant sources of variance in peer interaction are available (cf., Hartup, 1970, 1983, 1984; Berndt, 1986).

Settings and Activities as Contextual Determinants

The physical setting constrains child-child interaction from babyhood onwards. For example, the amount of social contact among children (both positive and negative) increases as the availability of toys decreases (Johnson, 1935). Different playthings afford different kinds of social interaction: In nursery schools, for example, art and book locations afford solitary and parallel activity to a greater extent than doll corners and outdoor activities. Doll corners (and most outdoor activities), in turn, afford more coordinated social interaction (Charlesworth and Hartup, 1967; Rubin, 1977). Crowding effects have been studied, too, but access to resources seems to be more important in determining the nature of child-child interactions than the space available (see pp. 62–63).

With increasing age, a sharing norm (i.e., the notion that children should share equally) constrains children's interactions with one another. Nevertheless, cooperation occurs most readily among school-aged children when rewards are equally available and sharing is stipulated by the adult in charge. Competition, on the other hand, occurs most commonly when rewards are assigned to "winners" only (French, Brownell, Graziano and Hartup, 1977). Competition under winner/loser conditions itself occurs according to the significance of the reward for the individuals involved and the nature of their relationships with one another (Tesser, Campbell, and Smith, 1984).

Children tend to interact in dyads rather than in larger sets. Three-child (and larger) enclaves are more common during middle than early childhood on playgrounds and in parks (Eifermann, 1971) but dyadic interaction remains common. Dyadic interaction, in contrast to interaction in triads or larger groups, is concentrated, intense, and more constrained by demands for intimacy and positive feedback (Weick and Penner, 1966). Consensus is easier to reach and leaders exert more extensive influence in small groups (Hare, 1953).

The existence of situational constraints on children's social interaction is thus well-documented. An integrated, ecological assessment of the peer context has not emerged but new work increasingly concerns contextual constraints on child-child interaction and we turn, next, to what is known about context and conflict.

Contextual Determinants of Children's Conflicts

Two kinds of contextual effects on children's conflicts can be identified: (a) constraints on the rate with which disputes occur and various tactics are used to settle them, and (b) constraints on the manifest issues involved in the disagreement. Psychologists have tended to pursue contextual effects on elicitation; sociolinguists, on the other hand, have pursued "contextualism" in the content and structure of children's disputes themselves (see Hay, 1984; Corsaro and Rizzo, 1990; Emihovich, 1986; Maynard, 1985).

As will be seen, "a conflict ecology" scarcely exists: setting effects on elicitation have been examined in a rather spotty fashion and with results that are not altogether consistent. In addition, settings almost always affect children's disagreements in combination with other conditions. Consider object struggles among young children: These disagreements suggest that attractive objects are important instigators of conflict and, in one sense, this is correct. Possession of objects, however, is not always what starts the dispute or keeps it going. Many conflicts over toys begin with one child wanting another child's toy when he or she already has one: the struggle, then, seems to involve control over the actions of the other child.

Children's conflicts are thus contextualized in one sense but not in another. Stated another way, children's conflicts almost always reflect the settings and relationships in which they are embedded, but settings and relationships don't account entirely for conflict elicitation or the strategies children choose to resolve them. We turn now to the matter of context and conflict with these considerations in mind.

Persons as Contextual Determinants of Children's Conflicts

Age and Sex Differences.   Conflicts vary in relation to both sex and age. Boys' conflicts differ from girls' conflicts and certain differences have been established between the conflicts of older and younger children. Since developmental trajectories in peer relations differ for boys and girls, and conflict variations seem to be manifestations of these differences, we consider age and sex differences simultaneously in this section.

Boys engage in more frequent conflicts than girls during early childhood (Dawe, 1934; Miller, Danaher, and Forbes, 1986; Shantz, 1986; Shantz and Shantz, 1985) but, within sex, rates remain fairly constant between the ages of 2 and 8 (Hay, 1984; Abramovitch, Corter, Pepler, and Stanhope, 1986; Howes and Wu, 1990). Comparable data for middle childhood and early adolescence are not available, but self-reports suggest that a rate change may occur during these years: Among sophomores and juniors in high school, girls report almost twice as many disagreements per day as boys (Laursen, 1989).

As children grow older, conflict issues gradually shift from control over objects to control over behavior. Toddlers disagree most often about possessions (Hay, 1984), but these disputes steadily decline in rate of occurrence until children start school, at which time conflicts are as likely to concern social issues as to concern objects (Shantz, 1987). Little is known about object struggles during middle childhood, although we know that they constitute a negligible proportion of peer conflicts during adolescence, having been replaced by social issues (Laursen, 1989).

Sex differences emerge relatively early in the social issues involved in conflict: Boys engage in more disagreements relating to power and abusive behavior than girls, while girls engage in more disagreements relating to interpersonal relations. These differences extend from the preschool years (Sheldon, 1990) through childhood (Maltz and Borker, 1982) to adolescence (Raffaelli, 1990; Youniss, 1980; Youniss and Smollar, 1985).

Conflict behaviors also vary according to age and sex. Goodwin and Goodwin (1987) observed friends, both preschoolers and early adolescents, in parks, yards, stoops, and street corners. Disagreements between males typically entailed power assertion (commands, threats, insults, and accusations) regardless of age. The disputes of older boys were only slightly more complex than those involving younger ones, as illustrated in the following exchange:

HUEY: Gimme the things.

CHOPPER: You shut up you big lips.

HUEY: Shut up.

CHOPPER: Don't gimme that. I'm not talkin ta you.

HUEY: I'm talkin ta you.

CHOPPER: Ah you better shut up with your little dingy sneaks.

HUEY: I'm a dingy your head. How would you like that?

CHOPPER: No, you won't you little—

(Goodwin and Goodwin, 1987)

Girls, in contrast, tended not to use confrontation with one another, reserving these behaviors for exchanges with boys. Instead, conflicts between girls were initiated indirectly, and bargaining and negotiation increased with age. Their disagreements revolved around long-running issues of interpersonal concern, with complicated interchanges carried forward across time and setting. The intricate structure of these disagreements is best illustrated by the ubiquitous "he said/she said" dispute [e.g., "And Stephen said that you said that I was showin off just because I had that blouse on"], which requires a convoluted process of checking and rechecking sources, witnesses, and assertions. Other studies show that power assertion, in general, declines as a form of conflict resolution during adolescence, while negotiation and withdrawal/disengagement increase (Selman, Beardslee, Schultz, Krupa, and Podorefsky, 1986; Youniss and Smollar, 1985; Blase, 1989). Power assertion remains more common, however, among males than among females.

Relatively little is known about the affective concomitants of children's conflicts as related to age and sex. Older children more commonly experience "after reactions" following disputes than younger children (Goodenough, 1931) and adolescent girls report frequently that negative affect persists following a disagreement while boys less often acknowledge affective lingering (Laursen, 1989). These results suggest that males may have a less mature understanding of peer relations than females, but it may also be the case that males do not associate threats, insults, and aggression with negative affect as consistently as females do.

Social interaction is as likely to be discontinued as continued following disagreements between preschool children (Laursen and Hartup, 1989). Adolescents, in contrast, almost always stay together and continue interacting following their conflicts (Laursen, 1989). While sex differences in these short-term outcomes are not evident among adolescents, perceptions of long-term outcomes differ: Boys are more likely than girls to report that, in the long run, disagreements don't affect their relationships very much. Girls, on the other hand, more often recognize long-term implications—both positive and negative ones (Laursen, 1989; Raffaelli, 1990).

Few investigators have considered the interaction between the child's age and sex and the companion's age and sex in relation to conflict management. By and large, the results summarized thus far in this section have not been reported separately by age and sex of the children's companions. Some investigators have reported that same-sex quarrels occur more frequently than those between members of the opposite sex (Dawe, 1934; Houseman, 1972; Sackin and Thelen, 1984), but social interaction baselines have not been controlled in most of the relevant comparisons. Conflict management styles also vary as a function of the child's sex and the companion's sex. For example, conflicts observed in mixed-sex groups of 5- and 7-year-olds (Miller, Danaher, and Forbes, 1986) showed that boys directed similar proportions of "heavy-handed" persuasion tactics (e.g., threats, physical force) to males (30%) and to females (22%), as well as proportions of conflict mitigation and compromise (8% each). Girls, however, discriminated according to the sex of their companions: mitigation was employed more frequently in conflict resolution with other females (26%) than with males (19%) while heavy-handed persuasion was used more with boys (24%) than with other girls (9%). Similar results were obtained by Goodwin and Goodwin (1987).

Overall, then, disagreements between young children typically arise over objects; tactics and strategies are used that underscore the transient nature of relationships at this time. As children grow older, conflicts increasingly center on interpersonal concerns. At the same time, tactics and strategies reflect a need to maintain good will as well as social interaction. Males do not embrace the shift to mutuality and trust in social relations as fully as females, perhaps because their close relationships are less intimate. These conclusions are tentative, however, since close relationships among males may be more variable in intimacy rather than modally different from females (Youniss and Smollar, 1985). Finally, girls employ strategies and tactics in conflict management that differ according to the sex of their companions; boys, on the other hand, are less discriminating.

Social reputation. Social interaction occurs mainly among children who know one another. Based on earlier encounters, children develop "schemata" or expectations about one another, among them schemata relating to aggression and contentiousness. Reputations for physical and verbal aggression are associated with being disliked by other children (Hartup, 1983), a connection which can be established very quickly as children get to know one another (Dodge, 1983). Once established, these social expectations remain relatively stable over time (Coie, Dodge, and Kupersmidt, 1990) and bias the attitudes and behavior of other children. Peers anticipate hostility and destructiveness from a child who has an aggressive reputation even when provocation is uncertain (Dodge, 1980).

According to an information-processing account developed by Dodge (1986), salient cues in every social act are encoded, mentally represented, and stored in a manner that establishes these biases. First, aggression and argumentativeness result in selective attention to these same behaviors in subsequent encounters, as well as selective inattention to other (less noxious) actions. Second, aggression and argumentativeness constrain subsequent interpretations of an individual's actions because perceivers tend to view succeeding actions as confirmations rather than disconfirmations of earlier impressions (Darley and Fazio, 1980). Third, unfavorable impressions are easy to acquire and difficult to disconfirm; positive impressions, on the other hand, are hard to acquire and difficult to disconfirm; positive impressions, on the other hand, are hard to acquire and difficult to disestablish (Rothbart and Park, 1986). Negative behaviors are also attributed by children to more stable causes when displayed by disliked rather than liked children, whereas positive behaviors are attributed to more stable causes when displayed by liked rather than disliked youngsters (Hymel, 1986). Fourth, aggressive interpretations of other children's actions are accompanied by biases in response selection that favor counteraggression (Dodge, 1980). Taken together, these notions constitute a strong argument to the effect that social reputations are important aspects of the social context.

Most of the empirical work suggesting that social reputations are important determinants of social interaction has dealt with aggression; virtually no distinction between aggression and conflict has been made in the relevant studies (see Dodge, 1986; Dodge, Coie, Pettit and Price, 1990). To argue that social reputations are important contextual elements in conflict management thus requires considerable extrapolation from the available evidence. On the other hand, we know that: (a) Large numbers of countervailing instances are required among adults to disconfirm the notion that other individuals are *argumentative* (Rothbart and Park, 1986). (b) Disliked children are viewed by their classmates as more likely to use angry retaliation strategies in conflict resolution than popular, neglected, or average children, and, conversely, popular children are viewed as more likely to use "calm" discussion strategies of conflict resolution than are rejected children (Bryant, 1989). (c) Socially rejected children, as compared to socially accepted children, also have more difficulty in resolving disputes with their friends (Asher and Parker, 1989). (d) Finally, we know that, when conflict and aggression rates are co-varied, conflict is significantly correlated with peer rejection while aggression isn't (Shantz and Shantz, 1985; Shantz, 1986). Taken together, these results strongly suggest that social reputation is a significant determinant of conflict management, as well as aggression and peer rejection.

Relationships as Contextual Determinants of Children's Conflicts

Conflict behavior is determined, in considerable measure, by the social relationships existing between the actors involved. When strangers or mere acquaintances disagree, individuals seek to maximize immediate benefits for themselves, each employing whatever tactics are necessary to prevail, with little regard for the other party (Deutsch, 1973). Within close relationships, however, winning may be less important than the rewards of continued social interaction (Berscheid, 1986). Short-term benefits of winning an argument thus must be balanced against long-term consequences.

Friends. Although children consider disagreements to be barriers in making friends, and certain evidence supports this claim (Gottman, 1983), the involvement of conflict in friendship relations is very complex. School-aged children, for example, believe that conflicts are inherent in close relationships and, when worked out, actually strengthen them (Selman, 1980). Older children and adolescents also differentiate between conflicts that are relatively minor (and that the relationship itself may serve to ameliorate) from those that threaten the very existence of the relationship (usually violations of trust).

Differences are clearly evident in the ways that children and adolescents manage their conflicts with friends and with acquaintances, but these differences vary according to the situation (Hartup and Laursen, 1989). In some settings, children seek to minimize the impact of conflict with their friends to a greater extent than with nonfriends. In other situations, friends appear to be "freer" in conflict interaction than nonfriends. Conflict rates, too, are related to friendship status, but also according to the setting in which the interaction occurs. For example, children have more frequent conflicts with their friends than with nonfriends during activities in which they are ego-invested, but fewer conflicts with friends during activities when ego-investment is absent (Tesser, Campbell, and Smith, 1984).

Owing to these situational variations, relationship strength by itself may be a poor predictor of conflict (Hinde, Titmus, Easton, and Tamplin, 1985) even though extreme conflict difficulties indicate the existence of dysfunctional relationships (Gottman, 1979; Robin and Foster, 1984; Rutter, Graham, Chadwick, and Yule, 1976). These interactions between friendship status and setting condition are discussed more specifically in the concluding sections of this chapter (pp. 71–73).

Siblings. Sibling relationships are similar to friendships in certain ways, but different in others. Siblings share possessions and responsibilities as well as share their parents, conditions that do not apply to friendships. Sibling relationships also have a permanence that friendships do not. Under ordinary circumstances, they cannot be terminated however dysfunctional they may be. And, finally, sibling relationships are also "mixed-age" relationships, meaning that brothers and sisters (twins excepted) differ in social skill to a greater extent than friends do.

Differences between sibling and peer relationships are not consistently evident in conflict rates; results vary according to the subjects' ages and the methodologies used. Observational studies, for example, show no differences between 4- to 10-year-old friends and siblings in rates of agonism, a somewhat less-than-perfect conflict index (Abramovitch et al., 1986; Stoneman, Brody, and MacKinnon, 1984), nor do self-report measures show consistent differences in conflict rates among younger school-age children (Buhrmester and Furman, 1990). In contrast, among preadolescents and adolescents, self-report methods indicate that conflicts occur more frequently between siblings than between friends (Furman and Buhrmester, 1985; Buhrmester and Furman,

1990). Even so, one investigator found the opposite (Blase, 1989), while another reported no differences (Laursen, 1989).

Additionally, it is not clear if sibling conflicts increase as children get older (Abramovitch et al., 1986) or decrease (Brody, Stoneman, MacKinnon, and MacKinnon, 1985). Sex differences are also uncertain, with some investigators reporting that cross-sex conflicts occur more often than same-sex disputes (Dunn and Kendrick, 1981, Whiting and Whiting, 1975), others reporting more frequent same-sex disputes (Minnett et al., 1983), some reporting more frequent conflicts among males than among females (Abramovitch, Corter, and Lando, 1979; Brody et al., 1985; Stoneman et al., 1984), and still others reporting no sex differences in conflict rates (Abramovitch, Corter, and Pepler, 1980; Lamb, 1978; Pepler, Abramovitch, and Corter, 1981). Everyone agrees, however, that older siblings initiate disagreements with their brothers and sisters more frequently than younger ones.

Sibling and friendship relations differ more clearly from one another in conflict issues than in conflict rates. Disagreements involving possessions and personal property remain common between siblings through childhood and adolescence (Laursen, 1989; Raffaelli, 1990), whereas objects become less and less salient in disagreements between friends. Conflicts between young siblings are also likely to be related to the mother or access to her (Dunn and Kendrick, 1981); no similar issue figures in friendship relations.

Siblings employ coercive tactics during their disagreements more frequently than friends (Raffaelli, 1990); their disagreements are also characterized by more intense affect (Laursen, 1989). These differences may account for the fact that parental intervention in sibling disputes is common (Dunn and Munn, 1985; Raffaelli, 1990; Sutton-Smith and Rosenberg, 1968), and why it is relatively uncommon during conflicts between friends. In most other respects, the conflict resolution strategies employed by friends and siblings are similar. Ranked in order of occurrence, these strategies include withdrawal, power assertion, and compromise (Montemayor and Hanson, 1985; Raffaelli, 1990; Vuchinich, 1987).

Finally, disagreements have a different impact on the social relations of siblings and friends. Friends are more likely than siblings to report continued social interaction and positive feelings following a disagreement (Laursen, 1989; Raffaelli, 1990).

But even though negative affect lingers after disputes between siblings, the sibling relationship is not generally as vulnerable to conflict as friendship relations. By its very nature, the sibling relationship is durable and enduring; negative affect and even aggression cannot change the fact that the obnoxious person is still your little brother, someone with whom you must "get along." On the other hand, aggression and disagreements routinely destroy children's friendships. Conflict, then, marks both friendships and sibling relationships in distinctive ways.

Group Arrangements as Conflict Determinants

Space and resources. Numerous crowding studies have been conducted over the years (see Smith and Connolly, 1981; Hartup, 1983; Parke and Slaby, 1983; Minuchin and Shapiro, 1983), most of them directed at two issues: (a) behavioral changes associated with increasing the number of individuals occupying a constant space, and (b) changes associated with variations in the space available to a constant number of individuals. Good experimental designs in this area require that resource densities be kept constant and that rough and tumble play, aggression, and conflict be examined separately. In most instances, aggression and conflict have *not* been disentangled, so that crowding effects on conflict can only be guessed at.

The weight of the evidence suggests that crowding large numbers of children into small spaces, especially with less than 20 square feet per child, is marked by more aggression than less crowded conditions. One investigator (Ginsburg, 1975) also reported that more fights, but shorter ones, occurred on a small playground than on a large one, suggesting that conflict durations and their intensities may be related to crowding as well as the frequency with which aggression occurs.

Variations in social densities are sometimes confounded with variations in the amount of play equipment available. Smith and Connolly (1981), however, varied social and resource densities separately and found that aggression increased with social density when resource availability was kept constant. Density had little effect, however, when resources were simultaneously increased. Resource densities seem to relate to both conflict and aggression. For example, Smith (1974) found that, among nursery school children, aggression most frequently occurred in the context of disagreements about toys and play equipment; the disagreements themselves increased as the number of toys was reduced (see also Smith and Connolly, 1981).

Crowding thus seems to increase aggression, especially when play equipment is scarce. The evidence is not entirely clear, however, as to whether the increases in aggression are independent of increases in conflict. Crowding does not always increase aggression, and sharing sometimes occurs more frequently when relatively little play equipment is available rather than when it is plentiful. Habituation may attenuate crowding effects, too (Fagot, 1977), in that children in some cultures seem not to be as affected by crowding as children in others. Overall, crowded conditions that force children into interdependent relations with one another appear to increase conflicts. But crowding effects would be better understood through investigations that separated conflicts from aggression.

Goal structures and group relations. Social climate and group relations have a bearing on conflict, as a series of well-known investigations shows. The social climate established by authoritarian leadership elevates both aggression and conflict among children, once they have been left to their own devices (Lewin, Lippitt, and White, 1938). Similarly, competitive goal structures ("winner take all" conditions) elicit blocking and task interference as well as aggression and self-enhancing statements ("I've done a lot more than you"; Bryant, 1977). Unfavorable social comparisons in some competitive situations, however, more commonly occur among "losers" than among "winners" (Ames, Ames, and Felker, 1977).

Relations between one group and another bear on the disagreements occurring within the groups, separately. Competition between groups initially increases intragroup conflicts, including blaming one another and scapegoating; these conflicts, however, decrease over time and group solidarity reemerges. Competition between groups, however, supports continuing conflict and disharmony between the collectives themselves: only cooperation in seeking common objectives ameliorates these disagreements (Sherif, Harvey, White, Hood, and Sherif, 1961).

Children separate themselves into small groups on playgrounds and in other situations in which numerous individuals are gathered together. Children prefer dyadic or triadic interaction for social intercourse, owing to the intensity and concentration that one-on-one situations permit (Peters and Torrance, 1972); games and play equipment must often be used by small enclaves, too. But these subdivisions are not fixed: Children understand that new children can enter them and new group arrangements made.

Group entry, however, is a difficult task: In fact, young children resist approximately 50% of other children's attempts to enter into their activities (cf. Corsaro, 1981). Children vary enormously in the success with which they gain group entry but, even so, the entry attempts of the most socially competent children are resisted 25% of the time (Putallaz and Gottman, 1981). Group entry thus exposes nearly everyone to social conflict. Moreover, these conflicts are difficult to resolve, requiring considerable skill by the entrant. Indeed, entry success is not a matter of choosing one "correct" overture, but a matter of undertaking a *series* of actions beginning with "hovering" (in order to make sure that one understands the group's frame of reference and the participation structure of the activity) and extending to mimicry and making relevant comments (in order to slip into the activity itself) (Dodge, Schlundt, Schocken, and Delugach, 1983; Garvey, 1984).

Resistance to the entry attempts of other children is not well understood. Among younger children, resistance is centered on property and territorial rights as well as on crowding; friendship rights, gender-related prerogatives, and unjustified refusals are also common. Same-sex groups, especially boys' groups, are difficult to enter by members of the opposite sex; mixed-sex groups are easier to enter by boys than by girls (Corsaro, 1981). Strange children have a harder time than old-timers; popular children have an easier time than rejected children. But little is known about the children's activities in relation to group resistance, an unfortunate omission since resistance may be grounded in children's notions than bringing others into an ongoing activity is likely to be disruptive.

Clearly, group entry is a significant social challenge, beginning in early childhood, owing mainly to the regularity with which it elicits conflict. We know little about why children seek entry into some groups more persistently than others, or why certain groups are harder to enter than others are. Much has been learned about individual differences in the success with which children negotiate group entry (Putallaz and Wasserman, 1990) but, at the same time, relatively little is known about group characteristics in relation to the instigation of entry conflicts.

Activities as Conflict Determinants

Intrinsic effects. Conflicts between children occur during play more often than during any other activity. Conflicts between siblings often involve the mother as a third party (see above) but even sibling conflicts occur more commonly in play than during any other activity (Hay, 1984; Shantz, 1987).

Conflicts occurring in the play of younger children involve two main issues—object control and social control (see Hay, 1984; Shantz, 1987). Social control issues can be classified according to whether access (group entry), play routines, or claims about opinions and beliefs are most salient (Corsaro and Rizzo, in press). Children thus oppose one another most frequently over who plays with whom and with what, as well as what one believes about the rules of the game and how to play it.

Among young children, play activities that involve shared space and equipment or that are markedly enriched by the presence of others elicit the highest rates of social interaction and, consequently, the most frequent conflicts. Block building, housekeeping, and dramatic play thus generate more frequent conflicts than painting, story time, puzzles, and table activities (Shure, 1963; Charlesworth and Hartup, 1967). Although activities inviting social interaction logically lead to more conflict than activities involving less extensive interaction, those involving space that must be shared, equipment that must be negotiated, or small groups that necessarily exclude others are especially conflict-prone (Houseman, 1972; Minuchin and Shapiro, 1983). Similar studies dealing with the role of toys and games in conflict instigation among older children are not available, although observations of preadolescents attending summer camps show that "robust" interactions, including assertiveness and blocking attempts, occur more frequently in swimming and certain sports activities than during crafts (Gump, Schoggen, and Redl, 1957).

Among adolescents, objects are not major conflict issues except between siblings, and these are mostly centered on the telephone and the television set. Organized games provoke conflicts but, otherwise, play does not provide a major setting for disagreements. On the other hand, "claims," including disagreements about ideas and opinions, standards of behavior, personal annoy-ances, and friendship responsibilities are prominent conflict is-sues among American teenagers (Laursen, 1989). These occur most frequently during "socializing," an activity that takes place in cars, shopping malls, school hallways and cafeterias, and other out-of-school and out-of-home locations (Medrich, Rosen, Rubin, and Buckley, 1982).

The evidence thus suggests these hypotheses: (a) Children's activities, especially play, constrain the occurrence of social con-flict through the amount and kind of social interaction elicited. (b) Conflicts occur more frequently during activities in which children and adolescents are socially interdependent than when they are not. (c) Play declines as a primary setting for children's conflicts, being replaced during preadolescence and adolescence by games and socializing (see also p. 55). No clear conflict differ-ences between indoor and outdoor settings are evident.

Mediated effects. Among older children and adolescents, ac-tivities elicit disagreements according to the individual's invest-ment in the activity and relationships with the other individuals involved. Most individuals strive to maintain positive views of themselves, and these self-views rest mainly on performance in *relevant* activities, for example, activities in which one is ego-invested. For example, performance on math tests or in soccer games may be relevant dimensions of self-evaluation for some individuals but not their piano playing; performance in piano playing, however, may be a relevant activity for others. But so-cial interaction rests on the *closeness* of relations between com-panions as well as the relevance of the activity in which they are engaged. Outstanding performance by a close friend may be threatening when the activity is especially relevant to one's self-esteem, whereas outstanding performance in the same activity by a more distant individual may not be.

These notions (Tesser, 1984) have been examined in a series of studies with preadolescents and adolescents showing that, during relevant tasks with friends and strangers, subjects make the task hard for their friends and easy for strangers whereas the reverse occurs on nonrelevant tasks (Tesser and Smith, 1980). Children also make biased comparisons between themselves and others, favoring their own performance over their friends' in rel-evant activities while favoring the performance of their friends in irrelevant ones (Tesser et al., 1984). Self-evaluation, too, is likely to be more negative following disagreements with a friend than following disagreements with a nonfriend (Aboud, 1989). These notions have been tested with competition rather than conflict behavior, but two hypotheses can be drawn from the existing data, namely, that: (a) conflicts are more intense between friends than between nonfriends when performance is relevant to self-definition but less intense when performance is not; and (b) self-evaluations will be more negative following conflict with friends than conflict with nonfriends but only when the disagreements concern relevant issues.

Should these ideas concerning the relevance of an activity be correct, other findings must be reinterpreted. For example, Berndt (1981) found that, among boys, competition for a scarce resource was greater between friends than between nonfriends; girls, on the other hand, did not differentiate between friends and nonfriends. While the results suggest sex differences in competitiveness, the data may also mean that the activity (being the first to finish a coloring task) was simply more relevant for the boys than for the girls (Tesser, 1984). In other words, the results may reflect sex differences in ego-involvement in the activity rather than sex differences in competitiveness.

This interaction between relevance and relationships in the instigation of conflict would apply to school-aged children and adolescents more extensively than to younger children. Preschoolers are known to engage in social comparisons in only limited ways (Feldman and Ruble, 1981), yet the self-evaluation model assumes their existence.

"Open" Versus "Closed" Settings

Settings vary in the degree to which individuals are free to choose or change companions, behave independently, or withdraw entirely from social interaction. On playgrounds, for example, children usually have considerable freedom to select their companions, their activities, and to determine the length of their interaction. Similar conditions occur indoors during "free play." Under these conditions, the actions of Child A do not completely constrain Child B's success in obtaining the objectives he or she desires. Settings such as these can be called *open.* In contrast, when an adult selects two children from a classroom and asks them to sit at a table and play Parchesi until a bell rings, the children are interacting under *closed* conditions, that is, with no choice concerning who their companions will be, whether to interact with them or not, and in which activities they should engage. Organized outdoor games also represent situations that are relatively closed. In closed situations, the children are especially interdependent: Whether one child obtains his or her desired objectives is heavily constrained by the actions of the other one.

Disagreements may differ in open and closed situations. First, closed situations sometimes elicit more frequent conflicts than open situations, simply because social exchanges occur more frequently in closed than in open circumstances. Second, closed situations confront children with mandated activities, that is, tasks in which they must engage together. We suggest that the likelihood of disagreements is greater in these situations, as compared with open ones, through the greater demands that mandated activities make for exploring different points of view, selecting among alternatives, and negotiating solutions. Third, disagreements in closed situations may be more intense than disagreements in open ones (and dominance behaviors more evident) since the children cannot withdraw as a means of conflict resolution. When children can't withdraw, disagreements recursively elicit other, more intense, disagreements through the successive frustrations they represent (Patterson, Littman and Bricker, 1967).

Open and closed situations have not been compared directly. Young children's conflicts have been observed by some investigators during free play in nursery schools and day-care centers (open situations) and by others in structured settings (closed situations). One survey (Hay, 1984) covered conflicts observed during free play in 31 different nursery school and day-care classes over a 50-year period: the median number of conflicts (mostly dyadic) occurring across groups was 4.6 per child per hour. Toddlers have also been observed in three instances interacting with one other child under closed conditions (i.e., the subjects could not withdraw). Hourly rates of conflict in these three cases were: (a) 18.6 between 2-year-olds (Maudry and Nekula, 1939); (b) 9.2 between 21-month-olds (Hay and Ross, 1982); and (c) 15.0 between 12- 18-month-olds and 10.0 between 18- and 24-month-olds (Russell, 1981). Comparisons across these studies must be made cautiously since the subjects in the two sets differed in age, the number of observation sessions differed, and definitions of conflict varied. Nevertheless, the number of conflicts occurring in closed situations appears to be substantially greater than the number occurring in open ones.

Among school-aged children observed during free play on playgrounds, conflict rates have not been reported apart from aggression. Aggression rates seldom average more than 1 or 2 per hour (Parke and Slaby, 1983). In contrast, the hourly disagreement rate occurring in one closed situation (a board game) was 35 per hour (Hartup et al., 1992).

Conflict durations do not seem to differ much according to situational openness. Quarrels in nursery school free play were observed in one investigation to last an average of 24 seconds (Dawe, 1934) while conflicts (using a more inclusive definition) were observed another time to last an average of 15–18 seconds (Green, 1933). At the same time, conflict durations in closed laboratory situations have been reported to average 22.7 seconds (Hay and Ross, 1982).

Toward a Contextual Theory of Children's Conflicts

Again and again, this review suggests that conflicts are especially evident when individuals are socially interdependent. When many children occupy a small space, when resources are limited, when play equipment requires coordinated activity or negotiation, and when the situation is "closed," conflict is likely to occur more frequently and be more intense than when interaction occurs in more open, "non-enmeshed" circumstances.

When friends interact with one another, in contrast to nonfriends, social interdependencies are especially great; equity and reciprocity are expected in the exchanges of friends with one another whereas these expectations do not exist between children who are "neutral associates," that is, who neither like nor dislike one another. Friends may also feel freer to criticize one another than nonfriends do, and be more secure in testing limits. Thus, conflict should be especially vigorous when friends, as compared with nonfriends, interact in closed situations. On the other hand, conflict should not be especially intense when friends, as compared with nonfriends, interact in open settings. This interaction effect has not been studied directly, but relevant studies can be examined separately according to whether the setting utilized was "closed" or "open."

Conflict Rates

A growing body of evidence shows that, in closed situations, conflicts and disagreements indeed occur more frequently between friends than nonfriends. Preschool friends have been shown to disagree with each other more frequently than nonfriends during conversations at play (Gottman, 1983). School-aged friends disagree more than nonfriends during discussions of social issues (Nelson and Aboud, 1985) and while playing a board game when previously taught different rules (Hartup et al., in press). These differences do not derive from the greater sociability of friends than nonfriends, since these friend/nonfriend differences in disagreement rates were sustained when sociability was partialled out.

Conflict rates differ less consistently between friends and nonfriends in open situations. Observations of nursery school children in two studies, controlling for the amount of time that the children spent together, revealed that conflicts occurred no more often between friends than between acquaintances (Hartup et al., 1988; Vespo and Caplan, 1988). In two other investigations, the stronger the "association" between two children (i.e., the more time spent together), the fewer conflicts (Green, 1933; Hinde et al., 1985). Observational data are not available for either school-aged children or adolescents, but teenagers' self-reports actually suggest that *more* conflicts occur with friends than with nonfriends, even when adjustments are made for time spent together (Laursen, 1989).

Conflict Management

Other data show that, as expected, conflicts are more intense in closed situations between friends than between nonfriends, and assertive exchanges more common. In one investigation (Hartup et al., in press), conflicts between friends during a board game were more intense and lasted longer than conflicts between nonfriends. Friends did not talk more during their conflicts than nonfriends but assertions were used selectively according to friendship and sex: With friends, girls used assertions accompanied by rationales more frequently than boys, whereas boys used assertions without rationales more frequently than girls. These sex differences were not evident during conflicts between non-friends. Nelson and Aboud (1985) reported that criticisms and explanations were exchanged more frequently during discussions of social issues by friends than nonfriends among both sexes.

Open situations, on the other hand, give rise to conflicts that are not as intense between friends as between nonfriends— both among young children in free play (Hartup et al., 1988) and among adolescents during out-of-class socializing (Laursen, 1989). Under open conditions, tactics and strategies used by friends are more flexible and "softer" than those used by nonfriends. Friends also are less likely to demand capitulation and more likely to disengage. Disagreements between friends are resolved more equitably (winner/loser outcomes are less common) than disputes between nonfriends (Hartup et al., 1988; Vespo and Caplan, 1988) and friends continue their interaction following disagreements whereas nonfriends don't. These results were obtained through observations in nursery schools, although adolescents' self-reports are similar, that is, social interaction commonly continues following disagreements between friends but not following disagreements between nonfriends. Adolescents' self-reports tell us something else about disagreements in open situations: When queried about long-term impact, these students indicate that disagreements usually improve relations with close friends while worsening relations with others (Laursen, 1989).

Comment

The existing data, while not extensive, thus support the hypothesis that situational openness and friendship relations interact as determinants of children's conflicts. In closed situations, (i.e., when social interdependencies are especially salient), children engage in more frequent and more intense conflicts with friends than with nonfriends. The current evidence is not completely consistent, however, concerning conflicts in open situations: Conflict rates do not differ between friends and nonfriends, even though disagreements occurring between friends are clearly not as intense and are resolved via "softer" tactics than disagreements occurring between nonfriends.

Conflict thus appears to differ between friends and nonfriends according to context. When social alternatives are available (i.e., the situation is "open"), friends manage conflicts in such a way as to minimize their impact. Conflicts themselves are inevitable in these situations, deriving from each child's efforts to obtain desired goals; thus conflict rates should not differ much between friends and nonfriends in open situations. Friends, however, are constantly in competition with other children to provide pleasant and rewarding exchanges for one another. Thus, when a conflict arises in an open situation, there is always the danger that one child may pick up his marbles and find someone else to play with. Conflict does not pose this same threat for nonfriends. Stated another way: friends have made a considerable investment of time, energy, and affect in one another, suggesting that they will make stronger efforts than nonfriends to minimize the damage resulting from social conflict. And the data show that, in open situations, they do.

When children cannot change partners or activities (i.e., when the situation is "closed"), friends can disagree with little risk. No danger exists, in these situations, that one's companion will take his or her marbles elsewhere. When the situation is closed, friends actually can be expected to disagree more intensely than nonfriends because they are "freer" and more secure with one another than nonfriends, and know one another better. It may also be that children wish to avoid the negative self-evaluations that are more likely to result from losing relevant arguments with friends than from losing such arguments with nonfriends (Tesser, 1984). Empirical studies do not yet specify the processes underlying the greater propensity for friends, as compared with nonfriends, to disagree with one another more frequently and more intensely in closed situations. Nevertheless, the evidence suggests that friendship and situational context combine as determinants of children's disagreements.

Playgrounds are generally open settings in that children can choose their playmates there, choose their activities, and determine how long they remain together. Consequently, what has been said about conflict in open situations may be more applicable to playground interaction than what has been said about conflict in closed situations. Playgrounds, however, are not single behavior settings but multiple ones; both open and closed conditions can be found there. Organized games with clear-cut rules and assigned positions, for example, are relatively closed social situations whereas free play is not. We also assume that, as applied to social situations, openness is a continuous variable rather than a categorical one. Playgrounds thus can be seen as containing many different behavior settings, varying considerably in the extent to which they are open or closed. Consequently, we believe that what we have said about *both* open and closed situations has relevance to children's socializing on the playground.

CONCLUSION

Children's conflicts are constrained by the social contexts in which they occur. Children's disagreements derive substantively from what they are doing with one another and the settings in which they interact. Among young children, conflict is most commonly embedded in play; among older children and adolescents, disagreements occur mainly in "socializing." Both quantitative and qualitative dimensions of these disagreements vary with the age and sex of the opponents, whether the disputants are friends or siblings, with goal structures, with group arrangements, and with the nature and importance of the activity to the individuals involved. Playground conflicts are presumably constrained by these same contextual elements.

Multivariate studies in this field are relatively rare, but the evidence suggests that contextual constraints on children's conflicts occur in combination with one another. Friendship relations, for example, appear to be related to both quantitative and qualitative dimensions of conflict in combination with the "openness" of the social situation and the relevance of the activities in which the children are engaged. New studies must examine these combinatorial effects directly: Inferring their existence from univariate studies is not appropriate. Nevertheless, we believe that the current evidence provides a range of interesting multivariate hypotheses that ought to be tested.

Rather consistently, *socially interdependent conditions* seem to intensify children's conflicts. Whether these interdependencies derive from close relationships (e.g., sibling relationships or friendships), from scarcity of resources and group arrangements, or from the closed nature of the social situation, interdependent conditions frequently are associated with elevated conflict rates and more intense disagreements. Other conditions sometimes moderate these effects and current results are not completely consistent concerning this issue. More direct investigation of these social interdependencies and their relation to conflict is needed, especially among the many behavioral settings found on ordinary playgrounds.

NOTE

1. Societal change involves similar disagreements between individuals and collectives, according to the tenets of dialectical materialism.

REFERENCES

Aboud, F. E. (1989). Disagreement between friends. *International Journal of Behavioral Development, 12*, 495–508.

Abramovitch, R., Corter, C., and Lando, B. (1979). Sibling interaction in the home. *Child Development, 50*, 997–1003.

Abramovitch, R., Corter, C., and Pepler, D. J. (1980). Observations of mixed-sex sibling dyads. *Child Development, 51*, 1268–1271.

Abramovitch, R., Corter, C., Pepler, D. J., and Stanhope, L. (1986). Sibling and peer interaction: A final follow-up and a comparison. *Child Development, 57*, 217–229.

Ames, C., Ames, R., and Felker, D. W. (1977). Effects of competitive reward structure and valence of outcome on children's achievement attributions. *Journal of Educational Psychology, 69*, 1–8.

Asher, S. R., and Parker, J. G. (1989). Significance of peer relationship problems in childhood. In B. H. Schneider, G. Attili, J. Nadel, and R. P. Weissberg (Eds.), *Social competence in developmental perspective* (pp. 5–23). Dordrecht, Netherlands: Kluwer Academic Publishers.

Baldwin, J. M. (1897). *Social and ethical interpretations in mental development*. New York: Macmillan.

Berndt, T. J. (1981). Effects of friendship on prosocial intentions and behavior. *Child Development, 52*, 636–643.

————. (1986). Sharing between friends: Context and consequences. In E. C. Mueller and C. R. Cooper (Eds.), *Process and outcome in peer relationships* (pp. 105–127). New York: Academic Press.

Berscheid, E. (1986). Emotional experience in close relationships: Some implications for child development. In W. W. Hartup and and Z. Rubin (Eds.), *Relationships and development* (pp. 135–166). Hillsdale, NJ: Erlbaum.

Blase, R. S. (1989). *Adolescents' perceptions of conflict and conflict resolution in three domains of social relationship.* Unpublished doctoral dissertation, Wayne State University.

Bowlby, J. (1969). *Attachment.* New York: Basic Books.

Brody, G. H., Stoneman, Z., MacKinnon, C. E., and MacKinnon, R. (1985). Role relationships and behavior between preschool-aged and school-aged sibling pairs. *Developmental Psychology, 21*, 124–129.

Bronfenbrenner, U. (1979). *The ecology of human development: Experiments by nature and design.* Cambridge, MA: Harvard University Press.

Bryant, B. K. (1977). The effects of the interpersonal context of evaluation on self- and other-enhancement behavior. *Child Development, 48*, 885–892.

————. (1989, April). *Conflict resolution strategies in relation to children's peer relations.* Paper presented at the biennial meetings of the Society for Research in Child Development, Kansas City, MO.

Buhrmester, D., and Furman, W. (1990). Perceptions of sibling relationships during middle childhood and adolescence. *Child Development, 61*, 1387–1398.

Charlesworth, R., and Hartup, W. W. (1967). Positive social reinforcement in the nursery school peer group. *Child Development, 38*, 993–1002.

Coie, J. D., Dodge, K. A., and Kupersmidt, J. B. (1990). Group behavior and social status. In S. R. Asher and J. D. Coie (Eds.), *Peer rejection in childhood: Origins, consequences, and intervention* (pp. 17–59). Cambridge, UK: Cambridge University Press.

Cooley, C. H. (1909). *Social organization.* New York: Scribners.

Corsaro, W. A. (1981). Friendship in the nursery school: Social organization in a peer environment. In S. R. Asher and J. M. Gottman (Eds.), *The development of children's friendships* (pp. 207–241). Cambridge, UK: Cambridge University Press.

Corsaro, W. A., and Rizzo, T. A. (1990). Disputes and conflict resolution among nursery school children in the U.S. and Italy. In A. D. Grimshaw (Ed.), *Conflict talk.* Cambridge, UK: Cambridge University Press.

Coser, L. A. (1967). *Continuities in the study of social conflict.* New York: Free Press.

Darley, J. M., and Pazio, R. H. (1980). Expectancy confirmation processes arising in the social interaction sequence. *American Psychologist, 35,* 867–881.

Dawe, H. C. (1934). An analysis of two hundred quarrels of preschool children. *Child Development, 5,* 139–157.

Deutsch. M. (1973). *The resolution of conflict.* New Haven, CT: Yale University Press.

Dodge, K. A. (1980). Social cognition and children's aggressive behavior. *Child Development, 51,* 162–170.

———. (1983). Behavioral antecedents of peer social status. *Child Development, 54,* 1386–1399.

———. (1986). A social information processing model of social competence in children. In M. Perlmutter (Ed.), *Minnesota Symposia on Child Psychology,* Vol. 18 (pp. 77–126). Hillsdale, NJ: Erlbaum.

Dodge, K. A., Coie, J. D., Pettit, G. S., and Price, J. M. (1990). Peer status and aggression in boys' groups: Developmental and contextual analyses. *Child Development, 61,* 1289–1309.

Dodge, K. A., Schlundt, D. G., Schocken, I., and Delugach, J. D. (1983). Social competence and children's social status: The role of peer group entry strategies. *Merrill-Palmer Quarterly, 29,* 309–336.

Dollard, J., and Miller, N. E. (1950). *Personality and psychotherapy.* New York: McGraw-Hill.

Dunn, J., and Kendrick, C. (1981). Social behavior of young siblings in the family context: Differences between same-sex and different-sex dyads. *Child Development, 52,* 1265–1273.

Dunn, J., and Munn, P. (1985). Becoming a family member: Family conflict and the development of social understanding. *Child Development, 56,* 480–492.

Eifermann, R. R. (1971). *Determinants of children's game styles.* Jerusalem: Israel Academy of Sciences.

Eisenberg, A. R., and Garvey, C. (1981). Children's use of verbal strategies in resolving conflicts. *Discourse Processes, 4,* 149–170.

Emihovich, C. (1986). Argument as status assertion: Contextual variations in children's disputes. *Language and Society, 15,* 485–500.

Erikson, E. (1950). *Child and society.* New York: Norton.

Fagot, B. I. (1977). Variations in density: Effect on task and social behaviors of preschool children. *Developmental Psychology, 13,* 166–167.

Feldman, N. S., and Ruble, D. N. (1981). The development of person perception: Cognitive and social factors. In S. S. Brehm, S. M. Kassin, and F. X. Gibbons (Eds.), *Developmental social psychology* (pp. 191–206). Oxford, UK: Oxford University Press.

Foot, H. C., Chapman, A. J., and Smith, J. R. (1977). Friendship and social responsiveness in boys and girls. *Journal of Personality and Social Psychology, 35,* 401–411.

French, D. C., Brownell, C. A., Graziano, W. G., and Hartup, W. W. (1977). Effects of cooperative, competitive, and individualistic sets on performance in children's groups. *Journal of Experimental Child Psychology, 24,* 1–10.

Freud, S. (1930). *Three contributions to the theory of sex.* New York: Nervous and Mental Disease Publishing Co. (originally published in 1905).

Furman, W., and Buhrmester, D. (1985). Children's perceptions of the personal relationships in their social networks. *Developmental Psychology, 21,* 1016–1024.

Garvey, C. (1984). *Children's talk.* Cambridge, MA: Harvard University Press.

Ginsburg, H. J. (1975, April). *Variations of aggressive interaction among male elementary school children as a function of spatial density.* Paper presented at the biennial meetings of the Society for Research in Child Development, Denver, CO.

Goodenough, F. L. (1931). *Anger in young children.* Minneapolis: University of Minnesota Press.

Goodnow, J., and Burns, A. (1988). *Home and school: Child's eye view.* Sydney: Allen and Unwin.

Goodwin, M. H., and Goodwin, C. (1987). Children's arguing. In S. Phillips, S. Steele, and C. Tans (Eds.), *Language, gender, and sex in comparative perspective* (pp. 85–117). Cambridge, UK: Cambridge University Press.

Gottman, J. M. (1979). *Marital interaction: Experimental investigations.* New York: Academic Press.

———. (1983). How children become friends. *Monographs of the Society for Research in Child Development, 48* (Serial No. 201).

Green, E. H. (1933). Friendships and quarrels among preschool children. *Child Development, 4,* 237–252.

Gump, P., Schoggen, P., and Redl, F. (1957). The camp milieu and its immediate effects. *Journal of Social Issues, 13,* 40–46.

Hare, A. P. (1953). Small group discussions with participatory and supervisory leadership. *Journal of Abnormal and Social Psychology, 48,* 273–275.

Hartup, W. W. (1970). Peer relations and social organization. In P. H. Mussen (Ed.), *Carmichael's manual of child psychology,* Vol. 2 (pp. 361–456). New York: Wiley.

———. (1983). Peer relations. In E. M. Hetherington (Ed.), P. H. Mussen (Series Ed.), *Handbook of child psychology,* Vol. 4 (pp. 103–196). New York: Wiley.

———. (1984). The peer context in middle childhood. In W. A. Collins (Ed.), *Development during middle childhood* (pp. 240–282). Washington, DC: National Academy Press.

———. (1989). Behavioral manifestations of children's friendships. In T. J. Berndt and G. W. Ladd (Eds.), *Peer relationships in child development* (pp. 46–70). New York: Wiley.

Hartup, W. W., French, D. C., Laursen, B., Johnston, K., and Ogawa, J. (in press). Conflict and friendship relations in middle childhood: Behavior in a closed-field situation. *Child Development*, in press.

Hartup, W. W., and Laursen, B. (1989, April). *Contextual constraints and children's friendship relations.* Paper presented at the biennial meetings of the Society for Research in Child Development, Kansas City, MO.

Hartup, W. W., Laursen, B., Stewart, M. I., and Eastenson, A. (1988). Conflict and the friendship relations of young children. *Child Development, 59,* 1590–1600.

Hay, D. F. (1984). Social conflict in early childhood. In G. Whitehurst (Ed.), *Annals of child development,* Vol. 1 (pp. 1–44). Greenwich, CT: JAI.

Hay, D. F., and Ross, H. S. (1982). The social nature of early conflict. *Child Development, 53,* 105–113.

Hinde, R. A. (1976). On describing relationships. *Journal of Child Psychology and Psychiatry, 17,* 1–19.

————. (1979). *Towards understanding relationships.* New York: Academic Press.

Hinde, R. A., Titmus, G., Easton, D., and Tamplin, A. (1985). Incidence of "friendship" and behavior with strong associates versus nonassociates in preschoolers. *Child Development, 56,* 234–245.

Houseman, J. (1972). *An ecological study of interpersonal conflicts among preschool children.* Unpublished doctoral dissertation, Wayne State University.

Howes, C., and Wu, F. (1990). Peer interactions and friendships in an ethnically diverse school setting. *Child Development, 61,* 537–541.

Hymel, S. (1986). Interpretations of peer behavior: Affective bias in childhood and adolescence. *Child Development, 57,* 431–445.

Johnson, M. W. (1935). The effect on behavior of variation in the amount of play equipment. *Child Development, 6,* 56–68.

Kelley, H. H., Berscheid, E., Christensen, A., Harvey, J. H., Huston, T. L., Levinger, G., McClintock, E., Peplau, L. A., and Peterson, D. R., (Eds.) (1983). *Close relationships.* New York: W. H. Freeman.

Kenney, D. A., and La Voie, L. (1984). The social relations model. In L. Berkowitz (Ed.), *Advances in experimental social psychology,* Vol. 19 (pp. 141–182). New York: Academic Press.

Lamb, M. E. (1978). Interactions between 18-month-olds and their preschool-aged siblings. *Child Development, 49,* 51–59.

Laursen, B. (1989) *Interpersonal conflict during adolescence.* Unpublished doctoral dissertation, University of Minnesota.

Laursen, B., and Hartup, W. W. (1989). The dynamics of preschool children's conflicts. *Merrill-Palmer Quarterly, 35,* 281–297.

Lewin, K. (1935). *A dynamic theory of personality.* New York: McGraw-Hill.

Lewin, K., Lippitt, R., and White, R. K. (1938). Patterns of aggressive behavior in experimentally created "social climates." *Journal of Social Psychology, 10,* 271–299.

Lougee, M. D., Grueneich, R., and Hartup, W. W. (1977). Social interaction in same- and mixed-age dyads of preschool children. *Child Development, 48,* 1353–1361.

Maltz, D., and Borker, R. (1982). A cultural approach to male-female miscommunication. In J. J. Gumperz (Ed.), *Communication, language and social identity* (pp. 196–216). Cambridge, UK: Cambridge University Press.

Maudry, M., and Nekula, M. (1939). Social relations between children of the same age during the first two years of life. *Journal of Genetic Psychology, 54,* 193–215.

Maynard, D. W. (1985). How children start arguments. *Language and Society, 14,* 1–30.

———. (1986). The development of argumentative skills among children. In Adler, P. A., and Adler, P. (Eds.), *Sociological studies of child development,* Vol. 1 (pp. 233–258). Greenwich, CT: JAI.

Mead, G. H. (1934). *Mind, self, and society.* Chicago: University of Chicago Press.

Medrich, E. A., Rosen, J., Rubin, V., and Buckley, S. (1982). *The serious business of growing up.* Berkeley, CA: University of California Press.

Miller, P. M., Danaher, D. L., and Forbes, D. (1986). Sex-related strategies for coping with interpersonal conflict in children aged five and seven. *Developmental Psychology, 22,* 543–548.

Minnett, A. M., Vandell, D. L., and Santrock, J. W. (1983). The effects of sibling status on sibling interaction: Influence of birth order, age spacing, sex of child, and sex of sibling. *Child Development, 54,* 1064–1072.

Minuchin, P. P., and Shapiro, E. K. (1983). The school as a context for social development. In E. M. Hetherington (Ed.), P. H. Mussen (Series Ed.), *Handbook of child psychology,* Vol. 4 (pp. 197–274). New York: Wiley.

Montemayor, R., and Hanson, E. (1985). A naturalistic view of conflict between adolescents and their parents and siblings. *Journal of Early Adolescence, 5,* 23–30.

Nelson, J., and Aboud, F. E. (1985). The resolution of social conflict between friends. *Child Development, 56,* 1009–1017.

Parke, R. D., and Slaby, R. G. (1983). The development of aggression. In E. M. Hetherington (Ed.), P. H. Mussen (Series Ed.), *Handbook of child psychology,* Vol. 4 (pp. 547–641). New York: Wiley.

Pastor, D. L. (1981). The quality of mother-infant attachments and its relationship to toddlers' initial sociability with peers. *Developmental Psychology, 17,* 326–335.

Patterson, G. R., Littman, R. A., and Bricker, W. (1967). Assertive behavior in children: A step toward a theory of aggression. *Monographs of the Society for Research in Child Development, 32* (Serial No. 113).

Pepler, D. J., Abramovitch, R., and Corter, C. (1981). Sibling interaction in the home: A longitudinal study. *Child Development, 52,* 1344–1347.

Peterson, D. R. (1983). Conflict. In H. H. Kelley, E. Berscheid, A. Christensen, J. H. Harvey, T. L. Huston, G. Levinger, E. McClintock, L. A. Peplau, and D. R. Peterson (Eds.), *Close relationships* (pp. 360–396). New York: W. H. Freeman.

Peters, R. W., and Torrance, E. P. (1972). Dyadic interaction of preschool children and performance on a construction task. *Psychological Reports, 30,* 747–750.

Piaget, J. (1932). *The moral judgment of the child.* London: Kegan Paul.

Putallaz, M., and Gottman, J. M. (1981). An interactional model of children's entry into peer groups. *Child Development, 52,* 986–994.

Putallaz, M., and Wasserman, A. (1990). Children's entry behavior. In S. R. Asher and J. D. Coie (Eds.), *Peer rejection in childhood.* (pp. 60–89). New York: Cambridge University Press.

Raffaelli, M. (1990). *Sibling conflict in early adolescence.* Unpublished doctoral dissertation, University of Chicago.

Robin, A. L., and Foster, S. L. (1984). Problem-solving communication training: A behavioral family systems approach to parent-adolescent conflict. In P. Karoly and J. J. Steffen (Eds.), *Adolescent behavior disorders: Foundations and contemporary concerns* (pp. 195–240). Lexington, MA: Lexington Books.

Rothbart, M., and Park, B. (1986). On the confirmability and disconfirmability of trait concepts. *Journal of Personality and Social Psychology, 50,* 131–142.

Rubin, K. H. (1977). The social and cognitive value of preschool toys and activities. *Canadian Journal of Behavioral Science/Review of Canadian Science, 9,* 382–385.

Russell, V. (1981). *The influence of age and sex on conflict episodes among toddlers.* Unpublished honors thesis, University of Waterloo (cited in Hay, 1984).

Rutter, M., Graham, P., Chadwick, O. F. D., and Yule, W. (1976). Adolescent turmoil: Fact or fiction? *Journal of Child Psychology and Psychiatry, 17,* 35–56.

Sackin, S., and Thelen, E. (1984). An ethological study of peaceful associative outcomes to conflict in preschool children. *Child Development, 55,* 1098–1102.

Selman, R. L. (1980). *The growth of interpersonal understanding.* New York: Academic Press.

Selman, R. L., Beardslee, W., Schultz, L. H., Krupa, M., and Podorefsky, D. (1986). Assessing adolescent interpersonal negotiation strategies: Toward the integration of structural and functional models. *Developmental Psychology, 22,* 450–459.

Shantz, C. U. (1987). Conflict between children. *Child Development, 58,* 283–305.

Shantz, C. U., and Hobart, C. J. (1989). Social conflict and development: Peers and siblings. In T. J. Berndt and G. Ladd (Eds.), *Peer relationships and child development* (pp. 71–94). New York: Wiley.

Shantz, C. U., and Shantz, D. W. (1985). Conflict between children: Social-cognitive and sociometric correlates. In M. W. Berkowitz (Ed.), *Peer conflict and psychological growth* (pp. 3–21). San Francisco: Jossey-Bass.

Shantz, D. W. (1986). Conflict, aggression, and peer status: An observational study. *Child Development, 57,* 1322–1332.

Sheldon, A. (1990). Pickle fights: Gendered talk in preschool disputes. *Discourse Processes, 13,* 5–31.

Sherif, M., Harvey, O. J., White, B. J., Hood, W. R., and Sherif, C. W. (1961). *Inter-group conflict and cooperation: The Robbers Cave experiment.* Norman, OK: University of Oklahoma Press.

Shure, M. B. (1963). Psychological ecology of a nursery school. *Child Development, 34,* 979–992.

Simmel, G. (1955). *Conflict and the web of group affiliations.* New York: The Free Press.

Smith, P. K. (1974). Aggression in a preschool playgroup: Effects of varying physical resources. In J. de Wit and W. W. Hartup (Eds.), *Determinants and origins of aggressive behavior* (pp. 97–105). The Hague: Mouton.

Smith, P. K., and Connolly, K. (1981). *The ecology of preschool behaviour.* Cambridge, UK: Cambridge University Press.

Stoneman, Z., Brody, G. H., and MacKinnon, C. E. (1984). Naturalistic observations of children's activities and roles while playing with their siblings and friends. *Child Development, 55,* 617–622.

Sullivan, H. S. (1953). *The interpersonal theory of psychiatry.* New York: Norton.

Sutton-Smith, B., and Rosenberg, B. G. (1968). Sibling consensus on power tactics. *Journal of Genetic Psychology, 114,* 63–72.

Tesser, A. (1984). Self-evaluation maintenance processes: Implications for relationships and for development. In J. C. Masters and K. Yarkin-Levin (Eds.), *Boundary areas in social and developmental psychology* (pp. 271–299). New York: Academic Press.

Tesser, A., Campbell, J., and Smith, M. (1984). Friendship choice and performance: Self-evaluation maintenance in children. *Journal of Personality and Social Psychology, 46,* 561–574.

Tesser, A., and Smith J. (1980). Some effects of friendship and task relevance on helping: You don't always help the one you like. *Journal of Experimental Social Psychology, 16,* 582–590.

Vespo, J. E., and Caplan, M. Z. (1988, March). *Preschooler's differential use of conflict resolution strategies with friends and acquaintances.* Paper presented at the Conference on Human Development, Charleston, SC.

Vuchinich, S. (1987). Starting and stopping spontaneous family conflicts. *Journal of Marriage and the Family, 49,* 591–601.

Weick, K. E., and Penner, D. D. (1966). Triads: A laboratory analogue. *Organizational Behavior and Human Performance, 1,* 191–211.

Whiting, B. B., and Whiting, J. W. M. (1975). *Children of six cultures: A psychocultural analysis.* Cambridge, MA: Harvard University Press.

Youniss, J. (1980). *Parents and peers in social development: A Piaget-Sullivan perspective.* Chicago: University of Chicago Press.

Youniss, J., and Smollar, J. (1985). *Adolescent relations with mothers, fathers, and friends.* Chicago: University of Chicago Press.

4

DAN OLWEUS

Bullies on the Playground: The Role of Victimization*

Bully/victim problems among schoolchildren ("mobbing") have been an issue of great concern in Scandinavia for almost two decades (Olweus, 1973a, 1978, 1986, 1992). A strong societal interest in bully/victim problems was first aroused in Sweden in the late 1960s and early 1970s (Heinemann, 1972, Olweus, 1973a), but it spread quickly to the other Scandinavian countries. Although interest in bully/victim problems has been largely confined to Scandinavia for quite some time, there are now clear indications of an increasing societal as well as research interest into these problems in several parts of the world, including Japan, England, the Netherlands, Canada, Australia, and the United States.

In Norway, bully/victim problems were an issue of general concern in the mass media and among teachers and parents for a number of years, but the school authorities did not engage themselves officially with the phenomenon. A few years ago, a marked change took place. In late 1982, a newspaper reported that three 10–14-year-old boys from the northern part of Norway had committed suicide, in all probability as a consequence of severe bullying by peers. This event aroused a lot of uneasiness and tension in the mass media and the general public. It triggered a chain of reactions which resulted in a nationwide campaign against bully/victim problems in Norwegian comprehensive schools (grades 1–9), launched by the Ministry of Education in the fall of 1983.

*The research reported was supported in various periods by grants from the William T. Grant Foundation, the Norwegian Ministry of Education, the Norwegian Council for Social Research, and the Swedish Delegation for Social Research (DSF).

In the latter part of this chapter, I will report some important outcomes of the intervention program developed in connection with the campaign, as evaluated in 42 schools in Bergen. I will also briefly describe the content of the program and some of the principles on which it was based. Before that, I will give an overview of some basic research findings on bully/victim problems among school children. I will mainly confine myself to results of the two recent large-scale studies I was commissioned by the Ministry of Education to conduct in that context.

A number of findings concerning developmental antecedents of bullying problems, characteristics of typical bullies and victims, and the veracity of some popular conceptions of the causes of these problems will be presented only briefly in this chapter, since these results have been described in detail in previous publications (e.g., Olweus, 1973a, 1978, 1980, 1981, 1983, 1984, 1986). It should be mentioned, however, that the findings from this earlier research have generally been replicated in several different samples and were obtained with a number of different methods, including peer ratings, teacher nominations, self-reports, grades, projective techniques, hormonal assays, and mother/father interviews about child-rearing practices. Most of these results were derived from my Swedish longitudinal project, which started in the early 1970s and is still continuing (see Table 4.1, p. 91).

BASIC INFORMATION

What Is Meant by Bullying?

The word used in Scandinavia for bully/victim problems is "mobbing" (Norway, Denmark) or "mobbning" (Sweden, Finland). This word has been used with several different meanings and connotations. The original English word stem "mob" implies that it is a (usually large and anonymous) group of people who are engaged in the harassment (Heinemann, 1972; Olweus, 1973a). But the term has also often been used when one person picks on, harasses, or pesters another. Even if the usage is not quite adequate from a linguistic point of view, I believe it is important to include in the concept of "mobbing" or bullying both situations in which a single individual harasses another and those in which a group is responsible for the harassment. Recent data collected in the large-scale study in Bergen (Olweus,

1985, 1986; below) showed that a substantial portion of victimized students were bullied primarily by a single student. Accordingly, it is natural to regard bullying from a single student and from a group as closely related phenomena—even if there may be some differences between them. In particular, it is reasonable to expect that bullying by several peers is more unpleasant and possibly detrimental to the victim.

I define *bullying* in the following general way: *A person is being bullied when he or she is exposed, repeatedly and over time, to negative actions on the part of one or more other persons.*

The meaning of the expression *negative actions* must be specified further. It is a negative action when someone intentionally inflicts, or attempts to inflict, injury or discomfort upon another—basically what is implied in the definition of aggressive behavior (Olweus, 1973b). Negative actions can be carried out by physical contact, by words, or in other ways, such as by making faces or dirty gestures or by refusing to comply with another person's wishes.

Even if a single instance of more serious harassment can be regarded as bullying under certain circumstances, the definition given above emphasizes negative actions that are carried out "repeatedly and over time." The intent is to exclude occasionally nonserious negative actions that are directed against one person at one time and against another on a different occasion.

It must be stressed that the term bullying is not (or should not be) used when two persons of approximately the same strength (physical or psychological) are fighting or quarreling. In order to use the term bullying, there should be an *imbalance in the strength or power relations:* The person who is exposed to the negative actions has difficulty in defending him/herself and is somewhat helpless against the person or persons who harass.

It is useful to distinguish between *direct bullying*—with relatively open attacks on the victim—and *indirect bullying* in the form of social isolation and exclusion from a group. It is important to pay attention also to the second, less visible form of bullying. In the present chapter the expressions bullying, victimization, and bully/victim problems are used synonymously.

Some Information about the Recent Studies

The basic method of data collection in the recent large-scale studies in Norway and Sweden has been a questionnaire[1] that I developed in connection with the nationwide campaign against bullying. The questionnaire, which can be administered by teachers, differs from several previous inventories on bully/victim problems in a number of respects, including the following:

• It provides a "definition" of bullying so as to give the students a clear understanding of what they are to respond to.
• It refers to a specific time period.
• Several of the response alternatives are quite specific, such as "about once a week" and "several times a day," in contrast to alternatives like "often" and "very often," which lend themselves to more subjective interpretation
• It includes questions about the environment's reactions to bullying as perceived by the respondents, that is, the reactions and attitudes of peers, teachers, and parents.

In connection with the nationwide campaign, all primary and junior high schools in Norway were invited to take the questionnaire. We estimate that approximately 85% actually participated. For closer analyses, I selected representative samples of some 830 schools and obtained valid data from 715 of them, comprising approximately 130,000 students from all over Norway. These samples constitute almost a fourth of the whole student population in the relevant age range (roughly 8 to 16; first-grade students did not participate, since they did not have sufficient reading and writing ability to answer the questionnaire). This set of data gives good estimates of the frequency of bully/victim problems in different school forms, in different grades, in boys as compared with girls, etc. In addition, it provides information on how differences between schools in these regards relate to the characteristics of the schools themselves and of the surrounding communities in terms of population density, degree of urbanization, economic resources, percentage of immigrants, and similar parameters. I will report here on some main findings from this study, but a number of more refined analyses remain to be done.

Roughly at the same time, a similar set of data was collected from approximately 17,000 Swedish students in grades 3–9, from 60 schools in the communities of Göteborg, Malmö, and Västerås. These three communities were selected to "match" in size as closely as possible the three largest cities in Norway: Oslo, Bergen, and Trondheim.

To get more detailed information on some of the mechanisms involved in bully/victim problems and on the possible effects of the intervention program, I also conducted a longitudinal project in Bergen. This study comprises some 2,500 boys and girls in four adjacent cohorts, originally in grades 4 through 7, from 28 primary and 14 junior high schools. In addition, we obtained data from 300–400 teachers and principals as well as some 1,000 parents. We collected data from these subjects at several points in time.

An overview of my main projects on bullying and related problems is given in Table 4.1.

One Student Out of Seven

I will now report some figures on the frequency of bully/victim problems in Norwegian and Swedish schools. It should be emphasized, however, that the percentages presented are dependent on the method and the definition of bullying that have been used. This fact may make it difficult to compare these percentages with other results obtained with different methods and other definitions or maybe no definitions at all. In calculating the percentages below, I have drawn the line between "now and then" and "more frequently." For a student to be considered bullied or bullying others, he or she must have responded that it happened "now and then" or more frequently (i.e., from "about once a week" to "several times a day").

On the basis of the Norwegian nationwide survey, one can estimate that some 84,000 students, or 15% of the total in the Norwegian comprehensive schools (568,000 in 1983–1984), were involved in bully/victim problems "now and then" or more frequently (autumn 1983)—as bullies or victims. This percentage represents one student out of seven. Approximately 9%, or 52,000 students, were victims, and 41,000, or 7%, bullied other students "now and then" or more frequently. Some 9,000 students were both bullies and victims (reporting that they both bullied other students and were victimized).

Assuming that we can generalize to Sweden as a whole (with a total of 959,000 grade 1–9 students in 1983–1984) from the three Swedish cities studied, we get the following rough estimates for Sweden: Approximately 145,000 students were involved as bullies or victims: some 100,000 were victims, 63,000 were bullies, and 18,000 were both bullies and victims.

	Nationwide Study In Norway (1983)	Large Scale Study in Sweden (1983/84)	Intensive Study in Bergen, Norway (1983–1985)	Study in Greater Stockholm, Sweden (1970–)
UNITS OF STUDY:	715 Schools, grades 2–9 (130,000 boys and girls)	60 Schools, grades 3–9 (17,000 boys and girls	4 Cohorts of 2500 boys and girls in grades 4–7 (1983) 3–400 teachers 1000 parents	3 Cohorts of boys (900 boys in all), originally in grades 6–8 (1973)
NUMBER OF MEASUREMENT OCCASIONS:	One	One	Several	Several
MEASURES INCLUDE:	Questionnaire on bully/victim problems (aggregated to grade and school level) data on recruitment area of the school: Population density, socioeconomic conditions percent immigrants, school size, average class size, composition of staff	Questionnaire on bully/victim problems School size, average class size	Self-reports on bully/victim problems, aggression, antisocial behavior, anxiety, self-esteem, attatchment to parents and peers, etc. grades, some peer ratings. Teacher data on characteristics of classroom climate, staff relations, etc.	Self-reports and reports by mothers on a number of dimensions, peer ratings, teacher nominations, official records on criminal offences, drug/abuse. For subgroups: interviews on early child rearing, hormonal data, psychophysiological data.

Table 4.1. Overview of studies on bully/victim problems conducted by the author.

Analyses from the Bergen study indicate that there are good grounds for placing a cutting point at "now and then" (and "more frequently.") But it is also useful to estimate the number of students who were involved in more serious bully/victim problems. We found that slightly more than 3% or 18,000 students in Norway were bullied "about once a week" or more frequently, and less than 2%, or 10,000 students, bullied others at that rate. Using this cutting point, only 1,000 students were both bullies and victims. A total of approximately 27,000 students (5%) in Norwegian elementary and junior high schools were involved in more serious bullying problems as victims or bullies—about 1 student out of 20.

It is natural to wonder if the reported results give an exaggerated picture of the frequency of bullying problems. This question can be examined by means of some findings from the Bergen study (Olweus, 1985). Each of some 90 form masters and mistresses was asked to assess which of the students in his or her class were bullied or bullied other students. The teachers used exactly the same response categories as in the students' questionnaire. The agreement between the percentages obtained from the teachers' assessments and from the responses of the approximately 2,000 students (in grades 4–7) was striking: There were differences on the order of only 1% to 2%. In short, the results indicated that "outside observers" of the relations among the students gave estimates that corresponded closely to what the students themselves reported.

In general, these findings suggest that the percentages reported were not inflated. Considering that the student (as well as the teacher) questionnaire refers only to the autumn term, it is likely that the figures actually underestimate the number of students who are involved in such problems during a whole year.

Against this background, it can be stated that, *in Norwegian and Swedish comprehensive schools, bullying is a considerable problem*, a problem that affects a very large number of students. Data from other countries such as Finland (Lagerspetz, Björkqvist, Berts, and King, 1982), England (Smith, 1991; Whitney and Smith, in press), the United States (Perry, Kusel, and Perry, 1988), Canada (Ziegler and Rosenstein-Manner, 1991) indicate that this problem exists also outside Scandinavia and with similar or even higher prevalence rates.

Bully/Victim Problems in Different Grades

If one drew a graph of the percentage of students in different grades who are bullied at school, a fairly smoothly declining curve is obtained for both boys and girls (see Figure 4.1). The decline is most marked in the primary school grades. Thus the percentage of students who are bullied decrease with higher grades. *It is the younger and weaker students who reported being most exposed.*

In junior high school (grades 7–9) the curves decline less steeply. The average percentage of students (boys and girls combined) who were bullied in grades 2–6 (11.6%) was approximately twice as high as that in grades 7–9 (5.4%). With regard to the way in which the bullying is carried out, there is a clear trend towards less use of physical means in the higher grades.

From the Bergen study it can also be reported that *a considerable part of the bullying was carried out by older students.* This is particularly marked in the lower grades: More than 50% of the bullied children in the lowest grades (2 and 3) reported that they

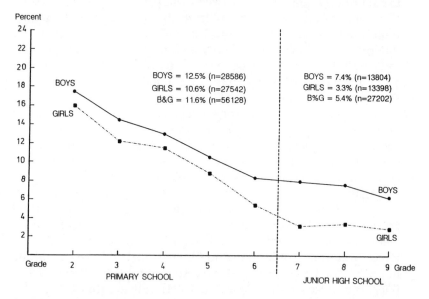

Figure 4.1. Percentage of students in different grades who reported being bullied (being exposed to direct bullying).

were bullied by older students. It is natural to invoke the latter finding, at least as a partial explanation of the form of the curves in Figure 4.1. The younger the students are, the more potential bullies they have above them; accordingly, the inverse relationship between percentage of victims and grade level seems reasonable. This is only a preliminary interpretation, however, and a more detailed analysis of the factors affecting the shape of the curves will be undertaken later.

As regards the tendency to bully other students, depicted in Figure 4.2, the changes with grades are not so clear and systematic as in Figure 4.1. The average percentage for the junior high school boys was slightly higher (11.3%) than for the boys in the lower grades (10.7%), whereas the opposite was true for the girls (2.5% in junior high vs. 4.0% in the lower grades). The relatively marked drop in the curves for grade 7, in particular for the boys, is probably a reflection of the fact that these students were the youngest ones in junior high school and accordingly did not have "access to suitable victims" in lower grades to the same extent. The trends demonstrated in the Norwegian material were confirmed in all essentials in the corresponding Swedish analyses.

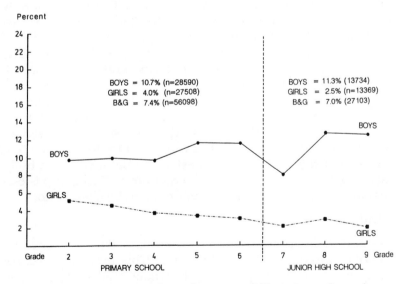

Figure 4.2. Percentage of students in different grades who reported having bullied other students.

The analyses above concern the distributions of victims and bullies across grades. The most remarkable result is that *bully/victim problems in primary schools were considerably more marked than previously assumed.*

Have Bully/Victim Problems Increased?

Several different methods, including questionnaires (for overviews in Scandinavian languages, see Raundalen and Raundalen, 1979; Roland, 1983; Pikas, 1975), teacher nominations (Olweus, 1973a, 1978), and peer ratings (Lagerspetz, et al., 1982), have been used in previous Scandinavian studies of the frequency of bully/victim problems. The samples have mainly consisted of students in grades 6 through 9. In summary, it can be stated that the percentages of bullied and bullying students, respectively, were found to be in the vicinity of 5–10%. By and large, the figures in these studies conducted chiefly in the 1970s are somewhat lower than the percentages obtained in the surveys reported on above. Whether this discrepancy reflects differences in methods, definitions, and the composition of the samples, or whether it shows that the frequency of bullying has actually increased in recent years, is difficult to know with certainty. There are no good data available to directly assess whether bully/victim problems have become more or less frequent in the 1980s. Several indirect signs, however, suggest that bullying takes more serious forms and is more prevalent nowadays than 10–15 years ago.

Whatever method of measurement used, there is little doubt that bullying is a considerable problem in Norwegian and Swedish comprehensive schools, one which must be taken seriously. At the same time, it is important to recognize that some 60–70% of the students (in a given semester) are not involved in bullying at all, neither as targets nor as perpetrators. This group is essential in efforts to counteract bully/victim problems at school.

Bullying among Boys and Girls

As is evident from Figure 4.1, there is a trend for boys to be more exposed to bullying than girls. This tendency is particularly marked in the junior high school grades. These results concern what was called direct bullying, with relatively open attacks on the victim. It is natural to ask whether girls were more often exposed to indirect bullying in the form of social

isolation and exclusion from the peer group. One of the questionnaire items makes it possible to examine this issue ("How
often does it happen that other students don't want to spend
recess with you and you end up being alone?"). The responses
confirm that girls were more exposed to indirect and more
subtle forms of bullying than to bullying with open attacks. At
the same time, however, the percentage of boys who were
bullied in this indirect way was approximately the same as
that for girls. In addition, a somewhat larger percentage of
boys was exposed to direct bullying, as mentioned above.
(It may also be of interest that there was a fairly strong
relationship between being a victim of direct and of indirect
bullying.)

It should be emphasized that these results reflect general
trends. There are, of course, a number of schools and classes in
which there are more girls, or an equal number of girls and boys
who are exposed to direct bullying. This also applies in junior
high school.

An additional result from the Bergen study is relevant in this
context. Here it was found that *a considerable part of the bullying
that girls were subjected to was carried out by boys.* More than
60% of bullied girls in grades 5–7 reported being bullied mainly
by boys. An additional 15–20% said they were bullied by both
boys and girls. The great majority of boys, on the other hand—
more than 80%—were bullied chiefly by boys.

These results lead in a natural way to Figure 4.2, which
shows the percentage of students who had taken part in bullying
other students. It is evident here that a considerably larger percentage of boys than girls had participated in bullying. In junior
high school, more than four times as many boys as girls reported
having bullied other students.

In summary, *boys were more often victims and, in particular,
perpetrators of direct bullying.* This conclusion corroborates what
can be expected from research on sex differences in aggressive
behavior (Ekblad and Olweus, 1986; Hyde, 1984; Maccoby and
Jacklin, 1980). It is well documented that relations among boys
are by and large harder, tougher, and more aggressive than among
girls (Maccoby, 1986). These differences have both biological and
social/environmental roots.

The results presented here should definitely not be construed
as implying that we need not pay attention to bullying problems

among girls. As a matter of course, such problems must be acknowledged and counteracted, whether girls are the victims of bullying or they themselves perpetrate such behavior. It should be recalled in this connection that girls were exposed to indirect bullying to about the same extent as boys.

How Much Do the Teachers Do and How Much Do the Parents Know?

The students' responses to one of the questionnaire items give information on how often the teachers try to interfere when a student is being bullied at school. Roughly 40% of bullied students in the primary grades and almost 60% in junior high school reported that the teachers tried to "put a stop to it" only "once in a while or almost never." And about 65% of bullied students in elementary school said that the form master/mistress had *not* talked with them about the bullying. The corresponding figure for junior high school students was as high as 85%. Almost the same results were obtained for students who bullied others. It can thus be established that *the teachers do relatively little to put a stop to bullying at school,* according to both the bullied and bullying students. Teachers also made only limited contact with the students involved in order to talk about the problems. This is particularly true in junior high school.

Once again, it should be stressed that these are main trends in the data. The results should not hide the fact that there are great individual differences among schools (and teachers): There were individual schools in which the teachers interfered with bullying and talked with the students involved much more often than the average. The other side of the coin is that there were also schools where the teachers did so considerably less than the average.

About 55% of bullied students in the primary grades reported that "somebody at home" had talked with them about the bullying. In junior high school, this percentage was reduced to approximately 35%. For students who reported having bullied others the figures were considerably lower. The conclusion can be drawn that *parents of students who are bullied and, in particular, who bully others, are relatively unaware of the problem and talk with their children about it only to a limited extent.*

Although these results do not speak directly to the issue of the frequency or causes of bully/victim problems, they are important pieces of information to consider when countermeasures are planned.

Bullying at School and on the Way to and from School

It is fairly often asserted that bullying chiefly takes place on the way to and from school rather than at school. The results from the recent studies in Norway and Sweden clearly show that this view is not valid. There were almost twice (in junior high school, three times) as many students who were bullied at school as on the way to and from school. (There is a fairly strong association here, however: Students who were bullied on their way to and from school tended to be bullied at school, too.) *The school is, no doubt, where most of the bullying occurs.*

The students reported, however, that they got considerably less help from others if they were bullied on their way to and from school. Accordingly, it is important to take effective measures against bullying there as well.

In a recent large-scale study of bullying in English schools using my Bullying Questionnaire, the students were also asked the question of *where in school* they had been bullied (Whitney and Smith, in press). The majority (76%) reported that most of the bullying had occurred on the playground. This was particularly true of students in the 8–11 year range, whereas for the somewhat older students, this percentage was only slightly higher (45%) than being bullied in the classroom (39%), or in the corridors (30%).

Comparison between Norway and Sweden

It is possible and meaningful to compare the responses of the 17,000 students from the three Swedish communities of Göteborg, Malmö, and Västerås, with the results from approximately 32,000 Norwegian students drawn from Oslo, Bergen, and Trondheim. The main impression is that there are great similarities. But there are also interesting differences, and I choose to focus briefly on the discrepancies here.

One marked finding is that the Swedish students were more exposed to indirect bullying in the form of social isolation and exclusion from the group. Eighteen percent of the Swedish primary school students (grades 3–6) as compared with scarcely 13% of students in corresponding grades in the Norwegian schools reported that "other students didn't want to spend recess with them and that they ended up being alone." There seems to be more loneliness and isolation among the Swedish youngsters.

The Swedish students were also to a greater extent victims of direct bullying (with open attacks) than the Norwegian students, in particular in junior high school. Furthermore, the Swedish junior high school students bullied other students slightly more. With regard to the more serious form of bullying ("once a week" or more frequently), a larger percentage of Swedish junior high school students bullied others or were bullied by others respectively.

By and large, then, bully/victim problems were somewhat greater and more serious in the Swedish schools than the Norwegian schools. This conclusion applies in particular to junior high school students and, as regards indirect bullying, to primary school students.

Other results worth mentioning are that the Norwegian teachers interfered to stop bullying slightly more often (junior high school) but that the Swedish teachers talked with bullied and bullying students somewhat more frequently than the Norwegian teachers (in both primary and junior high schools). The Swedish parents also talked with their bullied or bullying children slightly more often. The students' responses suggest that Swedish teachers and parents were somewhat more aware of bully/victim problems. Both Swedish and Norwegian results, however, must be considered clearly unsatisfactory in this regard.

Is Bullying Primarily a Big City Problem?

It has been commonly assumed that bullying occurs primarily in big city schools. Results from the nationwide Norwegian surveys show that this is a myth. The percentage of students in Olso, Bergen, and Trondheim (with populations varying from 150,000 to 450,000 inhabitants) who were bullied or who bullied others was approximately the same or somewhat lower than corresponding figures from the rest of the country. The "big city" children and youth were thus better than their reputation in this respect. It was also found that teachers as well as parents in the three cities talked more often with students involved in bullying problems than was done in other parts the country. These results point to a somewhat greater awareness of the problems in the cities.

In this context it is also of interest to consider the results from a comparison of 307 "ordinary" primary schools (with at least one class at each grade level) and some 90 one-room schools (with students from more than one grade level in the same class). The one-room schools, which constitute approximately 50% of the number of the primary schools in Norway but only 15% of the student population in that age range, are for the most part situated in the country. The average number of students who took the questionnaire was 43 in the one-room schools and 184 in the ordinary schools.

The basic finding from this comparison was that the percentage of bullied students in the small one-room schools was almost the same as in the larger, ordinary primary schools. The percentage of students who bully others was even slightly higher in the one-room schools. This finding certainly runs counter to the popular conception of the one-room school as an idyllic and conflict-free place.

The Size of the School and the Class

Another common view, popular in particular among teachers, is that bully/victim problems increase in proportion to the size of the school and the class. The data from 10 schools in Greater Stockholm that I presented in the beginning of the 1970s (Olweus, 1973a, 1978) gave no support to this hypothesis. Data from three schools in Finland also failed to show any relationship between percentage of bullied or bullying students on one hand and school or class size on the other (Ekman, 1977; Lagerspetz, Bjorkqvist, Berts, and King, 1982).

The recent Norwegian and Swedish surveys give new and considerably extended possibilities of testing the validity of these hypotheses. With the available data one can make comparisons among more than 700 schools and several thousand classes. It should be noted, however, that such comparisons must be carried out within the same kind or type of school (e.g., primary schools or junior high schools) in order to be meaningful.

The variations in school and class size among the units compared were quite substantial. For example, the smallest ordinary grade 1–6 school had only 43 students, whereas the largest had 930. With regard to average class size, the range was from approximately 7 to 27 students per class for schools of this kind.

The results were clear-cut: There were no positive relationships between level of bully/victim problems (the percentage of bullied and/or bullying students) and school or average class size.

The international research on the "effects" of class and school size agrees in suggesting that these factors are of no great significance, at least within the ranges of size variation typically found (e.g., Rutter, 1983). We can thus conclude that *the size of the class or school appears to be of negligible importance to the relative frequency or level of bully victim problems in the class or the school.* Accordingly, one must look for other factors to find the origins of these problems.

Supervision during Recess

In the Bergen study we have been able to explore the relationship between certain aspects of the supervision system during recess and the level of bully/victim problems in school. For the approximately 40 schools participating in this research we found a negative correlation of the order of –.45 between relative "teacher density" during recess time and the amount of bully/victim problems. That is: The greater the number of teachers (per, e.g., 100 students) supervising during recess, the lower the level of bully/victim problems in the school. This result indicates that it is of great importance to have a sufficient number of adults present among the students during recess time (probably on condition that the adults are willing and prepared to interfere with incipient bullying episodes).

At a more general level, this finding suggests that the attitudes of the teachers towards bully/victim problems and their behavior in bullying situations are of major significance for the extent of bully/victim problems in the school or the class. In the Bergen study, we will attempt to specify in more detail which components of the teachers' attitudes and behaviors are particularly important.

On Analyses at Different Levels

A good deal of what has been reported in this chapter is descriptive information about the distribution of bully/victim problems across various conditions. However, we have also briefly considered some possible causes of bully/victim problems, such as the size of the school or class and the way supervision during recess time is organized. In the latter cases, we examined characteristics of the environment or the system that can possibly influence the extent or level of bully/victim problems for a whole group of students such as the school or the class (*the group*, or aggregated data, is the *unit of analysis*). This is certainly an important set of issues to study, for example, in order to get more knowledge and ideas about what kinds of measures at the school or class level can reduce bully/victim problems.

Another set of issues is directed to the study of characteristics of different kinds of students, those who are bullies, victims, or neither (*the individual* is the basic *unit of analysis*). In these analyses, it is important to consider external characteristics and personality attributes of these kinds of students as well as whether there are differences in their situations or environments, for instance, as regards school and family conditions. Examples of questions to be examined are: Do external deviations such as fatness or red hair contribute to the student's becoming more easily victimized? Have bullied or bullying young people experienced a type of child-rearing which differs from what is characteristic of youngsters in general? It is essential to address both these sets of issues, which are complementary, in order to get a more complete understanding of the mechanisms involved in bully/victim problems and in order to design good programs of countermeasures.

As I stated in the beginning of the chapter, I will not go into detail here on the extensive findings related to the second set of issues. However, I will touch briefly on a couple of popular hypotheses about the causes of bully/victim problems that have not been supported by empirical data. I will also draw a thumbnail sketch of the characteristics of typical bullies and victims.

Two Nonsupported Hypotheses

In the general debate it has been commonly maintained that bullying is a direct consequence of competition and striving for grades in school. More specifically, it has been argued that the aggressive behavior of the bullies toward their environment can be explained as a reaction to failures and frustrations in school. A detailed casual analysis of data on 444 boys from greater Stockholm, who were followed from grade 6 to 9, gave no support at all for this hypothesis. Though there was an association between poor grades in school and aggressive behavior, there was nothing in the results to suggest that the behavior of the aggressive boys was *a consequence* of poor grades and failure in school (Olweus, 1983).

Further, a widely held view explains victimization as caused by external deviations. It is argued that students who are fat, are red-haired, wear glasses, or speak an unusual dialect, etc., are particularly likely to be targets of bullying. This explanation seems to be quite common among students. This hypothesis also failed to receive support from empirical data. In two samples of boys, victims of bullying were by and large found to be no more externally deviant (with regard to 14 external characteristics assessed by means of teacher ratings) than a control group of boys who were not exposed to bullying (Olweus, 1973a, 1978). The only "external deviation" that differentiated the groups was physical strength: The victims were physically weaker than boys in general, whereas the bullied were stronger than the average, and in particular stronger than the victims. This characteristic, however, has generally not been implicated in the hypothesis discussed. In spite of the lack of empirical support for this hypothesis, it seems still to enjoy considerable popularity. Some probable reasons why this is so have been advanced, and the interested reader is referred to this discussion (Olweus, 1978,1986).

A Sketch of the Typical Victim

The picture of the typical victim emerging from the research literature is relatively clear (see Olweus, 1978, 1986, 1992). Victims of bullying are more anxious and insecure than students in general. They are often cautious, sensitive, and quiet. When attacked by other students, they commonly react with crying (at least in the lower grades) and withdrawal. They have a negative view of themselves and their situation. They often look upon themselves as failures and feel stupid, ashamed, and unattractive.

Further, the victims are lonely and abandoned at school. As a rule, they don't have a single good friend in their class. They are not aggressive or teasing in their behavior; accordingly, one cannot explain the bullying as a consequence of the victims themselves being provocative to their peers. If they are boys, they are likely to be physically weaker than boys in general.

In summary, the behavior and attitude of the victims seem to signal to others that they are insecure and worthless individuals who will not retaliate if they are attacked or insulted. A slightly different way of describing the typical victims is to say that they are characterized by *an anxious reaction pattern combined* (in the case of boys) *with physical weakness.*

Detailed interviews with parents of victimized boys (unpublished) indicate that these boys were cautious and sensitive already at a young age. Boys with such characteristics (and maybe physical weakness in addition) are likely to have had difficulty in asserting themselves in the peer group. Thus, there are good reasons to believe that these characteristics directly contributed to their becoming victims of other children's aggression. At the same time it is obvious that the repeated harassment by peers must have considerably increased their anxiety, insecurity, and generally negative evaluation of themselves.

Data from the same interviews suggest that victimized boys have a closer contact and more positive relations with their parents, in particular their mothers, than boys in general. Sometimes teachers interpret this fact as overprotection on the part of the mothers. It is reasonable to assume that such tendencies toward overprotection are both a cause and a consequence of the bullying.

This is a sketch of the most common type of victim, whom I have called *the passive victim.* There is also another, smaller group of victims, *the provocative victims,* who are characterized by a combination of both anxious and aggressive reaction patterns. See Olweus (1973a, 1988) for more information about this kind of victim.

The Bullies

A distinctive characteristic of the typical bully is aggression toward peers; this is implied in the definition of a bully. They are also, however, often aggressive toward others: teachers, parents, and siblings. Generally, they have a more positive attitude toward violence and use of violent means than students in general. They are often characterized by impulsiveness and a strong need to dominate others. They seem to have little empathy with victims of bullying. If they are boys, they are likely to be stronger than boys in general, and victims, in particular.

In contrast to a fairly common assumption among psychologists and psychiatrists, we have found no indications that the aggressive bullies (boys) are anxious and insecure under a tough surface. Data based on several samples and using both direct and indirect methods such as projective techniques and hormonal assays, all pointed in the same direction: The bullies had unusually little anxiety and insecurity or were roughly average on such dimensions (Olweus, 1981, 1984). And they did not suffer from poor self-esteem.

These conclusions apply to the bullies regarded as a group. The results do not imply that there may not be (a certain, relatively small proportion of) bullies who are both aggressive and anxious.

It should be emphasized that there are students who sometimes participate in bullying but who usually do not take the initiative—they may be called *passive bullies, followers,* or henchmen. The group of passive bullies is likely to be fairly heterogeneous and can certainly also contain insecure and anxious students. In summary, the *typical bully* can be described as having *an aggressive reaction pattern combined* (in the case of boys) *with physical strength.*

Bullying can also be viewed as a *component of a more generally antisocial, conduct-disordered, and rule breaking behavior pattern.* From this perspective, it is natural to predict that youngsters who are aggressive and bully others in school run a clearly increased risk of later engaging in other problem behaviors such as criminality and alcohol abuse. Several recent studies confirm this general prediction (Loeber and Dishion, 1983; Magnusson, Stattin, and Duner, 1983).

In my own follow-up studies we have also found strong support for this assumption. Approximately 60% of boys who were characterized as bullies in grades 6–9 had at least one conviction at the age of 24, according to the official criminal registers. Even more dramatically, as much as 35–40% of the former bullies had three or more convictions at this age while this was true of only 10% of the control boys (those who were neither bullies nor victims in grades 6–9). Thus, as young adults, the former school bullies had a fourfold increase in the level of relatively serious, recidivist criminality. It may be mentioned that the former victims had an average or somewhat below average level of criminality in young adulthood.

Development of an Aggressive Reaction Pattern

In light of the characterization of bullies as having an aggressive reaction pattern—that is, they display aggressive behavior in many different situations—it becomes important to examine the question: What kind of child-rearing and other conditions are conducive to the development of an aggressive reaction pattern? Very briefly, the following four factors have turned out to be particularly important (based chiefly on research with boys; for details, see Olweus, 1980):

1. The basic emotional attitude of the primary caretaker(s) toward the child. A negative emotional attitude, characterized by lack of warmth and involvement, increases the risk that the child will later become aggressive and hostile toward others.
2. Permissiveness for aggressive behavior by the child. If the primary caretaker is generally permissive and "tolerant" without setting clear limits to aggressive behavior toward peers, siblings, and adults, the child's aggression level is likely to increase.
3. Use of power-assertive child-rearing methods such as physical punishment and violent emotional outbursts. Children of parents who make frequent use of these methods are likely to become more aggressive than the average child.

We can summarize these results by stating that *too little love and care and too much "freedom" in childhood are conditions that contribute strongly to the development of an aggressive personality pattern.*

4. The temperament of the child. A child with an active and hot-headed temperament is more likely to develop into an aggressive youngster than a child with an ordinary or more quiet temperament. The effect of this factor is smaller than those of the first two conditions mentioned.

The factors listed above can be assumed to be important for both younger and somewhat older children. It can be added that, for adolescents, it is also of great significance that the parents supervise the children's activities outside the school reasonably well (Patterson and Stouthamer—Loeber, 1984)—what they are doing and with whom.

It should also be pointed out that the aggression levels of the boys participating in the analyses above (Olweus, 1980) were not related to the socioeconomic conditions of their families, measured in several different ways. Similarly, there were no (or very weak) relationships between the four childhood factors discussed and the socioeconomic conditions of the family.

Some Group Mechanisms

When several students jointly engage in the bullying of another student, some group mechanisms are likely to be at work. Several such mechanisms have been discussed in detail in Olweus (1973a, 1978). Because of space limitations, they will only be listed here: (a) social "contagion," (b) weakening of the control or inhibitions against aggressive tendencies, (c) "diffusion" of responsibility, and (d) gradual cognitive changes in the perception of the victim.

A Wider Perspective on Bully/Victim Problems

In the nationwide survey we have found great differences in the extent of bully/victim problems among schools. In some schools the risk of being bullied was up to 4 or 5 times greater than in other schools within the same community.

More generally, such differences between schools or areas in the extent of bully/victim problems can be viewed as a reflection of the interplay between two sets of countervailing factors: Some conditions tend to create or enhance bully/victim problems, whereas other factors have controlling or mitigating effects.

Among the bullying or aggression—generating factors, poor childhood conditions in general and certain forms of child-rearing and family problems in particular are important. It is natural to postulate that schools with high levels of bullying are situated in areas where a relatively large proportion of children receive a "less satisfactory upbringing" and that there are many family problems. A less satisfactory upbringing implies, among other things, that the child gets too little love, care, and supervision, and that the caretakers do not set clear limits to the child's behavior (see above). Family problems can be conflict-filled interpersonal relationships between the parents, divorce, psychiatric illness, alcohol problems, etc.

The degree to which a school will manifest bully/victim problems is not only dependent on the amount of aggression-generating factors in the area, however. It is also largely contingent on the strength of the countervailing forces. The attitudes, routines, and behaviors of the school personnel, in particular the teachers, are certainly decisive factors in preventing and controlling bullying activities and in redirecting such behaviors into more socially acceptable channels. This generalization is supported, for example, by the clear negative correlation between teacher density during recess and amount of bully/victim problems in the Bergen schools, reported above. In addition, the attitudes and behaviors of the students themselves, as well as of their parents, can in important ways reduce the probability or extent of bully/victim problems in the school. And in a situation where bullying problems already exist, it is obvious that the reactions of students who do not participate in bullying can have a major influence both on the short-term and long-term outcome of the situation (see more on appropriate countermeasures below).

A Question of Fundamental Democratic Rights

The reported results demonstrate convincingly that bullying is a considerable problem in Scandinavian elementary and junior high schools, that the teachers (in 1983) did relatively little to counteract it, and that the parents knew too little about what their children were exposed to or engaged in. The *victims* of bullying are a large group of students who are to a great extent neglected by the school. We know that many of these youngsters are the targets of harassment for long periods of time, often for many years (Olweus, 1977, 1978). It does not require much imagination to understand what it is to go through the school years in *a state of more or less permanent anxiety and insecurity and with poor self-esteem.* It is not surprising that the victims' devaluation of themselves sometimes becomes so overwhelming that they see suicide as the only possible solution.

Bully/victim problems have even broader implications than those suggested in the previous paragraph. They really confront some of our *fundamental democratic principles: Every individual should have the right to be spared oppression and repeated, intentional humiliation, in school as in society at large.* No student should be afraid of going to school for fear of being harassed or degraded, and no parent should need to worry about such things happening to his or her child!

Bully/victim problems also relate to a society's general attitude toward violence and oppression. What kind of view of societal values will a student acquire who is repeatedly bullied by other students without interference from adults? The same question can be asked with regard to students who, for long periods of time, are allowed to harass others without hindrance from adults. *To refrain from actively counteracting bully/victim problems in school implies a tacit acceptance.*

In this context, it should be emphasized that it is also of great importance to counteract these problems for the sake of the aggressive students. As reported above, school bullies are much more likely than other students to follow an antisocial path. Accordingly, it is essential to try to redirect their activities into more socially acceptable channels. And there is no evidence to suggest that a generally "tolerant" and permissive attitude on the part of adults will help bullies outgrow their antisocial behavior pattern.

INTERVENTION

Main Goals and Components of Intervention Program

Up to this point, an overview of what is known about bully/ victim problems has been presented, based primarily on my own research. Against this background the effects of the intervention program that we developed in connection with the nationwide campaign against bully victim problems in Norwegian schools will be briefly described.

The *major goals of the program* were to reduce as much as possible existing bully/victim problems and to prevent the development of new problems. The *main components* of the program, which was aimed at teachers and parents as well as students, were the following:

1. A 32-page booklet for school personnel describing what is known about bully/victim problems (or rather: what was known in 1983) and giving detailed suggestions about what teachers and the school can do to counteract and prevent the problems (Olweus and Roland, 1983). Efforts

were also made to dispel common myths about the nature and causes of bully/victim problems which might interfere with an adequate handling of them. This booklet was distributed free of charge to all comprehensive schools in Norway.

2. A 4-page folder with information and advice to parents of victims and bullies as well as "ordinary" children. This folder was distributed by the schools to all families in Norway with school-age children.

3. A 25-minute video cassette showing episodes from the everyday lives of two bullied children, a 10-year-old boy and a 14-year-old girl. This cassette could be bought or rented at a highly subsidized price.

4. A short questionnaire designed to obtain information about different aspects of bully/victim problems in the school, as well as the frequency and readiness of teachers and students to interfere with the problems. The questionnaire was completed by the students individually (in class) and anonymously. Registration of the level and nature of bully/victim problems in the school was thought to serve as a basis and starting point for active interventions on the part of the school and the parents. A number of the results presented earlier in this chapter were based on information collected with this questionnaire.

Another "component" was added to the program as used in Bergen, the city in which the evaluation of the effects of the intervention program took place. Approximately 15 months after the program was first offered to the schools (in early October 1983) we gave, in a 2-hour meeting with the staff, individual feedback information to each of the 42 schools participating in the study (Manger and Olweus, 1985). This information derived from the students' responses to the questionnaire in 1983 focused on the level of problems and the social environment's reactions to the problems in the particular school as related to data from comparable schools obtained in the nationwide survey (October, 1983). At the same time, the main principles of the program and the major procedures suggested for intervention were presented and discussed with the staff. Since we know from experience that many (Norwegian) teachers have somewhat distorted views of the characteristics of the bullying students, particular emphasis was placed on a discussion of this topic and on appropriate ways of handling bullying behavior. Finally, the teachers rated different aspects of the program, in particular its feasibility and potential efficacy. Generally, this addition to the program as well as the program itself were quite favorably received by the teachers, as expressed in their ratings.

Subjects and Design

Space limitations prevent detailed presentation of methodological information including sampling scheme, definition of measuring instruments and variables, and significance tests. Only summary descriptions and main results will be provided in this context.

Evaluation of the effects of the intervention program is based on data from approximately 2,500 students originally belonging to 112 grade 4–7 classes in 42 primary and junior high schools in Bergen (modal ages at Time 1 were 11, 12, 13, and 14 years respectively). Each of the four grade/age cohorts consisted of 600–700 subjects with a roughly equal distribution of boys and girls. The first time of data collection (Time 1) was in late May 1983, approximately four months before the initiation of the campaign. New measurements were taken in May 1984 (Time 2) and May 1985 (Time 3).

Since the campaign was nationwide, it was not possible to set up a strictly experimental study with random allocation of schools or classes to treatment and control conditions. Instead, a quasi-experimental design was chosen, making use of "time-lagged contrasts between age-equivalent groups." In particular, for three of the cohorts data collected at Time 1 (see Figure 4.3) were used as a baseline with which data for age-equivalent cohorts at Time 2 could be compared. The latter groups had then been exposed to the intervention program for about 8 months. To exemplify, the data for the grade-5 cohort at Time 1 (modal age 12 years) were compared with the Time 2 data for the grade-4 cohort which at that time had reached approximately the same age as the baseline group. The same kind of comparisons were made between the grade-6 cohort at Time 1 and the grade-5 cohort at Time 2, and between the grade-7 cohort at Time 1 and the grade-6 cohort at Time 2.

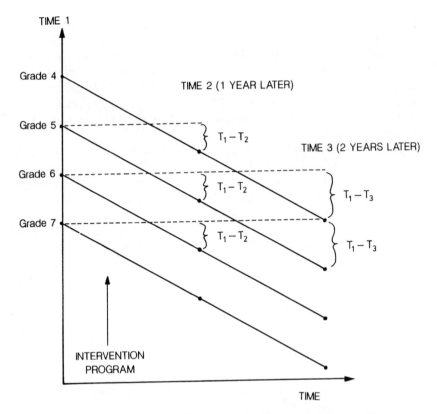

Figure 4.3. Design for evaluation of effects of intervention program. Fictitious data (which to some extent reflect the general trend of the empirical findings).

Comparisons of data collected at Time 1 and Time 3 permit an assessment of the persistence of possible decline or enhancement of the effects over a longer time span. For these comparisons data for only two of the cohorts could be used as a baseline, those of the grade-6 and grade-7 cohorts, which were contrasted with data collected at Time 3 on the grade-4 and grade-5 cohorts, respectively. The latter groups had been exposed to the intervention program during approximately 20 months at that time.

An attractive feature of the design is the fact that two of the cohorts serve as a baseline group in one set of comparisons and as a treatment group in another. This is the case with the grade-5 cohort at Time 1, the data for which are used as a baseline in comparison with the grade-4 cohort data collected at Time 2 (after 8 months of intervention). In addition, the grade-5 cohort data obtained at Time 2 serve to evaluate the possible effects of 8 months of intervention when they are compared with the data for the grade-6 cohort at Time 1. The same situation applies to the grade-6 cohort in comparisons with the grade-5 and grade-7 cohorts, respectively.

The advantage of this aspect of the design is that a possible bias in the sampling of the cohorts would operate in opposite directions in the two sets of comparisons, thus making it more "difficult" to obtain consistent "intervention effects" across co-horts as a consequence of such bias. There are, however, no grounds for expecting such bias since the classes/schools were distributed on the different cohorts by a basically random proce-dure. Accordingly, the cohorts should be essentially equivalent in important respects at Time 1. For certain variables, this assump-tion can and will be empirically tested. This aspect of the design would provide the same kind of protection against faulty conclu-sions in case the baseline data for one or both of these cohorts were unusually high or low simply as a function of chance.

To avoid erroneous conclusions due to possible selective attri-tion (more extreme or deviant individuals may be more likely to drop out in longitudinal studies) analyses were restricted to stu-dents for whom there were valid data at both time points in a particular comparison (both for the baseline and the intervention groups). In the present research, however, the results were basi-cally the same whether we controlled or did not control for such attrition.

It should also be noted that since selection of the subjects was not based on some kind of "extreme score" criterion, the problem with "regression toward the mean," which looms large in many evaluation studies, is not at issue in the present research. By the present design the common and serious problem of at-tempting to statistically adjust for initial differences between nonequivalent groups is also avoided.

Outcome Variables

The main variables on which possible effects of the intervention could be expected to show up are of course related to different aspects of bully/victim problems. In the present context only data for the key individual items reflecting these problems will be reported. In later publications analyses of more reliable composites of items will be presented.

The three key items were worded as follows:

1. How often have you been bullied in school? (Being exposed to direct bullying or victimization, with relatively open attacks on the victim.)
2. How often have you taken part in bullying other students in school? (Bullying or victimizing other students.)
3. How often does it happen that other students don't want to spend recess with you and you end up being alone? (Being exposed to indirect bullying or victimization by means of social isolation, exclusion from the group.)

As mentioned in the beginning of the chapter, to avoid idiosyncratic interpretations the students were provided with a detailed but simple "definition" of bullying before answering question 1. In both the written and the oral instruction, it was repeatedly emphasized that their answers should refer to the situation "this spring," that is, the period "from Christmas until now." All three questions had the same seven response alternatives, ranging from "it hasn't happened this spring" (scored 0) over "now and then" (scored 2) and "about once a week" (scored 3) to "several times a day" (scored 6).

Other items referred to being bullied or bullying others respectively on the way to and from school. Several items also concerned the individual's attitude toward victims of bullying (e.g., "How do you usually feel when you see a student being bullied in school?) and bullying students (e.g. "What do you think of students who bully others?")

With regard to the validity of self-reports on variables related to bully/victim problems, it may be mentioned that in my early Swedish studies (Olweus, 1978) composites of three to five self-report items on being bullied or bullying and attacking others, respectively, correlated in the range .40–.60 (unpublished) with reliable peer ratings on related dimensions (Olweus, 1977). Similarly, Perry, Kusel, and Perry (1988) have reported a correlation of .42 between a self-report scale of three victimization items and a reliable measure of peer nominations of victimization in elementary school children.

In the present study we also obtained a kind of peer ratings in that each student had to estimate the number of students in his or her class who had been bullied or had bullied others during the reference period. These data were aggregated for each class and the resulting class means correlated with the means derived from the students' own reports of being victimized or victimizing others. The two sets of class means were quite substantially correlated, the average correlations across the grade 5–7 cohorts being .61 for the victimization dimension and .58 for the bullying variable (Time 1). Corresponding coefficients for estimated average *proportion* of students in the class being bullied or bullying others (which measure corrects for differing number of students in the classes) were even somewhat higher, .62 and .68 respectively. Thus, there was considerable agreement across classes between class estimates derived from self-reports and from this form of peer ratings. *The results presented above certainly attest to the validity of the self-report data employed.*

Since a link has been established between bullying behavior and antisocial/criminal activities, it was hypothesized that the intervention program against bullying *might* also lead to a reduction in antisocial behavior. To measure different aspects of antisocial behavior in relatively young people, preadolescent and adolescents, a new self-report instrument was developed (Olweus and Endresen, 1987; Olweus, 1989). This questionnaire shows many similarities with the instruments recently developed by Elliot and Ageton (1980) and by Hindelang, Hirschi, and Weis (1981), but our questionnaire contained fewer items on serious crimes and more items related to school problems.

The 23 core items of the questionnaire were selected from two broad conceptual domains. One concerned disciplinary problems and other rule-breaking behavior in school, while the second covered more general and nonschool-related antisocial acts such as vandalism, theft, burglary, and fraud. Though it was possible and meaningful to divide the items into two separate scales roughly corresponding to the two conceptual domains, the results to be presented in this context only concern the Total Scale of Antisocial Behavior (TAS) consisting of all 23 items. Psychometric analyses of the questionnaire have given quite encouraging results indicating that the scales have satisfactory or good reliability, stability, and validity as well as theoretical relevance.

Finally, it was thought important to assess possible effects on student satisfaction with school life, in particular during recess time. (In Norwegian comprehensive schools, students usually have a break of approximately ten minutes every 45 minutes. In addition, they have a lunch break of 20–30 minutes in the middle of the day.) Since most of the bullying takes place at school (during recess and on the way to and from classes, and not on the way to and from school, see above), the following question was considered relevant: "How do you like recess time?"

Statistical Analyses

Since classes rather than students were the basic sampling units (with students nested within classes), it was considered important to choose a data analytic strategy that reflected the basic features of the design. Accordingly, data were analyzed with ANOVA (analysis of variance) with students nested within classes nested within schools nested within times/occasions (Time 1 vs. Time 2, Time 1 vs. Time 3). Sex of the subjects was crossed with times, schools (within times), and classes (within schools). Since several of the cohorts figured in two comparisons, the analyses had to be conducted separately for each combination of cohorts (for further information, see Olweus and Alsaker, 1991).

For several of the variables (or derivatives of them such as percentages), less refined (and in some respects, less informative) analyses with *t* tests and chi-square were also carried out. The findings from these analyses were in general agreement with those obtained in the ANOVAs.

Results

The results for some of the variables discussed above are presented separately for boys and girls in Figures 4.4–4.9. Since the design of the study is relatively complex, a few words about how to read the figures are in order.

The panel to the left shows the effects after 8 months of intervention, while the one to the right displays the results after 20 months. The upper curves (designated Before) show the baseline data (Time 1) for the relevant cohorts (the grade-5, grade-6, and grade-7 cohorts in the left panel and the grade-6 and grade-7 cohorts in the right). The lower curves (designated After) display

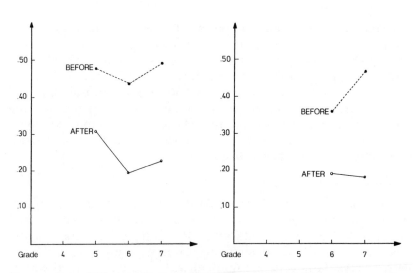

Figure 4.4.   Effects of intervention program on "Being exposed to direct bullying" for boys. Panel to the left shows effects after 8 months of intervention, and panel to the right displays results after 20 months of intervention. Upper curves (designated Before) show baseline data (Time 1), and the lower curves (designated After) display data collected at Time 2 in the left panel and at Time 3 in the panel to the right.

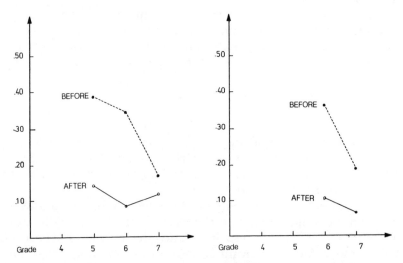

Figure 4.5.   Effects of intervention program on "Being exposed to direct bullying" for girls. See Figure 4.4 for explanation of the figure.

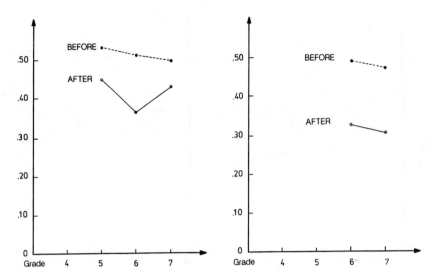

Figure 4.6.   Effects of intervention program on "Bullying other students" for boys. See Figure 4.4 for explanation of the figure.

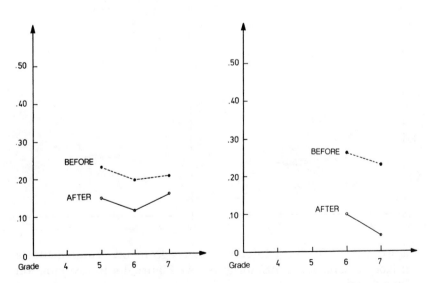

Figure 4.7.   Effects of intervention program on "Bullying other students" for girls. See Figure 4.4 for explanation of the figure.

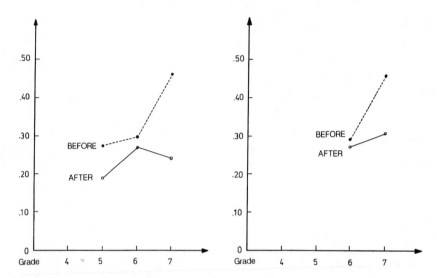

Figure 4.8.   Effects of intervention program on "Total Scale of Antisocial Behavior" (TAS) for boys. See Figure 4.4 for explanation of the figure.

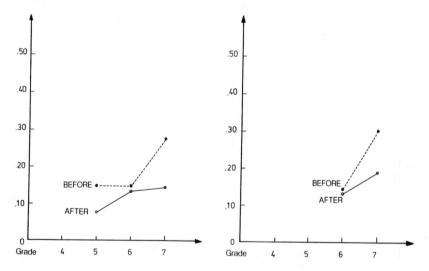

Figure 4.9.   Effects of intervention program on "Total Scale of Antisocial Behavior" (TAS) for girls. See Figure 4.4 for explanation of the figure.

data collected at Time 2 (after 8 months of intervention) in the panel to the left and at Time 3 (after 20 months of intervention) in the right-hand panel for the age-equivalent cohorts (the grade-4, grade-5, and grade-6 cohorts at Time 2 and the grade-4 and grade-5 cohorts at Time 3).

It should be noted that in some of the figures there are minor differences in baseline data (Before) for the grade-6 and grade-7 cohorts when presented in the left and right panels respectively. This is a consequence of the restriction of the analyses to subjects who had valid data at both time points; accordingly, it is not exactly the same subjects who entered the two sets of analyses.

The scales on the Y axis are in some sense arbitrary simply reflecting the system used in scoring the variables.

The *main findings* of the analyses can be summarized as follows:

• There were marked reductions in the levels of bully/victim problems for the periods studied, 8 and 20 months of intervention, respectively (Figures 4.4–4.9). By and large, reductions were obtained for both boys and girls and across all cohorts compared. For the longer time period the effects persisted in the case of "Being exposed to direct bullying" and "Being exposed to indirect bullying" and were strengthened for the variable "Bullying others."

• Similar reductions were obtained for the aggregated "peer rating" variables "Number of students being bullied in the class" and "Number of students in the class bullying others." There was thus consensual agreement in the classes that bully/victim problems had decreased during the periods studied.

• In terms of percentages of students reporting being bullied or bullying others, the reductions amounted to approximately 50% or more in most comparisons (Time 1–Time 3 for "Bullying others.")

• There was no displacement of bullying from the school to the way to and from school. There was a reduction or no change on the items measuring bully/victim problems on the way to and from school.

• There was also a reduction in general antisocial behavior (Figures 4.8 and 4.9) such as vandalism, theft, and truancy. (For the grade-6 comparisons the effects were marginal for both time periods.)

• At the same time, there was an increase in student satisfaction with school life as reflected in "liking recess time."
• In addition we could observe marked improvement as regards various aspects of the "social climate" of the class: improved order and structure, more positive social relationships, and a more positive attitude to schoolwork and the school.
• There were weak and inconsistent changes for the questions concerning attitudes to different aspects of bully/victim problems.

In the majority of comparisons for which reductions were reported above, the differences between baseline and intervention groups were highly significant or significant.

Quality of Data and Possible Alternative Interpretations

It is beyond the scope of this chapter to discuss in detail the quality of the data collected and the possibility of alternative interpretations of the findings. An extensive discussion of these matters can be found elsewhere (Olweus, 1991). Here I limit myself to summarizing the conclusions in the following "point statements":

• Self-reports, which were implicated in most of the analyses conducted so far, are in fact the best data source for the purposes of this study.
• It is very difficult to explain the results obtained as a consequence of (a) underreporting by the students; (b) gradual changes in the students' attitudes to bully/victim problems; (c) repeated measurement; and (d) concomitant changes in other factors. All in all, it is *concluded that the reductions in bully/victim and associated problems described above are likely to be a consequence mainly of the intervention program and not of some other "irrelevant" factor.*

In addition, a clear "dosage-response" relationship ($r = .51$, $n = 80$) has been established in preliminary analyses at the class level (which is the natural unit of analysis in this case): Those classes that showed larger reductions in bully/victim problems had implemented three presumably essential components of the intervention program (including establishment of class rules against bullying and regular class meetings) to a greater extent than those with smaller changes (additional information on these analyses can be found in Olweus and Alsaker, 1991). This finding certainly provides corroborating evidence for the effects of the intervention program. It will be followed up with more systematic and comprehensive analyses.

Basic Principles

Having reported the main goals and components of the intervention program as well as some of its effects, it is now natural to present its underlying principles and major subgoals.

The intervention program is built around *a limited set of key principles* derived chiefly from research on the development and modification of the implicated problem behaviors, in particular aggressive behavior. It is considered important to try to create a school (and ideally, also home) environment characterized by *warmth, positive interest, and involvement from adults* on one hand and *firm limits to unacceptable behavior* on the other. In cases of violations of limits and rules, *nonhostile, nonphysical sanctions* should be consistently applied. Implied in the latter two principles is also a certain degree of *monitoring and surveillance* of the students' activities in and out of school (Patterson, 1986). Finally, *adults* are supposed to *act as authorities at least in some respects.*

It can be seen that the first three of these principles largely represent the opposite of the child-rearing dimensions found to be important in the development of an aggressive reaction pattern discussed above: negativism on the part of the primary caretaker, permissiveness and lack of clear limits, and use of power-assertive methods (Olweus, 1980). The present intervention program can also be said to be based on an *authoritative adult-child interaction, or child rearing, model (cf. e.g., Baumrind, 1967).*

The principles listed above have been translated into a number of specific measures to be used at the *school, class,* and *individual levels.* It is considered very important to work on all of these levels, if possible. Figure 4.10 lists a number of such measures which were recommended in the intervention program. Space limitations prevent a detailed description of the various measures, but such an account can be found in a small book[2] designed for teachers and parents (Olweus, 1986, 1992).

COMPONENTS TO INTERVENTION PROGRAM AGAINST BULLYING

GENERAL PREREQUISITES: AWARENESS + INVOLVEMENT

SCHOOL LEVEL	CLASS LEVEL	INDIVIDUAL LEVEL
• Questionnaire survey • School conference day on bully/victim problems • Better supervision of recess • More attractive school playground • Contact telephone • Meeting staff-parents • Teacher groups for the development of the school climate • Parent circles (study and discussion groups)	• Class rules against bullying; clarification, praise, and sanctions • Regular class meetings • Cooperative learning • Meeting teacher—parents/children • Common positive activities • Role playing • Literature	• Serious talks with bullies and victims • Serious talks with parents of involved children • Teacher use of imagination • Help from "neutral" students • Advice to parents (parent brochure) • Discussion groups with parents of bullies and victims • Change of class or school

Figure 4.10. Overview of measures at the school, class, and individual levels.

With regard to implementation and execution, the program is mainly based on a *utilization of the existing social environment:* teachers and other school personnel, students, and parents. Nonexperts thus play a major role in the desired *restructuring of the social environment.* Experts such as school psychologists and social workers may also serve important functions as planners and coordinators, in counseling teacher and parent groups, and in handling more serious cases.

Additional Characteristics

Further understanding of the program and its way of working can be gained from a brief description of its four major subgoals (this entails some repetition of earlier material):

1. *To increase awareness of the bully/victim problem and advance knowledge about it* including to dispel some of the myths about it and its causes. Use of the questionnaire is an important step in obtaining more specific knowledge about the frequency and nature of the problems in the particular school.

2. *To achieve active involvement on the part of teachers and parents.* This implies among other things that the adults must recognize that it is their responsibility to control to a certain degree what goes on among the children at school. One way of doing this is to provide adequate supervision during recess time. Further, the teachers are encouraged to intervene in possible bullying situations and give a clear message to the students: Bullying is not accepted in our school. Teachers are also strongly advised to initiate serious talks with victims and bullies, and their parents, if a bully/victim problem has been identified in the class. Again, the basic message should be: We don't tolerate bullying in our school and will see to it that it comes to an end. Such an intervention on the part of the school must be regularly followed up and closely supervised; otherwise the situation may easily become worse for the victim than before the intervention.

3. *To develop clear rules against bullying behavior* such as: (a) We shall not bully others. (b) We shall try to help students who are bullied. (c) We shall make a point to include

students who become easily left out. Such a set of rules
may serve as a basis for class discussions about what is
meant by bullying behavior in concrete situations and
what kind of sanctions should be used for students who
break the rules. The behavior of the students in the class
should be regularly related to these rules in class meetings
("social hour"), and it is important that the teacher make
consistent use of sanctions (some form of nonhostile,
nonphysical punishment) in cases of rule violations and
also give generous praise when the rules have been
followed.

4. *To provide support and protection for the victims.* If followed, class rules against bullying certainly support
   children who tend to be victimized. In addition, the
   teacher may enlist the help of "neutral" or well-adjusted
   students to alleviate the situation of the victims in various ways. Also, teachers are encouraged to use their
   imagination to help victimized students to assert themselves in the class, to make them valuable in the eyes of
   their classmates. Parents of victims are exhorted to help
   their children develop new peer contacts and to teach
   them in detail how to make new acquaintances and to
   maintain a friendship.

It may be added that the present intervention program has
been evaluated by more than 1,000 Norwegian and Swedish teachers. In short, their reactions have generally been quite favorable,
indicating among other things that the teachers see the proposed
principles and measures as useful and realistic.

Concluding Words

The basic message of the reported findings is clear: *It is definitely possible to substantially reduce bully/victim problems in
school and related problem behaviors with a suitable intervention program.* In consequence, whether these problems will be
tackled or not no longer depends on whether we have the knowledge necessary to achieve desirable changes. It is much more a
matter of our willingness to involve ourselves and to use the
existing knowledge.

NOTES

1. There is an (expanded) English version of the Bully/Victim Questionnaire (one version for grades 1–4, and another for grades 5–9 and higher grades). This questionnaire as well as other materials related to the intervention program (see note 2, below) are copyrighted which implies certain restrictions on their use. For more details, please write to Dan Olweus, University of Bergen, Oysteinsgate 3, N-5007 Bergen, Norway.

2. The "package" related to the intervention program against bully/victim problems consists of the questionnaire for the measurement of bully/victim problems (note 1), a copy of a small book *Bullying at School—What We Know and What We Can Do* (Olweus, 1992) aiming at teachers and parents, a video about bullying, and a parent folder. (Additional materials are being developed.) These materials are copyrighted which implies certain restrictions on their use. For more information, please write to the author at the address given in note 1.

REFERENCES

Baumrind, D. (1967). Child care practices anteceding three patterns of preschool behavior. *Genetic Psychology Monographs, 75,* 43–88.

Ekblad, S., and Olweus, D. (1986). Applicability of Olweus' aggression inventory in a sample of Chinese primary school children. *Aggressive Behavior, 12,* 315–325.

Ekman, K. (1977). *Skolmobbning.* Pro gradu-arbete. Abo, Finland: Abo Akademi.

Elliott, D. S. and Ageton, S. S. (1980). Reconciling race and class differences in self-reported and official estimates of delinquency. *American Sociological Review, 45,* 95–110.

Heinemann, P. P. (1972). *Mobbning—gruppvåld bland barn och vuxna.* Stockholm: Natur och Kultur.

Hindelang, M. J., Hirschi, T., and Weiss, J. G. (1981). *Measuring delinquency.* Beverly Hills, CA: Sage.

Hyde, J. S. (1984). How large are gender differences in aggression? A developmental meta-analysis. *Developmental Psychology, 20,* 722–736.

Largerspetz, K. M., Björkqvist, K., Berts, M., and King, E. (1982). Group aggression among school children in three schools. *Scandinavian Journal of Psychology, 23,* 45–52.

Loeber, R., and Dishion, T. (1983). Early predictors of male delinquency: A review. *Psychological Bulletin, 94,* 69–99.

Maccoby, E. E. (1986). Social groupings in childhood: Their relationships to prosocial and antisocial behavior in boys and girls. In D. Olweus, J. Block, and M. Radke-Yarrow (Eds.), *Development of antisocial and prosocial behavior.* New York: Academic Press.

Maccoby, E. E., and Jacklin, C. N. (1980). Sex differences in aggression: A rejoinder and a reprise. *Child Development, 51,* 964–980.

Magnusson, D., Stattin, H., and Dunér, A. (1983). Aggression and criminality in a longitudinal perspective. In K. T. Van Dusen and S. A. Mednick (Eds.), *Prospective studies of crime and delinquency.* Boston: Kluwer-Nijhoff.

Manger, T., and Olweus D. (1985). Tilbakemelding til skulane. *Norsk Skoleblad* (Oslo, Norway), *35,* 20–22.

Olweus, D. (1973a). *Hackkycklingar och översittare: Forskning om skolmobbning.* Stockholm: Almqvist and Wiksell.

―――. (1973b). Personality and aggression. In J. K. Cole and D. D. Jensen (Eds.), *Nebraska symposium on motivation, 1972* (Vol. 20) (pp. 261–321). Lincoln: University of Nebraska Press.

―――. (1977). Aggression and peer acceptance in adolescent boys: Two short-term longitudinal studies of ratings. *Child Development, 48,* 1301–1313.

―――. (1978). *Aggression in the schools: Bullies and whipping boys.* Washington, DC: Hemisphere (Wiley).

―――. (1980). Familial and temperamental determinants of aggressive behavior in adolescent boys: A causal analysis. *Developmental Psychology, 16,* 644–660.

―――. (1981). Bullying among school boys. In N. Cantwell (Ed.), *Children and violence* (pp. 97–131). Stockholm: Akademilitteratur.

―――. (1983). Low school achievement and aggressive behavior in adolescent boys. In D. Magnusson and V. Allen (Eds.), *Human development. An interactional perspective* (pp. 353–365). New York: Academic Press.

―――. (1984). Aggressors and their victims: Bullying at school. In N. Frude and H. Gault (Eds.), *Disruptive behavior in schools* (pp. 57–76) New York: Wiley.

———. (1985). 80000 barn er innblandet i mobbing. *Norsk Sloleblad* (Oslo, Norway), *35*, 18–23.

———. (1986). *Mobbning—vad vi vet och vad vi kan göra.* Stockholm: Liber.

———. (1989). Prevalence and incidence in the study of antisocial behavior: Definitions and measurement. In M. Klein (Ed.), *Cross-national research in self-reported crime and delinquency* (pp. 187–201). Dodrecht, Netherlands: Kluwer.

———. (1991). Bully/victim problems among school children: Basic facts and effects of a school based intervention program. In D. Pepler and K. Rubin, *The Development and treatment of childhood aggression* (pp. 411–448). Hillsdale, NJ: Erlbaum.

———. (1992). *Bullying at school—what we know and what we can do.* Book manuscript.

Olweus, D., and Alsaker, F. D. (1991). Assessing change in a cohort-longitudinal study and hierarchical data. In D. Magnusson, L. Bergman, G. Rudinger, and B. Törestad (Eds.), *Problems and methods in longitudinal research* (pp. 107–132). New York: Cambridge University Press.

Olweus D., and Endresen, J. (1987). *Assessment of antisocial behavior in preadolescence and adolescence.* Manuscript.

Olweus D., and Roland, E. (1983). *Mobbing—bakgrunn op tiltak.* Oslo, Norway: Kirke-og undervisningsdepartementet.

Patterson, G. R. (1986). Performance models for antisocial boys. *American Psychologist, 41*, 432–444.

Patterson, G. R., and Stouthamer-Loeber, M. (1984). The correlation of family management practices and delinquency. *Child Development, 55*, 1299–1307.

Perry, D. G., Kusel, S. J., and Perry, L. C. (1988). Victims of peer aggression. *Developmental Psychology, 24*, 807–814.

Pikas, A. (1975). *Så stoppar vi mobbning.* Stockholm: Prisma.

Raundalen, T. S., and Raundalen, M. (1979). *Er du på vår side?* Oslo: Universitetsforlaget.

Roland, E. (1983). *Strategi mot mobbing.* Oslo: Universitetsforlaget.

Rutter, M. (1983). School effects on pupil progress: Research findings and policy implications. *Child Development, 54*, 1–19.

Smith P. (1991). The silent nightmare: Bullying and victimisation in school peer groups. *The Psychologist, 4*, 243–248.

Whitney, I., and Smith, P. K. (in press). A survey of the nature and extent of bullying in junior/middle and secondary schools. *Educational Research.*

Ziegler, S., and Rosenstein-Manner, M. (1991). *Bullying at school: Toronto in an international context* (Report No. 196). Toronto: Toronto Board of Education, Research Services.

PART III

PLAYGROUND BEHAVIORS AND PEER RELATIONS

5

GARY W. LADD AND JOSEPH M. PRICE

Playstyles of Peer-Accepted and Peer-Rejected Children on the Playground

Establishing positive relationships with the members of one's peer group is an important developmental task during childhood. Peer relations make unique contributions to the growth of social and emotional competence, to the acquisition of social skills and values, and to the development of the capacity to form relationships with others (see Berndt and Ladd, 1989). In addition, peers provide an important source of emotional support. However, the degree to which peer relationships provide these important contributions is dependent upon the quality of these relationships.

In the past decade there has been an accumulation of empirical evidence to indicate that the quality of children's peer relationships is, to a large extent, dependent upon the types of behaviors children display toward one another during social interaction. Prosocial exchanges (e.g., cooperative play, sharing, helping) between children facilitate the development of favorable impressions of one another and the formation of friendship, whereas aggression and negatively toned exchanges contribute to the development of negative impressions and antagonistic relationships.

Yet, in addition to the competencies children bring with them into peer interactions, the characteristics of the social context also have an impact on the quality of peer interactions. According to ecologically oriented psychologists (e.g., Barker, 1968; Bronfenbrenner, 1979), the social contexts or behavior settings in which people interact elicit and organize certain kinds of behavior. The kinds of behavior that are elicited depend upon the characteristics of that setting and are hypothesized to impact the formation of interpersonal perceptions and subsequent formation of relationships.

Included among the social contexts or settings in which children meet, interact, and form relationships are the neighborhood, clubs and organized community activities (e.g., scouts, dance classes, little league), and the school. During early and middle childhood, perhaps the most important of these social contexts is the school. With age, children spend increasing amounts of time with their peers at school—often the largest proportion of their waking hours. In addition, school offers a unique social context for the development of social behavior and relationships (Minuchin and Shapiro, 1983), fundamentally different from the context of the home. Within this context children interact with teachers who represent authority and leadership, who set the social climate of the classroom and the conditions of possible contact among class members (Minuchin and Shapiro, 1983). Children also have numerous opportunities to interact with the members of their peer group.

The school context is composed of a number of different behavioral settings, including the classroom, the lunchroom, and the playground. Of these settings, the two that appear to have the greatest impact on children's social behavior and peer interactions are the classroom and the playground. Each of these settings possess tangible characteristics and properties which elicit and organize certain kinds of behavior responses from children.

The classroom setting is distinguished by several important characteristics. First, teachers rather than children usually determine and organize the nature and direction of the activities. Second, the content of these activities typically involves learning specific material. Third, there tend to be a number of social conventions and rules that govern social behavior (e.g., talking with peers is only allowed during specified activities). Finally, children are not always free to choose work and play partners. Teachers often determine seating arrangements and select participants for group projects.

In contrast to the classroom setting is the playground. In this behavioral setting, children determine and organize the direction of their own activities, which almost exclusively involves various forms of play. In addition, there are typically only a few rules or regulations on the playground, and those that do exist usually set broad parameters for acceptable behavior (e.g., don't climb on the fence, don't throw sand). Perhaps the most important distinguishing characteristic of the playground is that children are free to choose play partners (King, 1987).

As is evident, playgrounds are essentially social environments intended for social rather than academic purposes. The characteristics of playgrounds afford children the opportunity not only to determine the nature of their play activities, but also the peers who serve as partners for these activities. In addition, children have the opportunity to display a wide array of social behaviors toward a sizable proportion of their classmates. Thus, peer interactions within this behavioral setting are likely to play an important role in the development of children's perceptions and impressions of their classmates and in the development of their peer relationships. Likewise, children's relationship histories with their classmates and their perceptions of those classmates would be expected to affect the quality of their interactions with those same peers on the playground.

PURPOSE AND SCOPE OF THIS CHAPTER

Although playgrounds appear to be an important context for social development, and most children spend considerable time on playgrounds as they grow up, researchers have seldom studied children's peer relations in this context. Thus, a major aim of this chapter is to provide a closer look at children's social experiences on playgrounds, and the role that these experiences may play in the formation and maintenance of certain types of peer relationships. Specifically, we will describe several recent studies that we have conducted to explore: (a) linkages among children's playground behaviors, play patterns, and social status among peers, and (b) variations in playgrounds and playground conditions and their relation to children's behavior and/or peer status in this setting.

Our work has been guided by an interest in both the potential antecedents and consequences of children's social status among peers. With respect to antecedents, we have begun to explore the question of how children become liked or disliked, or accepted or rejected by peers. A careful inspection of the literature on this topic (see Berndt and Ladd, 1989; Asher and Coie, 1990; Ladd and Crick, 1989) suggests that there may be many answers to this question. One promising explanation comes from the study of children's behavior in peer group settings. For example, there is growing evidence to suggest that differences in children's behaviors are related to their status or reputations among peers (see Coie, Dodge, and Kupersmidt, 1990). Progress toward understanding the antecedents of children's peer status has come primarily from studies in which children are observed longitudinally while interacting in play groups with unfamiliar peers (see Dodge, 1983;

Coie and Kupersmidt, 1983). This approach allows investigators to document behaviors that children employ prior to their eventual acceptance or rejection by peers in the group.

By using such designs, these studies have helped to eliminate important confounds inherent in past research. For example, until recently, most researchers tended to employ cross-sectional designs to study the relation between children's behavior and their status among peers, and these studies were often conducted with age-mates in classroom settings, and on occasions when children were already well-acquainted with peers (e.g., well after the start of a school year). As a result, it has been difficult for investigators to determine whether children's observed behavior patterns are a cause or consequence of their acceptance by peers.

In addition, the potential consequences of children's status among peers are not well understood. Most of the evidence we have about this issue comes from studies in which investigators have attempted to describe the interactions of children from existing status groups (e.g., how children who have become popular or rejected relate with peers). In many such studies, investigators have gathered data on children's status and behavior simultaneously. Although these investigations may provide some important clues about the behavioral outcomes of differing status groups, they suffer from many of the same problems outlined above. Advances in our understanding of this question also require that investigators employ longitudinal designs and examine the extent to which children's prior status predicts later peer behavior.

Another potential limitation of past research on the antecedents and consequences of children's peer status is that investigators have tended to conduct their observations in settings that are not conducive to children's play and social relations, and where the "players" tend to be segregated by age (i.e., classrooms). Thus, it is arguable that studies conducted in classrooms do not provide a representative picture of children's *social* behaviors and interaction patterns and, thus, perpetuate narrow and potentially inaccurate view of the antecedents and consequences of peer acceptance or rejection. Moreover, the possible effects of setting factors or conditions, such as the presence of adults, size of the play area, availability of companions that vary in age and gender, have seldom been studied. In response to these concerns, we have begun to observe children's social behaviors on playgrounds, and consider how potential setting factors may affect children's play in this context. Moreover, we have relied on both cross-sectional and longitudinal designs to probe both the potential antecedents and consequences of children's peer status.

PLAYGROUND ANTECEDENTS OF PEER SOCIAL STATUS

Because playgrounds are a context in which *play* is salient, children's play styles and skills may play an important role in peers' perceptions of them as "players." Children's play behaviors and skills may determine their value as play partners, and ultimately shape their reputations among many peers (to quote a recent songwriter, "how you play is who you are"). Consistent with this perspective, and past work on the origins of peer status (e.g., see Coie et al. 1990), we have hypothesized that children's playground behaviors and styles may be important antecedents of their status among peers.

To further examine this hypothesis, Ladd, Price, and Hart (1988, 1990) conducted a short-term longitudinal study of the playground behaviors and interaction patterns of 28 preschool children. Our primary objective was to chart children's playground behaviors and play patterns over the course of a school year, and determine whether early play behaviors and patterns were predictive of later peer status. Playground behaviors were defined as children's observed activities on the playground, and included both social and nonsocial forms. Play patterns referred to both the structure of children's contacts with peers (i.e., the number or range of different peers with whom children interacted; the number of companions with whom they had frequent or regular contact), and features of the context in which interactions occurred (i.e., group size; the relative age, sex, and status of one's partners).

Because children's playground behaviors have not been well studied, we also pursued several descriptive aims. Specifically, we were interested in knowing whether individual differences in children's playground behaviors and play patterns remained stable over time and thus could be construed as consistent play "styles" among individuals. Another important question was whether or not temporal trends occurred in children's play patterns, or interactive contexts over the course of the school year (e.g., whether children's range of partners, or the average number of peers present in their interactions tended to increase or decrease over time).

The subjects in this study were 28 preschoolers between the ages of 3½ and 4½ who were enrolled in four half-day preschool classrooms serving a total of 88 children ranging in age from 2½ to 5½. Half the children in the sample were males. The sample was also balanced with respect to children's familiarity with the school setting and enrollment in morning or afternoon sessions. Observations of children's playground behaviors and play patterns were conducted on three occasions: as children began school (early fall), midyear (winter), and at the end of the school year (spring). At each time of assessment, three trained observers and a reliability judge conducted observations during 18 40-minute free-play periods (approximately 3 per week for 6 weeks). Each play period was scheduled on the same playground with children from multiple ages and classrooms (the entire AM or PM enrollment), and children were free to choose their own play companions and activities.

Observers reliably recorded (Kappas > .86) children's playground behaviors during each assessment occasion using a mutually exclusive category scheme (see Ladd, 1983) consisting of four categories of interactive behavior (i.e., cooperative play, social conversation, rough play, argue) and five categories of noninteractive behavior (i.e., parallel play, solitary play, onlooking, teacher, or transition). Behaviors not represented in the scheme were coded as "other." The proportion of time subjects spent in each type of behavior at each time of assessment was calculated by summing the total number of entries within categories and dividing by the total number of observations.

To document children's play patterns, observers also recorded the names of children who were involved in each of the subject's observed interactions. Agreement between pairs of observers on the number of partners present in interactions ranged from $r = .84$ to .97 across assessment occasions. These data were used to estimate: (a) the number of different peers children interacted with at each time of assessment (range of contacts), (b) the number of frequent play companions (i.e., playmates present in more than 30% of the subject's interactions, and (c) the types of companions who tended to be present in their interactions (e.g., proportion of interactions conducted among older-, same-, or mixed-age partners; and among same-, opposite-, or mixed-sex partners).

At the end of each observational interval, an individual sociometric interview was conducted with each subject. Children were asked to nominate liked and disliked peers, and rate play-mates on a 3-point likability scale (see Asher, Singleton, Tinsley, and Hymel, 1979). The positive and negative nominations children received were summed and standardized within classrooms to yield measures of acceptance and rejection, and also subtracted (positive – negative) and summed (positive + negative) to create measures of social preference and impact, respectively (see Coie, Dodge, and Coppotelli, 1982). The ratings received by each child were summed over raters and standardized to create mean peer acceptance score.

Stability of Playground Behaviors and Play Patterns

To examine the stability of children's playground behaviors and play patterns, we correlated the scores children received for these measures both within (i.e., scores from each half of the interval) across the assessment intervals (e.g., fall to winter, winter to spring, and fall to spring). The resulting stability coefficients are reported in Table 5.1.

As can be seen in the top half of Table 5.1, individual differences in children's playground behaviors, with the exception of those coded as parallel play, onlooking, and transition, were relatively stable at each time of assessment. However, only individual differences in behaviors coded as cooperative play, unoccupied, and teacher remained relatively stable over the entire school year. Apparently, relative to peers, children who tended to be cooperative players, "tuned out" (e.g., wander aimlessly), or focused on the teacher, were likely to retain this style of behavior over long intervals. Other forms of behavior appeared to become more or less stable as the school year progressed. On the one hand, the hierarchy for "rough players" became somewhat more stable during the latter half of the school year. On the other hand, individual differences in behaviors such as social conversation and arguing became less stable later in the school year, and children who spent more time in these behaviors during the first half of the school year were not the same children who were extreme in their use of these behaviors during the second half of the school year.

Results for the stability of children's play patterns are shown in the bottom half of Table 5.1. Both the range of play companions and number of frequent playmates were relatively stable within assessment occasions and across each half of the school year (although less so over the entire year). Across short intervals, it would appear that there is some consistency both in children's tendencies to interact with larger (as opposed to smaller) numbers of play partners, and propensity to interact with the same play partners. Consistency in the interpersonal composition of children's interactions is also more apparent across brief as opposed to longer intervals (e.g., the entire school year). Among these measures, higher levels of stability can be seen for indices that reflect children's preferences for same-sex and same-age playmates.

Table 5.1   Stability Within and Between Assessment Intervals for Individual Differences in Children's Playground Behaviors and Play Patterns

Measure	Within Intervals			Across Intervals		
				Fall–	Winter–	Fall–
	Fall	Winter	Spring	Winter	Spring	Spring
Playground Behaviors						
Cooperative Play	.75	.75	.49	.75	.65	.52
Social Conversation	.65	.77	.38	.61	.17	.10
Rough Play	.82	.65	.51	.36	.53	.34
Argue	.60	.61	.53	.33	.31	.20
Parallel Play	– .06	.41	.50	.21	.26	.62
Solitary Play	.48	.54	.45	.52	.64	.34
Onlooking	.26	.38	.37	.78	.18	.24
Unoccupied	.53	.38	.31	.54	.61	.69
Teacher	.48	.74	.58	.82	.59	.44
Transition	.06	.29	– .01	.22	.29	– .10
Play Patterns						
Range of Contacts	.53	.65	.79	.48	.51	.33
Freq. Play Companions	.39	.66	.59	.50	.71	.41
Average Group Size	.48	.26	.39	.35	.33	.26
Same Sex	.69	.69	.55	.54	.43	.46
Opposite Sex	.70	.41	.57	.49	.42	.16
Mixed Sex	.15	.30	.19	.50	.38	.23
Same Age	.64	.59	.72	.54	.29	.30
Older	.63	.66	.39	.45	.27	.17
Younger	.58	.63	.74	.57	.22	.21
Mixed Age	.11	.47	.02	.30	.12	.08

Changes in Children's Playground Play Patterns over the Course of the School Year

Changes in children's play patterns over the school year were examined with a series of 2 (Sex) by 3 (Time) repeated measures analyses of variance (ANOVAs). More specifically, we were interested in determining whether the structure and composition of children's peer contacts on the playground changed over time, and whether these patterns and trends might differ by gender. Several analyses yielded significant main effects for time and/or gender, and the corresponding means are presented in Table 5.2.

Several important trends can be seen in the structure of children's peer contacts. First, the number of different peers with whom children interacted on the playground was greatest at the beginning of the school year, after which their range of contacts declined significantly. Second, the average number of companions present in children's interactions (excluding the subject) also declined significantly over time. Third, the number of companions present in boys' interactions was, on average, significantly larger than that observed for girls at all times of assessment. These data suggest that: (a) children's interactions become more focused over time—that is, they tend to interact with a smaller range of partners and in smaller groups as the year progresses, and (b) compared to girls, boys tend to interact in larger groups, or have more extensive play patterns (see also Waldrop and Halverson, 1975).

Trends were also found in the sex and age composition of children's interactive contexts. Whereas interactions conducted among same-sex and same-age companions increased significantly over time, contacts within mixed-sex groups or among older companions declined.

Table 5.2. Means for Play Patterns Measures that Achieved Significance

Measure	Fall	Winter	Spring	Males	Females
Range of Contacts	18.68	14.93	14.93		
Average Group Size	1.62	1.54	1.48	1.63	1.46
Same Sex	.46	.54	.58		
Mixed Sex	.27	.16	.15		
Same Age	.34	.44	.64		
Older	.23	.25	.06		

Playground Behaviors and Patterns and Children's Peer Status

Several sets of analyses were used to shed light on the potential determinants of children's peer status (see Ladd, Price, and Hart, 1988). First, we employed a series of hierarchical regression analyses to examine: (a) the extent to which early playground behaviors predicted changes in peer status (i.e., social preference and impact) over time, and (b) the extent to which early peer status predicted changes in playground behaviors over time. To predict changes in peer status from fall to winter, the playground behavior measures (fall) were used to predict social preference scores (e.g., winter), after first entering the prior social preference scores (fall) into the equation. The same analysis was also conducted with social impact scores, and changes in both sociometric measures from fall to spring were analyzed in the same manner. To predict changes in playground behavior from peer status, each of the prior peer status measures (fall) were used to predict later behaviors (e.g., winter), after first partialling the prior behavioral measures (fall). Changes in behavior from fall to spring were analyzed in the same manner.

Results indicated that two forms of interactive behavior, exhibited early in the school year, were predictive of later peer status. Higher levels of cooperative play at the outset of school predicted significant gains in social preference by the end of the school year. In addition, arguing during the early weeks of school forecasted significantly lower social preference scores by both the middle and end of the school year. Of the various nonsocial behaviors we assessed, only unoccupied behavior emerged as a significant predictor of children's peer status. Children who spent more time in unoccupied behaviors during the early weeks of school displayed lower levels of social impact by the end of the year (cf. Ladd, Price and Hart, 1990). Analyses that were used to explore the potential effect of early peer status on later behavior did not produce any significant findings.

An analogous set of regression analyses were employed to determine whether features of children's play patterns were predictive of changes in their peer status and vice versa. Findings from these analyses indicated that the children's range of peer contacts was not only predictive *of* their peer status, but also predicted *by* their peer status, depending on the time of assessment and the form of peer status measured. On the one hand, two aspects of children's play patterns were associated with changes in peer status. Children who interacted with a larger number of peers in the fall tended to receive higher social impact scores in the spring. On the other hand, the number of negative nominations children received at the beginning of the school year predicted their range of contacts at midyear, and the number of negative nominations received at midyear predicted their range of contacts at the end of the year. Across both intervals, higher negative nomination scores forecasted gains in the number of different play partners children interacted with at later points in time.

Thus, the hypothesis that children's playground behaviors influence their acceptance in the peer group receives some support from our data. Children who played cooperatively with peers at the outset of the school year also tended to do so at later points in time, and this style of interaction was associated with long-term gains in peer acceptance. In contrast, early arguing behaviors, although less stable over time, forecasted negative peer status as early as midyear. The thrust of these findings are consistent with studies of older children's playgroups (e.g., Dodge, 1983; Coie and Kupersmidt, 1983), and help to illustrate the potential functions of both prosocial and aggressive behaviors in the formation of social status in young children's playground environments. It would appear that cooperative behaviors facilitate positive peer perceptions because they serve as social reinforcers or help to perpetuate rewarding play activities on the playground. Arguing, in contrast, may foster negative peer attitudes because it is both aversive to children and disruptive of ongoing play themes and activities.

Our data also suggest that children who engage in higher levels of aimless solitary behavior on the playground (i.e., they tend to be unoccupied) fail to make much of an impression (in terms of likability) on their peers over the course of the school year. Instead of becoming either liked or disliked, they appear to be "overlooked" by their peers. Nonsocial behavior of this type may limit children's interactions with peers and, thus, restrict peers' opportunities to evaluate them as potential playmates.

In addition to children's play behaviors, it also appears that some aspects of their play patterns are related to their peer status. It would appear that more extensive contact patterns early in the school year enhance a child's social visibility in the peer group at later points in time. However, even though this play pattern may be predictive of later visibility, it appears that extensive contacts are not the rule as the school year progresses. On the average, the range or number of different peers children interacted with tended to decline over the course of the school year. Perhaps as children began the school year and were less familiar with peers, they tended to "sample" many different play partners and eventually gravitated toward smaller number of companions they preferred as playmates. Although typical for most children, it is interesting to note that this trend does not seem to describe what happens to children who become disliked by peers early in the school year. Early disliking or rejection forecasted a *larger* range of peer contacts at later points in the school year. Thus, unlike the norm, it would appear that disliked children have more difficulty focusing their social contacts, and even expand their search for partners as the year goes on. Perhaps once these children become disliked, they become "marginal" group members, and are forced to search out possible interaction partners among a broad range of peers.

THE PLAYGROUND BEHAVIORS OF CHILDREN IN EXISTING STATUS GROUPS

Another way that we have studied the relation between children's social behavior and status is by observing how children with established social reputations interact with peers on the playground. Unlike the longitudinal research described in the prior section, these investigations have cross-sectional designs and do not permit strong inferences about the direction of effect. However, because children are selected on the basis of their existing reputations (e.g., those who are popular vs. rejected by peers), and then observed on the playground, these studies may help us better understand whether children from differing peer strata experience differing social environments on the playground.

One such study was conducted by Ladd (1983) with a sample of 48 third- and fourth-grade children who were attending two small elementary schools in the midwestern United States. Children from these grade levels were selected because they represented the median grade levels in each school and, therefore, allowed us to observe children in a context where there were roughly equal numbers of older and younger companions present as potential playmates. At each site, observations of children's play behaviors and patterns were conducted on school playgrounds during times when children from all grade levels were present (i.e., lunch hour and recess times).

To select the sample, a sociometric rating scale (Oden and Asher, 1977) was administered in each classroom, and standard-score cutoffs were used to classify children into one of three sociometric groups, termed popular, average, or unpopular. Teachers were then asked to sort the names of unpopular children into the categories "neglected" or "rejected," based on observations of the children's behavior with classmates. Rejected children were defined as those who were actively disliked and rebuffed by other children, and only this group was included in the study. From these three groups, a total 16 popular, 16 average, and 16 rejected children were randomly selected from third- and fourth-grade classrooms and observed on the playground.

A friendship nomination questionnaire was also administered in all classrooms in each school in order to identify children's friends across classrooms and grade levels. Children were shown class pictures from each grade level and asked to nominate up to seven friends. These data were used to determine which of children's frequent companions on the playground were friends with the subject and with each other (dimensions termed network affinity and cliquishness in this study).

Observations were conducted on the playgrounds of the two grade schools over a 16-week period during the spring of a school year. One school had a large playground (approximately 150,000 square feet) that was largely grass-covered and organized into a variety of play and equipment areas (e.g., ball diamonds, basketball courts, sandbox area; swing and slide areas). The other school had a smaller playground (approximately 70,000 square feet) that contained some stationary play equipment, and was largely asphalt-covered. Observers gathered data on aspects of children's playground behaviors and play patterns that were similar to those described in the prior section, including: (a) four types of interactive behaviors (i.e., social conversation, cooperative play, arguing, and rough play) and four types of noninteractive behaviors (i.e., unoccupied, onlooking, solitary play, parallel play); (b) the number of peers present in each interaction; (c) the types of companions present in children's interactions (e.g., age and sex composition); and (d) the degree to which children's regular or frequent playground companions were friends with the subject and with each other (i.e., network affinity and cliquishness).

Analyses of children's playground behaviors revealed that popular and average status children tended to be more prosocial with peers than did rejected children. Specifically, popular and average status children spent significantly more time in cooperative play and social conversation than rejected children. Sex differences in these behaviors were also found for popular and average status children. Whereas boys in these two groups displayed higher levels of cooperative play than girls, popular and average girls evidenced higher levels of social conversation than boys. Thus, it would appear that children who are accepted by peers interact more positively with their playground partners than do children who are rejected, and that the form of these behaviors differs across gender.

In contrast, more negatively toned or conflictually oriented behaviors were more common in the playground interactions of rejected children. Rejected children argued with their playground companions more often than did their popular or average counterparts, and rejected males (but not females) engaged in higher levels of rough play. Apparently, children who are not well accepted by peers also have more difficult and conflict-ridden interactions on the playground.

Differences among the three status groups also emerged in the types of nonsocial behaviors they exhibited on the playground. Both rejected boy and girls spent more time in unoccupied behaviors (e.g., wandering aimlessly on the playground), and rejected girls were more likely to engage in parallel play (i.e., solitary play near other children). Popular children spent less time watching others play than children in either of the other two status groups. These findings suggest that children's status among peers is related to various forms of social "disengagement" on the playground. In general, rejected children, perhaps because they are disliked, spend more time wandering about, playing near but not with others, and watching others play than do more accepted children.

Play patterns are another way in which the lives of children from different sociometric strata differ on the playground. Observations of the number of companions present in children's inter-actions revealed that, on the average, rejected children tended to play in significantly smaller groups. Moreover, the relative age and status of rejected children's companions were significantly younger and less popular, respectively, than those of popular or average children. Popular children, in contrast, interacted among older and well-liked companions significantly more than children in the other two status groups. Also, compared to popular and average children, fewer of rejected children's play companions nominated them as friends in the friendship interviews, and fewer of their frequent playground companions were friends with each other. Therefore, it would appear that the play patterns of re-jected children do differ in important ways from their better-accepted counterparts. Our longitudinal studies show that re-jected children have difficulty establishing consistent play partners, and are more likely to seek out many different partners at times when other children have begun to focus their ties on a few "regular" companions. Data from this study are consistent with this picture, and may extend it by suggesting that rejected chil-dren eventually gravitate toward younger and less popular chil-dren in their search for playmates. The data also suggest that rejected children do not tend to be at the "hub" of peer activity—most often, their interactions tend to occur in small groups and with few partners. Moreover, these interactions do not appear to occur in a warm, affiliative "climate" in the sense that, whereas popular and average children interactions tend to occur among friends, rejected children's do not.

In another study of how children with established social repu-tations interact with peers on the playground, Price and Dodge (1989) examined the relation between peer-directed aggressive be-havior on the playground and children's classroom peer status. Two distinct subcategories of aggression were examined—reactive aggression and proactive aggression. Reactive aggression, which has theoretical roots in the frustration-aggression model (Dollard, Doob, Miller, Mowrer, and Sears, 1939), is a defensive reaction to a perceived threatening stimulus and is accompanied by some vis-ible form of anger (e.g., angry facial gestures or verbalizations). This form of aggression is similar to Hartup's (1974) category of "hostile' aggression. Proactive aggression, on the other hand, is considered an unprovoked aversive means of influencing or coercing another person and is more goal-directed than reactive aggression. In addition, proactive aggression may take one of two forms: instrumental or bullying. Instrumental aggression is "object-oriented" and is aimed at the retrieval of an object, territory, or privilege (Hartup, 1974). Bullying, on the other hand, is more "person-directed," with the aim of intimidating or dominating a peer in some manner. The theoretical roots of the proactive subtypes of aggression can be found in social learning theory (Bandura, 1973), which postulates that aggression is an acquired instrumental behavior that is controlled by reinforcements. Given that both reactive and bullying forms of aggression are person- rather than object-directed, it was hypothesized that each of these two forms of aggression would be more positively associated with social rejection than would object-oriented instrumental aggression.

The reciprocity of aggression and the play context in which aggression occurs were examined as well. Based on the findings of previous research (e.g., Dodge and Richard, 1985), it was hypothesized that a child who displayed aggression toward his/her peers would likely become a recipient of aggression from those peers. It was also hypothesized that aggression would occur most often in the context of rough play.

The sample for this study was composed of 70 5- and 6-year-old males from three kindergarten ($n = 31$) and three first-grade ($n = 39$) classrooms of a public elementary school located in a large metropolitan area. Females were excluded because previous research has demonstrated that among children 6 years of age and younger, females exhibit lower levels of both physical and verbal aggression than do males (see Maccoby and Jacklin, 1980). It was anticipated that an exclusively male sample would thus allow for a more adequate assessment of multiple forms of aggression.

Subjects were observed during regularly scheduled free play periods during the school day. The playground contexts in which the two samples were observed differed in several important respects. First, the children in each of the three kindergarten classes participated in separate free play sessions, whereas the children in the three first-grade classes participated in a joint free play session. Thus the total number of children present during free play differed for each grade level—about 20 for each kindergarten group and 80 for the first-grade group. Another difference was in the adult/child ratio during free play sessions. During kindergarten play sessions, at least one teacher was present on the playground. Occasionally, this teacher was joined by a teaching assistant. Thus, at least one teacher was present for every 20 children. In contrast, during the joint first-grade play sessions, there was usually only one teacher present, resulting in an adult/child ratio of 1 to 80. Finally, the area of the playground in which kindergartners and first graders were allowed to play differed. Kindergartner's play activities were restricted to the play equipment area, whereas first graders were allowed to play in any area of the playground (e.g., equipment area, field).

Behavioral observations were conducted during 15- to 20-minute periods, scheduled two to three times per week for a period of 7 weeks. Through a focal child approach, each subject was observed for a total of 9 or 10 3-minute intervals. Each time an aggressive act was exhibited by the focal child during a 3-minute interval, the following was recorded: (a) the type of aggression, (b) the name of the peer target, and (c) the peer target's response. At the end of each interval, the type of play activity in which the subject had been engaged for the majority of the 3-minute interval was coded into one of the following mutually exclusive and exhaustive categories: (a) unoccupied, (b) solitary play, (c) parallel play, (d) cooperative play, or (e) rough play. Kappas for the three aggressive behaviors were each greater than .84 and the Kappas for the play activity variables were each greater than .85. Six aggression variables were scored from the observations, including the rates (number of occurrences per minute of social time) of reactive, bullying, and instrumental aggression, and rates at which the subject was the target of each of these three behaviors. In addition to behavioral observations of aggression, classroom teachers were asked to fill out a 24-item rating (1 to 5 scale) instrument that included subscales for reactive and proactive bully aggression.

Two weeks prior to the observations, sociometric interviews were administered to at least 80% of each target subject's classroom peers. Using photographs of their classmates, each child was asked: (a) to rate each peer on how much he/she liked to play with that peer; (b) to nominate up to three liked classmates and three disliked classmates; and (c) to nominate up to three classmates who fit each of a number of behavioral descriptions (i.e., someone who starts fights, someone who gets angry easily, someone who is a good leader, someone who cooperates with others, and someone who cares about other kids). Two measures of classroom peer status were calculated—average group acceptance and social preference. These scores were then standardized within each classroom.

Given the important differences in the playground settings in which the two samples were observed, the first step in the analyses was to examine grade level differences in measures of play and aggression. As is indicated in Table 5.3, in comparison to kindergartners, first graders spent significantly more time in social interaction and cooperative play and significantly less time in parallel play. In addition, first graders display significantly higher rates of instrumental and bullying aggression during social interaction than did kindergartners. First graders also displayed a slightly higher rate of reactive aggression than did kindergartners, although this difference was not significant. These differences were most likely attributable to the differences in the free play/playground context rather than to actual developmental differences.

Table 5.3   Means and Standard Deviations for Measures of Playground Play* and Aggression by Grade

	Total *(n = 70)*	Kindergarten *(n = 31)*	First Grade *(n = 39)*
Playground Play			
Unoccupied	.06(.09)	.05(.09)	.07(.10)
Solitary	.07(.10)	.06(.08)	.07(.12)
Parallel	.09(.09)	.18(.17)	.00(.02)
Cooperative	.57(.20)	.52(.19)	.63(.21)
Rough Play	.20(.18)	.18(.16)	.22(.19)
Playground Aggression			
Reactive	.02(.03)	.02(.03)	.03(.03)
Bullying	.04(.05)	.02(.04)	.05(.05)
Instrumental	.03(.06)	.01(.03)	.05(.06)

*Note: Play behaviors were calculated as proportion of observed time engaged in particular kind of play. Aggressive behaviors were computed as the number of occurrences per minute of time observed in social interaction.

Relations between Measures of Aggression and Classroom Peer Status

Correlational analyses were conducted on the sample as a whole and then separately for each grade. For the sample as a whole, directly observed reactive aggression was associated with lower social preference scores and mean group ratings, although these correlations were not significant. Among first graders, however, reactive aggression was significantly related to lower social preference and mean group rating scores. Among kindergartners, reactive aggression was unrelated to either social preference or group ratings. The correlations among first graders were significantly different from those obtained for kindergartners (by z-score transformations, each p < .05). These differences were most likely attributable to the rate of aggression observed among kindergartners. For the whole sample, reactive aggression was marginally positively related to peers perceptions of "who starts fights" and "who gets angry." These correlations did not vary significantly across grade levels.

For the total sample, bullying aggression was unrelated to either measure of classroom status. Among kindergartners, however, bullying behavior was significantly related to higher social preference scores and mean group ratings. In contrast, among first graders, bullying behavior was associated with lower scores on these same measures of peer status. Furthermore, among first graders, bullying was significantly positively related to peers' perceptions of "who starts fights" and "who gets angry," whereas these measures were uncorrelated among kindergartners. The correlations were significantly different at the two grade levels. As expected, instrumental aggression was unrelated to either measure of classroom peer status.

Complementing these findings are the results from analyses of the relation between teacher ratings of reactive and bully aggression and classroom peer status. Due to the high correlation between the two teacher measures of aggression, two series of partial correlations were conducted. In the first set of analyses, the teacher rating of reactive aggression was correlated with each measure of social status, after the teacher rating of bullying was partialled out. Teachers' perceptions of who displayed reactive aggression were positively associated with lower scores on both measures of social status. This finding is consistent with the direct observations of behavior on the playground. Moreover, these relations were true for children at each age level.

In the second set of analyses, the teacher rating of bullying aggression was correlated with each of the measures of peer status, after partialing out the contribution of the teacher rating of reactive aggression. Teacher ratings of bullying aggression were related to higher scores on both measures of classroom peer status, although only the correlation with the mean group rating was significant.

Behavioral displays of reactive and proactive aggression toward peers on the playground were found to be differentially related to classroom peer status. In general, directing reactive aggressive behavior toward peers was associated with social rejection and negative peer evaluations. The utilization of instrumental aggression was positively related to classroom peer status. The findings were less clear about the relation between bullying aggression and social status in that the relation varied with grade level, and thus, setting conditions of the playground. Bullying was associated with peer acceptance among kindergartners, whereas among first graders bullying was associated with social rejection.

Based upon the findings of this investigation it appears that children who are disliked among the members of their peer group are more likely to display reactive aggression on the playground than are better liked peers. It is possible that the display of reactive aggression leads to or contributes to being disliked by one's peers. However, since the data were correlational, and equally plausible explanation is that being rejected by one's peers for whatever the reason may lead a child to display a higher rate of reactive aggression. Perhaps as a consequence of being rejected and rebuffed by the members of one's peer group, a rejected child perceives these peers as hostile, and, as a consequence, attributes hostility to their actions, even those that are accidental or benign. As a result, during the course of social interaction on the playground, the rejected child responds with retaliatory reactive aggression to a variety of peer initiated behaviors.

Reciprocity of Aggressive Behavior on the Playground

Only partial support was obtained for these hypotheses. Instrumental aggression was positively associated with being the recipient of instrumental aggression ($r = .37$, $p < .01$). This relation was significantly stronger for first graders ($r = .36$, $p < .05$) than for kindergartners ($r = -.17$). In addition, displaying bullying aggression was related to receiving bullying aggression ($r = .31$, $p < .01$. This relation was stronger for kindergarteners as opposed to first-graders ($r = .52$, $p < .01$ and $r = .16$, respectively).

These findings indicate that proactive rather than reactive aggression is more likely to be reciprocated by children on the playground. Perhaps as a consequence of reciprocal modeling (Parke and Slaby, 1983) or the establishment of an interpersonal norm, proactive aggression is responded to with a similar type of behavior. In contrast, reactive aggression may more likely be governed by social cognitive or temperamental factors than by interactive norms of social learning, and thus, it is less likely to be reciprocated by peers.

Play Activity Context of Aggression

Chi-square analyses were employed to address this hypothesis. The context for each occurrence of aggression was tallied and contrasted with the base rate occurrence of the context of aggression. Six analyses of the relation between play activity (i.e., unoccupied, solitary play, parallel play, cooperative play, and rough play) and aggressive behavior were conducted, one for each of the three categories of aggression at each grade level. Among kindergartners, none of the subtypes of aggression were associated with any particular type of play activity. Among first graders, however, each of the chi-square analyses indicated that each form of aggression was most likely to occur during rough play. Among kindergartners, there was no relation between the forms of aggression and the forms of play. It is possible that for these children the display of aggression is somewhat random. It is also possible that the low rate of aggression among kindergartners did not allow for an adequate assessment of these relations. In contrast, among first graders, all three forms of aggression were most likely to be displayed during rough play. Perhaps the high activity nature of rough play is conducive to the display of aggression, at least on the playground.

CONTEXTUAL FACTORS THAT COULD AFFECT THE QUALITY OF SOCIAL INTERACTIONS ON THE PLAYGROUND

As was pointed out earlier, it has been suggested that the social contexts and behavior settings in which people interact, elicit and organize certain kinds of behavior, depending upon the characteristics of that setting. It is evident, from the results of the studies reviewed in this chapter, that playground settings can elicit a variety of social behaviors from children, and that these behaviors play an important role in the development of children's peer relationships. Although all playgrounds are quite distinct from classroom settings, not all playgrounds are alike. Playgrounds can vary on a number of important characteristics, including size, type of playground equipment, number of children present, and teacher/child ratio. The dimensions on which playgrounds vary could be classified into one of two separate but related categories: characteristics of the physical environment (e.g., size of playground, amount of play materials available, and types of equipment present) and characteristics of interpersonal environment (e.g., number of children present, characteristics of these children, and teacher/child ratio).

There is a body of empirical evidence indicating that the physical characteristics of a play environment can affect children's interpersonal interactions, including the amount of space per child, the arrangement of space and materials, and the type of play area (i.e., indoor vs. outdoor) (see Christie, 1987 for a review of this literature). For example, Smith and Connolly (1980) found that among preschoolers less play material per child resulted in less solitary play, more parallel play, more sharing, and more aggressive behavior, whereas more materials per child resulted in the opposite patterns of behavior. Yet in addition to the physical features of a behavioral setting, people who inhabit a setting can also exert considerable influence on children's social behavior. In fact, some of the results from the studies reviewed in this chapter suggest that variations in a number of the interpersonal characteristics of playgrounds might affect the quality of children's social interactions on the playground. Several of these results will be discussed.

One type of interpersonal contextual variable that was examined in our research was the characteristics of the play partners, in particular the age and social status of the partner. The data from Ladd's (1983) investigation indicates that, in comparison to the play partners of popular and average children, the playmates of rejected children were younger and less popular. Given that the data in this investigation were correlational, it is possible to conjecture that the more negatively toned or conflictually oriented behaviors of rejected children may have been, in part, attributable to the characteristics of their play partners, who were likely to be less socially skilled than the older and better liked play partners of average and popular children. Continuing with this line of reasoning, it is possible that had the rejected children in this investigation been restricted to interacting with same age peers or better liked peers, their behavior may have been less negative.

Two additional interpersonal contextual variables that appeared in our research were the number of children present on the playground and, relatedly, the teacher/child ratio. In the Price and Dodge (1989) study, first graders displayed higher rates of aggression and spent more time in cooperative play and social interaction than did kindergartners. Because these two groups were so close in age it is possible to interpret these grade level differences in terms of variations in the interpersonal characteristics of the playground contexts in which these two samples were observed, rather than in terms of variations in development. The higher rates of aggression and higher percentage of social time among first graders may be attributable to the higher teacher/child ratio during play sessions. The greater the number of children per teacher, the larger the percentage of time spent by children in social interaction, and the higher the rate of aggression, especially instrumental and bullying aggression. It is more difficult to monitor the behavior of 80 children as opposed to 20 children. Thus, children have more freedom to behave in whatever manner they please—be it positive or negative. Conversely, in settings where there is a low teacher/child ratio the incidence of instrument and bullying aggression may be curtailed, but so might the percent of time children spend in social interaction and cooperative play.

One of the physical characteristics of the playgrounds in this study that may have interacted with a teacher/child ratio in affecting children's playground behavior was the size of the areas of the playground in which children were allowed to play. Kindergarten subjects were restricted to the equipment area of the playground, which constituted approximately 10 percent of the total playground area. Teachers and children were easily visible to one another, and as a consequence, teachers were effective in monitoring children's social interactions. In contrast, first graders were free to play anywhere on the playground. Thus, first-grade teachers were not very effective in monitoring children's behavior. In comparison to kindergartners, first graders were perhaps less inhibited in displaying a wide range of social behavior—both positive and negative.

Although the results from our research are far from conclusive, the data are, nevertheless, open to the interpretation that the characteristics of playgrounds may influence the quality of children's social behavior. Given this possibility, it seems plausible to suggest that these same characteristics may also serve to moderate the relation between children's social behavior and their classroom social status. This possibility will be discussed in the following section.

CONTEXTUAL FACTORS AS MODERATING VARIABLES IN THE RELATION BETWEEN PLAYGROUND BEHAVIOR AND CLASSROOM SOCIAL STATUS

Given that playground contextual factors may have an impact on the quality of children's social interactions on the playground, it is possible that these same variables might somehow affect the relation between playground behavior and the degree to which children are liked by their peers. Contextual variables might serve as moderating variables in this relation. Because of the lack of empirical data, however, only speculations can be offered in regard to the moderating influence of playground setting factors. Such speculations, however, might serve as a catalyst for future research. The possible moderating influences of three setting factors will be considered—the number of peers present on the playground, the age of the peer partners, and the teacher/child ratio.

To begin, the number of peers present on the playground could influence how a child's social behavior affects the development of peers' impressions of him or her. For instance, the presence of a large number of peers on the playground might serve to dissipate the impact of a child's aggressive acts. Because there are so many children, and so many ongoing activities, only one or two children may notice a child's act of instrumental aggression. (Yet it might also be argued the effect of a child's aggressive act might be wider ranging because there is the potential for a large audience.) In contrast, in a smaller group such an act may be more readily noticed and by a larger number of peers and, therefore, more likely to have a negative effect on a child's social status.

Another possible moderating variable is the age range of the peers available as play partners. Play in a mixed-age setting could have a number of different outcomes. Among older children, playing with a younger peer could be negatively perceived by age-mates and lead to less than favorable impressions. Alternatively, engaging in play with younger peers might provide an opportunity for a child to practice leadership skills that might later benefit the child in interactions with age-mates.

Playing with older children might also contribute to social acceptance. Older peers might serve as models of competent behavior and partners in practicing social skills. Additionally, by mere association, consistent interaction with older peers might enhance the social desirability of a particular child. In the eyes of age-mates, a child with older play partners is mature and competent.

Finally, the teacher/child ratio on the playground could serve as a moderating variable in the relation between social behavior and social status. On playgrounds where there is a high teacher/child ratio, the teacher is less effective in monitoring children's behavior, and therefore, less likely to influence the direction of children's behavior. In contrast, on playgrounds where there is a low teacher/child ratio, teachers are much better able to monitor children's behavior and to influence the direction of their behavior. As a consequence, teachers are more likely to influence the impact a particular child's behavior may have on the peer group. For instance, a child's apparent aggressive act of pushing another child could be accurately interpreted by the teacher as an accident and communicated to the group as such, thus lessening the negative impact of the behavior. Yet an opposing scenario is also possible. An accidental act on the part of a child could be misinterpreted by a teacher as intentionally hostile, which results in some sort of punishment for the child. This would call attention to a behavior that might otherwise had been ignored by the peer group. Calling attention to the behavior and to the subsequent discipline could contribute to the development of a negative impressions of the child among his/her peers.

In addition to these three contextual variables, the relation between children's social behavior and their peer status could also be moderated by another of the other physical and interpersonal characteristics of playgrounds, including the length of time children spend on the playground, familiarity of the teacher monitoring play activities, and the nature of the play activities. Unfortunately, little attention has been given to examining these and other contextual variables that may serve as moderating variables in the relation between children's social behavior and their social status. Clearly, more research in this area is necessary.

CONCLUSIONS AND FUTURE DIRECTIONS

Findings from the studies we have reviewed in this chapter reveal that playgrounds serve as a context for many important social developments during childhood. Playgrounds are essentially social environments, and as such provide both the physical and interpersonal resources that allow children to meet, interact, and form relationships with peers.

Of the questions we have tried to address in this chapter, one is whether children's playground behaviors play an important role in the social reputations they form with peers. The evidence we have presented is consistent with the view that children develop certain behavioral styles on the playground, and that these styles may affect the way they are perceived by playmates. Whereas prosocial, cooperative players tend to become liked by peers and favored as play partners, children who rely on aggressive, disruptive, and argumentative tactics are more often disliked and rejected by their companions. By comparison, children who do not tend to interact with peers on the playground, especially those who display high levels of aimless solitary behavior, often fail to engender feelings of liking or disliking among potential playmates. These children seem to be overlooked or ignored by peers.

The findings from our research also suggest that when examining the relation between aggression on the playground and peer status, it is important to distinguish among various categories of aggressive behavior. In our research two subtypes of aggression, reactive and proactive, were found to be differentially related to peer status. Directing reactive aggressive behavior toward peers on the playground was associated with social rejection. Less clear were the findings regarding proactive aggression. Whereas the use of instrumental aggression was unrelated to peer status, the use of bullying was associated with acceptance among kindergartners and with rejection among first graders. This particular pattern of findings should, however, be viewed tentatively. It is possible that the low frequency of the two forms of proactive aggression observed among kindergartners did not allow for an adequate assessment of each behavior. Larger samples of children observed for longer periods of time are needed to confirm these findings. In addition, as the findings suggest, before firm conclusions can be drawn regarding the relation between aggression and peer status, children should be observed in a number of different playground contexts.

A second question we have explored concerns the possible consequences of children's peer reputations for their experience on the playground. Some of the evidence we have cited suggests that the kinds of relationships children form with the members of their peer group may be related to the quality of their interactions on the playground, and the types of play opportunities and partners they are afforded in this context. In particular, it appears that the problematic and often aggressive interactions that may lead to negative peer reputations continue long after children have been rejected, and children who are rejected by their playmates appear to develop lasting difficulties at finding play partners and maintaining peer companionship. Part of the reason for the continued difficulties of a rejected child may be that once peer group members have developed stereotyped perceptions of the child, they may persist at interpreting his or her intentions and behavior as hostile or aggressive, even in the face of disconfirming evidence (Hymel, Wagner, and Butler, 1990; Price and Dodge, 1989). For example, once a child develops a reputation as being aggressive and becomes rejected as a consequence, peers may be more likely to attribute hostile intentions to the actions of the child, even though his or her behavior or intentions may not be hostile. Once formed, peers who hold these perceptions may be inclined to behave aggressively toward the rejected child; as a means of retaliating for perceived threats, or simply avoid interacting with him or her altogether on the playground. The usefulness of longitudinal designs for examining the *development* of children's social reputations was demonstrated in this chapter. The use of longitudinal designs may also prove fruitful in understanding the various forces that contribute to the *maintenance* of a children's social reputations.

A third issue that we have considered is the potential impact of playground environments on both children's peer interactions and relationships. Results from the studies reviewed in this chapter suggest that the characteristics of the playgrounds on which children are observed can influence the quality of their social behavior, and as a consequence, their peer relationships. Although the findings we consider do not permit strong inferences about playground variations and their effects, they nonetheless raise the possibility that both the physical and interpersonal features of playgrounds may affect the quality of children's interactions with peers. Moreover, because the quality of children's peer inter-actions may affect the types of relationships they form, it will also be important for investigators to determine whether setting vari-ables moderate the relation between children's social behavior and their reputations or status among peers.

Our findings highlight several of the features of playgrounds that might serve as a starting point for more systematic examina-tion of the effects of the contextual features of playgrounds. One of the sets of features of playgrounds examined in our research were the characteristics of playground playmates. More specifi-cally, the age and social status of children's playground play-mates were addressed. It was found that the play companions of rejected children tended to be younger and less popular than those of popular or average children. In contrast, the play part-ners of popular children were older and more well-liked than the partners of children in the average or rejected groups. What re-mains unclear is whether these particular play patterns are an antecedent to or consequence of children's social status. Based upon the revealing results of Ladd, Price, and Hart's (1988) longi-tudinal study on the development of peer status, a longitudinal examination of the development of children's social status *and* these specific play patterns could prove fruitful in unraveling this bidirectional issue.

Another set of interpersonal features that was addressed in our research and which needs to be addressed in the future is the number of children on the playground, and relatedly, the ratio of teachers to children on the playground. The findings from our research imply that these two features of playground settings might influence both the quality and rate of social interaction on the playground. However, since neither of these features were examined with sufficient control for the effects of other influencing factors (e.g., the size of the playground), the true impact of these contextual features is still unknown. In future research, it will be important for investigators to employ designs that provide a more controlled and systematic examination for the effects of these important interpersonal features of playgrounds.

Beyond these questions, investigators should begin to explore child and setting effects by comparing the types of behaviors children exhibit and the quality of the relationships they form in a variety of developmental settings (e.g., classrooms, playgrounds, neighborhoods, sports and competitive activities, etc.). Currently, there is very little research on the development of peer reputations and status in differing peer environments. It will be important to determine whether children tend to behave in similar ways and develop similar peer relationships across settings (i.e., findings that will support a child effects interpretation), or whether the quality of their interactions and relationships vary by context (i.e., a child by context interpretation). For example, it may be the case that children who are rejected by peers in the classroom, where academic issues are salient, develop more favorable reputations on the playground. Alternatively, children who are favored among peers in competitive situations (e.g., sports) may do less well in the classroom. Were this the case, it might be possible for children to compensate for problematic relationships in one context by forming more supportive ones in another. Conversely, it may also be the case that children's behavioral styles are relatively stable across contexts, and precipitate the same relationship successes or difficulties regardless of the setting. At present, although there is data from research with preschool and elementary-age children that lends support to a child effects interpretation (see Coie and Kupersmidt, 1983; Ladd and Price, 1987), there are also findings to suggest that the reputations children form are dependent on the context (Wright, Giammarino, and Parad, 1986). Clearly, systematic attempts to compare children's interactions and relationships across contexts are needed.

To conclude, it is clear that playground environments have an important impact on children's social development and peer interactions. The extent of this impact and the specific features of playgrounds that may affect the degree and quality of this impact have yet to be determined. Although the task may not be an easy one, fortunately children are always ready and willing to provide opportunities for investigators to observe their behavior and social interactions on the playground.

REFERENCES

Asher, S. R., and Coie, J. D. (1990). *Peer rejection in childhood.* New York: Cambridge.

Asher, S. R., Singleton, L. C., Tinsley, B. R., and Hymel, S. (1979). A reliable sociometric measure for preschool children. *Developmental Psychology, 15,* 443–444.

Bandura, A. (1973). *Aggression: A social learning analysis.* Englewood Cliffs, NJ: Prentice-Hall.

Barker, R. G. (1968). *Ecological psychology: Concepts and methods for studying the environment of human behavior.* Stanford, CA: Stanford University Press.

Berndt, T. J., and G. W. Ladd (1989). *Contributions of peer relationships to children's development.* New York: Wiley.

Bronfenbrenner, U. (1979). *The ecology of human development.* Cambridge, MA: Harvard University Press.

Christie, J. F. (1987). Preschool play. In J. H. Block and N. King (Eds.), *School Play* (pp. 109–142). New York: Garland.

Coie, J. D., Dodge, K. A., and Coppotelli, H. (1982). Dimensions and types of social status: A cross-age perspective. *Developmental Psychology, 18,* 557–570.

Coie, J. D., Dodge, K. A., and Kupersmidt, J. B. (1990). Group behavior and social status. In S. R. Asher and J. D. Coie (Eds.), *Peer rejection in childhood.* (pp. 17–59). New York: Cambridge.

Coie, J. D., and Kupersmidt, J. (1983). A behavioral analysis of emerging social status in boys' groups. *Child Development, 54,* 1400–1416.

Dodge, K. A. (1983). Behavioral antecedents of peer social status. *Child Development, 54,* 1386–1399.

Dodge, K. A., and Richard, B. A. (1985). Peer perceptions, aggression, and the development of peer relations. In J. B. Pryor and J. D. Day (Eds.), *Social developmental perspectives of social cognition* (pp. 35–38). New York: Springer-Verlag.

Dollard, J., Doob, L. W., Miller, N. E., Mowrer, O. H., and Sears, R. R. (1939). *Frustration and aggression.* New Haven, CT: Yale University Press.

Hartup, W. W. (1974). Aggression in childhood: Developmental perspectives. *American Psychologist, 29,* 336–341.

Hymel, S., Wagner, E., and Butler, L. J. (1990). Reputational bias: View from the peer group. In S. R. Asher and J. D. Coie (Eds.), *Peer rejection in childhood* (pp. 156–186). New York: Cambridge.

Hymel, S., Wagner, E., and Butler, L. J. (1990). Reputational bias: View from the peer group. In S. R. Asher and J. D. Coie (Eds.), *Peer rejection in childhood* (pp. 156–186). New York: Cambridge.

King, N. R. (1987). Elementary school play: Theory and research. In J. H. Block and N. King (Eds.), *School Play* (pp. 143–165). New York: Garland.

Ladd, G. W. (1983). Social networks of popular, average, and rejected children in school settings. *Merrill-Palmer Quarterly, 29,* 283–307.

Ladd, G. W., and Crick, N. R. (1989). Probing the psychological environment: Children's cognitions, perceptions, and feelings in the peer culture. In C. Ames and M. Maehr (Eds.), *Advances in motivation and achievement* (Vol. 6, pp. 1–44). Greenwich, CT: JAI Press.

Ladd, G. W., and Price, J. M. (1987). Predicting children's social and school adjustment following the transition from preschool to kindergarten. *Child Development, 58,* 1168–1189.

Ladd, G. W., Price, J. M., and Hart, C. H. (1988). Predicting preschoolers' peer status from their playground behaviors. *Child Development, 59,* 986–992.

———. (1990). Preschooler's behavioral orientations and patterns of peer contact: Predictive of Peer Status? In S. R. Asher and J. D. Coie (Eds.), *Peer rejection in childhood* (pp. 90–115). New York: Cambridge.

Maccoby, E. E., and Jacklin, C. N. (1980). Sex differences in aggression: A rejoinder and reprise. *Child Development, 51,* 964–980.

Minuchin, P. P., and Shapiro, E. K. (1983). The school as a context for social development. In P. H. Mussen (Ed.), *Handbook of child psychology* (Vol. 6), (pp. 195–274). New York: John Wiley and Sons.

Oden, S. L., and Asher, S. R. Coaching children in social skills for friendship making. *Child Development, 48,* 1977, 495–506.

Parke, R. D., and Slaby, R. G. (1983). The development of aggression. In P. H. Mussen (Ed.), *Handbook of child psychology* (4th ed.) (Vol. 4) (pp. 547–642). New York: Wiley.

Price, J. M., and Dodge, K. A. (1989). Reactive and proactive aggression among young children: Relations to peer status and social context dimensions. *Journal of Abnormal Child Psychology, 17,* 455–471.

———. (1989). Peers' contributions to children's social maladjustment: Description and intervention. In T. J. Berndt and G. W. Ladd (Eds.), *Peer relationships in child development* (pp. 341–370). New York: John Wiley and Sons.

Smith, P. K., and Connolly, K. (1980). *The ecology of preschool behavior.* Cambridge, England: Cambridge University Press.

Waldrop, M. F., and Halverson, C. F. (1975). Intensive and extensive peer behavior: Longitudinal and cross-sectional analyses. *Child Development, 46,* 27–38.

Wright, J. C., Giammarino, M., and Parad, H. W. (1986). Social status in small groups: Individual-group similarity and the social "misfit." *Journal of Personality and Social Psychology, 50,* 523–536.

6

LISA A. SERBIN, KEITH MARCHESSAULT, VALERIE MCAFFER,
PATRICIA PETERS, AND ALEX E. SCHWARTZMAN_____

Patterns of Social Behavior on the Playground in 9- to 11-Year-Old Girls and Boys: Relation to Teacher Perceptions and to Peer Ratings of Aggression, Withdrawal, and Likability*

INTRODUCTION

In an initial observational study of the playground behavior of 9- to 11-year-old children identified by peers as extremely aggressive and/or withdrawn (Lyons, Serbin, and Marchessault, 1988; Serbin, Lyons, Marchessault, Schwartzman, and Ledingham, 1987), we found that the distinctive behavior patterns of these extreme groups could be readily observed on the playground. Moreover, distinct patterns of peer behavior toward these children and many sex differences in play styles were apparent. In the present chapter, we briefly summarize these findings and present further analyses of these data using a multivariate approach. These analyses allow for an in-depth analysis of the relation between peer perceptions and playground behavior patterns. Teachers perceptions of the children were also examined and related to patterns of playground behavior.

Because very distinctive patterns and relationships emerged

_____
*This research was partially supported by grants from Health and Welfare Canada, and the National Institute of Mental Health, United States. The Concordia Longitudinal Risk Research Program was originated in 1976, under the direction of Jane Ledingham, Ph.D., and Alex Schwartzman, Ph.D. We are extremely grateful for the cooperation of the participating students and staff of the schools of the Commission des Ecoles Catholiques de Montreal. Correspondence may be addressed to Lisa A. Serbin, Ph.D., Centre for Research in Human Development, Department of Psychology, Concordia University, 1455 de Maisonneuve Blvd. West, Montreal, Quebec, Canada H3G 1M8.

from the observations of our initial sample of extreme groups, we subsequently felt a strong need to replicate our findings and extend them to a more normally distributed, nonpreselected group. The literature on playground behavior, or any other form of unstructured free play in naturalistic settings, is very limited for school-aged children, particularly for children over 7 or 8 years old. A number of researchers (e.g., Dodge, Coie, and Brakke, 1982; Ladd, 1983) have investigated the free play social behavior of children in the late primary grades (i.e., grades 4–6). However, these studies have typically focused on children preselected on the basis of criteria such as sociometric nominations. Except for our own "contrast group," who had been identified and preselected as close to "average" (50th percentile) on aggression and withdrawal, we found no normative or descriptive studies with which to compare the free play behavior of our deviant samples. That is, we could find no comparable study of playground behavior in a nonpreselected sample of 9- to 11-year-olds.

Further, there was little information available concerning the relation between peer nomination or sociometric instruments and observable play behavior in children of this age group. Our own study used extreme groups, and no one had examined this issue in a nonpreselected sample, where patterns of aggression and withdrawal could be expected to vary along a continuum. The relation between teacher assessments of problem behavior and playground behavior for this age group had also not been established in a nonpreselected, nonclinical sample.

Finally, sex differences in unstructured play patterns, particularly in aggressive and withdrawn behavior on the playground, had rarely been studied using naturalistic observations in older school-aged children. From our study of extreme groups, we had reason to believe that the dimensions of aggression and withdrawal might have different contextual significance for boys and girls, and we hoped to explore this in a normative sample.

The present chapter contains an overview of two observational studies: one using a sample of 117 peer-identified aggressive, withdrawn, aggressive/withdrawn, and contrast children aged 9–11, the second involving a randomly selected sample of 60 girls and boys the same age, observed over the school year under the same conditions. We present, first, brief descriptions of the play patterns of each sample, focusing on aggressive and withdrawn behavior.

We also explore and compare the relation between teacher and peer perceptions and aggressive and withdrawn play behavior in the two samples. Finally, since sex differences in both play patterns and interrelations with peer and teacher measures were found in both studies, we discuss differences in the significance aggressive playground behavior appears to have for boys and girls.

STUDY 1: PLAYGROUND BEHAVIOR IN AGGRESSIVE AND WITHDRAWN BOYS AND GIRLS

Method

Subjects. Subjects were 117 children in grades 4–6 at two French-language elementary schools located in working-class neighborhoods in Montreal, Canada. These subjects were selected from the total enrollment of 456 children in those grades, based on the administration of a French translation of the Pupil Evaluation Inventory (PEI) (Pekarik, Prinz, Leibert, Weintraub, and Neale, 1976). The PEI is a peer nomination instrument consisting of 34 items which load onto one of three factors: Aggression (20 items), Withdrawal (9 items), and Likability (5 items). The inventory was administered twice, once for nominations of up to four same-sex classmates, and once for nominations of up to four opposite-sex classmates. Each child's total scores on the Aggression and Withdrawal factors of the PEI were converted to standard scores relative to those of same-sex classmates.

The 16 boys and 13 girls selected for the aggressive group included all children who scored above the 90th percentile on Aggression and below the 75th percentile on Withdrawal. The mean percentile scores for the aggressive group were 98 on Aggression and 43 on Withdrawal. For the withdrawn group, the reverse criteria were applied, yielding 15 boys and 12 girls, with mean percentile scores of 98 on Withdrawal and 25 on Aggression. For the aggressive/withdrawn group, children scoring above the 75th percentile on both dimensions were selected, yielding a sample of 14 boys and 14 girls with means of 94 on Aggression and 95 on Withdrawal. Finally, contrast children were selected from among those children receiving scores between the 25th and the 70th percentile. The mean percentile scores for the 16 boys and 17 girls selected for this group were 36 on Aggression and 42 on Withdrawal. The specific percentile scores used as deviant group selection criteria (i.e., 75th and 90th) are the result of a compromise between efforts to select only cases that were sufficiently extreme on the dimensions of interest, and the need to maintain an adequate sample size for statistical analyses.

Videotaping procedure. Videotaping was carried out by two-person teams. One person used binoculars to locate the target children on the playground, and also timed each segment using a stopwatch. The second team member operated the telephoto color video camera and portable video cassette deck. The teams positioned themselves in second story windows overlooking the playground, so as to be minimally intrusive. From the second floor, and with the aid of the telephoto lens, we were able to record the children's activities in even the most remote corners of the playground. Although the children were aware of the teams' presence, they were unaware of the individual targets of videotaping, and generally took little notice of our activities. In effect, we were able to conduct fully naturalistic observations of children's playground activity while minimizing reactivity. However, a limitation of the observational procedure was our inability to capture the content of the children's conversation. Although the cameras were equipped with microphones, they were by no means sensitive enough to record sufficient verbal detail for later coding.

The children had outdoor recess 10–15 minutes each morning and afternoon, weather permitting. Segments of 2 minutes in length were videotaped throughout the school year, using a random order of subjects to ensure uniformity of data collection across the fall, winter, and spring seasons. The importance of balancing data collection for subjects across seasons was confirmed by our observation that far more aggression occurred during the winter months (possibly due to the soft blanket of snow on the playground). In total, an average of 20 minutes of playground observation was collected on each target child (i.e., approximately 10 segments of 2 minutes). However, the mean number of minutes of observation per target child varied considerably from School 1 (approximately 10 minutes of observation) to School 2 (approximately 28 minutes). The fewer observational segments at School 1 was due to limited resources during the pilot year of the project, while increased funding for the second year allowed for an increased number of observations at School 2.

Observational coding of videotapes. A quantitative observational code was developed which focused on both the target child's behavior and on the peers' behavior which was directed toward the target. Due to the complexity of the observational code, scoring of each 2-minute video segment involved four passes, one for context, and three passes to cover each of three categories of playground behavior. The first category tapped the nature of the group surrounding the target child including group size, sex of peers, and nature of the group's activity.

The second category included measures of the frequency of aggressive and nonaggressive physical contact, and whether aggression was incited or retaliated. It is important to note that aggressive behavior, as defined in this study, included "play fighting" or "rough and tumble play," as well as moderate to severe forms of aggression with intent to inflict injury. These two levels of aggression were combined because we initially believed that the absence of verbal and subtle facial cues would make it difficult to reliably differentiate the more serious forms of aggression from the playful sparring. We acknowledge that recent research by Pellegrini (1988), demonstrating rough and tumble play to be positively correlated and serious aggression to be negatively correlated with social competence, would suggest that a combined aggression category is a limitation of our study. However, a subsequent recoding of the severity of aggressive incidents in our videotaped observations (Marchessault, Serbin, and Schwartzman, 1989) indicated that the more serious forms of aggression accounted for less than 7% of all aggressive incidents. We, therefore, decided that the rates were too low to permit analysis of serious aggression as a distinct behavioral category.

Finally, a third category of measures involved ratings of levels of target motor activity, target involvement with peers, target solicitation of peer attention, and peer attention to the target. Coded observations were recorded on More data microprocessing units (Observational Systems, Seattle, WA). Each segment of videotape was coded by two randomly paired observers, and data from the two observers were then averaged. Moskowitz and Schwarz (1982) have found that averaging across multiple coders in this way helps to reduce error variance and thus increases the reliability and validity of the data. Based on Pearson product moment correlations, the average level of interrater agreement across all code categories was .77, while rates of agreement on individual categories were above .70 for all but two variables.

Teacher ratings. A French translation of the Teacher Report Form (TRF) of the Child Behavior Checklist (CBCL) (Edelbrock and Achenbach, 1984) was completed for target subjects by their primary teachers. The TRF consists of 113 brief descriptions of problem behaviors scored on eight first-order factors (e.g., Anxious, Social Withdrawal, Inattentive, Aggressive) and two second-order factors (Internalizing and Externalizing). T-scores for the first- and second-order factors, based on the authors' scoring profiles, were used in subsequent analyses. The TRF was administered at only one of the two schools. Thus, analyses involving teacher ratings of the subjects are based on a reduced sample of 74 children.

Results

The initial aim of Study 1 was to identify differences in the playground behavior of children in each of the socially deviant groups. The following description is a summary of the distinct play styles displayed by children in the aggressive, withdrawn, and aggressive/withdrawn groups. A more detailed presentation of these results can be found in earlier reports by Serbin and her colleagues (Lyons et al., 1988; Serbin et al., 1987). A taxonomy of the measures used in both Study 1 and Study 2 appears in Table 6.1.

Children identified by peers as aggressive were generally highly active and very involved in social interaction. They were more likely to initiate physical contact, both aggressive and nonaggressive, and were also more likely to retaliate when peers initiated aggression against them. The aggressive group displayed a high level of motor activity relative to peers, and more frequently attempted to solicit peer attention.

Peer-identified withdrawn children, in comparison, spent more time alone on the playground than did peers in the other target groups or the contrast group. They were less involved with other children and made fewer attempts to gain the attention of peers. Similarly, the other children on the playground were less involved with the withdrawn children.

Although children within the aggressive group and the withdrawn group showed play styles which were intuitively consistent with their peer-identified classification group, children identified as both aggressive *and* withdrawn displayed an unexpected behav-

Table 6.1.   Taxonomy of Measures (Study 1 and 2)

a) Pupil Evaluation Inventory (Pekarik et al., 1976)

Aggression (z-score based on 20 items)
Withdrawal (z-score based on 9 items)
Likability (z-score based on 5 items)

b) Observational measures (Serbin, Lyons, and Marchessault, 1987)

Characteristics of the peer group
   Group size (multiple peers, single peer, solitary)
   Sex of peer group (same-, opposite-, mixed-sex)
   Group activity (social play, conversation)

Physical contact
   Nonaggressive touching
   Aggressive contact including rough and tumble
      (scored as incited or retaliated by target or by peer)

Level of involvement of target (rated on 3-point scale)
   Target involvement with peers
   Target solicitation of peer attention
   Peer attention to target

Target level of motor activity (rated on 3-point scale)

c) Teacher Report Form of the CBCL
   (Edelbrock and Achenbach, 1984)

First-order factors
   Anxious
   Withdrawal
   Depressed (girls) Obsessive-compulsive (boys)
   Unpopular
   Self-destructive
   Inattentive
   Nervous—overactive
   Aggressive
Second-order factors
   Internalizing
   Externalizing

ioral pattern on the playground. While their own behavior did not differ significantly from the contrast subjects on any of our coded measures, the aggressive/withdrawn children appeared to be more frequent victims of peer incited aggression. In fact, the ratio of peer incited to target incited aggression for the aggressive/withdrawn children was almost 2:1. That is, they received twice as much aggression from peers as they delivered, perhaps indicative of a "whipping boy" status on the playground (Olweus, 1978; Chapter 4, this volume). In comparison, the withdrawn group and the contrast group were the targets of approximately 40% more aggression than they initiated, while the aggressive group actually doled out 50% more aggression than they received from peers.

The above descriptions of the behavior of the four groups applied to both the boys and girls. That is, there were no significant sex by classification group interactions on any of our playground measures. Boys and girls within each peer-identified deviant group had similar play styles relative to same-sex children in the other groups, and these patterns were consistent in samples drawn from two different schools. However, there were several significant main effects of sex in the rates of various behavioral categories. In particular, the amount of nonaggressive touching, target-incited aggression, peer-incited aggression, and the level of motor activity all showed significant sex effects with boys scoring higher than girls. On the aggression variables, it is noteworthy that the magnitude of the sex difference was actually highest within the contrast group, where boys engaged in three times more aggression than girls. Thus, the observed sex difference in aggression was not due primarily to the contribution of a subgroup of highly aggressive boys.

While the above "group differences" approach to analysis identified many important characteristics of our aggressive, withdrawn, and aggressive/withdrawn samples, we were left with further questions about the relation among assessment sources. In particular, we were surprised by the absence of sex by classification group interactions in the results of our analyses of variance. Intuitively, we had anticipated that peer-rated aggressive and/or withdrawn boys would show playground behaviors that were different from their female counterparts. This expectation was based on our belief that the dimensions of aggression and withdrawal might have different contextual significance for boys and girls (i.e., "rough and tumble" interactions may be a specific, socially acceptable form of play within particular contexts for boys, but not for girls). If so, we would expect to find sex differences in the behavioral profiles associated with each dimension.

A possible reason for our failure to find such differences in these analyses was our use of a group comparison design which ignored the range of variability in levels of aggression and withdrawal within groups. For example, in using a group differences approach, the scores of children who barely met the selection criterion within a deviant group were weighted equally with those who fell at the extreme upper end of the continuum. Consequently, observed variation among children within a group on a given playground measure was regarded as within group error, rather than meaningful variance.

As an alternative to the group comparison approach, a multivariate canonical correlation analysis contrasting the peer-rated aggression and withdrawal measures with the observed playground measures was carried out in order to more adequately examine relations between these sets of variables. Sex differences in these relations could then be examined through comparison of the canonical solutions generated in separate analyses for boys and girls. The nature of these correlations would be of theoretical interest in terms of the manner in which boys and girls perceive dimensions of deviance and might eventually have practical implications for programs of early intervention and prevention. In a final step, parallel analyses involving teacher ratings were carried out, contrasting teachers' perceptions with peer perceptions and playground observations.

Peer ratings and playground observation: Peer perceptions of aggression and withdrawal for boys and girls. Canonical correlation analyses, conducted for boys and girls separately, enabled us to provide a fine-grained description of the nature of the relation between children's ratings and observed playground behavior for each sex (Marchessault, 1985). We hypothesized that aggression and withdrawal might have different contextual "meanings" for boys and girls, as reflected in the relations between observed behavior and peer ratings. It should be noted that the four peer-identified groups were collapsed for the purposes of the canonical analyses: we created a single group of males and a single group of females, each covering the full range of scores on the aggression and withdrawal dimensions of the PEI.

For the girls, two highly distinct canonical correlations emerged featuring aggression and withdrawal, respectively, as independent dimensions. The first significant canonical correlation, $X^2(24) = 52.47$, $p < .001$, indicated that girls who are perceived as withdrawn by their peers show a distinct pattern of low rates of nonaggressive physical contact, few attempts to solicit attention from others, and limited attention from peers. The second canonical correlation, $X^2(14) = 26.29$, $p < .05$, indicated that girls perceived by peers as aggressive spend more time in mixed-sex groups, less time with same-sex peers, display a higher rate of incited and retaliated aggression, and more frequently attempt to solicit peer attention.

For the boys, only a single significant canonical correlation emerged, X^2 $(24) = 43.68$, $p < .01$, featuring peer ratings of aggression and withdrawal as opposite extremes on the same dimension. Peer ratings of aggression in boys were associated with increased attempts to solicit attention, more attention from peers, high levels of motor activity, and less time spent alone. Withdrawal, on the other hand, was associated with the opposite poles of the same variables, specifically: few attempts to solicit attention, low levels of attention from peers, low levels of motor activity, and increased time spent alone. Target-incited aggression on the playground was only marginally related to peer ratings of aggression by boys, perhaps reflecting the perceived "normality" and acceptable nature of aggressive physical contact among males at the elementary school level. This interpretation is supported by the fact that peer ratings of likability showed a positive relation to playground aggression for boys, r $(37) = .31$, $p < .05$. Furthermore, given that the vast majority of aggression observed in this study was "mild" in nature, the finding is consistent with the positive relation between rough and tumble play and indices of social competence noted by Pellegrini (1988). In contrast, a weak negative correlation between likability and playground aggression was found for girls, r $(32) = -.16$, ns.

The results of these analyses indicate that peers make a clear distinction between aggressive and withdrawn behavioral styles in girls, with separate sets of playground correlates corresponding to each dimension. In contrast, peer perceptions of aggression and withdrawal in boys appear to load on a single dimension, featuring aggression and withdrawal at opposite ends of the same continuum, and characterized by a single set of playground measures. This finding is possibly explained by the fact that playful aggression is a very high frequency form of social interaction for boys, averaging almost three incidents every 2 minutes per child, whereas it is considerably less frequent in girls' playground activity, with an average rate of one incident every 2 minutes. Since the overwhelming majority of aggression observed on the playground was of the rough and tumble type, for boys the distinction between aggression and withdrawal simplifies to a single continuum which might be more appropriately labelled "intensity of involvement." Those boys who fall at the high end of the involvement continuum are more likely to engage in aggressive play, while boys at the low end are less likely to be involved in aggression. Girls, on the other hand, appear to be sensitive to elevated levels of aggression, even of the playful type, and appear to rate along distinct dimensions of involvement/withdrawal and of aggression. That is, peers do not perceive aggression as part of a general pattern of "social involvement" for girls. It is not just one extreme of the dimension of social play, nor is it simply a function of the level of involvement with peers.

In summary, perceptions of boys' and girls' play differ in that peers appear to be very sensitive to distinct dimensions of involvement/withdrawal and aggression in girls, whereas in boys the two dimensions are combined on a continuum of social involvement.

Ratings by Teachers and the Relation with Peer Ratings and Playground Observation. Teacher ratings are commonly used in the initial screening of children experiencing adjustment difficulties. However, teacher ratings, like any other assessment source, are subject to their own unique set of biases. Biases in teacher ratings are a function of the teacher's classroom priorities, the environment within which he/she is exposed to the children, and personal expectations of appropriate behavior for boys and girls. For this reason, teacher ratings may differ considerably from peer perceptions of play behavior or from the actual observed patterns of aggression and withdrawal on the playground (see Coie and Dodge, 1988; Hymel and Rubin, 1985; McConnell and Odom, 1986). In the next set of analyses, we attempted to identify the nature of the relation between teacher ratings and our two alternative sources of assessment, peer ratings and playground observation, for boys and girls, using the same sample of peer-rated aggressive, withdrawn, aggressive/withdrawn and contrast children.

Teacher and Peer Ratings of Aggression and Withdrawal. Analyses of teacher ratings and peer ratings of boys indicated strong agreement between the two sources for both aggression and withdrawal, a finding which is consistent with research by Coie and Dodge (1988). The teacher-rated internalizing measure was highly correlated with peer ratings of withdrawal r (37) = .59, p < .01, and teacher-rated externalizing behavior showed a strong association with peer-rated aggression r (37) = .70, p < .01. In comparison, while teacher and peer ratings of girls showed strong agreement between the externalizing and aggression dimensions, r (32) = .69, p < .01, the association between teacher-rated internalizing behavior and peer ratings of withdrawal was weak and failed to reach significance, r (32) = .17, ns.

Thus, from the perspective of peer ratings, teachers appear to reliably identify both major dimensions of maladjustment in boys, but clearly are unable to identify "withdrawal" in girls. A possible explanation for this effect lies in the frequently reported sex role stereotypes of boys' and girls' behavior held by many adults: that is, aggression, competence, and dominance are viewed as male characteristics, while affection, nurturance, and passivity are seen as characteristics of females. As a result, quiet, passive behavior by girls would less likely be considered deviant by an adult than would withdrawal in males, and might not be noticed or rated as problematic by teachers on a behavior problem checklist. In contrast, while aggression in boys may be viewed by teachers as "normal," it would still be disruptive and hence salient to teachers.

Teacher Ratings and Playground Behavior. Agreement between teacher ratings and playground behavior was generally stronger for aggressive behavior than for withdrawal. In canonical correlation analyses for each sex separately, aggression was featured in a statistically significant canonical solution (boys: X^2(12) = 25.16, p < .05; girls: X^2(12) = 29.05, p < .05). That is, children who tended to be among the more active and aggressive on the playground were readily identified as aggressive or externalizing by teachers. In contrast, the canonical correlations between teacher ratings and playground observations of withdrawn behavior were weak for both the boys and the girls in our sample, and failed to reach statistical significance (boys: X^2(5) = 10.94, ns; girls: X^2(5) = 10.32, ns). One reason for this inconsistency may be that teacher ratings are based primarily on student behavior exhibited in the classroom, while playground observations involve an entirely different milieu. There may be children who thrive on the structure of the classroom but have difficulties socially when it is time for less structured play. Since peers have opportunities to interact with their classmates in both classroom and playground settings, their perceptions may more closely relate to observed playground behavior than those of teachers, especially concerning withdrawn behavior which is less likely to present problems or be noticed in the classroom setting.

In summary, Study 1 identified distinct play styles for a sample of children identified by peers as aggressive, withdrawn, and aggressive/withdrawn, suggesting the validity of peer ratings of children's behavior problems. In addition, through canonical correlation of the full continuum of peer ratings on aggression and withdrawal, we were able to describe the nature of the relation among teacher and peer ratings, and actual playground behavior. These analyses suggest that both teachers and peers perceive dimensions of aggression and withdrawal differently for boys and girls, and that these differences may have important implications for the concurrent and predictive validity of each assessment source.

However, we recognized that the relations reported above were derived from a sample of children rated as extreme on aggression and withdrawal, and that the strength and nature of correlations among measures may have been influenced by the large number of extreme scores. Consequently, we undertook a second observational study to determine whether the same relations would be found in a randomly selected, normative sample of children. The normative sample, with a presumably normal distribution of aggression and withdrawal scores on the PEI, would allow us to confirm patterns observed in the extreme groups sample or, alternatively, describe the dimensions of aggression and withdrawal that hold for the elementary school population as a whole.

STUDY 2: PLAYGROUND BEHAVIOR, PEER PERCEPTIONS, AND TEACHER EVALUATIONS IN A RANDOMLY SELECTED SAMPLE OF 9- TO 11-YEAR-OLDS

Study 2 involved playground observations and peer and teacher assessments of a group of randomly selected boys and girls of the same age range, in the same situational context as in Study 1. The first goal of the study was to provide information on "normative" play patterns in this age group during free play, in a sample that was not based on extreme groups or any other preselected criterion. In addition, using this sample, we could determine whether the correlational patterns found in Study 1 would replicate using a nonpreselected sample. The statistical design of Study 2 is somewhat different from that used in Study 1, due to expected differences in the distribution of scores between the randomly selected and extreme groups samples. The findings of the two studies are generally consistent, although there are several interesting differences in the pattern of results.

Method

Subjects. Subjects for Study 2 were 30 boys and 30 girls in grades 4 and 5 at a French-language elementary school located in a working-class neighborhood of Montreal. Three boys and three girls were randomly selected for observation from each of 10 classes (5 at each of two grade levels). Ages ranged from 9 to 11 years.

The observational procedure followed in Study 2 was identical to the methodology reported above for Study 1 (Lyons et al. 1988; Serbin et al., 1987). The PEI was again administered to all children in each of the 10 participating classes. For this study of "normal," randomly selected children, the resulting peer ratings on aggression and withdrawal were reserved for later analyses and were not used as subject selection criteria. Mean percentile scores on the Aggression factor were 54 for the boys and 56 for the girls, while mean scores on Withdrawal were 56 and 52 for boys and girls, respectively. Thus, overall, the sample was close to "average" (i.e., 50th percentile) on both behavioral dimensions. The TRF of the Child Behavior Checklist was also completed for each of the randomly selected children by their primary teachers.

Results

Types of Activities. During the fall and spring, play was mainly focused around highly organized games with formal rules, such as dodgeball or jump rope, which typically involved large numbers of children. The teachers on duty encouraged participation in these activities and provided the play materials necessary. Because of this imposed structure, it was possible and common for children to be technically "participating" in a large group game without being very actively involved (e.g., a child could be "playing" dodgeball while actually wrestling with a peer or while passively watching others move towards or away from the ball). This allowed for considerable variability in behavior, despite the high degree of imposed structure. In the winter, when the playground was snow-covered (December through March), play was very different. There were fewer large, highly structured games. Children played in smaller groups or dyads, and there was a great deal of physical contact and rough and tumble play in the snow.

How Children Distributed Their Time on the Playground. Children averaged approximately 60% of their recess time actively engaged in play. The remainder of their time was spent "proximal" to peers (in conversation or watching others, 27%), or alone (11%). Examining peer contexts, 70% of time was spent with a group (either playing or proximal to others), 16% of time with a single peer. Analysis of sex composition of groups showed that 58% of group time included children of both sexes, while 42% of group play was gender segregated.

Physical Contact. In general, physical contact was very frequent. Children averaged 1.15 nonaggressive touches per minute. Aggressive contacts (e.g., punch, slap, kick, push) occurred on average once every 2 minutes, per child, with peers retaliating aggressively to these acts about 30% of the time.

Sex Differences in Playground Behavior. Many statistically significant sex differences were observed in the rates of play behavior. Girls spent 34% of their time watching or talking to others versus 54% engaged in play, while boys spent 20% of their time watching/talking versus 66% engaged in play. This sex difference is consistent with the Boulton and Smith (Chapter 8, this volume) study indicating that boys spent more time in "rule games," but less time in "positive social contact" than girls. Despite these sex differences in proportions of time spent "playing" versus "watching," girls and boys spent similar amounts of time in a dyad, and similar amounts of time in larger groups.

Boys aggressed at a rate of .64 per minute, while girls displayed about half that rate, or .33 aggressive acts per minute (t (58) = 4.11, $p < .001$). Boys retaliated aggressively more frequently than girls (t (58) = 2.28, $p < .05$). However the sex difference in aggressive retaliation was due to the boys' overall higher rate of aggression rather than a higher probability of retaliation following an aggressive initiation by peers. In fact, girls and boys were found to be equally likely to retaliate aggressively when aggression was initiated by peers. Peers of both sexes were more likely to retaliate aggressively to any type of initiation by boys than by girls (t (58) = 3.53, p < .001).

Finally, boys averaged higher on physical activity ratings than girls (t (58) = 4.94, p < .001). This is consistent with their higher rates of involvement in play, as opposed to watching or talking with peers.

Individual Differences: Factors That Characterize Play Patterns of Individual Children. A factor analysis was carried out to see whether specific playground behaviors tended to intercorrelate. This analysis served to reduce the number of observational variables for use in further correlational analyses with peer and teacher ratings. Children's scores on the factors derived from this analysis could then be used to relate playground behavior patterns to teacher and peer ratings on a variety of dimensions. In addition, this factor analysis allowed us to evaluate whether certain types of play and peer interaction tended to occur within a particular "context," and to compare these contextual patterns for girls and boys.

Using this approach, the behavior categories clustered into three distinct oblique factors. The first was labeled "Aggression," and consisted of high levels of aggressive initiation, aggressive responses to initiation by peers, and included high levels of aggressive initiations towards the target by peers. In addition, the degree to which peers focus attention on the target during play loaded positively on this factor.

A second factor was labeled "Involvement/physical contact." This factor included high levels of proximity to same-sex children, nonaggressive touching, peer involvement with the target, and low levels of physical activity. In other words, this factor reflects involvement with same-sex peers, in a positive context, including talking, watching, and nonaggressive touching.

Finally, factor three, "Withdrawal," included spending time alone, not being physically active, and not eliciting or giving attention to peers.

Sex Differences in Play Patterns: The Contextual Meaning of Play. Interesting sex differences occurred in the intercorrelation of the play factors, particularly between Aggression and Involvement, suggesting that the behaviors in each factor may have different significance for each sex. For boys, there was a significant relation between the factors of Aggression and Involvement/ physical Contact, r (29) = .31, p < .05. That is, there was a relation between levels of playground aggression and high levels of play, proximity to other boys, and nonaggressive touching. In contrast, playground Aggression was not related to either of the two other play factors for girls.

This suggests that boys may have a situational context for aggression which girls lack. Given the much higher frequency of aggression by boys towards each other, it appears that boys accept aggression as a normal and pervasive element of play within the same-sex play context. For girls, however, aggression seems to be unrelated to other specific behavioral contexts. It does occur with some frequency (averaging one initiation every three minutes by each girl), but appears to happen in almost any playground context. That is, girls' aggression is not associated with any distinct play situation. For this reason, it may be that girls' aggression has a different meaning for them, and is interpreted differently by peers. It is not simply part of a distinct and predictable type of interaction, as it is for boys.

In sum, boys' aggression may be perceived by children as part of the ongoing "give and take" of rough and tumble peer interaction. In contrast, girls' aggression may reflect or indicate more "serious" or negative intent, which is not incorporated into predictable patterns of playground interaction. Peers may thus respond more negatively to girls who act aggressively than to boys. Teachers also may view aggressive girls as having serious social/emotional problems. This possibility was explored further by correlating the playground factors with peer ratings of aggression, withdrawal, and likability, and with teacher ratings on problem behavior scales.

Relation Between Peer Evaluations (PEI) and Playground Behavior Within the Normative Sample. Correlations between playground factors and peer ratings confirm that the playground behavior of boys and girls is perceived differently by their peers. Similar to the results of Study 1, peer perceptions of aggression on the PEI scale were positively correlated with boys' aggressive free play behavior, r (29) = .37, p < .05, and negatively correlated with boys' withdrawal on the playground, r (29) = −.32, p < .05.

That is, boys who are seen as aggressive by their peers behave aggressively on the playground and do not spend a lot of time on their own, away from peers. Also consistent with Study 1, peer perceptions of withdrawal were positively associated with boys' withdrawn behavior on the playground, r (29) = .54, p < .001. Finally, for boys, peer ratings of likability in Study 2 were not associated with either aggressive or withdrawn playground behavior patterns.

The correlations between peer ratings and playground behavior showed a very different pattern for girls. Playground aggression was positively related to peer perceptions of *both* aggression, r *(29)* = .36, p < .05, and withdrawal, r (29) = .36, p < .05, and negatively related to peer likability, r (29) = −.31, p < .05. In other words, girls in this randomly selected sample who exhibited aggressive behavior on the playground were viewed by peers as having a wide variety of problems in peer relations, including patterns of both aggression and of withdrawal, and were not liked by their peers. This contrasts with the results of Study 1, where peer ratings of aggression were unrelated to playground withdrawal in girls. As in Study 1, girls' withdrawn behavior on the playground was positively related to peer ratings of withdrawal, r (29) = .37, p < .05, and showed a weak negative association with nominations for peer likability, r (29) = −.27, p < .10.

Relation Between Teacher Evaluations and Playground Behavior. The T-score results from the teacher form of the CBCL indicated that teachers perceived the majority of our normative sample as generally falling well within the nonclinical range (T-scores < 70) on the twelve behavior problem scales (average T-scores on these scales ranged from 49.6 to 62.7). Correlations between teacher ratings on the CBCL and playground factors revealed that, like peers, teachers may also have different perceptions of boys' and girls' playground behavior. Teachers rated boys who were observed to engage in high levels of aggressive behavior on the playground as high on the following scales of the CBCL: Aggressive, r (29) = .49 p < .01; Unpopular, r (29) = .41, p < .05; Inattentive, r (29) = .35, p < .05; and the summary scales Externalizing, r (29) = .33, p < .05; and Total Problems, r (29) = .37, p < .05. Interestingly, however, teachers associated girls' aggressive behavior on the playground with twice as many scales, indicating a larger variety of problems: Depressed, r (29) = .56, p <

.001; Social Withdrawal, r (29) = .54, p < .001; Anxious, r (29) = .50, p < .01; Unpopular, r (29) = .42, p < .01; Self-Destructive, r (29) = .34, p < .05; Inattentive, r (29) = .34, p < .05; Other Problems, r (29) = .51, p < .01; and the summary scales, Internalizing, r (29) = .59, p < .001; Externalizing, r (29) = .32, p < .05; and Total Problems, r (29) = .50, p < .01. In other words, like peers, teachers see girls' aggressive playground behavior as indicative of a range of both internalizing and externalizing problems, while they associate boys' free play aggression with a more obviously similar cluster of externalizing problems.

Teachers also demonstrated some discrepancy in their perceptions of boys' and girls' withdrawn behavior on the playground. Withdrawn boys were rated by teachers as low on the CBCL Aggressive scale, r (29) = –.36, p < .05, and were not rated as having any particular problems in the classroom. In contrast, withdrawn playground behavior in girls was associated with the Self-Destructive scale, r (29) = .32, p < .05, and with Other Problems on the CBCL, r (29) = .35, p < .05. In general, however, the Withdrawal playground dimension failed to correlate with the corresponding "Internalizing" dimension of the CBCL, or with the corresponding subscales. This lack of association between the CBCL and the withdrawal dimension of playground behavior is quite consistent with the results of Study 1. Teachers' ratings seem to be relatively "insensitive" to this aspect of social relations, possibly because a withdrawn style creates fewer problems and is less salient in the classroom. This contrasts with peer ratings on the PEI in both studies, which were relatively sensitive to predictions of withdrawal on the playground.

DISCUSSION

The results of the two studies confirm that there is substantial agreement between peer ratings of aggression and withdrawal and distinct patterns of playground behavior. This is true both in the identification of extremely withdrawn and aggressive groups of children, and also within the normal range on these dimensions. However, there are sex differences in these patterns.

For boys in both studies, peers seem to perceive the trait of "aggression" as positively related to a continuum of playground behavior, ranging from a passive, isolated style at the low extreme to an active socially involved style which incorporates a good deal of rough and tumble aggressive play at the high end. Aggressive play seems to be accepted as a component of "normal" play for boys, in that it is either unrelated or positively related to likability.

For girls, peer perceived "aggression" is unrelated to degree of social involvement, but does directly predict aggressive behavior on the playground. In Study 2, girls' playground aggression was negatively related to likability, indicating that peers dislike girls who are particularly aggressive on the playground, possibly because this aggression tends to occur outside of a well-defined social context.

Similarly, in both samples, peer perceptions of withdrawal predict playground behavior of this type, for both sexes. However, in the normative sample, peer perceptions of aggression also positively predicted girls' withdrawn playground behavior. The general interpretation of these results is that girls who are perceived as aggressive by peers show a variety of extreme patterns of playground behavior, not just aggression. Further, as noted above, they are disliked by peers.

Teacher perceptions similarly confirm that girls who display aggressive playground behavior are seen as having a wide variety of problems in the classroom, not just problems within the "externalizing" spectrum. Allowing for sex-stereotyped bias, which might cause both teachers and peers to view aggressive girls in a generalized negative perception, it remains likely that girls showing aggressive behavior may be having a variety of problems which merit careful assessment. It should be noted, also, that girls' aggression levels, overall, are lower than boys'. In other words, "highly aggressive" girls in these studies were aggressive *relative to other girls*, not relative to overall levels of aggression on the playground. Thus, in identifying extremely aggressive girls, it is important to use relevant norms (i.e., base rates of aggression for girls).

The weakness of teacher perceptions seems to be insensitivity to patterns of withdrawal on the playground. The classroom does not seem to be a setting in which behavior of this type is salient, for either sex. However, there is evidence from Study 1 that teachers do see the relation between boys' internalizing spectrum behaviors and peer perceptions of withdrawal, at least within an extreme sample of highly withdrawn boys.

These findings are somewhat disturbing in view of the likelihood that girls having psycho-social problems may display relatively more internalizing than externalizing spectrum disorders, compared with boys. Peers can identify these problems in girls, and their isolated, withdrawn behavior is distinctive on the playground, but teachers, apparently, do not notice this pattern unless the girl is also aggressive. Teachers may fail to refer children with "internalizing" disorders for treatment, and a relatively high percentage of these neglected children may be girls. Further, teachers may be very inaccurate raters of problems of this type, which could lead to underreporting of the frequency of girls' problems in studies which utilize teacher ratings as outcome measures.

In conclusion, it is clear that observations of playground behavior add a valuable dimension in assessing problem behaviors. Playground observations add a richness of detail and perspective beyond what is offered by more standard teacher and peer ratings. A second major conclusion from these studies is that boys' and girls' aggressive behavior may have very different significance, which can best be assessed in a context where relevant baselines of behavior for each sex can be assessed, such as the playground.

REFERENCES

Coie, J. D., and Dodge, K. A. (1988). Multiple sources of data on social behaviour and social status in the school: A cross-age comparison. *Child Development, 59,* 815–829.

Dodge, K. A., Coie, J. D., and Brakke, N. P. (1982). Behaviour patterns of socially rejected and neglected preadolescents: The roles of social approach and aggression. *Journal of Abnormal Child Psychology, 10,* 389–410.

Edelbrock, C. S., and Achenbach, T. M. (1984). The teacher version of the Child Behavior Profile: I. Boys aged 6–11. *Journal of Consulting and Clinical Psychology, 52,* 207–217.

Hymel, S., and Rubin, K. H. (1985). Children with peer relationships and social skills problems: Conceptual, methodological, and developmental issues. In G. J. Whithurst (Ed.), *Annals of Child Development* (Vol. 2), Greenwich, CT: JAI Press.

Ladd, G. W. (1983). Social networks of popular, average, and rejected children in school settings. *Merrill-Palmer Quarterly, 29*, 283–307.

Lyons, J. A., Serbin, L. A., and Marchessault, K. (1988). The social behavior of peer-identified aggressive, withdrawn, and aggressive/withdrawn children. *Journal of Abnormal Child Psychology, 16*, 539–552.

Marchessault, K. (1985). *Teacher reports and naturalistic observations of peer-identified patterns of aggression and withdrawal.* Unpublished master's thesis. Concordia University, Montreal.

Marchessault, K., Serbin, L. A., and Schwartzman, A. E. (July, 1989). The intensity of playground aggression: A naturalistic study of peer-identified aggressive and withdrawn children. Paper presented at the Tenth Biennial Meeting of the International Society for the Study of Behavioural Development, Jyvaskyla, Finland.

McConnell, S. R., and Odom, S. L. (1986). Sociometrics: Peer-referenced measures and the assessment of social competence. In P. Strain et al. (eds.), *Children's Social Behaviour,* Academic Press.

Moskowitz, D. S., and Schwarz, J. C. (1982). Validity comparison of behavior counts and ratings by knowledgeable informants. *Journal of Personality and Social Psychology, 42*, 518–528.

Olweus, D. (1978). *Aggression in the schools: Bullies and whipping boys.* Washington, DC: Hemisphere.

Pekarik, E. G., Prinz, R. J., Liebert, D. E., Weintraub, S., and Neale, J. (1976). The Pupil Evaluation Inventory: A sociometric technique for assessing children's social behavior. *Journal of Abnormal Child Psychology, 4*, 83–97.

Pellegrini, A. D. (1988). Elementary school children's rough-and-tumble play and social competence. *Developmental Psychology, 24*, 802–806.

Serbin, L. A., Lyons, J. A., Marchessault, K., Schwartzman, A. E., and Ledingham, J. E. (1987). An observational validation of a peer nomination technique for identifying aggressive, withdrawn, and aggressive/withdrawn children. *Journal of Consulting and Clinical Psychology, 55*, 109–110.

7

STEVEN R. ASHER AND SONDA W. GABRIEL_____

Using a Wireless Transmission System to Observe Conversation and Social Interaction on the Playground*

Sarah, a regular education third-grade girl, has just come out of the lunchroom to the playground for recess. She sees Jean, a mildly retarded fourth-grade girl, walking alone nearby and crying.[1]

SARAH: What's the matter?

JEAN: Nobody wants to play with me.

SARAH: I'll play (Jean doesn't respond; Sarah and Jean continue walking near each other).

SARAH: Jean.

JEAN: What?

SARAH: Do you like to play with puppies? I can get you in the Puppy Club (the Puppy Club, in which boys pretended to be puppies, and girls were their masters, was a popular club at the school this spring).

JEAN: Yeah, I like 'em.

SARAH: Okay (Sarah runs to where some members of the Puppy Club are playing; Jean follows her).

Jean and Sarah approach three other girls, members of the Puppy Club. The girls, who had been sitting down, get up and run away screaming and yelling "Cooties" as Jean and Sarah come toward them. Jean and Sarah do not follow the girls.

_____

*Preparation of this chapter was supported by a grant from the W.T. Grant Foundation and by the National Institute of Child Health and Human Development Research Grant HD05951.

SARAH: I don't know why they're doing that (Sarah sits down; Jean sits next to her).

JEAN: I don't know either. It's like, it's just how people feel sometimes. You know? When they run away, and stuff? And I don't under, understand why. Do you understand why?

SARAH: They just don't like you (Sarah says this gently).

SARAH: You stay here, okay? I'll be back (Sarah leaves Jean and runs over to Alice, another member of the Puppy Club).

SARAH: Alice. Alice. I know how you feel about um, Jean, you know?

ALICE: Who?

SARAH: The one that's retarded you know? (Sarah whispers).

SARAH: You know how you feel about Jean you know? That everybody's scared? Of her, you know? I don't think that that's right.

ALICE: Well, she can't be one of the dogs I don't think. Well, maybe. Does she want to be?

SARAH: She wants to, she doesn't have nobody to play with.

ALICE: Do you want her to?

SARAH: If she wants to.

ALICE: You stay here. I'll, I'll go.

SARAH: Okay.

Alice leaves to go talk to Jean. A few moments later Jean and Alice return, with Jean crawling on her hands and knees, pretending to be a puppy. Alice had agreed to let Jean play in the Puppy Club.

The conversation presented above was recorded on an elementary school playground by means of a wireless transmission system that enabled the observer to record children's speech at a great distance. Simultaneous videotaping provided information about nonverbal behavior and context. This wireless transmission methodology offers special opportunities for researchers interested in children's social interactions on the playground and in other school contexts. Indeed, the methodology is ideally suited

for exploring the hidden world of children's everyday conversations. Our goal in this chapter is to describe the observational
methodologies most commonly used to record children's conversations, to review the strengths and limitations of each approach,
and to demonstrate the ways in which wireless transmission
methodology successfully meets the challenges of playground research.

RECORDING CHILDREN'S CONVERSATIONS

Despite the many interesting topics that have been explored by
playground researchers (see Pellegrini, 1987, for a review), there
have been remarkably few studies of children's conversations
on the playground. Investigators of children's playground behavior have typically employed live observational coding systems to record children's behavior. This limits the type of conversational data playground researchers can obtain, since it is
quite difficult without recording devices to record verbatim the
complex conversations that are typical of children's playground
discourse.

Even when recording techniques such as videotaping have
been employed in playground research, the camera has typically
been at such a great distance from the children being observed
that conversations have not been recorded. Researchers have
filmed or videotaped children's behavior on their school playgrounds from a vehicle parked near the playground (e.g., Aldis,
1975; Ginsburg, 1980), or from second-story windows inside the
school building (Lyons, Serbin, and Marchessault, 1988). Such
viewing-at-a-distance techniques reduce the visibility of the video
camera and thereby minimize reactivity. These techniques are
also of value for events or behavioral categories that do not require conversational analysis to code children's behavior. For example, Aldis (1975) employed this technique to analyze nonverbal
components of children's play, such as wrestling, chasing, and
vestibular stimulation (e.g., play on slides, swings, and merry-go-
rounds). Ginsburg (1980) focused on children's agonistic playground interactions with this technique, including comparisons
of children chosen last by their peers for games (referred to as
"omega" children) with their higher-ranking peers.

However, for conversational analysis, some means of recording children's speech to one another is needed. In this chapter we
will discuss four observational techniques that can be used to

record children's conversations: (a) field notes, (b) audiotape recordings, (c) videotape (with audio) recordings, and (d) a wireless transmission system that provides both audio and videorecording. Because these techniques have been infrequently used in playground research, we will illustrate their various strengths and limitations with studies of children's conversations that have been conducted in nonplayground as well as playground contexts. After discussing these techniques, we will describe how wireless transmission technology has been employed in our playground research on children's everyday social interactions at school.

Field Notes

The field note or *ad libitum* technique has a long history of extensive use in ethological and ethnographic research (Altmann, 1974; Jacob, 1987; Martin and Bateson, 1986). With this method, the observer simply describes, in prose, the behavior of the individual or individuals who are being observed. Unlike a formal coding system, field notes are a continuous record, typically recorded in ordinary language, of an individual's behavior over a set period of time.

Field notes have certain limitations as a method for recording conversations. This method can be effective when the goal is to record representative samples of children's conversations rather than complete, verbatim sequences of conversation. However, it is very difficult for an observer to obtain a complete and accurate transcript of speech when the observer is taking written notes as speech occurs. The challenge is even more formidable when the observer makes notes later and must rely on memory to reconstruct what each child has said. Still, the method can serve well for noting impressions and ideas for later analysis, and its relative unobtrusiveness makes it an excellent method for early phases of observation and for hypothesis generation. The field note method is also well suited for situations where children's physical activity is limited, and where children are conversing in dyads rather than larger groups.

There are several variations of the field note technique. In one approach, written notes are taken to describe the behavior of an individual as it occurs (Barker and Wright, 1951; Bryan, Wheeler, Felcan, and Henek, 1976; Grant, 1985; Schofield, 1981). A remarkable example of research involving field notes is *One Boy's Day* (Barker and Wright, 1951), a volume which is a complete, virtually minute-by-minute accounting of one day's activities and conversations of a 7-year-old boy in his home, at school, and in the community. This documentation of a child's everyday behavior and conversations was achieved by using multiple, consecutive observers, following the child from place to place, and taking continuous field notes. Multiple observers were also employed in research by Bryan et al. (1976) on learning disabled children's conversations. Two observers simultaneously wrote down all of a subject's social interactions, one recording all statements made by the subject, and the other noting all statements made by others to the subject.

The field note technique has also been employed by researchers who are participant observers. Here the observer participates in the activities of the individuals who are being observed (e.g., playing or eating lunch with a group of children), and typically does not take notes during the period of observation. After an activity has ended, the participant observer leaves the setting and writes brief notes. These brief notes are then transformed into full field notes at a later time. This field note/participant observation methodology has been used by many contemporary ethnographic researchers interested in the peer relationships of children and adolescents (e.g., Fine, 1987; Thorne, 1986; Zetlin and Murtaugh, 1988). However, there has been relatively little emphasis on children's conversations in this research. Conversations are presented primarily in the form of illustrative examples, rather than as sequences of conversation.

One noteworthy exception is Corsaro's research, which has included considerable emphasis on recording and analyzing children's social conversations (Cook-Gumperz and Corsaro, 1977; Corsaro, 1981, 1985). Corsaro has been particularly interested in preschool children's entry strategies in the context of their friendships, and has found that children use claims of friendship as a means of gaining access to peer activities, and use denial of friendship as a means of exclusion and protection of interactive space from their peers. Corsaro's work points to the importance of recording and analyzing children's conversations in natural settings as a means of understanding children's everyday social relations.

The field note/participant observation methodology has also been used by Eder to record children's conversations in middle school (e.g., Eder, 1985; Evans and Eder, 1989). Eder and her colleagues recorded the lunchroom conversations of middle school students over a 3-year period of time. Eder was interested in social processes such as the development of social stratification (Eder, 1985) and social isolation (Evans and Eder, 1989). Evans and Eder (1989) found that socially isolated students typically were initially rejected by their peers because of perceptions of deviance in isolates' appearance, intellectual development, or gender-appropriate behavior. Isolated students faced significant problems in overcoming their isolation, particularly the unwillingness of other students to associate with individuals labeled as deviant.

Another variant of the field note technique for recording behavior is that of dictating notes into an audiotape recorder which is carried by the observer. Although this technique has not been utilized as frequently as the written field note method, it may be more practical in many circumstances, since the observer is able to watch continuously and is not diverted by writing, and since dictation is often more quickly accomplished than is note-taking. This method has been used to record free play in preschool classrooms (Krasnor, 1982; Laursen and Hartup, 1989), and by several playground researchers (e.g., Humphreys and Smith, 1987; Pellegrini, 1988; Sluckin, 1981; Smith and Lewis, 1985), although only Sluckin (1981) includes conversations in his descriptions of children's social interactions. Sluckin (1981) observed on school playgrounds during recess, speaking quietly into a small audiotape recorder to record behavioral sequences and samples of conversations. Much of Sluckin's book, *Growing up in the Playground*, is devoted to describing children's play and games, including considerable material on children's playground rituals. His book is a rich collection of children's lore, presented with numerous excerpts from children's conversations. Sluckin's work demonstrated that it is possible to be a nonparticipant observer on the playground and to be accepted by the children as a normal part of the school environment in a relatively short period of time.

Audiotape Recordings

Audiotape recording is another frequently used method for recording children's conversations. This technique has been used to record spontaneous conversation between children in natural settings (e.g., Goodwin, 1990; Gottman, 1983). Goodwin (1990) recorded children's conversations in their neighborhood peer groups, focusing on how children use language in their everyday activities. Goodwin (1990) has been particularly interested in gender differences in children's disputes. For example, Goodwin has found that girls typically make use of indirect methods in their discussions of offenses committed against them, whereas boys are more likely to directly confront an offending party.

Audiotape recording has also been employed to record conversations where children are brought together by a researcher and asked to discuss specified topics (e.g., Brenneis and Lein, 1977; Eckert, 1990; Kernan, 1977; Ransohoff, 1975). For example, Eckert (1990) brought together a group of six girls she had observed as part of her long-term participant observation at their high school (Eckert, 1989). Eckert (1990) focused particularly on the girls' discussion of boys that occurred as part of this session, and identified underlying themes in their talk (e.g., the view that a girl's status is measured by her familiarity with popular boys).

Audiotape recording has several advantages compared to recording children's conversations with the field note method. The most important of these is the increased accuracy and completeness of the record that can be obtained when recording lengthy or complex speech episodes or rapid speech. Other advantages include the capability of recording less audible speech (e.g., whispering and private speech) than can be heard by a live observer, and the ability to record paralinguistic aspects of conversation (e.g., pitch, volume, rate of speech).

There are also advantages of audiotape recording in comparison with videotape recording. Habituation is likely to be achieved more readily with an audiotape recorder, since it is somewhat less intrusive. In addition, audiotape recorders are much less costly, enabling research in which audiotape recordings are made simultaneously at many different research sites. Audiotape recorders can also be left at several research sites with the subjects, and thus the researcher's presence is not inevitably required, increasing the efficiency of data collection.

One noteworthy example of research using audiotape recording of children's conversations is the work of Gottman and his colleagues (e.g., Gottman, 1983; Gottman and Parkhurst, 1980). Gottman (1983) audiotaped young children playing in their homes in dyads with either a best friend or a stranger. The presence of a live observer or a video camera was judged to be intrusive and to inhibit children's conversations. However, since the children played in dyads and in a specified environment (a room in the home of one of the children), the potential problems associated with the lack of a visual record were minimized. Accordingly, Gottman left a tape recorder with the mother of the child at whose home the dyad played, and asked her to turn it on when her child's dyadic partner arrived at her home to play. The goal of Gottman's research was to identify and describe the social processes that account for variation in the progress of previously unacquainted children toward friendship. Gottman and his colleagues have also extended their observations to friendship development processes in adolescents (Gottman and Mettetal, 1986) and college roommates (Ginsberg and Gottman, 1986).

Despite the advantages of audiotape to obtain recordings of children's conversation, there are certain limitations to this methodology as well. One of the most significant is the lack of a visual record when audiotape recording alone is used. As a result, one loses information about the nonverbal component that accompanies speech, and one faces the problem of identifying the speaker and the target of the speech. The lack of a visual record also means that the social and environmental context, a very significant influence on conversation, is much more difficult to determine, especially in large group contexts such as the playground.

These problems can be addressed by combining audiotape recording with simultaneous field notes taken by a live observer. Several researchers have used this methodology to record children's arguments (Genishi and DiPaolo, 1982; O'Keefe and Benoit, 1982). The technique of combining audiotape recording with field notes has also been used by Rizzo (1989) in his ethnographic observations of young elementary school children's friendship development. Rizzo audiotaped children's conversations in an interesting manner. At recess on the playground, Rizzo wore a small microphone and tape recorder and adopted the role of a peripheral child, remaining on the fringes of a social group, yet close enough to record the conversations of the children in the group. Rizzo supplemented these audiotape recordings by waiting until an interactive episode ended and then leaving the area and writing brief field notes. In the classroom, Rizzo would ask children if he could work next to them. He then placed a tape recorder on their table or desk, sat down nearby, and began audiotaping and simultaneously taking field notes.

Another creative way of combining audiotape recording with field notes was used by Ross and Lollis (1989). They were interested in whether children's interactive style in a dyad varied as a function of the interactive partner. Children were observed in their homes for a large number of lengthy play sessions. An observer followed the children around the home, recording the children's speech on one track of a stereo tape recorder, and dictating a description of the children's behavior on the other track.

It is also possible to combine audiotape recording with live coding of children's behavior using a formal coding system (i.e., assigning a predetermined code to specific behaviors) and noting the identity of the speaker and target of speech (Abramovitch, Corter, Pepler, and Stanhope, 1986; McCabe and Lipscomb, 1988). For example, Abramovitch et al. (1986) used this technique to examine patterns of dyadic sibling and peer interaction in the children's homes. An observer recorded the children's initiations and responses to prosocial, agonistic, and play behaviors, simultaneously with the audiotaping of their speech.

Audio-Videotape Recordings

Audio-videotape recording has several important features. The resulting complete visual as well as auditory record means that the identity of the speaker, the target of speech, and the directionality of speech can be more reliably identified. In addition, the social and environmental context in which the conversation is taking place can be more clearly determined. Nonverbal communicative elements such as gestures, body postures, and facial expressions can also be recorded using a video camera. Lastly, by audio-videorecording, conversation and nonverbal behavior can be recorded in synchrony, a very important consideration for conversational analysis.

Audio-videotape recording has been frequently employed by peer relations researchers in experimentally arranged contexts (e.g., Coie and Kupersmidt, 1983; Dodge, 1983; Eckerman, Davis, and Didow, 1989; Hazen and Black, 1989; Parker, 1986; Rubin, 1979; Shantz and Shantz, 1985; Vogel, Keane, and Conger, 1988). The advantages of using audio-videotape recording techniques can be seen, for example, in Putallaz's detailed examination of the verbal and nonverbal entry behaviors used by popular and unpopular children (Putallaz, 1983; Putallaz and Gottman, 1981). Putallaz audio-videotaped popular and unpopular children's attempts to enter a dyad composed of either popular or unpopular children. Verbatim transcripts of children's speech were made from the videotapes and coded using a complex coding system. Putallaz found that popular and unpopular children differed in their entry strategies and that popular children were able to enter groups more quickly, more often, and with fewer entry bids.

Audio-videotape recording has also been frequently used by researchers in natural settings such as schools (e.g., Cook-Gumperz and Corsaro, 1977; Eisenberg and Garvey, 1981; Maynard, 1985; Shultz and Florio, 1979; Strayer and Strayer, 1980; Wilkinson, Clevenger, and Dollaghan, 1981), homes (Ervin-Tripp, 1982; Howes, Unger, and Seidner, 1989; Kramer and Gottman, 1992; MacDonald and Parke, 1984; Miller and Sperry, 1987; Vuchinich, Emery, and Cassidy, 1988), or in both schools and homes (Schultz, Florio, and Erickson, 1982). For example, Wilkinson et al. (1981) audio-videotaped children's unsupervised reading groups in their first-grade classrooms. Two observers were also present, taking field notes to supplement the audio-videotape recordings. Children's use of requests for action and information and the influence of gender variables on children's requests were examined. Wilkinson's detailed transcripts of children's speech clearly show the value of audio-videotaping in reliably identifying the speaker and the target of speech, as well as the social and environmental context in which the conversation is taking place.

Despite the advantages of audio-videotape recording, certain challenges must be faced when attempting to record children's behavior and conversations on the playground. One challenge is that children may range over a very large area, with the potential to move outside the recording range of the audio-video recorder. A second challenge is that because there is often considerable background noise on the playground, a focal child's speech can be masked when the child is some distance from the camera.

One solution to these problems is to have a child wear a self-contained recording unit that stays with the child as the child moves about. This technique has been used in classroom observational research. For example, Mishler (1979), in his research on first-grade children's conversations related to food trading, had children wear a small backpack containing a cassette tape recorder, with a microphone attached to the chest strap of the backpack. A similar system was used by Garnica (1981) in her research focusing on the communicative interactions of "omega" children with their peers and teachers in their kindergarten classrooms. A variation of this technique was also employed by Cherry (1975) in her research on gender differences in teacher-child dyadic verbal interaction. Here the teacher carried a small cassette tape recorder over her shoulder as she moved about the classroom. There is at least one researcher who has used this technique on the playground. Borman (1979) audiotaped children's speech on their school playground during games such as tag and hopscotch by having children wear a lightweight backpack that contained a tape recorder. Although Borman's system did not include an external microphone, this element could easily be added to the procedure.

Researchers using self-contained recording units have not typically mentioned the weight of their audiotape recorders. Certainly this is a practical consideration for playground research. The advent of extremely lightweight microcassette recorders makes the procedure of having children carry a recorder quite feasible, since the units are fairly light and small enough to be contained in a relatively unobtrusive pouch. Nonetheless, a major limitation remains when this type of audiotape recording technique is used. The technique does not facilitate the synchronization of the audio material with a visual picture that could be provided by independently videotaping. The method to be described next, the wireless transmission system, is designed to solve this problem.

Wireless Transmission Systems

Wireless transmission systems represent a significant methodological advance in techniques for recording children's conversations. These systems typically involve the individual who is being observed wearing a small microphone and lightweight transmitter. The speech of the individual and the speech of others who converse with that individual are then transmitted to receiving and recording units which are some distance away. This technology allows the individual being observed to roam freely, relatively unencumbered by equipment, and usually far enough away from the researcher to reduce problems of reactivity.

One early example of the use of a wireless transmission system is Soskin and John's (1963) audiorecordings of the conversations of two couples at a summer resort. In their system, the transmitter was worn on a shoulder strap, with a small microphone attached to the front of the strap. The receiving and recording station was in a small building on the resort grounds. The building was equipped with a high tracking antenna, and, as a result, the individual wearing the device was free to range over virtually the entire resort area. Couples were asked not to leave the resort area grounds, although they could turn off and remove the transmitter if they wished. This observational procedure maximized the privacy of each couple, since no observer was nearby to simultaneously make field notes or to film their behavior.

A different type of wireless transmission methodology that combined audio- and videorecording was used by Saville-Troike (1986) in her sociolinguistic studies of young children's conversations. Saville-Troike had children wear a lightweight vest with a microphone clipped to the front of the vest and a wireless transmitter contained in a hidden pocket in the back of the vest. The behavior and conversations of nursery school and kindergarten children were simultaneously audiotaped and videotaped, with the wireless transmission system output relayed to an audio receiver, which in turn supplied the sound directly to the videotape. Saville-Troike's research was conducted in a university-operated nursery school and in a public school kindergarten, both of which enrolled English-speaking and non-English-speaking children from a variety of ethnic backgrounds (e.g., Japanese, Chinese, and Korean). Saville-Troike was particularly interested in the phenomenon of "dilingual discourse" which she defined as mutually unintelligible conversations by speakers of different languages which are responded to by the participants in the conversation as though the conversation was intelligible.

Guralnick and Groom (1987) also employed wireless transmission technology with videotaping. In their research, mildly developmentally delayed preschool-aged boys were paired with other same-aged mildly delayed boys, with younger nonhandi-

capped boys, or with same-aged nonhandicapped boys and observed during eight dyadic play sessions. Guralnick and Groom
used a vest and pocket wireless transmission system similar to
that of Saville-Troike (1986). Children were brought to a playroom, and their behavior was videotaped and speech recorded
from an adjacent observation room through a one-way mirror.
Guralnick and Groom (1987) found that in play sessions with
same-aged, nonhandicapped play partners, the frequency and
quality of mildly delayed children's social play improved considerably, compared with only limited social interactions in play sessions with other delayed peers.

Sheldon (1990) has utilized wireless transmission technology
with videotaping in research on gender differences in preschool
children's conflicts. Sheldon also used a vest and pocket arrangement for the microphone and transmitter. Children were grouped
into twelve same-sex triads, and each triad was videotaped on
three different occasions in one of the children's usual play areas.
Each child's voice was recorded on a separate audio cassette at
the same time that the three voices were recorded together on the
videotape sound channel. This recording technique facilitates the
transcription of conversation, since each child's voice can be distinguished more clearly than would be possible with only a mixed
recording. Sheldon (1990) specifically examined two lengthy disputes, one that occurred in a triad of girls, the other in a triad of
boys. The triad of girls used negotiation to arrive at a resolution
of their conflict, whereas the boys used coercive tactics such as
threats and physical intimidation.

In summary, of the various techniques for recording children's
conversation discussed above, the wireless transmission system
is ideally suited for meeting the challenges of playground observation. Using the wireless transmission system enables the observer to stay at a distance that minimizes reactivity, and facilitates the recording of children's conversations as the children
move freely over large areas, such as the playground. These systems can also be remarkable light in weight and thereby minimally constrain the children being observed.

WIRELESS TRANSMISSION ON THE PLAYGROUND

In this section, we will describe the wireless audio-video transmission system we employed to observe and record children's
social interactions and conversations on the playground. Our

research, now at the transcription and coding phase, was moti-
vated by an interest in learning about the day-to-day rejection
experiences of children at school. A considerable number of
elementary school children have serious peer relationship problems in school (see Asher and Coie, 1990, for reviews). For
example, about 10% of elementary school children have no one
name them as a friend on sociometric measures (e.g., Hymel
and Asher, 1977). The percentage is considerably higher for
mildly retarded students and other students with serious learning difficulties (Bryan, 1976; Gottlieb and Leyser, 1981; Taylor,
Asher, and Williams, 1987). We know from recent research that
peer rejected, nonhandicapped students (Asher and Wheeler,
1985; Cassidy and Asher, 1992; Crick and Ladd, in press) and
mildly retarded "mainstreamed" students (Taylor et al., 1987;
Williams and Asher, 1992) are especially likely to report strong
feelings of loneliness and social dissatisfaction in school. However, we know very little about the actual content of children's
daily rejection experiences at school, or about the antecedents,
consequences, and contexts of rejection.

Two different samples of third- through sixth-grade children
participated in our research. One sample included 22 children in
regular education classrooms, half of whom were highly rejected
by their peers and half of whom were average in their sociometric
status. The second sample was comprised of 13 mildly retarded
children who were observed as they interacted with peers in their
special education classrooms, and in regular education (main-
stream) contexts. For both samples, observations were made in
several school settings, including the playground, lunchroom,
gymnasium, classroom, library, and in music and art classes.
Observations were made throughout the school year, beginning
in October and ending in early June. Altogether, we collected
approximately 6 hours of observational data on each of our focal
children. Individual observation sessions averaged approximately
45 minutes in length. Children were observed in the same setting
no more than once per week, and at least 1 day elapsed between
successive observations of the same child. The observations were
made using a focal-child behavior sampling technique, an adaptation of the focal-animal technique (Altmann, 1974; Martin and
Bateson, 1986). The focal-child technique facilitates the collection
of data on the frequency, duration, and sequencing of behavior,
and thus was particularly well suited for our research.

The components of the wireless transmission system worn by the child included a small, lavaliere microphone (Sony ECM-44), and a pocket transmitter (Samson TH-1 Belt Pack). The microphone was attached to the collar of the child's clothing, and the transmitter was contained in a small padded pouch on a belt fastened around the child's waist. The transmitter was actually designed to fit in a pocket or on a belt without the use of a pouch. However, the padded pouch made the transmitter more stable and reduced the risk of damage if it was dropped. We used a pouch and belt arrangement because the pouch was somewhat less conspicuous than a vest. Children wearing the microphone and transmitter were able to move about freely, since the devices together weighed only 7 ounces.

The observer positioned herself so that she had a clear view of the child being observed and the group of children he or she was with, while remaining as far away from the child as possible to reduce the intrusiveness of the recording equipment. The observer carried a backpack containing the necessary receiving equipment, which included a battery pack (SAFT NPP-1245C) that powered a specially adapted audio receiver (Samson RH-1 VHF-FM), and a small audiotape recorder (Toshiba KT-P22). Children's behavior was videotaped with an 8 mm camcorder (Minolta CR-8000). To synchronize the audio and videorecording, a cable ran from the audio receiver directly to an input on the video camera. In this way, the audio channel of the videotape was filled with input from the child's transmitting unit, rather than from the camera's built-in microphone. Additionally, the observer wore an earphone which was connected by a thin cable to the video camera. This enabled the observer to monitor audio input at all times. The audiovisual technology we employed solved the problem of recording children's conversation very effectively, and proved to be quite unobtrusive, since with our audio transmission equipment the observer could be as much as 300 feet away from the child wearing the microphone and transmitter.

With our particular wireless transmission system, sound did not pass through walls and other solid structures. Thus, if the child wearing the microphone went around a corner of the school building on the playground, sound was momentarily lost until the observer rounded the same corner. The presence of power lines, interfering radio frequencies, and large metal objects could also cause a momentary loss of audio input. Since the observer monitored audio input at all times, if an audio loss occurred the observer moved a short distance to eliminate the problem.

Before beginning formal observations, the observer spent 3 weeks at the school to acclimatize the children, their teachers, and the other school staff to her presence. This time spent in the school was important for several reasons. First, it gave the observer an opportunity to familiarize herself with the school and school routines. This time was also spent in meeting and learning the names of the teachers, the school support staff (e.g., teacher aides, secretaries, lunch and recess monitors), and other school professional staff (the librarian, school social worker, speech and occupational therapists). Since the observer planned to spend virtually an entire year at the school, it was essential to foster a good working relationship with these individuals, so that they felt comfortable with the observer's presence in their school and would, indirectly, help the children to feel comfortable with the observer.

This time was also spent in learning the names of all 287 children in third through sixth grade at the school. This information was critical because we were interested in the identities and characteristics of the children who interacted with the focal children (see Ladd, 1983). To assist in learning the children's names, the observer obtained copies of the previous year's school pictures and distributed these to each of the teachers, asking them to indicate which children were in their class during the current year. The observer then went to each of the third- through sixth-grade classrooms on several occasions and sat in class, matching names on the class list with faces in the class and on school pictures. On these occasions, the teachers were asked, whenever possible, to call on children by name rather than pointing or using a nonspecific term of address for the children.

This preliminary time spent in the school was perhaps most important in allowing the children themselves to become accustomed to the observer's presence in the school. Although the observer was friendly with the children and answered the children if spoken to, she did not initiate interactions with the children or engage in extended conversations. The observer also did not direct the children's activities in any way. Children were told that the observer would not tell their teachers, peers, parents, or anyone else what they did or said. There were several signs that the children came to trust the observer, and to behave very naturally in her presence. For example, children occasionally swore, discussed sexual topics, behaved aggressively, gossiped about other children and their teachers, and talked about personally sensitive matters (e.g., parental divorce).

The acclimatization and data-collection phases of our research involved a considerable time commitment. This level of commitment continues during the data analysis phase. We find, for example, that it requires approximately 20 hours to transcribe each hour of audio-videotaped playground conversation. It is also important for the person who collected the data to be involved with the transcribing process, since that individual is most familiar with the children's voices and identities, as well as references children may make to certain topics, individuals, or locations.

Finally, it should be understood that despite extensive efforts to habituate the children to the recording equipment, there was a small amount of occasional reactivity to the wireless transmission system and video camera. Fortunately, reactivity was minimized by the unobtrusiveness of our system and our observational techniques. Reactivity was also greatly reduced by the fact that the observer and the equipment were present every day, all day long, in several different settings at the school, thus becoming a normal part of the school environment. The children's reactivity was also reduced by the fact that the adult staff at the school showed little reactivity to our presence or our recording system. Signs of reactivity by the children, when they did occur, were usually limited to children making a brief comment about the observer, the microphone, or the video camera, after which children resumed their normal activities and conversation.

This pattern of momentary reactivity followed by the resumption of previous activities is illustrated by the following transcript. The transcript, like the one at the beginning of the chapter, also illustrates the richness of the conversational material that can be obtained by a wireless transmission system.

Scott, a fifth-grade boy, is on the playground during recess, talking to a fifth-grade girl, Betsy, about a fight he had with his girlfriend, whom Betsy knows. After graphically describing the fight to Betsy, using considerable obscene language, Scott briefly reacts to the observer's presence.

SCOTT: Look what I've got on (Scott shows Betsy the transmitter pouch he is wearing).

BETSY: I know. I could see her watching (Betsy looks over at the observer, then back at Scott, and laughs).

SCOTT: I hope that thing, that thing's waterproof. That one, that one, excuse me, that she has with her because she sent out, she's a, she's out (a light rain has started to fall, and Scott seems to be talking about the observer's video camera).

BETSY: We have to go in early because we lost recess because of some big mouths. One of them was Susie Anderson (this is a girl in Betsy's class that a lot of other girls don't like).

SCOTT: Why does Susie Anderson think that she can beat Carol up? (Carol is Scott's girlfriend).

BETSY: I don't know. She thinks she can beat me up and she bosses me around because she's just the Wagon Train master (Wagon Train is an activity that Betsy's class was doing).

SCOTT: Wagon Train?

BETSY: And then, yeah we're like doing a Wagon Train now, and she thinks she's the boss of everybody at our table. I said "Come on, try to beat me up" and she goes "I don't want to get a detention" and I said "Oh I'm not worried about detention, I'm talkin' about at home."

SCOTT: Don't get near me Bill (Bill is a mildly retarded boy that Scott intensely dislikes, who is now approaching Scott and Betsy).

SCOTT: I'll kick you flat on your face (Scott gives Bill another warning as he continues approaching him).

Despite these warnings, Bill continued approaching Scott and then stood a few feet away from him. After more threats, Scott finally chased Bill away from him, telling him he would find out where he lived.

CONCLUSION

In this chapter, we have discussed the strengths and limitations of several different methods of recording children's conversations. Our particular emphasis has been on the advantages of wireless transmission methodology. This method is ideally suited for capturing the hidden world of children's conversations in settings such as the playground or the lunchroom. It is important to analyze children's conversations in settings such as these, since many of the social interactions that take place in school are in relatively unstructured settings. We hope that future researchers will make use of this promising technology, and that the description we have provided of its implementation will be a useful guide.

NOTE

1. All names given in the transcripts are pseudonyms.

REFERENCES

Abramovitch, R., Corter, C., Pepler, D. J., and Stanhope, L. (1986). Sibling and peer interaction: A final follow-up and a comparison. *Child Development, 57,* 217–229.

Aldis, O. (1975). *Play fighting.* New York: Academic Press.

Altmann, J. (1974). Observational study of behavior: Sampling methods. *Behaviour, 49,* 227–267.

Asher, S. R., and Coie, J. D. (Eds.). (1990). *Peer rejection in childhood.* Cambridge: Cambridge University Press.

Asher, S. R., and Wheeler, V. A. (1985). Children's loneliness: A comparison of rejected and neglected peer status. *Journal of Consulting and Clinical Psychology, 53,* 500–505.

Barker, R. G., and Wright, H. F. (1951). *One boy's day.* New York: Harper and Brothers.

Borman, K. M. (1979). Children's interactions on playgrounds. *Theory into Practice, 18,* 251–257.

Brenneis, D., and Lein, L. (1977). "You fruithead": A sociolinguistic approach to children' dispute settlement. In S. Ervin-Tripp and C. Mitchell-Kernan (Eds.), *Child discourse* (pp. 49–65). New York: Academic Press.

Bryan, T. H. (1976). Peer popularity of learning disabled children: A replication. *Journal of Learning Disabilities, 9*, 307–311.

Bryan, T., Wheeler, R., Felcan, J., and Henek, T. (1976). "Come on, dummy": An observational study of children's communications. *Journal of Learning Disabilities, 9*, 53–61.

Cassidy, J., and Asher, S. R. (1992). Loneliness and peer relations in young children. *Child Development, 63*, 350–365.

Cherry, L. (1975). Teacher-child verbal interaction: An approach to the study of sex differences. In B. Thorne and N. Henley (Eds.), *Language and sex: Difference and dominance* (pp. 172–183). Rowley, MA: Newbury House.

Coie, J. D., and Kupersmidt, J. (1983). A behavioral analysis of emerging social status in boys' groups. *Child Development, 54*, 1400–1416.

Cook-Gumperz, J., and Corsaro, W. A. (1977). Social-ecological constraints on children's communicative strategies. *Sociology, 11*, 411–434.

Corsaro, W. A. (1981). Friendship in the nursery school: Social organization in a peer environment. In S. R. Asher and J. M. Gottman (Eds.), *The development of children's friendships* (pp. 207–241). New York: Cambridge University Press.

———. (1985). *Friendship and peer culture in the early years.* Norwood, NJ: Ablex.

Crick, N. R., and Ladd, G. W. (In press). Children's perceptions of their peer experiences: Attributions, social anxiety, and social avoidance. *Developmental Psychology.*

Dodge, K. A. (1983). Behavioral antecedents of peer social status. *Child Development, 54*, 1386–1399.

Eckerman, C. O., Davis, C. C., and Didow, S. M. (1989). Toddlers' emerging ways of achieving social coordinations with a peer. *Child Development, 60*, 440–453.

Eckert, P. (1989). *Jocks and burnouts*. New York: Teachers College Press.

———. (1990). Cooperative competition in adolescent "Girl Talk." *Discourse Processes, 13*, 91–122.

Eder, D. (1985). The cycle of popularity: Interpersonal relations among female adolescents. *Sociology of Education, 58*, 154–165.

Eisenberg, A. R., and Garvey, C. (1981). Children's use of verbal strategies in resolving conflicts. *Discourse Processes, 4*, 149–170.

Ervin-Tripp, S. (1982). Structures of control. In L. C. Wilkinson (Ed.), *Communicating in the classroom* (pp. 27–47). New York: Academic Press.

Evans, C., and Eder, D. (1989, August). *"No exit": Processes of social isolation in the middle school.* Paper presented at the meeting of the American Sociological Association, San Francisco.

Fine, G. A. (1987). *With the boys: Little League baseball and preadolescent culture.* Chicago: University of Chicago Press.

Garnica, O. (1981). Social dominance and conversational interaction— the omega child in the classroom. In J. Green and C. Wallat (Eds.), *Ethnography and language in educational settings* (pp. 229–253). Norwood, NJ: Ablex.

Genishi, C., and DiPaolo, M. (1982). Learning through argument in a preschool. In L. C. Wilkinson (Ed.), *Communicating in the classroom* (pp. 49–68). New York: Academic Press.

Ginsberg, D., and Gottman, J. M. (1986). Conversations of college roommates: Similarities and differences in male and female friendships. In J. M. Gottman and J. G. Parker (Eds.), *Conversations of friends: Speculations on affective development* (pp. 241–291). New York: Cambridge University Press.

Ginsburg, H. J. (1980). Playground as laboratory: Naturalistic studies of appeasement, altruism, and the omega child. In D. O. Omark, F. F. Strayer, and D. G. Freedman (Eds.), *Dominance relations* (pp. 341–357). New York: Garland STPM Press.

Goodwin, M. H. (1990). Tactical uses of stories: Participation frameworks within girls' and boys' disputes. *Discourse processes, 13*, 33–71.

Gottlieb, J., and Leyser, Y. (1981). Friendships between retarded and non-retarded children. In S. R. Asher and J. M. Gottman (Eds.), *The development of children's friendships* (pp. 150–181). New York: Cambridge University Press.

Gottman, J. M. (1983). How children become friends. *Monographs of the Society for Research in Child Development, 48* (3, Serial No. 201).

Gottman, J. M., and Mettetal, G. (1986). Speculations about social and affective development: Friendship and acquaintanceship through adolescence. In J. M. Gottman and J. G. Parker (Eds.), *Conversations of friends: Speculations on affective development* (pp. 192–237). New York: Cambridge University Press.

Gottman, J. M., and Parkhurst, J. T. (1980). A developmental theory of friendship and acquaintanceship processes. In W. A. Collins (Ed.), *Minnesota symposia on child psychology* (Vol. 13) (pp. 197–253). Hillsdale, NJ: Lawrence Erlbaum.

Grant, L. (1985). Race-gender status, classroom interaction, and children's socialization in elementary school. In L. C. Wilkinson and C. B. Marrett (Eds.), *Gender influences in classroom interaction* (pp. 57–77). Orlando, FL: Academic Press.

Guralnick, M. J., and Groom, J. M. (1987). Dyadic peer interactions of mildly delayed and nonhandicapped preschool children. *American Journal of Mental Deficiency, 92*, 178–193.

Hazen, N. L., and Black, B. (1989). Preschool peer communication skills: The role of social status and interaction context. *Child Development, 60*, 867–876.

Howes, C., Unger, O., and Seidner, L. B. (1989). Social pretend play in toddlers: Parallels with social play and with solitary pretend. *Child Development, 60*, 77–84.

Humphreys, A. P., and Smith, P. K. (1987). Rough-and-tumble play, friendship and dominance in school children: Evidence for continuity and change with age. *Child Development, 58*, 201–212.

Hymel, S., and Asher, S. R. (1977). *Assessment and training of isolated children's social skills.* Paper presented at the biennial meeting of the Society for Research in Child Development, New Orleans (ERIC Document Reproduction Service No. ED 136 930).

Jacob, E. (1987). Qualitative research traditions: A review. *Review of Educational Research, 57*, 1–50.

Kernan, K. (1977). Semantic and expressive elaboration in children's narratives. In S. Ervin-Tripp and C. Mitchell-Kernan (Eds.), *Child discourse* (pp. 91–102). New York: Academic Press.

Kramer, L., and Gottman, J. M. (1992). Becoming a sibling: "With a little help from my friends." *Developmental Psychology, 28*, 685–699.

Krasnor, L. R. (1982). An observational study of social problem solving in young children. In K. H. Rubin and H. S. Ross (Eds.), *Peer relationships and social skills in young children* (pp. 113–132). New York: Springer-Verlag.

Ladd, G. W. (1983). Social networks of popular, average, and rejected children in school settings. *Merrill-Palmer Quarterly, 29*, 283–307.

Laursen, B., and Hartup, W. W. (1989). The dynamics of preschool children's conflicts. *Merrill-Palmer Quarterly, 35*, 281–297.

Lyons, J., Serbin, L. A., and Marchessault, K. (1988). The social behavior of peer-identified aggressive, withdrawn, and aggressive-withdrawn children. *Journal of Abnormal Child Psychology, 16*, 539–552.

MacDonald, K., and Parke, R. D. (1984). Bridging the gap: Parent-child play interaction and peer interactive competence. *Child Development, 55*, 1265–1277.

Martin, P., and Bateson, P. (1986). *Measuring behaviour. An introductory guide.* Cambridge: Cambridge University Press.

Maynard, D. W. (1985). On the functions of social conflict among children. *American Sociological Review, 50*, 207–223.

McCabe, A., and Lipscomb, T. J. (1988). Sex differences in children's verbal aggression. *Merrill-Palmer Quarterly, 34*, 389–401.

Miller, P., and Sperry, L. L. (1987). The socialization of anger and aggression. *Merrill-Palmer Quarterly, 33*, 1–31.

Mishler, E. G. (1979). "Wou' you trade cookies with the popcorn?" The talk of trades among six year olds. In O. Garnica and M. King (Eds.), *Language, children, and society: The effects of social factors on children's learning to communicate* (pp. 221–236). Elmsford, NY: Pergamon Press.

O'Keefe, B. J., and Benoit, P. J. (1982). Children's arguments. In J. R. Cox and C. A. Willard (Eds.), *Advances in argumentation theory and research* (pp. 154–183). Carbondale, IL: Southern Illinois University Press.

Parker, J. G. (1986). Becoming friends: Conversational skills for friendship formation in young children. In J. M. Gottman and J. G. Parker (Eds.), *Conversations of friends: Speculations on affective development* (pp. 103–138). New York: Cambridge University Press.

Pellegrini, A. D. (1987). Children on playgrounds: A review of "What's out there." *Children's Environments Quarterly, 4,* 2–7.

———. (1988). Elementary-school children's rough-and-tumble play and social competence. *Developmental Psychology, 24,* 802–806.

Putallaz, M. (1983). Predicting children's sociometric status from their behavior. *Child Development, 54,* 1417–1426.

Putallaz, M., and Gottman, J. M. (1981). Social skills and group acceptance. In S. R. Asher and J. M. Gottman (Eds.), *The development of children's friendships* (pp. 116–149). New York: Cambridge University Press.

Ransohoff, R. (1975). Some observations on humor and laughter in young adolescent girls. *Journal of Youth and Adolescence, 4,* 155–170.

Rizzo, T. A. (1989). *Friendship development among children in school.* Norwood, NJ: Ablex.

Ross, H. S., and Lollis, S. P. (1989). A social relations analysis of toddler peer relationships. *Child Development, 60,* 1082–1091.

Rubin, K. (1979). The impact of the natural setting on private speech. In G. Zivin (Ed.), *The development of self-regulation through private speech* (pp. 265–294). New York: Wiley.

Saville-Troike, M. (1986). Children's dispute and negotiation strategies: A naturalistic approach. In J. A. Fishman, A. Tabouret-Keller, M. Clyne, B. Krishnamurti, and M. Abdulaziz (Eds.), *The Fergusonian impact* (Vol. 1, pp. 135–152). Berlin: Mouton de Gruyter.

Schofield, J. W. (1981). Complementary and conflicting identities: Images and interaction in an interracial school. In S. R. Asher and J. M. Gottman (Eds.), *The development of children's friendships* (pp. 53–90). New York: Cambridge University Press.

Shantz, C. U., and Shantz, D. W. (1985). Conflict between children: Social-cognitive and sociometric correlates. In M. Berkowitz (Ed.), *Peer conflict and psychological growth* (pp. 3–21). San Francisco: Jossey-Bass.

Sheldon, A. (1990). Pickle fights: Gendered talk in preschool disputes. *Discourse processes, 13,* 5–31.

Shultz, J., and Florio, S. (1979). Stop and freeze: The negotiation of social and physical space in a kindergarten/first grade classroom. *Anthropology and Education Quarterly, 10,* 166–181.

Shultz, J. J., Florio, S., and Erickson, F. (1982). Where's the floor? Aspects of the cultural organization of social relationships in communication at home and in school. In P. Gilmore and A. Glatthorn (Eds.), *Children in and out of school: Ethnography and education* (pp. 88–123). Washington: Center for Applied Linguistics.

Sluckin, A. (1981). *Growing up in the playground.* London: Routledge.

Smith, P. K., and Lewis, K. (1985). Rough-and-tumble play, fighting, and chasing in nursery school children. *Ethology and Sociobiology, 6,* 175–181.

Soskin, W. F., and John, V. P. (1963). The study of spontaneous talk, In R. G. Barker (Ed.), *The stream of behavior: Explorations of its structure and content* (pp. 228–281). New York: Appelton-Century-Crofts.

Strayer, F. F., and Strayer, J. (1980). Preschool conflict and the assessment of social dominance. In D. R. Omark, F. F. Strayer, and D. G. Freedman (Eds.), *Dominance relations: An ethological view of human conflict and social interaction* (pp. 137–157). New York: Garland STPM Press.

Taylor, A. R., Asher, S. R., and Williams, G. A. (1987). The social adaptation of mainstreamed mildly retarded children. *Child Development, 58,* 1321–1334.

Thorne, B. (1986). Girls and boys together. . .but mostly apart: Gender arrangements in elementary school. In W. W. Hartup and Z. Rubin (Eds.), *Relationships and development* (pp. 167–184). Hillsdale, NJ: Erlbaum.

Vogel, J., Keane, S. P., and Conger, J. C. (1988). A content analysis of the conversational behavior of accepted and rejected children. *Journal of Psychopathology and Behavioral Assessment, 10,* 49–64.

Vuchinich, S., Emery, R. E., and Cassidy, J. (1988). Family members as third parties in dyadic family conflict: Strategies, alliances, and outcomes. *Child Development, 59,* 1293–1302.

Wilkinson, L. C., Clevenger, M., and Dollaghan, C. (1981). Communication in small instructional groups: A socio-linguistic approach. In W. P. Dickson (Ed.), *Children's oral communication skills* (pp. 207–240). New York: Academic Press.

Williams, G. A., and Asher, S. R. (1992). Assessment of loneliness at school among children with mild mental retardation. *American Journal on Mental Retardation, 96,* 373–385.

Zetlin, A. G., and Murtaugh, M. (1988). Friendship patterns of mildly learning handicapped and nonhandicapped high school students. *American Journal on Mental Retardation, 92,* 447–454.

8

MICHAEL J. BOULTON AND PETER K. SMITH _____

Ethnic, Gender Partner, and Activity Preferences in Mixed-Race Schools in the U.K.: Playground Observations*

The actual setting in which children meet and interact has been shown to play a crucial role in determining the nature of their interactions and their outcomes, both proximal and in the longer term (see Bloch and Pellegrini, 1989). One setting that has been underresearched is the school playground. We believe that this is an important location for many different reasons, not least because it is here that many children meet with only minimal adult supervision and hence they are free to behave in ways that lack many of the usual adult-imposed constraints. From a methodological point of view, we have never been in a better position to study children in these environments (e.g., Boulton and Smith, 1989).

In free play situations, such as the playground, research suggests that children do not select their partners on a random basis. Rather they appear to actively seek out the company of peers or avoid them on the basis of certain characteristics. In this chapter we shall present details and data that relate to this issue, with particular reference to race and sex. Our data come from a longitudinal project on aspects of peer relations in three ethnically mixed middle schools in the United Kingdom. In addition to considering play partner preferences, we shall also examine preferences shown by subgroups of children for engaging in certain types of activities on the playground, as well as the relationship between children's stated and observed preferences. Specifically, the aims of our investigation were:

---

*The data reported in this chapter were collected as part of a study supported by the Economic and Social Research Council, Swindon, U.K. We are grateful to Louise Boulton for helpful comments on earlier drafts of this chapter, and to Jenny Brown for assistance with data collection.

1. to compare observed own-sex and own-race preferences, in the playground of British boys and girls, of both white and Asian origin.
2. to investigate observed race and sex differences in preferred group size, and categories of playground behavior.
3. to relate observed partner preferences to stated partner preferences (obtained from interview).

SEX OF PREFERRED PARTNERS

One of the most obvious and well-documented aspects of the social structuring of children's peer groups is a propensity for same-sex partners. In a comprehensive review of 16 studies that examine sex segregation within the school environment among 3- to 11-year-old children, Lockheed and Klein (1985) noted that a preference for same-sex peers emerged during the third year (although slightly earlier in girls than boys) and lasted till the end of the middle school period. Scott (1984) also documented a similar pattern of preference in children's play throughout the preschool and elementary school years.

While this sex cleavage may hold in a general sense, other data suggest that age and sex may be important mediating variables. For example, whereas Macobby and Jacklin (in press) reported that the extent of same-sex preference was equal among preschool boys and girls, data obtained by Daniels-Beirness and LeShano (1988) suggested that 8-year-old elementary school girls may have more cross-sex interactions than do boys. Similarly, LaFreniere, Strayer, and Gauthier (1984) did not find a sex difference in the degree of same-sex segregation at 3 to 4 years of age, but by 5 to 6 years of age the boys exhibited a significantly greater same-sex bias than did the girls.

Gottman (1986) has argued that ecological factors may also influence the degree of cross-sex friendship. He observed that they were more likely to appear in nonschool settings than within school, and suggested that on entering school, close friendships with the opposite sex are broken off or only manifest themselves at home. Several other studies have found that even within school, relatively low level setting and social parameters can influence this aspect of children's partner preference; Lockheed and Klein (1985) found a more pronounced same-sex preference on the playground than in the classroom, and in the absence of adults compared to when they were present; and Bianchi and Bakeman (1978) found a greater sex cleavage in traditional school settings than in open school settings. Swadener (see Swadener and Johnson, 1989) conducted an ethnographic case study of two day-care centers, in which weekly observations over a 9-month school year and interviews with teachers and children were carried out. The extent of gender segregation was found to differ depending on the activity or setting; for example, at one of the centers, children associated with same-sex peers 75% of the time on the playground, 72% of the time at snack, and 65% of the time during table activity. Smith and Connolly (1980) found that sex cleavage was less in smaller preschool groups in the United Kingdom (of about 10–15 children) than in lager groups (of about 20–30 children).

To date, few studies have considered gender segregation as a function of race. One recently reported study (Bloch, 1989) examined children's play in two communities—an American midwestern, middle-class suburban community, and a rural West African village in Senegal. Bloch used Whiting's (1980) cultural-ecological model as an explanatory framework to investigate the influence of the ecological context on children's activities, and more specifically how the social and physical parameters of the settings they typically experience can affect the activities and patterns of social interactions they learn during their childhood years. Among the American sample of 83 children aged up to 6 years, there were no significant age or sex differences in time spent with children of either sex, but the descriptive data from the 5- to 6-year-olds showed a tendency for the boys to spend less time with their sisters or with other females than was the case with girls. The Senegalese sample consisted of 54 children aged between 2 and 6 years, and among the 5- to 6-year-olds there was a tendency for them to be in same-sex groups in a range of activities.

In our study, we set out to compare the extent of own-sex preferences in British children, among both white boys and girls, and those of Asian origin.

RACE OF PREFERRED PARTNERS

Following school desegregation in the United States, many researchers have examined children's interracial attitudes, and several reviews of the literature were published in the 1970s (Amir, 1976; Carithers, 1970; Cohen, 1975; St John, 1975;

Stephan, 1978). St John noted the great variety of results that had been obtained. Some studies reported evidence that desegregation facilitated more positive interracial attitudes (e.g., Gardner, Wright, and Dee, 1970) but others that it led to more negative attitudes (e.g., Barber, 1968). Some even reported that desegregation improved the attitudes of blacks but had a negative impact on whites (e.g., Crooks, 1970) or vice versa (e.g., McWhirt, 1967).

Up until recently, relatively few studies have examined racial preferences in racially mixed schools by means of direct observations. Previously, most investigators relied on sociometric measures. For example, in his review of 19 studies, St John (1975) noted that only two actually involved direct observations of intergroup behavior. Schofield (1978; Schofield and Sagar, 1977; Schofield and Francis, 1982) has suggested several reasons why this trend was "unfortunate." She noted that most data suggesting a correspondence between sociometric indices and actual behavior have come from all white groups; social desirability biases and/or evaluation apprehension may have influenced the validity of sociometric data; and sociometric measures were usually focused on assessing "fairly intensive positive relationships," but "less intense acquaintance relationships are both more numerous and more likely to be open to change (Schofield and Francis, 1982, p. 723).

Partly in response to these concerns, from the late 1970s onwards, observational methodologies were incorporated into several studies in order to directly investigate interracial behavior. At the younger age range, Finkelstein and Haskins (1983) observed 38 black and 25 white kindergarten children during classroom instruction and during recess on the school playground. Observations were made during the fall and then during the following spring. Talk, Negative, and Command categories were scored, and in the classroom, observers recorded group work when children worked together at the same or adjoining desks, or took part in instructional groups led by the teacher. On the playground, they recorded when subjects played with objects together, shared toys or playground apparatus, or participated in games with formal rules with peers. The results indicated that the 5-year-olds entered kindergarten with a clear own-race preference, and that moreover, this preference increased over the school year.

Schofield and Sagar (1977) observed spontaneous seating patterns within a desegregated middle school cafeteria. They found that "race is an extremely important grouping criterion even for children who have chosen to attend a desegregated school" (p. 136). Schofield and Francis (1982) investigated the quantity and quality of cross-race interactions in four racially mixed eighth-grade classrooms. They coded the race and sex of partners, the mutuality (one-sided, mutual), the affective tone (positive, neutral, negative), and the orientation (task, social, ambiguous) of the interactions. Overall, the children were found to interact significantly more with own-race than with other-race peers, and the patterns of behavior shown by the four subgroups of sex/race subjects indicated that cross-race interactions tended to be more task-related than within race interactions, whereas within race interactions had a more social orientation than cross-race interactions.

These two studies by Schofield and her colleagues also found that sex may be an important mediating variable. In the earlier study, boys were found to have significantly more cross-race interactions than girls, and similarly in the latter study, planned comparisons revealed the strong own-race preference of the girls was responsible for the overall significant own-race preference in the total sample of boys and girls; the boys did not show a corresponding significant preference.

In the study reported in this chapter, we also investigated racial preferences as a function of race/sex. Moreover, our study was deemed important because most, if not all, studies carried out to date have involved black and white American subjects. There is clear need to examine racial preferences in children from a variety of ethnic backgrounds. Our sample was made up of white children and those whose parents are of Asian origin.

There is some evidence to suggest that the racial mix within a school may exert an influence on children's racial preferences, and this was examined in our study. However, because the available evidence is mixed on this issue, no firm predictions were made (see Aboud, 1988).

PREFERRED GROUP SIZE AND NUMBER
OF DIFFERENT COMPANIONS

Another robust finding from studies investigating the social structure of children's peer groups is in terms of preferred group size. For example, Lever (1976, 1978) observed that among 11-year-old boys, groups of 10–25 were common, and that they were usually involved in team games, whereas girls were mostly to be found with one or two others. A similar sex difference was obtained by Laosa and Brophy (1972) with 5–7-year-olds, by Waldrop and Halverson (1975) with 7-year-olds, and Omark, Omark, and Edelman (1975) with 5- to 9-year-olds. This propensity for engaging in play or other activities with relatively few or many peers by boys and girls could be one factor that is responsible for the typically observed sex cleavage reported above.

A result from the study by Bloch (1989), already discussed, suggests that cultural variability may also mediate any sex difference in preferred size of group; in contrast to the results with United States children, among 5- to 6-year-old Senegalese children, there was no sex difference in the size of play groups. Clearly more data are needed, so we assessed the preferred group size of white and Asian boys and girls in the United Kingdom. Data on this issue are important since it is possible that a preference for interacting in groups of a certain size could contribute to the own-race preference typically shown by children, in the same way as has been suggested for own-sex preferences.

PLAY/ACTIVITY PREFERENCES AS A FUNCTION OF RACE AND SEX

Another possible factor that could contribute to the own-race and/or the own-sex preference shown by children is a preference for engaging in different types of play and other activities. A number of studies have shown that boys and girls differ in the type of activity they prefer or at least engage in. In a study of infant school children in the United Kingdom, Tizard, Blatchford, Burke, Farquhar, and Plewis (1988) found a near significant tendency ($p < .06$) for boys to engage in permitted play activities, such as sand and water play and play in the home corner, more than girls. Lever (1976) reported that formal rule-governed games constituted 65% of the play of fifth-grade boys but only 35% of girl's play. The latter preferred turn-taking games that were characterized by a lack of competition and little role differentiation. Bloch (1989) found that 5- to 6-year-old boys' and girls' social play in Senegal differed. Girls preferred social pretence whereas boys engaged in more gross motor play. In a review of the literature on rough and tumble play (i.e., play fighting and chasing), Humphreys and Smith

(1984) reported that boys are usually observed to engage in more of this type of play than girls.

Outside of school, fifth-grade American girls were observed to spend more time in organized activities, including shopping with mother, whereas boys preferred unorganized activities including watching television and unsupervised play (Long and Henderson, 1973). Similarly, Timmer, Eccles, and O'Brien (1985) reported that boys spent more of their time on sport and less on housework and in personal care activities than girls. A recent study by Carpenter, Huston, and Spera (1989) also looked at gender preferences in daily activities, as well as amount of adult supervision and involvement. Children filled in a diary of out-of-school activities for seven consecutive days, and in an attempt to increase the internal validity, the 7–11-year-old participants received detailed training and financial incentive for filling in their diaries. Girls were found to spend significantly more time in away-from-home organized activities (such as clubs, outings, and parties), lessons and practice, and personal hygiene, but significantly less time in team games and out-of-home unorganized activities than boys.

With respect to own-race preference, few studies have provided data to assess the possibility that preferences for different activities could be responsible. One in the United Kingdom by Child (1983), involved children from similar ethnic backgrounds to those used in the present study, but younger (2–5 years). Observations of children's play behaviors were different 'play buses' in five different inner-city locations were made. Asian children were found to engage in less pretend play, were more likely to be passive (i.e., not playing), were less often actively engaged, and were less playful overall than white children. In infant school classrooms in the United Kingdom, Tizard et al. (1988) reported that black boys were more likely to "fool around" than their female counterparts or white boys and girls. Ariel and Sever (1980) compared and contrasted the contents, color, and dynamity of the pretend play of rural (indigenous) and urban Arabic children, and Israeli kibbutzim children. The two groups of Arabic children were found to differ in all three respects from the Israeli children. The authors pointed out that the rural children were likely to have less opportunity for extensive peer group contacts than the urban children, and that the ties between families of rural children that play together would have been weaker than between those of urban children. They concluded that "the content, structure and development of individual and social play are not universal, but culture-bound" (p. 174). This factor could contribute to the racial segregation observed in groups of children from different cultural backgrounds (or those from families with different cultural backgrounds).

More data are needed to assess the causal influence of activity preferences on race/gender cleavage in children's peer groups. The present study examined time spent in different categories of playground behavior as a function of both race and sex. In an attempt to improve the generalizability of our findings, data were collected at two schools. Thus, the influence of school differences, such as school climate, could be considered.

VALIDITY OF CHILDREN'S STATED PREFERENCES

We have already noted some of the possible limitations of sociometric indices of children's racial preferences, and it is likely that these may also relate to other reflective methods. In order to assess this possibility, we set out to measure the association between children's stated partner preferences for participating in a range of play and other activities, and their actual preferences observed during free play. Some earlier studies (Goodman, 1964) reported that children show more prejudice in projective tests than in real-life situations, and Hraba and Grant (1970) found no association between doll choice and actual friendship patterns. Due to the lack of recent studies, and to differences between the procedures of earlier investigations and our own, no firm predictions were made.

METHOD

Subjects

Altogether, 93 children from two classes in two schools (called here A and B) participated in this study. Most children were aged 8 or 9, although some were 10 years of age. At school A, there were 12 girls and 14 boys of parents born on the Indian subcontinent but who now resided in the United Kingdom. They were mainly Muslim[1] and the children are here called "Asian." There were also 11 girls and 7 boys of indigenous British parents, who are here called "white." At school B, there were 6 Asian girls, 9 Asian boys, 18 white girls, and 16 white boys. Altogether, there were 18 Asian girls, 23 Asian boys, 29 white girls, and 23 white boys. In addition to our subjects in the four target classes, at schools A and B there were 9 and 3 other/mixed race children respectively. The children came from mainly working-class backgrounds. The large majority of the Asian children had been born in Britain and were fluent in English. The racial composition of the two schools differed slightly, but in all cases they contained mainly Asian and white children with only about 10% of other or mixed race children. At school A, 44% of the children were Asian and 44% were white, and at school B the values were 21% and 70% respectively. The schools were located in the suburbs of a large industrial city in England.

Playground Observations

Playground observations were carried out from November to March. In each school, an observer recorded the activities and companions of each child in turn in a predetermined random order that was changed on successive observation periods. Each observation consisted of the observer locating a child, observing them for 1 minute to determine the activity in which they were participating, and recording what this activity was along with the number of male-female, Asian-white companions. If the child either changed activities or partners within this 1-minute period, the observer only recorded the details that were applicable at the end of this period. The 1-minute scans, during which no data were collected, were included to ensure that the observer could determine exactly what a focal child was doing, and who were their actual partners. We found that without this period, it was very difficult to do so, and observer reliability was low. As an example, if a focal child was engaged in a game of hide-and-seek as the seeker, the observer might erroneously record them as being alone and wandering aimlessly about the playground.

Observations were made during the mid-morning (10:00–10:15 A.M.) and lunch time (12:00 A.M.–1:00 P.M.) recesses. Each observation period was terminated when the whistle signaling the end of playtime was heard. The final complete 1-minute scan marked the end of data collection for that period. One observer (M. J.

Boulton) favored recording observations on a portable tape recorder, the tapes being later transcribed, whereas the other observer (a female undergraduate) favored writing down details of her observations on prepared data sheets. Most children were observed on 25 occasions, although for a small proportion of children the number of observations were slightly lower due to such things as absence from school or going home for lunch.

In order to ensure that the children's behavior was not influenced by the presence of an observer, the latter spent time on their respective playground during the two recesses each day for 4 weeks prior to the main data collection phase. The observers neither initiated interactions with the children nor responded with anything other than a brief reply to their initiations. Within this 4-week habituation period, the children appeared to lose interest in the observers, who were then free to move around the playground without changing their behavior. Only data collected after the habituation period are reported. This lead in time prior to data collection proper also enabled the first observer (the first author), who had had previous experience of this type of methodology, to train the second observer, who had not, and served as practice for the second observer. Measures of observer reliability were taken at the end of this period. The two observers recorded the activities and partners of 10 children on five occasions in the way described. For the number of male, female, Asian, and white partners each focal child had on each occasion, reliability estimates were based on the following 'categories': 0–2, 3/4, 5/6, and 7+ partners. To assess observer agreement, Cohen's Kappa was calculated. For companions, the Kappa value was significant at .87; for activity engaged in the reliability estimate was based on the five molar categories shown in Table 8.1, and Kappa was significant at .86. These significant Kappa's indicate that the difference in the way the data were recorded by the two observers did not influence what was recorded.

Preference Test

During November and December, children were taken individually from their classroom to a quiet room in the school. They were seated at a desk and asked if they would "play a game" with the experimenter. All consented. The interview that followed lasted about 20 minutes per child, but only the details of

Table 8.1.   Behavioral Categories

Rule games	*Positive social contact*
Skipping	Talk with peer
Clapping songs	Walk with peer
Chanting songs	Run with peer
Tag	Sit with peer
Delavio	Stand with peer
Marbles	Contact comfort
Soccer	Groom peer
Rounders	Swap collector's cards
Hopscotch	
Hide-and-seek	
Cricket	
Tennis	
Nonlocomotor Active	*Solitary*
Ball play	Any activity performed alone
Climb	
Dance	
Piggyback	
Gymnastics	
Support peer	

Other
Any activity which does not fall into another category

the Preference Test will be reported here. The children were shown six photographs, an Asian boy and girl, a boy and girl of parents with Afro-Caribbean origins, and a white boy and girl. All were unknown children of about the same age as the subjects. Each subject was asked to point to the photograph of the child they would "most like to play with in the playground"; this photograph was removed; and the child asked to indicate their second choice. This procedure was repeated for "sit next to in class," "invite home to your house," "have in your team for a game," and "ask for help with school work." For each subject, their first choice received a score of 2 and their second choice a score of 1 point. The total score for all these five activities given to each photograph were tallied and constituted the primary dependent variable. The maximum score for a particular type of child was therefore 10, and the minimum score 0.

RESULTS[2,3]

Sex of Preferred Partners[4]

In school B only, Binomial tests were used to determine whether children played with proportionally more same- or other-sex peers. For all groups, there was a significant preference for same-sex peers (Asian girls, n = 6, x = 0, p < .05; white girls, n = 18, x = 0, p < .001; Asian boys, n = 9, x = 0, p < .001; and white boys, n = 16, x = 0, p < .001; all 1 = tailed tests). A 2 (Race) X2 (Sex) analysis of variance (ANOVA) was also carried out to investigate possible race and sex differences in the proportion of opposite sex playground companions in this school. The Race main effect ($F[1,41]$ = 10.97, p < .002) was significant, but not the main Sex or interaction effect; white children (mean proportion of opposite-sex companions = 6.47) had more opposite sex playground companions than did Asian children (mean = 2.01).

Playmate Preference, Group Size, Number of Different Playmates, and Activity Preference Analyses

For each subject, the mean proportion of Asian and white companions, the mean group size (regardless of race and sex), the mean number of different companions (regardless of race and sex), and the mean proportion of time spent in the four main activities were calculated. Group means for Asian and white and female and male subjects were then calculated (see Table 8.2). Each of these measures was analyzed using a 2 (School) X2 (Race) X2 (Sex) ANOVA, and main effects are also shown in Table 8.2. Significant two-way interactions are discussed in the text.

Proportion of Asian Playmates

Boys and girls did not differ in the proportion of Asian peers they played with, but Asian children associated with Asian peers to a significantly greater extent than did white children (Table 8.2). There was a significant SchoolXRace interaction ($F[1,82]$ = 25.4, p < .001), indicating that the own-race preference was greater among the Asian children at school B (mean proportion of Asian playmates = 90.7) than at school A (mean = 78.7), whereas the preference for Asian peers was greater among

Table 8.2.   Mean Group Size, Number of Different Playmates, Proportion of White and Asian Playmates, and Proportion of Time Spent in Three Activities by Female and Male Asian and White Children, and School, Race, and Sex Main Effects

						F values	
	Female	Male	Asian	White	School	Race	Sex
Proportion of Asian playmates	48.3%	49.9%	84.7%	13.4%	1.61	498.7***	0.05
Proportion of white playmates	46.9%	39.5%	12.8%	73.5%	0.14	391.4***	3.31
Group size	3.1	6.6	3.8	5.8	.12	14.9***	44.5***
No. of playmates[a]	4.8	7.6	3.9	8.5	1.35	30.7***	12.0***
Proportion of time in rule games	35.6%	64.7%	46.4%	53.9%	0.12	1.75	32.2***
Proportion of time in positive social	44.2%	12.8%	33.4%	23.6%	1.63	5.97*	60.3***
Proportion of time alone	9.8%	11.0%	10.7%	10.8%	30.2***	0.01	0.26

d.f. = 1,82, except [a] d.f. = 1,81. *p < .05, **p < .01, ***p < .001.

white children at school A (mean = 21.6) than at school B (mean = 5.2). There was also a significant RaceXSex interaction ($F[1,82] = 17.21$, $p < .001$); Asian girls (mean = 89.6) played with more Asian peers than did Asian boys (mean = 79.9), whereas white boys (mean = 19.9) played with more Asian peers than did white girls (mean = 7.0).

Proportion of White Playmates

White children played with a greater proportion of white peers than did Asian children, and girls played with a greater proportion of white peers than was the case for boys (Table 8.2). A significant SchoolXRace interaction ($F[1,81] = 12.93$, $p < .001$) indicated that white children at school B (mean proportion of white playmates = 80.7) played with a greater proportion of white peers than was the case at school A (mean = 66.3), whereas Asian children at school A (mean = 17.3) played with a greater proportion of white peers than was the case at school B (mean = 8.3). A significant RaceXSex interaction ($F[1,81] = 25.11$, $p < .001$) showed that whereas white girls (mean = 84.4) had a greater proportion of white playmates than white boys (mean = 62.7) had, Asian boys (mean = 16.2) had more white playmates than was the case for Asian girls (mean = 9.4).

Preferred Group Size, and Number of Different Playground Companions

Regardless of the race and sex of peers, white children played in significantly lager groups than Asian children, and boys played in significantly larger groups than girls (Table 8.2).

Mirroring the results for preferred group size, white children played with a significantly greater number of different peers than did Asian children, and boys played with significantly more peers than did girls did (Table 8.2).

Preferred Activities on the Playground

Boys spent a significantly greater proportion of their time in *games with rules* than girls. The opposite was the case for time spent in *positive social contact* (Table 8.2). In this latter group of activities, there was also a significant main effect for race, with Asian children showing more *positive social contact* than white children, and a significant SexXSchool interaction ($F[1,82] = 6.220$, $p < .05$); boys and girls did not differ at school B whereas at school A, boys spent more time in *positive social contact* than girls. For time spent *alone*, only the school main effect was significant, with children at school A spending significantly more time *alone* than those at school B.

Stated Activity Partner Preferences

Mean preferences scores from the Preference Test for Asian and white boys and girls are shown in Table 8.3, along with the outcomes of Kruskall-Wallace H tests and multiple comparisons. For each of the four groups of children at the two schools, there was a highly significant preference. For both boys and girls, there was a clear preference for sharing activities with same-sex children over other-sex children. Superimposed on this own-sex preference was an own-race preference in most of the groups; for four out of the eight groups, these children showed a significant preference for selecting children that were of similar race *and* gender to themselves. For the other four groups, similar race/gender children were preferred to the same

Table 8.3. Results of Preference Test: Mean Preferences Shown by White and Asian Boys and Girls at Each School, and Results of Kruskall-Wallace H Tests and Multiple Comparisons

	WB^a	WG^b	AB^c	AG^d	CB^e	CG^f	H^g	Multiple comparisons
White girls at A	.6	6.5	0.0	2.5	.5	4.7	39.0*	WG = CG > AG > WB = CB > AB
White girls at B	1.0	6.9	.7	2.1	.4	3.9	21.9*	WG > CG > AG = WB > CB > AB
Asian girls at A	.4	5.9	.7	7.0	0.0	1.0	51.2*	AG > WG > CG > AB > WB > CB
Asian girls at B	.8	6.2	.3	5.8	.2	1.8	22.5*	WG = AG > CG > WB = AB = CB
White boys at A	4.9	.3	3.0	.1	5.9	.4	31.0*	WB = CB > AB > CG = WG = AG
White boys at B	8.2	1.2	2.5	0.0	2.8	.4	34.0*	WB > CB > AB > WG = CG = AG
Asian boys at A	4.9	0.0	5.7	.1	3.8	.4	63.8*	AB = WB > CB > CG > AG > WG
Asian boys at B	4.6	.2	8.1	.3	1.6	.2	40.1*	AB > WB > CB > AG > WG = CG

[a]White boys; [b]White girls; [c]Asian boys; [d]Asian girls; [e]Afro-Caribbean boys; [f]Afro-Caribbean girls. [g]d.f. = 5. *p < .001.

extent as another "type" of child; at school A, the white girls and the white boys preferred same-sex Afro-Caribbean children to the same extent as they preferred white same-sex children, and Asian boys at School A and Asian girls at school B preferred same-sex white children to the same extent as they preferred Asian same-sex children.

Correlation between Stated and Observed Activity Partner Preferences

Data from the Preference Test were correlated with observed preferences using Spearman's Rank Correlation Coefficient, that is, individual children's preference score for the two Asian children shown in the Preference Test were correlated with the mean proportion of Asian playmates they had on the playground, and then their preference score for the two white children in the Preference Test were correlated with the mean proportion of white playmates they had. Separate tests were performed for Asian and white girls' and boys' preferences for Asian and white children. The correlations between white girls' (n = 29) stated and observed preferences for whites (r_s = .16) and for Asians (r_s = .05), and those between Asian girls' (n = 16) stated and observed preferences for whites (r_s = −.34) and for Asians (r_s = − .04) were all nonsignificant.

The correlations between these two measures for white boys' (n = 23) preference for Asians (r_s = .16), and Asian boys' (n = 21) preference for whites (r_s = .04) were also nonsignificant. However, the correlations for white boys' preferences for whites (r_s = .50, p < .05) and for Asian boys' preferences for Asians (r_s = .57, p < .01) were both significant.

DISCUSSION

Sex of Preferred Partners

At school B, in line with previous findings, children were found to spend more of their free time on the playground with same-sex peers. Our data also indicated a significant effect of race on this measure; white children had more opposite-sex companions on the playground than did Asian children. There is no obvious way of accounting for this differential sex cleavage in the two racial groups studied here, but socializing practices could be an important factor.

Race of Preferred Partners

Both the Asian and white children in our sample exhibited a very highly significant preference for spending time with other own-race peers. This result extends the similar own-race preferences shown by black and white children in the United States. Clearly, the bringing together of children of disparate racial backgrounds and origins in schools is of itself an insufficient condition to foster appreciable levels of cross-race interactions. The idea that desegregation can by itself promote more positive attitudes and behavior between children of different racial origins in the United States has been shown to be naive, and our data suggest the same to be true in the United Kingdom. As long ago as 1954, Allport, in his Contact Theory, proposed that desegregation may actually bolster existing negative stereotypes and/or lead to more hostility being directed towards the outgroup, if the majority group enjoyed greater status than the minority group. In order to foster cross-race interactions and perceptions of a positive nature, Allport argued the need for institutional support and encouragement. Some studies (e.g., Schofield, 1982) have shown that cross-race interactions can be increased if school authorities take steps to ensure that within school, racial differences are played down and cross-race interactions supported. Cohen (1982) has even suggested that in those situations where negative attitudes are strong and deeply entrenched, it may be necessary for the status of the minority group to be, at least temporarily, elevated above that of the majority group. This approach is held to increase the self-esteem of the former, while at the same time reducing mutual hostility and rejection.

Our results have also shown that the two sexes differ in the extent to which they favor own-race peers. Both Asian and white boys played with proportionally more other-race peers, and proportionally fewer own-race peers, than did their female counterparts. These findings are consistent with those of Schofield and Sagar (1977) and Schofield and Francis (1982) for black and white children in the United States.

Significant interaction effects involving the school factor were also obtained, notably the own-race preference among both Asian and white children at school B was stronger than that at school A. This finding suggests that more equal racial mixes may result in greater cross-race preferences in school settings, at least for this age group and racial mix of children. However, it should not be freely generalized to other age groups and/or racial mixes, as the available evidence is mixed (see Aboud, 1988). Another variable that could be influential in this respect is the climate created by school personnel. Clearly school differences need to be examined in more detail in relation to the mixing of children from different racial backgrounds.

Size of Preferred Group, and Number of Different Playground Companions

In line with previous research findings, we found that boys played or associated with peers in larger groups than girls. We have also demonstrated that white children preferred to be in larger groups than Asian children. These findings are probably responsible for the corresponding results that boys had a greater number of different playground companions than did girls, and that white children had significantly more than Asian children.

Preference for groups of a certain size could be one factor that is responsible for the sex and race cleavage reported above. Taken together with the findings for differences in activity preferences (see below), researchers need to consider in the future whether, say, the preference for larger groups by boys precedes their greater preference for rule games such as soccer, or conversely, whether their preference for such games precedes their preference for larger groups.

Preferred Activities on the Playground

With respect to race, Asian and white children did not differ significantly in the proportion of time they spent in *rule games*, or were *alone*. However, Asian children spent significantly more time in *positive social contact* than did white children. In terms of sex differences, boys spent significantly more time in *rule games*, but less time in *positive social contact* than girls. The latter two results can possibly explain the differences in own-race preferences shown by boys and girls which was reported above. The findings that boys were more likely to interact with other-race peers relative to girls could be a consequence of a differential preference for engaging in certain playground activities. Boys spent about two-thirds of their time in *rule games*, girls about half that amount. Typically, this class of activity for boys consisted of soccer and to a lesser extent rule-bound chase games. In these activities, groups of 10 or more were commonplace. Within such a context, racial considerations may be less important for the children than in situations where fewer peers are present, as is typically the case for girls. For example, "real" soccer involves teams of 11 players and therefore in children's groups, other-race peers may be accepted in order to make the game more realistic. Moreover, participants in such a large-scale game as soccer do not have to talk to one another. Thus, the greater degree of cross-race contact shown by boys relative to girls may not necessarily reflect a greater tolerance or preference for other-race peers, but instead may be a consequence of their desire to take part in games that require many participants. This idea has similarities with the proposition of Finkelstein and Haskins (1983) who found that both black and white kindergarten children preferred same-color peers, and that the former emitted relatively more negative behaviors and commands, but talked less than the latter. They stated that their findings may "imply that black and white children are characterized by different styles of social interaction. It may follow that such differences . . . contribute to the development of children's preferences for same-color peers" (p. 508).

Few researchers have considered racial interactions as a function of activity engaged in. One that has, though, is Polgar (1978), who looked at the process of game playing among sixth graders in U.S. schools in three contexts: games in which all the children are of the same race, those in which the group or team includes individuals of different races, and those in which a team of one race opposes a team of a different race. Details of how the teams were formed, how the rules developed, and how game progressed, in terms of duration and interruptions, were noted. Polgar reported that mixed-race teams were the least stable, had problems with their organization, suffered frequent interruptions and disputes over the rules, and were mostly of short duration. However, these data were descriptive and more importantly were based on only seven examples of games involving mixed race teams. In our study, although formal data were not collected on this issue, it appeared that games involving mixed-race teams were not as unsatisfactory for the participants as was the case for Polgar's subjects. Such games typically lasted for long periods, often for the whole of a recess period, and involved relatively few disputes. The latter tended to be centered on such things as whether or not a goal should be allowed, or a tackle should be penalized, rather than on the rules per se. This difference between the behavior of the children in our sample and those of Polgar might be due to the fact that for our subjects, soccer was such a well-known game that the rules were clearly understood by all the children at this age, whereas Polgar's subjects may have engaged in activities that were less common or well-known by one or other racial group. On the basis of this rather limited evidence, it is tempting to speculate that different styles of interaction and/or different degrees of preference/familiarity for certain activities could contribute to the race cleavage reported here and elsewhere.

Stated Racial Preferences

In both schools investigated in this study, the four subgroups of female-male Asian-white children showed clear and significant preferences for sharing activities with unknown children that were of similar sex and race to themselves. Photographs of children who were of similar sex *and* race to the subject were selected as either the first or second choice. On this test, then, despite the fact that our subjects were asked about sharing activities with *unknown* children, whose personal characteristics and suitability for the activities in question could only be guessed, race and sex were of paramount importance. Although we tried to ensure that the children in the photographs were equal in such respects as physical attractiveness, facial expressions, and standard of dress, the influence of these factors cannot be ruled out. Nevertheless, the fact that *both* the Asian and white children showed mostly own-race preferences suggests that these influences were minimal.

Another interesting aspect of our results concerns the relative preference of the white subjects for Asian and black children. In all four cases, black children were preferred significantly more than Asian children. Given that each school contained only a small proportion of black children but that Asian children made up 21% and 44%, one implication of this result may be that mere contact will not on its own bring about positive attitudes and behavior on the part of the majority group. As such, Allport's Contact Theory, discussed above, has received some support from our data.

The data for the Asian children indicate that, like the white children, they clearly preferred own-race children, but in addition, they also preferred white children significantly more than black children. In an attempt to improve their feelings of self-worth, their perceptions of another minority group (in this case blacks) could have been negative.

Correlations between Stated and Observed Racial Preferences

Some early studies found little correspondence between preferences for known and unknown children (Goodman, 1964; Hraba and Grant, 1970). A more recent study by Davey and Mullin (1980), however, reported that children who named no other-race peers as friends were significantly more likely to pick a photograph of an unknown own-race (rather than an other-race) child as the "one they would most like to be." Nevertheless, when they considered the data from the white and West Indian children separately, only those from the white children reached significance. Thus, most of the available data suggest only minimal correspondence between preferences based on projective tests and those actually observed. A similar trend was obtained in our study. In only two cases out of eight (Asian boys' preferences for Asian children, and white boys' preferences for white children) were the correlations between stated preferences for unknown children and observed preferences for known children significant. Are we to interpret these findings as suggesting that the validity of stated preferences is low? Certainly this possibility needs to be kept in mind, but several other factors need also to be considered. Here, we correlated the proportion of actual Asian/white playmates a child had with a composite preference score made up of their preferences for sharing a range of different activities (such as sitting next to a child in class, and asking for help with schoolwork). As we suggested earlier, it is possible that racial preferences may vary as a function of activity, so that, for example, racial considerations may not influence who children would ask for help with their schoolwork as much as who they would chose to play with on the playground. While these contentions must remain speculative at present, they would seem to suggest a fruitful area for empirical enquiry.

A second reason for the lack of association between stated and observed preferences by most of our subgroups of children could be because the Preference Test was based on preferences for unknown children, whereas we observed their preferences for known peers. It is possible, though as yet untested, that in contrast to perceptions of unfamiliar peers, perceptions of known peers may be less likely to be influenced by racial considerations. Instead, how good a peer is at soccer, for example, may be a more important determinant of him/her being selected as a playmate than his/her ethnic origin. This view is similar to that proposed by Teplin (1977) when he considered the lack of association between choices of unknown children in photographs and desired friendship choices of known peers (measured with sociometry).

Davey and Mullin (1980) have proposed that we should be more disturbed if there *was* a close correspondence between preferences for known and unknown children. They stated, "a close relationship between imaginary photo-choice and choice in a real-life situation would imply that children's stereotypes were already so inflexible that the children were no longer amendable to the discovery of characteristics which conflict with their own ethnic expectations" (pp. 249–250). This idea ties in with research in social psychology on the relationship between attitudes and overt behavior. Generally, this relationship is found to be only slight (see Wicker, 1969, for a review). Wicker suggests that factors other than attitudes per se can influence behavior. He divides these personal factors (such as competing motives) and situational factors (such as expected consequences of various acts).

Given this perspective, our results should, perhaps, not be taken as challenging the validity of children's stated preferences, but instead as evidence for some, albeit limited, flexibility in children's selection of who to play with, above simple racial considerations.

Methodological Limitations

The present study can be criticized in several ways on methodological grounds. The sample size was small, and some of the subgroups (e.g., Asian girls) were only just acceptable, in terms of size, for statistical analyses. Moreover, the extended sampling period of November through March may mean that developmental and/or social competence effects have been confounded with the children's behavior over time.

All these points mean that the conclusions drawn in this chapter must remain tentative until a larger scale study, that overcomes the methodological limitations, has been carried out. Nevertheless, the results presented here do suggest that such an investigation would be a worthwhile venture.

SUMMARY AND CONCLUSIONS

Our data indicate that children's preferences for partners and activities vary strongly as a function of sex and race. We have demonstrated that in ethnically mixed schools in the United Kingdom, own-sex and race preferences are as apparent as those reported in the United States. Own-race choices are less marked in boys, perhaps because of situational factors.

We also found a considerable lack of correspondence between children's stated and observed racial preferences, and some reasons for this were discussed. This finding reinforces our belief that direct observations of children in relatively unconstrained situations, such as the school playground, are essential in our attempts to understand children's experiences in the peer group, and their relations with other-race peers in particular. Interview data have their own intrinsic interest and value as regards children's beliefs, but observational data can reliably inform us of their actual behavioral experiences in this domain.

NOTES

1. We included a note on the religion of the Asian children because of the trend in the (UK) literature, and the advice of Asian researchers, to differentiate between subgroups of Asian peoples (Weinreich, P., and Kelly, A. "Collectivism and individualism in identity development: Muslim British and Anglo-Saxon British identities." Paper presented at the Workshop on Individualism and Collectivism, Seoul, Korea, July 9–13, 1990). We did not enquire as to the religious backgrounds of the white children as we have no reason to suppose it would be an important factor. However, his is an interesting empirical question that should perhaps be pursued.

2. The unequal cell sizes were controlled for in the Analysis of Variance. Contact scores were "corrected" for the different number of same and opposite race children in each school.

3. Arc-sine transformations were used on the proportion scores.

4. At school A, data on the sex of the companions of focal children were not recorded.

REFERENCES

Aboud, F. E. (1988). *Children and prejudice.* Oxford: Basil Blackwell Ltd.

Allport, G. (1954). *The nature of prejudice.* Cambridge, MA: Addison-Wesley.

Amir, Y. (1976). The role of intergroup contact in change of prejudice and ethnic relations. In P. Katz (Ed.), *Towards the elimination of racism.* New York: Pergamon.

Ariel, S., and Sever, I. (1980). Play in the desert and play in the town: On play activities of Bedouin children. In H. Schwartzman (Ed.), *Play and culture* (pp. 164–174). West Point, NY: Leisure Press.

Barber, R. W. (1968). The effects of open enrollment and anti-negro and anti-white prejudices among junior high school students in Rochester, New York. Unpublished doctoral dissertation, University of Rochester.

Bianchi, B., and Bakeman, R. (1978). Sex-typed affiliation preferences observed in preschoolers: Traditional and open school differences. *Child Development, 49,* 910–912.

Bloch, M. N. (1989). Young girls and boys play at home and in the community: A cultural-ecological framework. In M. N. Bloch and A. D. Pellegrini (Eds.), *The ecological context of children's play* (pp. 120–154). Norwood: Ablex Publishing Corporation.

Bloch, M. N., and Pellegrini, A. D. (1989). Ways of looking at children, context, and play. In M. N. Bloch and A. D. Pellegrini (Eds.), *The ecological context of children's play* (pp. 1–15). Norwood: Ablex Publishing Corporation.

Boulton, M. J., and Smith, P. K. (1989). Issues in the study of children's rough-and-tumble play. In M. N. Bloch and A. D. Pellegrini (Eds.), *The ecological context of children's play* (pp. 57–83). Norwood: Ablex Publishing Corporation.

Carithers, M. W. (1970). School desegregation and racial cleavage, 1954–1970: A review of the literature. *Journal of Social Issues, 26,* 25–47.

Carpenter, C. J., Huston, A. C., and Spera, L. (1989). Children's use of time in their everyday activities during middle childhood. In M. N. Bloch and A. D. Pellegrini (Eds.), *The ecological context of children's play* (pp. 165–190). Norwood: Ablex Publishing Corporation.

Child, E. (1983). Play and culture: A study of English and Asian children. *Leisure Studies, 2,* 169–186.

Cohen, E. (1975). The effects of desegregation on race relations. *Law and Contemporary Problems, 39,* 271–299.

———. (1982). Expectation states and interracial interaction in school settings. *Annual Review of Sociology.* Palo Alto, CA: Annual Review.

Crooks, R. C. (1970). The effects of an interracial preschool program upon racial preference, knowledge of racial differences and racial identification. *Journal of Social Issues, 26,* 137–144.

Daniels-Beirness, T. M., and LeShano, S. (1988). Children's social relationships outside of school. Paper presented at the NATO Advanced Study Institute: Social Competence in Developmental Perspective, Savoy, France.

Davey, A. G., and Mullin, P. N. (1980). Ethnic identification and preference of British primary school children. *Journal of Child Psychology and Psychiatry, 21,* 241–251.

Finkelstein, N. W., and Haskins, R. (1983). Kindergarten children prefer same-color peers. *Child Development, 54,* 502–508.

Gardener, B. B., Wright, B. D., and Dee, R. (1970). *The effect of busing black ghetto children into white suburban schools.* ERIC Document Reproduction Service No. ED 048 389.

Goodman, M. E. (1964). *Race awareness in young children.* New York: Collier Books.

Gottman, J. M. (1986). The world of coordinated play: Same- and cross-sex friendship in young children. In J. M. Gottman and J. G. Parker (Eds.), *Conversations of friends: Speculations on affective development* (pp. 139–191). Cambridge, UK: Cambridge University Press.

Hraba, J., and Grant, G. (1970). Black is beautiful: A re-examination of racial preference and identification. *Journal of Personality and Social Psychology, 16,* 398–402.

Humphreys, A. P., and Smith, P. K. (1984). Rough and tumble in preschool and playground. In P. K. Smith (Ed.), *Play in animals and humans.* Oxford, England: Basil Blackwell.

LaFreniere, P., Strayer, F. F., and Gauthier, R. (1984). The emergence of same-sex affiliative preferences among preschool peers: A developmental/ethological perspective. *Child Development, 55,* 1958–1965.

Laosa, L. M., and Brophy, J. E. (1972). Effects of sex and birth order on sex-role development and intelligence among kindergarten children. *Developmental Psychology, 6,* 409–415.

Lever, J. (1976). Sex differences in the games children play. *Social Problems, 23,* 478–487.

———. (1978). Sex differences in the complexity of children's play. *American Sociological Review, 43,* 471–483.

Lockheed, M., and Klein, S. (1985). Sex equality in classroom organization and climate. In S. Klein (Ed.), *Handbook for achieving sex equality through education* (pp. 263–284). Baltimore: John Hopkins University Press.

Long, B. H., and Henderson, E. H. (1973, January). Children's use of time: Some personal and social correlates. *Elementary School Journal,* 193–199.

Maccoby, E. E., and Jacklin, C. N. (in press). Gender segregation in childhood. In H. Reese (Ed.), *Advances in child behavior and development.*

McWhirt, R. A. (1967). The effects of desegregation on prejudice, academic aspiration and the self-concept of tenth grade students. Unpublished doctoral dissertation, University of South Carolina.

Omark, D. R., Omark, M., and Edelman, M. S. (1975). Formation of dominance hierarchies in young children: Action and perception. In T. Williams (Ed.), *Psychological anthropology* (pp. 289–315). The Hague: Mouton.

Polgar, S. K. (1978). Modeling social relations in cross-color play. *Anthropology and Education Quarterly, 9*, 283–289.

Schofield, J. W. (1978). School desegregation and intergroup relations. In D. Bar-Tal and L. Saxe (Eds.), *Social psychology of education: Theory and research.* Washington, DC: Hemisphere Press.

————. (1982). *Black and white in school: Trust tension or tolerance?* New York: Preager.

Schofield, J. W., and Francis, W. D. (1982). An observational study of peer interactions in racially mixed "accelerated" classrooms. *Journal of Educational Psychology, 74*, 722–732

Schofield, J. W., and Sagar, H. A. (1977). Peer interaction patterns in an integrated middle school. *Sociometry, 40*, 130–138.

Scott, K. P. (1984). *Teaching social interaction skills: Perspectives on cross-sex communication.* ERIC Document No. AN ED 252445.

Smith, P. K., and Connolly, K. J. (1980). *The ecology of preschool behaviour.* Cambridge, England: Cambridge University Press.

Stephan, W. G. (1978). School desegregation: An evaluation of predictions made in Brown v. Board of Education. *Psychological Bulletin, 85*, 217–238.

St John, N. (1975). *School desegregation: Outcomes for children.* New York: Wiley.

Swadener, E. B., and Johnson, J. E. (1989). Play in diverse social contexts: Parent and teacher roles. In M. N. Bloch and A. D. Pellegrini (Eds.), *The ecological context of children's play* (pp. 214–244). Norwood: Ablex Publishing Corporation.

Teplin, L. A. (1977). Preference versus prejudice: A multi-method analysis of children's discrepant racial choices. *Social Science Quarterly, 58*, 390–406.

Timmer, S. G., Eccles, J., and O'Brien, K. (1985). How children use time. In F. T. Juster and F. P. Stafford (Eds.), *Time, goods, and well-being.* Ann Arbor: University of Michigan, Institute for Social Research.

Tizard, B., Blatchford, P., Burke, J., Farquhar, C., and Plewis, I. (1988). Young children at school in the inner city. London and Hillsdale (NJ): Lawrence Erlbaum Associates.

Waldrop, M. F., and Halverson, C. F. (1975). Intensive and extensive peer behavior: Longitudinal and cross-sectional analyses. *Child Development, 46,* 19–26.

Whiting, B. B. (1980). Culture and social behavior. *Ethos, 2,* 95–116.

Wicker, A. W. (1969). Attitudes versus actions: The relationship of verbal and overt responses to attitude objects. *Journal Social Issues, 25,* 41–78.

PART IV

FAMILY BACKGROUND INFLUENCES AND CHILDREN'S PLAYGROUND BEHAVIOR

9

GREGORY S. PETTIT AND AMANDA W. HARRIST

Children's Aggressive and Socially Unskilled Playground Behavior With Peers: Origins in Early Family Relations*

INTRODUCTION

The importance of peer relations in children's social development is now widely acknowledged. As will become apparent
later in this review, research focusing on children's playground
behavior has been particularly instrumental in illuminating the
link between peer interaction and subsequent developmental
outcomes. When peer-directed behaviors are competence-
enhancing (i.e., leading to positive evaluations by peers and
teachers), children profit by being viewed as desirable playmates, which in turn provides significant socialization benefits
(e.g., more frequent and high-quality interactions with a variety
of peers; see Berndt and Ladd, 1989). Conversely, children's
behaviors that antagonize peers, or result in exclusion from
play with peers, are much less likely to lead to social benefits.
In fact, these patterns of behavior instead may lead to rejection
by one's peers and the concomitant social disadvantages associated with peer rejection (Parker and Asher, 1987).

Given the apparent developmental significance of children's
playground interactions with peers, the question as to the origins
of these interactional styles looms as one of great importance.
Several recent reviews (e.g., Cohn, Patterson, and Christopoulos,
1991; Putallaz and Heflin, 1990) have documented both direct
and indirect influences that parents may have on their children's

*Preparation of this chapter was supported in part by NIMH Research Grant
MH42498, awarded to K. A. Dodge, G. S. Pettit, and J. E. Bates. Thanks are due
Melinda Raab, Beverly Cree, and Michael Rodin for their assistance in data
collection and coding. Jacquelyn Mize provided helpful commentary on an earlier version of this chapter.

development of social interactional styles. One of the most extensively studied and perhaps most complex sources of influence is that of the child's relationship with the parent(s). Research in this area generally is based on the assumption that children acquire a set of social-behavioral orientations as a consequence of their repeated and familiar interactions with their parents, and that these orientations somehow carry over into the peer group. The critical issue thus becomes one of identifying those features of the parent-child relationship that are most important for the development of peer competence.

Our work in this area has been guided by recent findings emerging from studies of parent-child interaction patterns in families with antisocial children (e.g., Gardner, 1989; Wahler and Dumas, 1986). We believe that these findings provide new insights into the processes by which children acquire competent (or incompetent) interactional styles. Central features of this literature are the notions of social contingency and circumspection. Here, social contingency refers to the synchronization or matching of individuals' behavior within an interactional episode. Circumspection is defined as the appropriate use of situational cues to guide interpersonal behavior.

In the sections that follow we first present a review of selected research on the behavioral predictors of children's peer competence, emphasizing the role of interactional synchrony and circumspection. We argue that children judged to be socially competent by peers and teachers are more likely than socially ineffective children to (a) engage their peers in situationally appropriate (i.e., context dependent) ways, and (b) have interactions with peers that are characterized by "positive" synchrony (i.e., interactions in which the children respond in a positive way to peer behavior and/or initiate positive behavior that elicits positive behavioral responses from peers). We then examine evidence of deficiency in use of social-contextual cues and an absence of interactional synchrony in families with behavior problem children. These family characteristics are shown to bear close resemblance to the interpersonal deficits found among children with peer relationship problems. We conclude by presenting data from our own ongoing longitudinal study of family influences on children's development of social competence. These data are drawn from naturalistic observations of families interacting with their preschool-aged children in their homes and observations of the children's playground and classroom interactions with peers several months later in kindergarten.

BEHAVIORAL CORRELATES OF PEER ACCEPTANCE: THE ROLE OF SYNCHRONY

Children's behavioral orientations in peer interaction have been observed in a variety of contexts. Children's naturally occurring behavior at school has been examined in both classroom and playground settings (e.g., Dodge, Pettit, McClaskey, and Brown, 1986; Pettit, McClaskey, Brown, and Dodge, 1987; Ladd and Price, 1987; Ladd, Price, and Hart, 1988), with the aim of discovering which aspects of social behavior are most predictive of children's competence with peers (based on teacher, observer, or peer assessments). In other studies children have been observed (and their behavior typically videorecorded) in laboratory analogue (e.g., Dodge, Schlundt, Schocken, and Degulach, 1983; Dodge et al., 1986) and experimental play group (e.g., Dodge, Coie, Pettit, and Price, 1990; Pettit, Bakshi, Dodge, and Coie, 1990) settings, with the goal of capturing variations in children's social behaviors that are either infrequent or difficult to observe in more naturalistic contexts, but that may nonetheless have important consequences for peer interaction. Taken as a whole, the results from these studies have been consistent (with some exceptions; see below) in suggesting that socially competent children behave in more positive or prosocial ways with peers, whereas children who are rejected by their peers tend to display higher rates of antisocial, aggressive behavior (Dodge et al., 1990; Ladd, 1983; Ladd et al., 1988; Putallaz, 1983). It is important to note that results from longitudinal studies (e.g., Dodge et al., 1990; Ladd et al., 1988) suggest that the direction of influence in these relations runs from behavior to social status. That is, behavioral qualities of children's interactions with peers determine subsequent status to a greater degree than status determines variations in later peer-directed behavior.

The above conclusions represent a simplification of what is no doubt a considerably complex social-interactive process. Why, for example, do aggressive children continue to behave in an antisocial manner in the face of continued rejection by peers?

What have aggressive children learned about social relationships that leads them to behave in such ways in the first place? Conversely, what rules and expectations have socially effective children learned in their early experiences, and how are these expectations translated into successful behavioral performance with peers? We have found Asher's (1983) characterization of competent functioning to be useful as a framework for further examination of the behavioral-correlates issue in the peer relations literature. Asher describes three dimensions of social effectiveness with peers. First, competent children behave with peers in ways that are *relevant* to the ongoing peer activity. This requires that children "have the ability to read the social situation and adapt their behavior to the ongoing flow of interaction" (1983, p. 1428). The second social-behavioral dimension is *responsiveness*, or responding positively and appropriately to the social initiations of peers. The third dimension reflects a process view whereby competent children move toward greater familiarity (or friendship) with peers in a gradual, indirect way.

The first two dimensions described by Asher correspond to the social contingency-circumspection perspective guiding our own current work. A substantial body of observational research findings supports the contention that competent children are more "tuned in" to contextual-situational contingencies and are more likely to synchronize their behavior with that of their peers. Socially ineffective children, on the other hand, are less attentive to social-environmental cues and achieve synchrony only by engaging their peers in increasingly coercive aggressive cycles. In a comparison of the classroom and playground behavior of popular, rejected, and neglected elementary school-aged children, Dodge, Coie, and Brakke (1982) found that rejected children made more social approaches than did popular children in the classroom (and were rebuffed at a high rate), but fewer such approaches on the playground. Rejected children also were more likely to engage in task-inappropriate solitary activity (classroom only), and were more aggressive than other children, especially on the playground. Dodge et al. interpret these findings as suggesting that "rejected children have not learned to discriminate the work context from the play context. Indeed, the behavior of the rejected children varied less as a function of context than did the behavior of the popular children" (1982, pp. 406–407).

Ladd (1983) also observed the playground behavior of popular and rejected elementary school-aged children, with special focus on the social network characteristics of the children's groups. Playgrounds provide a unique setting for observing naturally occurring configurations of peer contact, since mixing with a variety of children—especially children of different ages—is usually possible at school only on playgrounds. Rejected children were found to engage in high levels of aversive exchanges with peers, and low levels of relationship-enhancing (i.e., cooperative) exchanges. Rejected children also spent more time disengaged from their peers. The social networks of rejected children were less mature than those of other children, inasmuch as they were marked by play in smaller groups composed of younger and/or unpopular children. Ladd (1983) speculates that the comparatively impoverished social networks of rejected children may limit their ability to develop the knowledge and skills necessary for success in the broader peer context. Indeed, the networks of popular children, with their more complex play and egalitarian structure, likely require a higher degree of social sophistication (e.g., awareness, context discrimination, perspective taking) than is the case for rejected children's networks.

In a subsequent study, Ladd and Price (1987) demonstrated that preschoolers' behavioral orientations with peers during classroom free play were stable over time, and predictive of subsequent kindergarten adjustment. Social competence (based on teacher ratings and peer sociometrics) was positively related to cooperative play and the extensivity of peer contacts. That is, socially competent children engaged in cooperative play and social conversation with a variety of different peers. Peer rejection and teacher-rated aggression were predicted by observed rough play (preschool only), aggression, and negative contacts with peers. Since these positive and negative behavioral orientations were found to be stable (the former especially for girls; the latter mainly for boys) from preschool to kindergarten, Ladd and price conclude that they reflect social dispositions that are maintained across time and partners.

Other studies have examined aspects of child-peer behavioral matching variously termed synchrony, behavioral decentration, and interactional coherence. In two separate laboratory studies (one a group entry analogue and the other an experimental play group) comparing popular, rejected, and neglected children, Dodge et al. (1983) found that popular children were less likely to disrupt the group or otherwise draw unfavorable attention to themselves. Rejected children engaged in 10 times as many disruptive entry attempts (e.g., by physically asserting themselves at inopportune times) as popular children. Neglected children were more likely to hover on the periphery and to be ignored by the other children. Interestingly, even when popular and rejected children used the same tactic, peers were more likely to respond negatively to the rejected children. These findings led Dodge et al. (1983) to propose a pattern of successful play with peers they termed *behavioral decentration*, as indicated by mimicking the behavior of the group and making group-relevant statements.

Putallaz (1983) also employed the peer group entry analogue technique to examine relations among social behavior, "perceptual" accuracy, and social status in first-grade boys. Boys whose behaviors were coded as most relevant to the ongoing peer play had higher sociometric ratings 4 months later than boys whose behaviors were irrelevant or tangential. Surprisingly, interfering behavior (i.e., acting in ways that were disruptive to the group's activity) did not predict sociometric status. The strongest prediction of social status was found for the interaction of behavioral relevance and perceptual accuracy. This latter measure reflects the ability to accurately identify the general content of the other boys' behavior (based on a post-session review of a videotape of the session). Boys who were comparatively accurate in their assessments of the peers' behavior *and* whose observed behavior was most relevant to ongoing peer play subsequently obtained the highest sociometric scores in their classrooms. Putallaz notes that, in this study, it was not the specific content of the behavior (e.g., agreeable, disagreeable, questioning, self-statements) that discriminated between high- and low-status children, but whether the behavior was used in a relevant manner. Thus, children who are preferred as playmates appear to understand better the social-contextual settings in which they find themselves, and are better able to adapt their behavior to that of their peers.

Similar patterns of findings have emerged from studies conducted within more naturalistic settings. Asarnow (1983) compared the social behaviors of unpopular and popular fourth- and sixth-grade boys observed during in-class seatwork, physical education, and transitional periods. Unpopular boys (especially sixth graders) initiated fewer positive contacts and more negative contacts with peers, and were participants in fewer friendly mutual exchanges than were popular boys. Unpopular boys were also more often off-task and more likely to receive negative teacher attention. Sequential analyses of the boys' behaviors indicated the presence of negative interactional reciprocity for unpopular boys only. That is, when popular boys' behaviors were negative, their peers tended to respond in a nonnegative (i.e., neutral or positive) way, and when a peer directed a negative behavior toward them, popular boys tended to respond in a nonnegative manner. The reverse pattern was seen for unpopular boys: their negative behavior was likely to result in a negative peer response, and their behavioral response to negative peer behavior was most likely to be negative. These findings suggest that unpopular boys achieved interactional synchrony only in negative (i.e., coercive) ways.

Two sets of studies merit special attention because they examined high- and low-status elementary school-aged children's social-behavioral orientations in both naturalistic (classroom and playground) *and* analogue settings. Dodge et al. (1986) found that children's successful (i.e., competent) group entry in an analogue setting was predicted by low levels of disagreements and high levels of behavioral sequences denoting positive reciprocity and "connectedness." Moreover, high-status children more often engaged in nonverbal synchrony (indexed as matching child-peer behavior) with their peer hosts and less often disengaged from peer play. Results from a second study in which aggressive children were contrasted with nonaggressive, popular children replicated and extended these findings. Aggressive children were more antisocial and disruptive at school, and their social initiations were more likely to be rebuffed by peers. In the group entry situation aggressive children engaged in less nonverbal synchrony with their host peers. Furthermore, for all children, ratings of group entry competence and overall acceptance by the host peers were most highly predicted by synchronous, connected interactions.

The Dodge et al. (1986) findings indicate that aggressive children behave in incompetent (e.g., disconnected, antisocial) ways in both laboratory and school settings. However, the extent to which behavior in one setting was predictive of behavior in another (generalizability) could not be determined. Pettit et al. (1987)

specifically addressed this issue by relating molar and molecular assessments of elementary school-aged children's behavior in two analogue situations (peer group entry and response to an ambiguous peer provocation) to observations of the children's behavior in the classroom and on the playground. Agreeable, coherent (i.e., predictable) behavior in the laboratory group entry analogue setting predicted success in that setting, as well as group entry success at school. Lower levels of attention-seeking behaviors at school also predicted school group entry success. Molar-level assessments (representing global laboratory ratings and proportional scores for group entry success and aggressiveness at school) were found to be situationally-specific: Analogue group entry success predicted global school group entry success, but not school aggressiveness; laboratory ratings of aggressiveness in response to provocation predicted school aggressiveness, but not group entry success at school. These findings indicate that molar-level measures (but not molecular measures) of children's social behavior evidence cross-setting, situationally specific generalizability. Group entry success (in either setting) was best predicted by measures of behavioral coherence/predictability.

Taken together, the findings described above suggest that socially competent children, in comparison to socially incompetent children, are better able to "read" social situations and coordinate their social behavior with that of their peer partners. Thus, it is not a simple matter of generally being agreeable or disagreeable that leads to social status in the group. Rather, successful adaptation to the peer group requires an appreciation for social contingencies and a high degree of social sensitivity. Although parents may directly coach their children in the use of these skills (see Finnie and Russell, 1988), it would appear more likely that the socialization origins of these orientations lie in the quality of the parent-child relationship, and specifically, whether that relationship is marked by the presence or absence of harmony, sensitivity, and coherence. Socialization literature relevant to these possibilities will be examined next.

FAMILY INTERACTION AND CHILDREN'S SOCIAL ADJUSTMENT

Traditional conceptualizations of family influences on children's social development emphasize the role of discipline (e.g., power assertion vs. inductive reasoning) and affection (warmth vs.

hostility). There is ample literature documenting the relation between these parenting styles and children's interpersonal behavior (see review by Maccoby and Martin, 1983). For example, power assertive disciplinary styles have been shown to predict children's hostility toward others (Chapter 10, this volume; Hoffman, 1960), whereas more inductively oriented discipline has been linked to children's prosocial orientations (Bryant and Crockenberg, 1980).

Several investigators recently have sought to examine more explicitly the relations among disciplinary technique, affective qualities of the parent-child relationship, and children's behavioral competence with peers. One of the first studies of this type was conducted by MacDonald and Parke (1984). In this study, mothers and fathers were observed in their homes interacting with their preschool-aged children and then attributes of these interactions were correlated with the children's adaptation among peers, as noted by teachers and as observed in a laboratory playroom. Competent boys had fathers who were physically playful, eliciting positive affect during play, and mothers who were verbally stimulating. The fathers (but not mothers) of competent girls also were verbally stimulating. Boys who engaged in high levels of "harmonious play" with peers (defined in terms of ratings of coordinated, harmonious, agreeable interactions) had fathers who were physically playful and mothers who actively engaged them in play.

In a subsequent study, MacDonald (1987) examined additional attributes of parent-child physical play as related to the preschool-aged boys' sociometric status. Parent and child behaviors were coded during a brief laboratory play session. Parents of popular boys engaged them in high levels of physical play, and the boys displayed positive affect during these encounters. Rejected boys more often were overstimulated and their interactions with their parents were more one-sided (i.e., less mutually coordinated). Parents of neglected boys engaged them in less physical play and the boys approached them less often. Neglected boys were generally passive in their interactions with parents. These findings suggest parents of both rejected and neglected boys are somewhat less attentive to child cues—as evidenced by their either under- or overstimulating the boys—and are less successful in facilitating the boys' regulation of affective arousal.

Putallaz (1987) sought to identify the family interaction correlates of first-grade children's sociometric status and social behavior with peers. Mother-child and child-peer interactions were observed in a laboratory playroom. Children with higher sociometric ratings in their first-grade classrooms had mothers who displayed high rates of agreeable, "feeling" behavior, and low rates of disagreeable, demanding behavior. Positive, agreeable mothers also had children who engaged in comparatively high rates of agreeable behavior with peers. These findings suggest that children acquire affective dispositions similar to those displayed by their mothers.

The potentially important role of maternal disciplinary strategy in children's development of peer competence recently has been highlighted by two interview-based studies. Hart, Ladd, and Burleson (1990) asked mothers of elementary school-aged children to respond to stories depicting hypothetical conflict situations; these responses were scored for the degree of induction versus power assertion. Maternal power assertion predicted low levels of peer acceptance (based on sociometric ratings). Similar findings were reported by Pettit, Dodge, and Brown (1988), who assessed mothers' disciplinary practices through the use of hypothetical stories and a semistructured interview. Peer competence was evaluated on the basis of sociometric ratings and teacher ratings. Both indices of peer competence were inversely related to mothers' restrictive discipline and mothers' endorsement of aggression as an acceptable solution to interpersonal problems.

The studies described above have been important in calling attention to the possible role of parenting in children's acquisition of social skills. This research is not without its limitations, however. The central limitation is the absence of naturalistic observational data, either of the parents interacting with their children, or of the children interacting with their peers. Thus, little is known at the present about the relations among naturally occurring patterns of parent-child interaction and children's playground (or classroom) behavioral orientations. These studies also have been somewhat limited in their operationalization of the key parent-child interaction variables. As mentioned earlier, disciplinary style and affective tone represent two broad dimensions of parenting that have received extensive research attention, but other parenting dimensions also may be consequential for children's development of peer competence. In particular, the notion of parent-child *synchrony* deserves special consideration as a possible precursor of children's behavioral orientations with peers.

Synchrony is used here as a general term to describe a variety of observed phenomena. This parent-child interactional quality has been discussed under several different rubrics, including consistency (Gardner, 1989), responsiveness (e.g., Bakeman and Brown, 1980; Dowdney, Mrazek, Quinton, and Rutter, 1984), sensitivity (e.g., Ainsworth, Blehar, Waters, and Wall, 1978; Egeland, 1985), and predictability (Wahler and Dumas, 1986). In spite of wide differences in focus (e.g., age of child, outcome being predicted) and measurement technique, each of these perspectives emphasizes the role of a contingent and predictable social environment in healthy social development.

We have found it useful to distinguish between what might be referred to as positive synchrony (behavioral matching with predominately negative affect), negative synchrony (behavioral matching with predominately negative affect), and nonsynchrony (nonmatching of behavior with nonextreme affect). Attachment theorists and mother-infant interaction researchers have stressed the importance of a positively synchronous mother-infant relationship for children's optimal social adaptation (including a secure attachment) (e.g., Ainsworth et al., 1978; Egeland, 1985; Isabella, Belsky, and von Eye, 1989). Nonoptimal social-developmental outcomes—including insecure attachment and later aggression and/or social disengagement—have been linked to extended exposure to nonsynchronous (unresponsive, insensitive, or irrelevant) parenting (Ainsworth et al., 1978; Bakeman and Brown, 1980; Egeland, 1985; Gianino and Tronick, 1988; Isabella et al., 1989). The typical explanation for the links between synchrony and later social outcomes is that the infant or child internalizes a sense of trust about (and confidence in) relationships as a consequence of the caregiver's provision of a predictable social environment. Further, the sensitive caregiver appears to foster a "rhythmicity" in the interaction (Censullo, Bowler, Lester, and Brazelton, 1987) that, because it makes the interaction more predictable, allows the child to better coordinate his or her behavior with that of the caregiver. This in turn allows for more extended episodes of interaction, and prepares the child for more complex social encounters in the future. Rocissano, Slade, and

Lynch (1987) suggest that sensitivity to children's needs may be especially important (and particularly challenging) during the toddler years, when children need structure but also need to develop autonomy. These researchers note that, "For mothers, synchrony reflects a capacity to remain available to the child, and for children, it indicates an ability to assume the role of a social partner" (p. 702).

Positive synchrony also has been assessed in studies of interactions between older children and their parents. Parpal and Maccoby (1985) examined the relations among mothers' social-interactive styles and their preschool-aged children's compliance orientations. Mothers were observed in one of three laboratory conditions: (a) a free play situation in which mothers were encouraged to interact with their children as they normally would; (b) a play situation in which mothers had been trained to be responsive (i.e., mothers were instructed to imitate and describe the child's behavior, to follow the rules and suggestions made by the child, and to minimize commands and criticisms); and (c) a noninteractive situation. A standard compliance task followed each session. Children whose mothers were in the responsive condition were the most compliant; children in the free play condition were the least compliant. These findings were replicated and extended by Lay, Waters, and Park (1989), who found evidence supporting a mood induction interpretation of the effects of maternal responsiveness on children's compliance (i.e., when mothers were responsive their children were more likely to comply with their instructions because their mood was more positive, and hence their behavior more agreeable).

These findings are in general agreement with those reported in Baumrind's (1971) classic work. The authoritative family type identified by Baumrind contains elements of responsivity/synchrony in that these parents encouraged verbal give-and-take, satisfied their children's needs, and communicated respect for their children's decisions. These mothers had children who were compliant and cooperative in the nursery school setting. According to Baumrind, when parents are sensitive and encourage reciprocity, their children view the parents' authority as more legitimate and are more likely to model themselves after their parents.

Other researchers—especially those interested in the familial origins of antisocial behavior— have focused on negative synchrony (coercion) and the absence of synchrony. Work in this area has relied on detailed observational analyses of the social contingencies operating within families of aggressive children (e.g., Gardner, 1989; Patterson, 1982; Snyder, 1977; Wahler and Dumas, 1986). Patterson's (1982) seminal research has shown how aggressive children and their parents become entrapped within ever-escalating cycles of negativity. Within the present framework these coercive cycles are conceptualized as instances of negative synchrony, that is, the synchronization of aversive behaviors between family members. Patterson (1982) suggests that, once a parent and child are engaged in an escalating, coercive exchange, the coercion itself is reinforced, regardless of the outcome of the struggle. These extended coercive exchanges include situations where the parent makes a demand, the child resists, and the cycle repeats until the parent fails to enforce the directive, or where the child makes a demand and the parent initially resists but subsequently capitulates in the face of continued child demands.

It is clear that parents who participate in such coercive episodes are not behaving in a consistent fashion with their children. In a detailed study of the contingency systems operating in such families, Snyder (1977) reported that "problem" families experienced more aversive and fewer positive consequences for pleasing (positive) behavior, and more positive and fewer aversive consequences for displeasing behavior than did nonproblem families. Snyder concluded that *no* contingency systems were operating in these families. Wahler and Dumas (1986) recently have argued for an alternative interpretation of the inconsistency-reinforcement hypothesis. These researchers have reported home observational data on multistressed mother-child dyads that reveal the operation of the characteristic indiscriminate parenting pattern *except* during extended coercive (and hence, synchronous) episodes. They have hypothesized that the children were misbehaving in order to reduce maternal indiscriminate attention, that is, the children found unpredictability more aversive than involvement in a coercive bout. Additional support for this hypothesis was obtained by Wahler, Williams, and Cerezo (1990). Analyses of mother-child behavioral sequences (derived from detailed home observations) provided evidence of alternating sequences of indiscriminate attention and mother-child coercion. Apparently, indiscriminate maternal attention set the stage for subsequent escalations in children's aggressive behavior, leading to coercive (and predictable) mother-child exchanges. According to Wahler et al. (1990), the child coerces the mother "to create a predictable social dance for the dyad. Although this dance is judged to be unpleasant by all concerned, it also brings a familiar sense of order within an otherwise disordered relationship" (p. 406).

Wahler and his colleagues (summarized in Wahler and Dumas, 1989) also have found evidence of attentional deficiencies in mothers of problem children. Wahler and Dumas (1989) conceptualize mothers' attentional skills in terms of *surveillance*. Mothers whose surveillance skills are limited are less able to provide accurate descriptions of their child's behavior; they use global and diffuse terms when describing the nature of their child's "problem"; and they are less able to distinguish the multiple social contexts in which they and their children live. That is, these mothers cannot readily discriminate between events occurring in the child care arena and those occurring in other facets of their lives, such as their interactions with a spouse, relative, or social service worker. Thus, the mothers lack the observational skills that would allow them to pinpoint the source of their social difficulties with their children, and lack the discrimination skills that would allow them to distinguish among the varied social demands made of them in disparate social contexts (e.g., child rearing, work, marriage). Similar types of attentional skill deficiency in mothers of problem children have been reported by Patterson (1982) and by Holleran, Littman, Freund, and Schmaling (1982).

As this review indicates, children's social adaptation is associated with a broad range of parenting styles. We have proposed the notion of parent-child synchrony as an organizational device for summarizing some important aspects of this literature. Furthermore, we have highlighted research indicating an absence of both parent-child synchrony and parental attentional skill in families of children experiencing social and behavioral difficulties. In general, then, the literature we have examined suggests the following: Competence-promoting interactions in the family may be described in terms of positive synchrony, or the extent to which parents and their children engage in reciprocally positive interactional exchanges. Competence-inhibiting interactions may be characterized either by negative synchrony, or mutual negative exchanges, or by parent-child nonsynchrony (i.e., indiscriminate parental initiations or responses).

Earlier we summarized literature suggesting that children's competence with peers is based in part on children's attentional skills (circumspection) and ability to coordinate their behavior with that of their peers. Are variations in these skills associated with early patterns of family relations? Little research specifically has been directed to the identification and description of naturally occurring patterns of family interaction that are predictive of variations in children's behavior with peers at school. Consequently, the possible familial origins of children's playground and classroom behavioral orientations have yet to be articulated.

PREDICTING PLAYGROUND BEHAVIOR FROM FAMILY INTERACTION PATTERNS: AN OBSERVATIONAL STUDY

Based on the literature reviewed above, we speculated that children's experience of positively synchronous family interactions would facilitate their development of competent behavioral orientations with peers, whereas family experiences marked by comparatively high levels of negative synchrony or nonsynchrony would contribute to children's social inadequacies with peers. We examined these possibilities in a naturalistic study of family interaction patterns and children's subsequent classroom and playground behaviors with peers. Our specific predictions were as follows: Family interactions marked by high levels of positive responsivity (synchrony) were predicted to be associated with high levels of children's cooperative behavior and low levels of aggressive behavior. Children from these families also were predicted to be rated by teachers as socially competent in their peer interactions and as especially attentive to social cues. Coercive (negatively synchronous) family interactions were expected to be associated with high levels of children's aggressive behavior and low levels of cooperative behavior. These children were expected, in turn, to be rated by their teachers as aggressive and socially insensitive in their peer interactions. Abrupt and intrusive (nonsynchronous) family interactions were predicted to be associated with both social disengagement (solitary and onlooker behavior) and aggressive behavior, and teacher ratings of inattentiveness in peer interactions.

Subjects

Subjects for this study were 30 4- and 5-year-old children (15 were boys) and their families who are participating in a larger longitudinal project. Families were recruited during the 1987 spring roundup for kindergarten at four elementary schools representing diverse socioeconomic regions of Knoxville, Tennessee. A total of 101 families initially agreed to participate. Observations were conducted in the homes of a subset of these families. Inclusion in the home observation pool was determined by having both parents (in two-parent homes) complete the Achenbach Child Behavior Checklist (CBCL; Achenbach and Edelbrock, 1981), from which we selected high-, low-, and medium-aggressive children (10 of each) on the basis of their scores on the aggression subscale of the CBCL. Socioeconomic status scores for these families (based on the Hollingshead four-factor index) ranged from 17 to 66 ($M = 47$). Families were observed in their homes during the latter part of the summer and early fall. School observations of the children were conducted the following winter and spring. Teacher ratings of the children's social skillfulness with peers also were obtained at this time.

Procedures

Home observations. Each family was observed during and after the evening meal by an experienced observer for two, 2-hour sessions. The observer wrote a detailed narrative record of ongoing social transactions in the family involving the target child. After completing the observation the observer made clarifying remarks and provided additional contextual description where appropriate and segmented the narrative into social-interactive "events" (see Pettit and Bates, 1990). The narratives provide a contextually rich description of the location, activity, participants, interactional "theme," and affect of each event, as well as a summary of conversation and nonverbal behavior. Each narrative was coded by a trained undergraduate with no prior knowledge of the children or their families.

Events were coded using the Social Events Coding (SEC) system developed by Pettit and Bates (1989, 1990). In this system, interactional events are conceptualized as meaningful units distinguished not by intervals of time but by thematic content and apparent intentions of the interactants. The current version of the SEC system focuses on four types of events: (a) *control* events, defined as explicit influence attempts directed from one individual to another; (b) *teaching* events, which in this system are limited to extended and intentional didactic exchanges (e.g., mother instructs child in how to play a game); (c) *social contact* events, represented by nonmanipulative social play and conversation (e.g., mother and child discuss the day's events); and (d) *reflective listening* events, defined as parental responsiveness to child cues in which no effort is made to redirect or otherwise modify ongoing child behavior (e.g., mother responds with sympathetic concern when child is obviously frustrated). Each event is further coded according to specific descriptive aspects of the interaction. Coding was facilitated by the use of an interactive computer program designed especially for this project (Pettit, Raab, and Habibi, 1990). Analyses to be reported here focus only on those events involving the mother and child.

Four family interaction measures were derived from these data for the current report. *Negative synchrony* (coercive control) represents the proportion of all observed events in which one family member responds to the demands of another in an aversive manner. *Positive synchrony* (responsivity) is indexed as the total frequency of high quality reflective listening events. *Nonsynchrony* (instrusiveness) is represented as the proportion of all control events in which the child seeks to avoid or terminate (nonaversively) intrusive or interfering maternal behavior. The fourth measure is *proactive involvement,* and is indexed by the frequency of teaching and mother-initiated social contact events. This latter observational measure was included because it reflects the active-initiating component of positive synchrony (insofar as it describes active maternal involvement in play, social conversation, and teaching), and because in past research (Pettit and Bates, 1989) it has been shown to be associated with children's positive social adaptation.

Reliability of the home observational codes was checked in two ways. First, interobserver agreement was assessed by contrasting the narrative protocols made by two independent observers during five home visits. The degree of "concordance" (see Pettit and Bates,

1990) was estimated by having a separate coder identify matches (events described by both observers) and nonmatches (events described by one observer but not the other). Concordance agreements ranged from .68 to .74, with a mean of .71. Next, intercoder reliability was evaluated by having two coders independently code eight narratives. Kappa coefficients (all $p < .05$) were calculated for event type (kappa = .67), initiating circumstances of control events (demand/antagonism vs. interference/intrusion; kappa = .65), type of control used (aversive vs. nonaversive; kappa = .42), and qualities of listening events (kappa = 1.0).

Teacher Ratings. During the latter half of the school year kindergarten teachers completed the Teacher's Checklist of Peer Relationships (Dodge and Somberg, 1987), which consists of 12 items rated on 5-point Likert-type scales, half of which pertain to social competence (e.g., "this child gets along well with peers") and half of which describe various aggressive behaviors (e.g., "this child threatens or bullies others in order to get his/her own way"). The aggression items were summed to create a composite measure of teacher ratings of *aggression* (alpha = .89). The social competence items were summed to form a teacher rating-based measure of *social competence* (alpha = .87).

An additional set of items described children's social attentiveness and social problem-solving skills (e.g., "accurately interprets what a peer is trying to do"). These seven items were summed to form a teacher-based measure of *attentiveness to social cues* (alpha = .94).

Playground/Classroom Observations. Children were observed during indoor (classroom) and outdoor (playground) free play by trained undergraduates using a focal-child, event-based system. Each child was observed for 12, 5-minute periods, divided into 10-second intervals. Observations were scheduled so that each child was observed over a minimum of six different days (i.e., no more than two, 5-minute periods per day); same-day observations on a child were separated by at least 10 minutes. Observers noted the occurrence of solitary (child plays alone), parallel (child engages in activity that mirrors or mimics that of a peer), cooperative (prosocial, competent social interaction and play), and rough (roughhousing, good natured jostling, or wrestling) play, as well as play that could not be coded into a meaningful category because it was ambiguous (e.g., inaudible, such as when a child mumbled, or talked at the same time as another child), transitional, or nonsensical (called "other" play). Observers also noted instances where the child engaged in reactive aggression (angry, hostile aggression in response to a stimulus provided by a peer) or proactive aggression (aggressive behavior in the service of some other goal; includes bullying and dominating behavior), or was the target of one of these types of aggression. In addition, all instances in which the teacher interacted with the child were noted. Separate scores were created for the unsupervised playground context and for the unsupervised (i.e., unstructured) classroom context. Both contexts allowed for free play activity. Preliminary analyses revealed no consistent differences between scores derived from the two contexts in their relation to one another or to the family interaction measures. Therefore, the analyses to be reported below are based on the combined behavioral scores.

Reliability observations were conducted for 20% of the sessions. Correlations were computed between the two observers' summary scores for each session. This was judged to be the appropriate level for assessing interobserver reliability since all reported analyses are based on session totals, not sequences. These correlations ($M = .69$) ranged from .40 (for rough play) to .88 (teacher contact), all $p < .05$.

Results and Discussion

Relations Within Domains. We first examined the interrelations of measures within the home and school settings. For the family interaction measures, the strongest correlation was between negative synchrony and nonsynchrony ($r = .53$), as would be expected on the basis of findings reported by Wahler et al. (1990). Negative synchrony was also negatively related to proactive involvement ($r = -.32$). Families characterized by high rates of coercive exchanges were thus prone to higher rates of indiscriminate, intrusive interactions and a relative absence of positive social involvement.

Strong patterns of relations were found among the teacher rating measures. Children rated by teachers as competent with peers were seen by teachers as less aggressive ($r = -.77$) and more socially aware (attentive) in their interactions with peers ($r = .78$). Children rated as aggressive were viewed by teachers as less attentive to relevant social cues ($r = -.53$). The finding of a relation between child aggression and lower levels of social sensitivity (i.e., use of relevant social cues) is consistent with prior observational studies (e.g., Dodge et al., 1986; Putallaz, 1987).

Intercorrelations among the school behavior measures were numerous and in keeping with prior literature. Solitary play was associated with lower levels of cooperative play (r = -.43), rough play (r = -.44), and reactive aggression (r = -.35), and higher levels of "other" play (r = .34). Rough play was positively correlated with reactive aggression (r = .69), proactive aggression (r = .56), and being the object of both reactive (r = .61) and proactive (r = .42) aggression. "Other" play was associated with more frequent contacts with the teacher (r = .33). Finally, the aggression measures were related to one another in modest-to-moderate ways: Reactive aggression correlated with proactive aggression (r = .28), and with being the object of both reactive (r = .46) and proactive (r = .47) aggression. Proactive aggression was also associated with being the object of reactive aggression (r = .57). These findings suggest that the playground/classroom observational variables covary in reasonable ways, but the relations are not strong enough to justify the combining of the variables into more general categories.

Relations Between Domains. Relations among family interaction patterns, the teacher ratings, and the classroom/playground behavioral orientations were examined next. Correlations between the teacher ratings of children's social behavior and social attentiveness and the home observational measures are shown in Table 9.1.

As can be seen in the table, children's social competence with peers, as rated by teachers, was significantly associated with high levels of positively synchronous and proactive family interactions, and low levels of negatively synchronous and nonsynchronous interactions. Children's aggressive orientations were predicted by high levels of negatively synchronous and nonsynchronous interactions. Children's attentiveness to their peers' social cues was significantly related to high levels of positive synchrony and low levels of both negatively synchronous and nonsynchronous interactions. These correlations suggest that variations in children's social competence—as rated by teachers— have social precursors in distinctive patterns of family interaction observed several months earlier. As we predicted, socially competent and socially attentive children were more likely than socially

Table 9.1. Intercorrelations Among Family Interaction Measures, Teacher Ratings, and Playground/Classroom Behavior

	Family Interaction Measures					Teacher Ratings	
	Positive Synchrony	Proactive Involve	Negative Synchrony	Non-Synchrony	Aggressive	Competent	Attentive
Teacher Ratings							
Aggressive	-.22	-.11	.40*	.37*		-.77*	-.53*
Competent	.39*	.37*	-.36*	-.27+			.78*
Attentive	.30*	.18	-.52*	-.36*			
Playground/Classroom Behavior							
Solitary Play	-.17	-.15	.25+	.26+	.15	-.29+	-.30+
Parallel Play	.03	.17	-.28+	.00	-.15	.12	.09
Cooperative	-.08	.33*	-.38*	-.14	.05	.23	.27+
Rough Play	.15	.13	-.15	-.13	-.11	.16	.15
Other Play	-.22	-.09	.07	.10	.51*	-.58*	-.55*
Reactive Aggression	.18	.04	.11	-.05	-.01	-.13	-.12
Proactive Aggression	.28+	.23	.07	.24+	.09	.13	-.02
Object of Reactive Aggression	.33*	.10	.03	.03	.02	.15	.02
Object of Proactive Aggression	.06	.04	-.18	.01	-.06	-.05	.18
Teacher Attention	-.36*	.01	.40*	.22	.36*	-.14	-.33*

$+p < .10$ $*p < .05$

ineffective children to have experienced harmonious family interactions. Socially ineffective children (including aggressive children), on the other hand, were more likely to have experienced
nonsynchronous and/or coercive styles of family interaction.

In our next set of analyses we examined the relations among
the teacher ratings and children's observed free play behavior.
These correlations are also shown in Table 9.1. Children viewed
as more competent and socially "tuned-in" (attentive) by their
teachers engaged in lower rates of solitary and "other" play. Also,
attentive children required less teacher attention, and were more
cooperative in their play with peers. These findings are congruent
with earlier observational studies of the behavioral bases of peer
status, based on sociometric data (e.g., Ladd et al., 1988; Pettit et
al., 1987). To determine the combined predictive relation between
the free play behaviors and the teacher ratings, we conducted a
series of stepwise multiple regression analyses. In order to reduce
the overall number of predictor variables we selected a subset of
the observational measures for inclusion in these analyses. These
measures were selected on the basis of empirical relations (i.e., at
least one significant or near-significant correlation) with the criterion variables, or because of conceptual relevance (i.e., an interest in including measures indicative of both positive and negative
behavioral orientations). These measures were solitary play, cooperative play, "other" play, proactive and reactive aggression,
and teacher attention. These behavioral measures were entered
into the regression equation as a single set. The teacher rating of
competence was highly related to these observational measures,
overall $R^2 = .41$, $p = .04$, as was the rating of social attentiveness,
overall $R^2 = .39$, $p = .056$.

Teacher-rated aggression was associated with "other" play and
teacher attention, but surprisingly, not with observed classroom
and playground aggression and rough play. In order to assess
whether teacher ratings of aggression might be more highly related
to observations of children's aggression in the classroom setting
(where, presumably, teachers would be better situated to observe
the children's behavior), we computed correlations separately for
each context (classroom and playground). Observed aggression was
unrelated to teacher ratings of aggression in either context. The
multiple correlation between the entire set of observational measures and the aggression rating was nonsignificant ($R^2 = .57$).

Our final set of analyses concerned the predictability of the children's free play behaviors observed at school from the family interaction patterns observed in the home. These correlations (see Table 9.1) were generally in predicted directions. Negatively synchronous (coercive) family interactions were associated with higher rates of solitary play and attention from the teacher, and lower rates of cooperative and parallel play. Nonsynchronous interactions predicted solitary play and proactive aggression. Positively synchronous family interactions forecasted lower rates of teacher attention and somewhat higher rates of proactive aggression and being the object of reactive aggression. Proactive family interactions predicted higher rates of cooperative play.

These findings indicate that, for the most part, children displaying behavioral orientations with peers that prior literature suggests are associated with positive peer outcomes (i.e., low levels of solitary play and high levels of cooperative play) had experienced sensitive and responsive (i.e., positively synchronous) family interactions. Conversely, children who displayed behavioral styles with peers that are associated with negative outcomes (i.e., high levels of solitary play and aggression) were more likely to have experienced coercive and intrusive (i.e., negatively synchronous and nonsynchronous) family interactions. The unexpected correlations between positive family synchrony and the two aggression measures (initiating proactive aggression and being the object of reactive aggression) may indicate that children from these families are highly involved with their peers, sometimes crossing the boundary between active play and proactive aggression. This exuberance may then have sometimes led other children to respond negatively. The children from positively synchronous homes, being inexperienced in coercion, may have difficulty avoiding being the occasional target of others' reactive aggression.

We had expected stronger patterns of relations between negative synchrony in the family and children's observed aggression with peers. It is worth noting that aggression was infrequently observed in our sample, and its occurrence was not associated with teachers' ratings of the children's aggressiveness. As Serbin (Chapter 6, this volume) notes, teachers may be less aware of aggression (and other playground behavior) than peers, perhaps accounting for the lack of relations between the teacher ratings and the observational measures. At the same time, it may be the case that our measures of playground (and classroom) aggression are not sensitive indicators of the children's actual aggressive behavioral orientations. However, it is also possible that children from negatively synchronous families were aggressive in their initial encounters with peers in the fall, but that peers had learned to avoid these children by the winter and spring (when the observations were conducted), resulting in fewer opportunities for aggression. This possibility seems all the more plausible given Ladd et al.'s (1988) finding that arguing predicted children's social preference scores during the fall but not during the spring.

CONCLUSION

We began this chapter by noting that children's playground behavior with peers serves an important function in social development, namely, that children reap benefits (e.g., greater opportunities to practice social skills with a variety of partners) when their behavior leads to positive evaluations by teachers and peers, and that children suffer (in terms of increasingly diminished social opportunities) when their behavior leads to adverse reactions by teachers and peers. A review of the literature revealed that children most likely to be viewed by others as socially competent engage in high rates of mutually rewarding and reciprocal interactions with their peers. Moreover, these children are circumspect in the sense that they are peceptually attuned to relevant social-environmental cues. Socially ineffective children, on the other hand, more frequently engage in aggressive and irrelevant behavior with peers, and seem less "tuned-in" to relevant contextual detail.

We have speculated that the likely origins of these playground interaction styles are to be found in early family relations. When parents are sensitive to their children's needs, when they provide their children with a predictable and coherent social environment, and when they teach (and model) surveillance skills, their children are apt to be better equipped to engage in successful peer interaction. When parents are inattentive, unpredictable, or coercive with their children, the children may fail to acquire skills in reading and interpreting social-environmental cues. But these children do learn the value of being manipulative and aggressive, since such behavior often results in short-term payoffs (e.g., termination of aversive parental behavior). These children also acquire an important tool for combating ambiguity in new social settings: they have learned that, when unsure of a peer's behavior, act aggressively, because a predictable (albeit aversive) response will follow.

As we see it, interpersonal relationships—whether in the context of the family or the peer group—are more likely to "work" (i.e., lead to positive social outcomes for all participants) when the interacting persons behave in ways that are relevant and connected to one another. This inherent striving for connectedness in social interaction has been noted by writers from divergent theoretical camps, including communication theorists (Watzlawick, Beavin, and Jackson, 1967), psycholinguists (Clark and Clark, 1977), and family therapists (Minuchin, 1985). In order for optimal social development to occur, children must learn how to mesh their own behavior and goals with that of significant others. Our reading of the socialization literature—and our own observational data—suggest that early family relations are pivotal in this learning process.

The data we have presented here are longitudinal, and indicate that school behavior (as rated by teachers and observed in free play settings) is predictable from family interaction patterns assessed several months earlier. Nonetheless, we recognize the correlational nature of these data, and the fact that characteristics of the children themselves (e.g., temperament) may be responsible for the patterns observed both at home and school.

Our data are limited in several other important respects. Owing to the small number of subjects we were unable to examine potentially important moderators of our family interaction and school behavior measures, including child sex and family social class. The small N also precluded the use of more sophisticated analytic strategies (e.g., path analysis). As part of our ongoing longitudinal investigation we have collected home and school observational data on a much larger sample of families (> 160). These data currently are being coded. Use of the larger data set should also make possible a more typological analysis of family interaction patterns, such as has been used so profitably by Baumrind (1971).

Some of the patterns of relations were weaker than we expected, based on our own and other's prior work. The modest levels of interrater agreement for our observational data may partly be responsible. That is, measurement error may have contributed to an underestimation of the magnitude of some of the relations between family interaction and school behavior. In the absence of replication (with more psychometrically robust measures), the current set of findings must be interpreted cautiously.

It also will be important in our subsequent work to examine father-child interaction patterns. Previous research has shown that different aspects of mother-child and father-child interaction predict children's peer competence (MacDonald and Parke, 1984). Moreover, it has been speculated that same-sex parents exert greater influence on children's socialization outcomes due to sex-role identification (Biller, 1981). In future analyses we will examine the impact of interactional events involving family dyads (i.e., mother-child and father-child) and triads.

Finally, we will continue to refine our procedures for identifying synchronous and nonsynchronous patterns of interaction in both family and peer contexts. In family research it has been the case that molar-level measures (e.g., global ratings) of responsivity and sensitivity better predict later social outcomes than do more discrete behavioral indicators (e.g., see Bakeman and Brown, 1980). In developing the SEC system we sought to bridge the molar and molecular levels of analysis by first describing in contextually rich ways the ongoing flow of interaction, and then later applying specific behavioral codes. We are now developing additional coding schemes that focus explicitly on the degree of interactional synchrony and affective quality at the level of the individual event (Harrist, 1991). We consider this to be a reasonable compromise between the interval-based, affective matching procedures typically used to define synchrony/predictability (e.g., as used by Snyder, 1977; and Wahler and Dumas, 1986), and the global ratings procedures typically used to assess responsivity/sensitivity (cf. Bakeman and Brown, 1980). Measures derived from this new coding system will allow us to cross-validate our current indices of positive synchrony, negative synchrony, and nonsynchrony.

Greater attention also will be devoted in future research to the development of playground observational systems that will allow for the creation of synchrony measures analogous to our family measures. We currently are testing the utility of the narrative (SEC) approach for describing peer interaction. Our goal is to develop procedures whereby children's interpersonal behavior in school settings can be reliably described in terms of context appropriateness, affective and content matching of exchanges, and positive and negative reciprocity. Such measures should enable more direct comparisons of synchrony-based family interaction styles and child-peer behavioral orientations.

REFERENCES

Achenbach, T. M., and Edelbrock, C. S. (1981). Behavioral problems and competencies reported by parents of normal and disturbed children aged four through sixteen. *Monographs of the Society for Research in Child Development, 46* (1, Serial No. 188).

Ainsworth, M. D. S., Blehar, M. C., Waters, E., and Wall, S. (1978). *Patterns of attachment.* Hillsdale, NJ: Erlbaum.

Asarnow, J. (1983). Children with peer adjustment problems: Sequential and non-sequential analyses of school behavior. *Journal of Consulting and Clinical Psychology, 51,* 709–717.

Asher, S. R. (1983). Social competence and peer status: Recent advances and future directions. *Child Development, 54,* 1427–1434.

Bakeman, R., and Brown, J. V. (1980). Early interaction: Consequences for social and mental development at three years. *Child Development, 51,* 437–447.

Baumrind, D. (1971). Current patterns of parental authority. *Developmental Psychology Monographs, 4* (1, Pt. 2).

Berndt, T. J., and Ladd, G. W. (Eds.) (1989). *Peer relationships in child development.* New York: Wiley.

Biller, H. B. (1981). The father and sex role development. In M. E. Lamb (Ed.), *The role of the father in child development* (pp. 319–358). New York: Wiley.

Bryant, B. K., and Crockenberg, S. B. (1980). Correlates and dimensions of prosocial behavior: A study of female siblings and their mothers. *Child Development, 51,* 529–544.

Censullo, M., Bowler, R., Lester, B., and Brazelton, T. B., (1987). An instrument for the measurement of infant-adult synchrony. *Nursing Research, 36,* 244–248.

Clark, H. H., and Clark, E. V. (1977). *Psychology and language: An introduction to psycholinguistics.* New York: Harcourt Brace Jovanovich.

Cohn, D. A., Patterson, C. J., and Christopoulos, C. (1991). The family and children's peer relationships. *Journal of Social and Personal Relationships, 8,* 315–346.

Dodge, K. A., Coie, J. D., and Brakke, N. P. (1982). Behavior patterns of socially rejected and neglected preadolescents: The roles of social approach and aggression. *Journal of Abnormal Child Psychology, 10,* 389–409.

Dodge, K. A., Coie, J. D., Pettit, G. S., and Price, J. M. (1990). Peer status and aggression in boys' groups: Developmental and contextual analyses. *Child Development, 61,* 1289–1309.

Dodge, K. A., Pettit, G. S., McClaskey, C. L., and Brown, M. M. (1986). Social competence in children. *Monographs of the Society for Research in Child Development, 51* (2, Serial No. 213).

Dodge, K. A., Schlundt, D. G., Schocken, I., and Degulach, J. D. (1983). Social competence and children's sociometric status: The role of peer group entry strategies. *Merrill-Palmer Quarterly, 29* 309–336.

Dodge, K. A., and Somberg, D. R. (1987). Hostile attributional biases among aggressive boys are exacerbated under conditions of threats to the self. *Child Development, 58,* 213–224.

Dowdney, L., Mrazek, D., Quinton, D., and Rutter, M. (1984). Observation of parent-child interaction with two- to three-year-olds. *Journal of Child Psychology and Psychiatry, 25,* 379–407.

Egeland, B. (1985, April). *The impact of an interfering style of parenting behavior on the later development of the child.* Paper presented at the biennial meeting of the Society for Research in Child Development, Toronto.

Finnie, V., and Russell, A. (1988). Preschool children's social status and their mother's behavior and knowledge in the supervisory role. *Developmental Psychology, 24,* 789–801.

Gardner, F. E. M. (1989). Inconsistent parenting: Is there evidence for a link with children's conduct problems? *Journal of Abnormal Child Psychology, 17,* 223–233.

Gianino, A., and Tronick, E. Z. (1988). The mutual regulation model: The infant's self and interactive regulation coping and defensive capacities. In T. Field, P. McCabe, and N. Schneiderman (Eds.), *Stress and coping* (pp. 47–68). Hillsdale, NJ: Erlbaum.

Hart, C. H., Ladd, G. W., and Burleson, B. R. (1990). Children's expectations of the outcomes of social strategies: Relations with sociometric status and maternal disciplinary styles. *Child Development, 61,* 127–137.

Harrist, A. W. (1991). Synchronous and nonsynchronous parent-child interaction: Relations with children's later competence with peers. Unpublished doctoral dissertation, University of Tennessee, Knoxville.

Hoffman, M. L. (1960). Power assertion by the parent and its impact on the child. *Child Development, 31,* 129–143.

Holleran, P. A., Littman, D. C., Freund, R. D., and Schmaling, K. B. (1982). A signal detection approach to social perception: Identification of negative and positive behaviors by parents of normal and problem children. *Journal of Abnormal Child Psychology, 10,* 547–558.

Isabella, R. A., Belsky, J., and von Eye, A. (1989). Origins or infant-mother attachment: An examination of interactional synchrony during the infant's first year. *Developmental Psychology, 25,* 12–21.

Ladd, G. W. (1983). Social networks of popular, average, and rejected children in school settings. *Merrill-Palmer Quarterly, 29,* 283–307.

Ladd, G. W., and Price, J. M. (1987). Predicting children's social and school adjustment following the transition from preschool to kindergarten. *Child Development, 58* 1168–1189.

Ladd, G. W., Price, J. M., and Hart, C. H. (1988). Predicting preschoolers' peer status from their playground behavior. *Child Development, 59,* 986–992.

Lay, K., Waters, E., and Park, K. A. (1989). Maternal responsiveness and child compliance: The role of mood as mediator. *Child Development, 60,* 1405–1411.

Maccoby, E. E., and Martin, J. A. (1983). Socialization in the context of the family: Parent-child interaction. In E. M. Hetherington (Ed.), P. H. Mussen (Series Ed.), *Handbook of child psychology: Vol. 4. Socialization, personality, and social development* (pp. 1–101). New York: Wiley.

MacDonald, K. B. (1987). Parent-child physical play with rejected, neglected, and popular boys. *Developmental Psychology, 23,* 705–711.

MacDonald, K. B., and Parke, R. D. (1984). Bridging the gap: Parent-child play interaction and peer interactive competence. *Child Development, 55,* 1265–1277.

Minuchin, P. (1985). Families and individual development: Provocations from the field of family therapy. *Child Development, 56,* 289–302.

Parker, J. G., and Asher, S. R. (1987). Peer acceptance and later personal adjustment: Are low-accepted children "at risk"? *Psychological Bulletin, 102,* 357–389.

Parpal, M., and Maccoby, E. E. (1985). Maternal responsiveness and subsequent child compliance. *Child Development, 56,* 1326–1334.

Patterson, G. R. (1982). *Coercive family process.* Eugene, OR: Castalia.

Pettit, G. S., Bakshi, A., Dodge, K. A., and Coie, J. D. (1990). The emergence of social dominance in young boys' play groups: Developmental differences and behavioral correlates. *Developmental Psychology, 26,* 1017–1025.

Pettit, G. S., and Bates, J. E. (1989). Family interaction patterns and children's behavior problems from infancy to 4 years. *Developmental Psychology, 25,* 413–420.

———. (1990). Describing family interaction patterns in early childhood: A "social events" perspective. *Journal of Applied Developmental Psychology, 11,* 395–418.

Pettit, G. S., Dodge, K. A., and Brown, M. M. (1988). Early family experience, social problem solving patterns, and children's social competence. *Child Development, 59,* 107–120.

Pettit, G. S., McClaskey, C. L., Brown, M., and Dodge, K. A. (1987). The generalizability of laboratory assessments of children's socially competent behavior in specific situations. *Behavioral Assessment, 9,* 81–96.

Pettit, G. S., Raab, M. M., and Habibi, A. (1990). *ACCESS: An interactive computer program for coding narrative records of complex social events.* Unpublished manuscript, Auburn University. (Available from G. S. Pettit.)

Putallaz, M. (1983). Predicting children's sociometric status from their behavior. *Child Development, 54,* 1417–1426.

———. (1987). Maternal behavior and children's sociometric status. *Child Development, 58,* 324–340.

Putallaz, M., and Heflin, A. (1990). Parent-child interaction. In S. R. Asher and J. D. Coie (Eds.), *Peer rejection in childhood* (pp. 217–249). New York: Cambridge University Press.

Rocissano, L., Slade, A., and Lynch, V. (1987). Dyadic synchrony and toddler compliance. *Developmental Psychology, 23,* 698–704.

Snyder, J. J. (1977). Reinforcement analysis of interaction in problem and nonproblem families. *Journal of Abnormal Psychology, 86,* 528–535.

Wahler, R. G., and Dumas, J. E. (1986). Maintenance factors in coercive mother-child interactions: The compliance and predictability hypotheses. *Journal of Applied Behavior Analysis, 19,* 13–22.

———. (1989). Attentional problems in dysfunctional mother-child interactions: An interbehavioral model. *Psychological Bulletin, 105,* 116–130.

Wahler, R. G., Williams, A. J., and Cerezo, A. (1990). The compliance and predictability hypotheses: Sequential and correlational analyses of coercive mother-child interactions. *Behavioral Assessment, 12,* 391–407.

Watzlawick, P., Beavin, J., and Jackson, D. (1967). *Pragmatics of human communication.* New York: Norton.

10

CRAIG H. HART, MICHELE DEWOLF,
AND DIANE C. BURTS _____

Parental Disciplinary Strategies
and Preschoolers' Play Behavior in
Playground Settings

Much of the research presented in this volume suggests that naturally occurring patterns of child behavior on the playground are related to indices of peer competence. Over the past several years, researchers have also targeted many family characteristics that may be linked to children's behavior and competence with peers. However, few of these studies have investigated ways that familial characteristics may be related to children's behavior in naturalistic play contexts. One area within the family domain that has been linked to child behavior and has received increasing attention is that of parental disciplinary strategies. The purpose of this chapter is to further explore literature and present data that call attention to the possible role that both maternal and paternal disciplinary strategies play in children's acquisition of social skills that are displayed in naturalistic settings such as the playground.

A preponderance of evidence has already been gathered over the years suggesting that disciplinary strategies are related to children's behavior and competence with peers (see Brody and Shaffer, 1982; Ladd, 1992, 1991; Maccoby and Martin, 1983; Putallaz and Heflin, 1990, for reviews). Why then were linkages between parental discipline and child playground behavior selected for further study? Although much is known about relations involving maternal discipline, little is known about ways that *both* maternal and paternal disciplinary strategies contribute to children's behavioral orientations while taking into account conceivably different strategies on the part of both parents (see Hart, DeWolf, Wozniak, and Burts, 1992a). Moreover, few studies have examined the relations between naturalistic child behavior in less structured child-, rather than adult-guided environments and parental disciplinary strategies.

271

Little is also known about whether or not child behavioral data collected in playground settings would yield results similar to data gathered in past research exploring relations between parental discipline and child behavior. Much of the child behavioral data in past research has been derived from parent or teacher questionnaires or from analogue situations, observations in the home or in indoor classroom settings. We felt that the less constrained environments provided by playgrounds not only offer children the opportunity to be less inhibited in their expression of social skills or the lack thereof, but also allow children opportunities to create, organize, and control their own play experiences (cf. King, 1987). It stands to reason that such contexts would be well suited for studying children's naturalistic social interactions.

One of the major purposes of this chapter is to present data linking children's behavioral orientations on the playground and peer status to both maternal and paternal disciplinary strategies. Before discussing our work on power assertive and inductive discipline, it is hoped that an overview of the related literature will serve as a springboard for further investigation of linkages between other aspects of parenting and children's behavior that is manifested in naturalistic play contexts. Specifically, this chapter was designed to: (a) overview pathways to peer competence; (b) discuss roles that global parenting styles play in the development of peer competence; (c) present theoretical considerations addressing how children acquire social knowledge and behavior from parental inductive and power assertive disciplinary strategies; (d) discuss situational and child determinants of disciplinary strategies; (e) present results of a study designed to assess linkages between parental discipline, preschooler's playground behavioral orientations, and peer status; and (f) point to new directions for future work.

PATHWAYS TO PEER COMPETENCE

To further our understanding of the interface between family and peer systems, recent research has been devoted to searching for antecedents within the family that may be linked to aspects of peer competence that have been discovered in the peer relations literature. Some of this research has been conducted in the context of models involving "pathways" that help investigators better conceptualize ways that families may influ-ence children's peer relations and vice versa. As Ladd (1992) suggests, these pathways "refer to processes that may impinge on the child in one context (e.g., family relations), and the mechanisms of mediating variables that may be responsible for transmitting the effects of such processes to another context (e.g., peer relations)."

These pathways between family and peer contexts are cur-rently thought of as being "direct" or "indirect" (see Ladd, 1992; 1991). As Parke, MacDonald, Beitel, and Bhavnagri (1988) have pointed out, direct pathways are activities and processes that parents use to control or enhance their children's social skills and relationships with peers. These could include efforts to en-hance children's social lives by providing access to play partners and planning or supervising children's interactions with peers (see Bhavnagri and Parke, 1991; Ladd, Profilet, and Hart, 1992; Ladd and Hart, 1992). In contrast, indirect pathways are those aspects of the parent-child relationship that are not explicitly designed to foster competence with peers. Among those discussed in detail by Ladd (1992) are interactional styles during parent-child play (e.g., MacDonald and Parke, 1984; MacDonald, 1987); parent-child synchrony (e.g., Chapter 9, this volume; Pettit, Harrist, Bates, and Dodge, 1991); the affective tone of parents' social interactions with the child and with other persons (e.g., Eisenberg, Fabes, Schaller, Carlo, and Miller, 1991; Putallaz, 1987; Cassidy, Parke, Butkovsky, and Braungart, 1992); parental perceptions, attitudes, and beliefs (e.g., Rubin, Mills, and Rose-Krasnor, 1989); and parental disciplinary strategies (e.g., Hart, Ladd, and Burleson, 1990).

In conjunction with these two types of pathways, the family domain consists of many processes and characteristics that op-erate both within and outside of the family. These may produce variations in ways that family and peer systems are linked to-gether with regard to direct and indirect pathways. Research findings suggest that cultural differences, divorce, marital dis-cord, affective disorders, abusive versus nonabusive backgrounds, and economic and life stress may all play a role in the develop-ment of children's peer competence (see Ladd, 1992, for a review). These factors and others including child characteristics (e.g., tem-perament), family size, personal social networks, parental dis-

agreements about child-rearing practices, and parental recollections of childhood peer relationships may also serve to influence
parenting practices in ways that mediate the role of direct and
indirect pathways from parenting skill to children's competence
with peers (e.g., Bell and Chapman, 1986; Belsky, 1984; Crnic
and Greenberg, 1990; Dishion, 1990; Dix, Ruble, and Zambarano,
1989; Cochran and Brassard, 1979; Jouriles et al., 1991; Putallaz,
Costanzo, and Smith, 1991; Roberts, 1989; Rubin, Hymel, Mills,
and Rose-Krasnor, 1991; Rubin, LeMare, and Lollis, 1990).

Indeed, some negative family characteristics have been found
to disrupt important parenting and socialization activities that
play both direct and indirect roles in fostering children's competence with peers (e.g., Belsky, Steinberg, and Draper, 1991; Ladd,
1992; Rubin, et al. 1989). For instance, with regard to the direct
pathway, parents who are economically deprived appear to be
less able to help their children initiate and sustain interactions
with playmates (cf. Cohn, Patterson, and Christopoulos, 1991;
Ladd, Hart, Wadsworth, and Golter, 1988). Similarly, family stress
and socioeconomic factors also appear to disrupt the indirect
path going from parental discipline to peer competence. Dishion
(1990) found that such factors contributed to negative parental
discipline practices, which, in turn, were related to child adjustment problems.

Beyond this, more work is needed to advance formal, complex
models describing ways that child characteristics, as well as family
processes and characteristics, interact with *both* direct and indirect pathways through which parents contribute to the socialization of their children. These models will likely focus on direct and
indirect pathways involving parenting practices that are embedded
in the context of intervening familial processes and characteristics
such as those described above. Current models should be used as
a foundation for future endeavors in this regard (cf. Rubin et al.
1989, 1990, 1991; Putallaz and Heflin, 1990). Moreover, such
models should take into account the fact that the direction of effect
may not always be from parent to child (Bell and Chapman, 1986;
Rubin et al., 1990, 1991). More will be said about this later.

PARENTING STYLES

Most of the research that has been conducted on parenting
(or child-rearing) styles would fall under the indirect influence

pathway (Ladd, 1992). As with other family characteristics, the construct of parenting styles is multifaceted in nature and consists of many affective, cognitive, and behavioral components (Maccoby and Martin, 1983; Chapter 9, this volume; Putallaz and Heflin, 1990; Rubin et al., 1989). To provide clarity and cohesion to the many components of parenting that have been studied, Putallaz and Heflin (1990) point out that many components of parenting style can be classified under the two major dimensions of acceptance-rejection and dominance-submission (cf. Symonds, 1939). Corresponding dimensions have also been referred to as warmth and control (see Becker, 1964; Baumrind, 1973; and Maccoby and Martin, 1983 for a historical overview).

Dimensional Components

Warmth-hostility, warmth-coldness, and responsiveness versus unresponsiveness are components that have generally been investigated under the warmth or acceptance-rejection dimension. Restrictiveness-permissiveness, control-autonomy, and high demandingness-low demandingness are components that have been studied under the control or dominance-submission dimension (cf. Maccoby and Martin, 1983).

Expanding on models and typologies constructed by Becker (1964) and Baumrind (1967, 1971, 1973), Maccoby and Martin (1983) developed four typologies that emerged from the two-dimensional warmth and control scheme: authoritarian (i.e., demanding rather than responsive; high control, low warmth), authoritative (i.e., demanding and responsive; high control, high warmth), indulgent (i.e., more responsive than demanding; low control, high warmth), and indifferent-uninvolved or neglected (i.e., undemanding and unresponsive; low control, low warmth).

Research on parenting styles has been fairly consistent in showing that socially competent children are those who have authoritative parents who rate higher on both warmth and nonpunitive control dimensions. In contrast, children who are less socially competent tend to have parents who are either authoritarian or permissive in the sense of being indulgent or neglectful (see Lamborn, Mounts, Steinberg, Dornbusch, 1991; Maccoby and Martin, 1983; Putallaz and Heflin, 1990 for reviews).

Pathways Involving Parenting Styles

Going beyond parenting typologies that appear to be associated with children's social competencies, Putallaz and Heflin (1990) advanced a model describing pathways through which parenting styles may work to help children develop social motivation, behavior/skills, and social cognitions that enhance or diminish the quality of peer relations. For instance, parental warmth and responsiveness is thought to facilitate children's emotional development through classical conditioning by enhancing their ability to trust and care about others, thereby increasing their tendency to engage in social interaction with peers.

Likewise, appropriate parental modeling and a judicious use of operant conditioning (i.e., rewarding socially desirable behavior and punishing or ignoring undesirable behavior), may serve to help children acquire socially competent behaviors that may enhance successful interactions with peers. Coaching, which includes reasoning with the child about emotional reactions as well as appropriate and inappropriate interaction strategies, may help children regulate and select more socially desirable behavior and be more cognizant of the thoughts and feelings of others. This, in turn, may enhance the quality of peer interactions. This model was based upon a review of literature indicating that successful parenting styles include components involving (a) warmth; (b) gentle rather than punitive parental control; (c) sensitivity, responsiveness, and involvement; and (d) inductive reasoning in a democratic framework (Putallaz and Heflin, 1990).

While all components appear to be important, recent evidence suggests that individual components may make separate and individual contributions to child competence with peers, even though all of these components may not be mutually exclusive in an overall parenting style framework. In a recent study, Pettit and Mize (in press) gathered extensive data from videotaped assessments of 23 mother-child pairs in which preschool-age children were selected from a larger sample according to their sociometric status. These mother-child pairs took part in a laboratory assessment procedure involving three mother-child interaction contexts in which mothers were observed helping their children work through social problem solving situations with peers and a cognitive task. Videotapes were reliably coded and measures were derived for mother-child *interactional synchrony* (i.e., responsiveness to one another's cues and engagement in smooth and reciprocal behavioral exchanges), *positive parenting* (e.g., enthusiasm and sensitivity), and *maternal coaching skill* (e.g., reasoning about and encouraging socially desirable strategies and helping with interpretation of outcomes associated with a particular social event).

Is a warm, synchronous relationship style by itself adequate for providing children with the skills necessary for successful peer interaction? Results from the Pettit and Mize study suggest that it is not. Direct verbal guidance provided by mothers (as indexed by *maternal coaching skill*) was found to not be significantly correlated with mother-child *interactional synchrony*. However, both *maternal coaching skill* and *interactional synchrony* were significantly related to child peer competence. Results of hierarchical regression analyses (controlling one variable for the other and vice versa) also showed that synchrony and coaching made independent contributions to peer competence. Similar to findings by Barocas et al. (1991), these results suggest that maternal affect and teaching strategies represent separate paths and work through different mechanisms to contribute to different but perhaps overlapping aspects of competence.

Results from the Pettit and Mize study also indicated that parental warmth and responsiveness as characterized by *interactional synchrony* and *positive parenting* were not only significantly related to each other but also to children's peer competence. Similar to Putallaz and Heflin (1990), Pettit and Mize concluded from their data that a warm, responsive, and synchronous style of interaction may contribute to a child's positive view of relations with others, thereby increasing a child's propensity to engage in positive social interactions with peers. Being rewarded for and having many opportunities to practice reading cues from the caregiver may contribute to interpersonal sensitivity in peer group settings. In contrast, children involved in asynchronous interactions "may fail to develop skills for reading social cues, may learn that social relationships are unpredictable, and may withdraw or respond with hostility in order to protect the self from further unrewarding relationships (p. 147)."

As seen above, although warmth and responsiveness in parenting is important, findings from Pettit and Mize (in press) indicated that children also need direct guidance (i.e., coaching) in order to be able to interpret and respond to the complex world of human relations. They further suggest that parents can encourage children to attend to social cues by explaining the rationale underlying certain parental actions or prohibitions (cf. Brody and Shaffer, 1982). As Putallaz and Heflin (1990) theorize, such guidance can also enhance the effects of other modes of parental influence including operant conditioning and modeling processes. For instance, past research indicates that punishment accompanied by reasoning has been found to be more effective than punishment alone (cf. Hetherington and Parke, 1979). In contrast, prohibitions, threats, or rules without reasoning or justification provide little information for children to build repertoires of social strategy information that will enhance competent behavioral interactions with peers (cf. Hoffman and Saltzstein, 1967; Hart et al., 1990; Pettit and Mize, in press).

THEORETICAL CONSIDERATIONS

How is social knowledge transferred from parenting styles to child behavior with peers? In conjunction with the notion that children build repertoires of social strategy information, several theorists have proposed that an important aspect of children's social development entails gathering information about one's social world (Damon, 1977; Higgins, 1981; Turiel, 1977). During the early years, a large part of this information gathering may take place through interactions with parents. As children grow older, information may also be gathered from parents in combination with or in addition to experiences with peers and siblings (Hartup and Moore, 1990; Piaget, 1926; Mead, 1934).

Social Knowledge Structures

In accordance with this assumption, Higgins (1981) argues that social knowledge structures change qualitatively as they become progressively elaborated and sophisticated over the course of development through interactions with the environment. Information to build these structures could be extracted from several avenues of social stimulation in the indirect pathway leading from parenting skill to child competence with peers. Among others, these could include information derived through: (a) observing others in modeling contexts, (b) participating in either warm and responsive interactions or hostile-nonresponsive interactions with others, (c) being exposed to conditioning paradigms where information about rewarding and punishing consequences of certain behaviors is acquired, and (d) taking in communicated information from parents and other significant individuals (cf. Bandura, 1986; Putallaz and Heflin, 1990; Turiel, 1977; Pettit and Mize, in press).

By whatever means social cognitive and behavioral information is gleaned from parents, the enactment of behavior in peer group situations may be further modified and/or sustained by the peer group. For instance, biased perceptions of behavior by peers may occur in accordance with the peer status of the target child (see Hymel, Wagner, and Butler, 1990). Children who are rejected by peers due to biased first impressions based on their own aggressive, disruptive behavior may respond to peers with more hostile behavior that serves to confirm peers' initial perceptions. Recent evidence suggests that these perceptions tend not to change, regardless of any prosocial behaviors the rejected child might later exhibit (Hymel et al. 1990).

The social knowledge base of stored schematic representations derived from experiences with parents and peers may set the stage for the development of ways that children represent and process social experiences (Hartup, Brady, and Newcomb, 1983). According to several models of social information processing, children respond to social stimuli by first encoding relevant cues, then interpreting those cues, accessing possible behavioral responses from memory, evaluating the consequences of possible behaviors, and finally selecting and enacting a behavior (e.g., Dodge, 1986; Ladd and Crick, 1989; Rubin and Krasnor, 1986). In some instances, however, stored schematic representations of social interaction that are acquired through interaction with parents may serve to override or restructure any social information being presented in social situations with peers, thus having an impact on social-information processing patterns (cf. D'Andrade, 1972, cited in Hartup et al., 1983).

For example, Dodge, Bates, and Pettit (1990) recently theorized that, based on attachment theory, insecure attachments associated with abusive parenting may lead to deviant patterns of encoding relevant social cues. Such deficiencies may be based on internal models of hostility and dominance that children have constructed based on information gathered from consistent exposure to abusive parent-child interactions. Social learning theory would also suggest that consistent exposure to physical abuse would lead to later aggression based on these stored schematic representations that were gathered from parent modeling of hostile means to resolve interpersonal issues (cf. Bandura, 1986).

Stored schematic representations have also been referred to as scripts, a kind of "shorthand" that streamlines the complexity of social stimuli into manageable means for processing social information and enacting social strategies (Glick, 1978; Hartup et al., 1983; Schank and Abelson, 1977). Scripts help children to actively transfer or represent selected information in ways that make social information more useful. Such selective streamlining of information may lead to social cognitive processing biases. From this viewpoint, it is conceivable that varying ways that parents provide information to their children concerning social behavior at home may influence habitual ways that children develop to represent and process social information in peer group interactions.

Research Support

Data supporting this perspective includes recent work by Dodge et al. (1990). In a prospective study of 309 children, physically harmed children (relative to nonharmed children) were found to be significantly less attentive to and more likely to misinterpret relevant social cues; specifically, these children were more biased toward attributing hostile intent to benign or ambiguous social cues displayed by other children. In addition, they were less likely to generate competent solutions to interpersonal problems. Such information processing deficits were also found to serve as mediational mechanisms between parental physical abuse and children's aggressive behavior with peers. Similar findings were obtained in a recent study by Weiss, Dodge, Bates, and Pettit (1992). Moreover, significant relations between harsh parental discipline at age four and children's aggression toward peers at kindergarten held true even when several child biological and family ecological factors had been statistically controlled. Findings presented by Pettit and Harrist (Chapter 9, this volume) were also consistent with prior work demonstrating that coercive parent-child interactions are related to less attentiveness to peers' social cues and to less competent interactions with peers.

Other supportive research suggests that social cognitive mechanisms may mediate relations between several aspects of parenting skill and indices of peer competence. Several studies have statistically tested potential paths of influence. For instance, Pettit, Dodge, and Brown (1988) found that social problem-solving skills mediated relations between maternal endorsement of aggression and lower levels of competence with peers. In later work, Pettit et al. (1991) investigated relations involving both responsive and intrusive parent-child interactional styles. They found that these styles were related to children's perceptions of how easy it would be to enact socially competent and aggressive behavior. This, in turn, contributed to children's actual performance of such behavior with peers.

Other research has been devoted to exploring mediational relations involving consequential thinking skills. Hart et al. (1990) discovered that children who expected to get their way by being hostile with peers not only had mothers who were power assertive in their discipline strategies but were also more rejected by peers. More recent findings reported by Hart, DeWolf, and Burts (1992b) suggest that such outcome expectancies for hostile social strategies were linked not only to power assertive disciplinary strategies, but also to preschoolers' hostile behavior with peers. In contrast, preschoolers of inductive mothers envisioned prosocial strategies as leading to both instrumental gains and enhanced relations with peers. Children with such outcome expectancies were also found to exhibit more prosocial behavior with peers.

Although an effort has been made to identify potential mediating roles that social cognitive mechanisms play in relations between several aspects of parenting and peer competence, little is known about ways that behavioral mechanisms mediate this relationship. Notable exceptions to this include results reported by MacDonald and Parke (1984), MacDonald (1987), and Putallaz (1987). Taken together, findings indicated that excessive directive, negative, and controlling behavior with children was linked not only to hostile interactions with peers, but also to lower levels of peer status. In contrast, positive maternal verbal interactive styles appeared to be linked to enhanced interactions with and acceptance by peers. However, statistical, mediational linkages have not yet been explored in these lines of research.

Studies in which mediational paths involving parenting skill, child behavior, and peer status were statistically tested include recent work by Dishion (1990). In a study involving lower socioeconomic status 10-year-old boys, Dishion reported that the combined effects of maternal and paternal power assertion may work through antisocial behavior to promote peer rejection. However, few studies have explored possible roles that positive features of parental discipline may play in facilitating prosocial behavior with peers that, in turn, is related to positive peer status outcomes. We will now turn attention to exploring not only the role that parental power assertion may play in facilitating children's hostile behavior and subsequent rejection by peers but also to ways that inductive discipline may enhance prosocial interactions with and acceptance by peers. Although there is evidence that children acquire social cognitions and behavior from parents through other means (Putallaz and Heflin, 1990), the remainder of this chapter will be narrowed to focus exclusively on inductive and power assertive disciplinary strategies.

Inductive Strategies

Induction is a multifaceted disciplinary strategy that can be adapted to a wide range of disciplinary circumstances. Although inductive strategies are generally classified outside the realm of overall parenting styles and included more in the realms of parent-child communication, or disciplinary techniques (cf. Maccoby and Martin, 1983; Putallaz and Heflin, 1990), there is some evidence to suggest that inductive strategies are associated with authoritative parenting styles that were discussed earlier (Coppersmith, 1967; Maccoby and Martin, 1983). Moreover, elements of Baumrind's authoritative parenting style including parents encouraging verbal give-and-take, communicating their point of view, and allowing children to express their own viewpoint is not far akin from inductive discipline (Baumrind, 1967, 1971; Maccoby and Martin, 1983;). Although verbal interactions of this nature may be classified under responsive aspects of parenting, such communications likely set the stage for children to be more open to reasoning about their behavior.

It may be recalled that prior work by Pettit and Mize (in press) indicated that verbally articulated instruction makes contributions to peer competence in ways that appear to be independent of warm, responsive aspects of parenting style although both are important for nurturing socially competent children (cf. Dix, 1991; Rollins and Thomas, 1974). Induction is a verbal means through which parents may provide children with specific instruction regarding how to negotiate their social world and understand the consequences of their actions for themselves and others. When used to facilitate social skills, induction would likely fall into the direct rather than the indirect pathway of influence that was discussed earlier.

What is the nature of induction? No single inductive strategy can be used to define the necessary and sufficient conditions for this disciplinary mode (cf. Eisenberg and Miller, 1990; Rushton, 1980). Instead, researchers have identified specific inductive strategies that parents may use independently or simultaneously in regulating their child who has done something (or wants to do something) that is contrary to parental desires and expectancies.

In general, parents who use inductive strategies for regulating children's behavior coach children by introducing claims and consequences and then supplying rationales that support them (Burleson, 1983). This is done by limit setting, setting up logical consequences, explaining, and eliciting ideas from the child rather than by focusing upon coercive means to regulate behavior. More specifically, inductive strategies can include the act of pointing out to the transgressor the consequences of his or her behavior for himself or herself and for other persons (Saltzstein, 1976), the explanation of and reasoning about the perspectives and feelings of others (e.g., Applegate & Delia, 1980), the elicitation of alternative behaviors from the child that could be enacted in similar situations (Spivack, Platt, and Shure, 1976), the encouragement of verbal give-and-take and the offering of alternatives to the child (Baumrind, 1971; see also Rollins and Thomas, 1979), limit setting and following through with consequences articulated by the parent or the child (Applegate, Burke, Burleson, Delia, and Kline, 1985; Biller, 1981), and the direct explanation of rules and restrictions that are prevalent in society (Turiel, 1983).

The basis for parental control when using inductive means is *internal* for the child because "the goal of the disciplinarian is to [help] children understand why their transgressions are wrong, why they should follow various rules and regulations, and how they might alter their behavior to achieve that end" (Brody and Shaffer, 1982, p. 37). In accordance with the viewpoint expressed earlier that children build social knowledge structures by extracting information from parental stimulation, induction provides children with the opportunity to regulate their own behavior by acting in accordance with the social knowledge base that has been acquired from parental instruction through reasoning practices. As Hoffman (1970) stated:

> The effectiveness of induction as discipline, as compared to power assertion, appears to be based less on the fear of punishment and more on the child's connecting its cognitive substance to his own resources for comprehending the necessities of the situation and controlling his own behavior accordingly. (p. 286)

An explication of reasons for one's conduct not only assists the child in attempts to extract, interpret, and understand parental rationales for specific expectancies but also provides children with opportunities to consider alternative strategies for social interaction and to practice contriving strategies and considering subsequent consequences. Induction also serves to focus children on the perspectives, feelings, thoughts, desires, attitudes, plans, motivations, needs, and other psychological qualities of those whom the child's behavior affects (e.g., Bearison and Cassel, 1975). Consider the following example of a parent reasoning with a child:

> "How do you feel when someone calls you names? You shouldn't call Johnny names because it hurts his feelings. That makes him mad, and then he wants to hurt back, just like you do when someone hurts your feelings. And if you hurt people, then they won't like you and won't want to play with you." What can you say to Johnny to help him feel happy? (modified from Burleson, 1983, p. 9).

Over time, these reasons concerning how others usually respond to particular behavioral strategies may become internalized principles and standards by which conduct is governed as opposed to being governed by external forces and constraints. These reasons also help children focus on the less visible qualities of their social-psychological world that are manifested in concrete behavioral ways that are more salient to the child.

Attention to these invisible qualities can be enhanced through inductive parenting strategies. Although the effectiveness of induction appears to begin early (by 1.5 to 2.5 years of age), young children have natural tendencies to think of others in terms of concrete behavioral and physical characteristics rather than in terms of their invisible psychological qualities (e.g., Burleson, 1983; Harter, 1982; Zahn-Waxler et al., 1979). Studies that have explored children's conceptions of friends have shown that as children grow older they tend to focus less on physical manifestations of how others might be thinking and feeling and more on the psychological characteristics themselves (e.g., Bigelow, 1977; Bigelow and LaGaipa, 1975; Furman and Bierman, 1983). These invisible psychological qualities then become a basis for action as the child begins to attend to them first within a behaviorally oriented framework and then later within an abstract, person-centered orientation (Applegate et al., 1985; Applegate, Burke, Burleson, and Delia, 1992).

Given the above, it does not seem unreasonable that through induction, parents provide information that will help children build social knowledge structures concerning less visible qualities of others that will enhance various components of the social information processing models mentioned earlier (Dodge, 1986; Rubin and Krasnor, 1986). These include social cue interpretation, having access to a variety of social strategies in the memory repertoire, evaluating possible consequences of behavior, and enacting appropriate behavior. For example and as mentioned earlier, with regard to evaluating possible consequences and enacting appropriate behavior, recent research findings suggest that parents who focus their children on consequences of their actions through inductive rather than power assertive means, have both preschool and school-age children who have consequential thinking styles that are more flexible and socially adept (Hart et al., 1990; Hart, et al., 1992b).

Other research, involving primarily mothers, has also shown positive relations involving parental induction and child developmental outcomes. For example, results of past research have indicated that parents who typically employ inductively oriented interactive strategies have children who are relatively more empathic (e.g., Feshbach, 1974), altruistic (e.g., Hoffman, 1975a; Mussen, Rutherford, Harris, and Keasey, 1970), generous

(Dlugokinski and Firestone, 1974), and considerate of others (e.g., Hoffman, 1963). Research has also linked inductive discipline to greater self-control, enhanced communication skills, and positive social interactions with peers (Bearison and Cassel, 1975; Burleson, Delia, and Applegate, 1992; Hoffman, 1975b; Zahn-Waxler, Radke-Yarrow, and King, 1979). Moreover, induction, accompanied by other nondisciplinary procedures including prosocial modeling, moral exhortations, assigning responsibilities, helping older children acquire prosocial self-attributions, and providing warmth and supportiveness appear to go far in enhancing children's prosocial behavior (cf. Eisenberg and Miller, 1990).

Power Assertive Strategies

In contrast to inductive strategies, power assertion is *externally* oriented for the child as the parent is involved in demanding an immediate modification of their child's behavior. It is generally linked with the authoritarian parenting style discussed earlier. Operationally, power assertive strategies include the deprivation of material objects or privileges, the direct application of force including physical punishment (e.g. spanking, slapping, grabbing, shoving) and/or threats thereof, yelling, belittling, and stating directives with little or no justification (e.g., Hoffman, 1982; Saltzstein, 1976; Straus, 1991). Other parental power assertive strategies could include the overuse of material or physical rewards in order to bring about conformance. Such strategies are used to promote the valuing of obedience and respect for authority by attempting to shape children's behavior in accordance with an absolute set of standards (Maccoby and Martin, 1983). Thus, the child conforms with parental expectancies that are instrumentally focused in order to avoid (or obtain) parent-controlled punishment (or rewards) (Burleson, 1983).

Rather than sending information cues that will assist the child in constructing adaptive social knowledge structures, heavy reliance on power assertive discipline strategies provides little or no information that the child can draw from that would be helpful in internalizing social knowledge that would be necessary for establishing positive relationships with others. Instead, parental power assertion models a rigid and hostile interactional style as an efficacious means of resolving interpersonal issues. (Eisenberg and Miller, 1990). Consistent exposure to parents getting their way by power assertive means in disciplinary contexts may also lead children to view consequences for hostile behavior as leading to instrumental gains, excluding interpersonal relationship considerations (cf. Hart et al., 1990; Hart, et al., 1992b).

It may be recalled that research reviewed earlier indicates that abusive and power assertive parenting is also associated with other social cognitive deficits, which, in turn, are related to hostile interactions with and rejection by peers (e.g., Dodge et al., 1990; Dishion, 1990; Hart et al., 1990; Pettit et al., 1988). Some children may also respond to power assertion with social withdrawal (cf. Maccoby and Martin, 1983). In addition, many other studies have documented low self-regulation and negative childhood interactions with peers as being associated with this disciplinary strategy (e.g., Baumrind, 1967, 1971; Becker, Peterson, Luria, Shoemaker, and Hellmer, 1962; Sears, Whiting, Nowlis, and Sears, 1953; Sears, Maccoby, and Levin, 1957). Such hostile interpersonal styles also appear to be compounded by coercive familial interactional patterns (e.g., Patterson, 1982; Patterson, Reid, and Dishion, 1992; Dishion, 1990; Chapter 9, this volume).

In contrast, recent findings reported by Kochanska (1991) suggest that the deemphasis of power assertion in parental discipline capitalizes on the child's internal arousal associated with wrongdoing. This appears to promote more self-regulation in children due to a more internalized conscience and more intense feelings of discomfort associated with wrongdoing. Overreliance on strict, forceful methods of discipline such as threats and punishment appeared to shift the child's attention away from the internal discomfort associated with wrongdoing to a focus on salient external contingencies, such as threats and punishments (cf. Loeb, 1975). Moreover, although power assertion may produce conformity in the immediate situation, both verbal and physical power assertion by parents has been linked to a variety of psychosocial problems in children including aggression, delinquency in adolescence, and violent crimes both inside and outside the family over the lifespan (Straus, 1991; Vissing, Straus, Gelles and Harrop, 1991).

SITUATIONAL AND CHILD DETERMINANTS OF DISCIPLINARY STRATEGIES

Do parents use either inductive or power assertive strategies exclusively? There is fairly conclusive evidence that for abusive parents, punishment tends to be the predominant type of discipline regardless of the types of child misbehavior (Gerris and Janssens, 1987; Trickett and Kuczynski, 1986). For more normative parenting, Maccoby and Martin (1983) cite several studies suggesting that parents use power assertive or inductive methods depending on the disciplinary situation (e.g., Grusec and Kuczynski, 1980). Although some of this work has been criticized on methodological grounds (see Burleson, 1983), it seems reasonable, for example, that parents would be more power assertive in situations where physical harm to self or others might be intended and more inductive in situations where psychological or emotional harm might be inflicted by the child. In our own research, however, we have found a surprising degree of consistency in the ways that parents responded to a variety of hypothetical disciplinary situations (either power assertively or inductively—see Hart et al., 1990, 1992a). Similar findings have been obtained by Applegate et al. (1985) and Burleson et al. (1992).

The issue is further complicated, however, by recent data suggesting that attributions of child competence mediate variations in mothers' inductive and power assertive discipline across children's ages, children's behaviors, and mothers' child-rearing ideaologies (Dix et al., 1989). Since most research on parenting and child competence has been correlational in nature, the results can be interpreted as providing an equally plausible explanation that child characteristics beyond situational determinants of varying disciplinary contexts (e.g., temperament) influence parents to select specific child regulative strategies (e.g., Bell and Chapman, 1986).

However, others have argued that studies supporting child effects on discipline practices are inconclusive (e.g., Burleson, 1983; Hoffman, 1975b, 1984; Lytton, 1980). Because parents have far more power to place constraints on the child than the other way around, it has been argued that it is unlikely that child behavior could substantially mold enduring parental personality characteristics or general behavioral dispositions. Moreover, according to this line of reasoning, characteristics of the child cannot negate the positive or negative influence of disciplinary strategies anyway. Until more conclusive evidence is obtained that supports the reciprocity or unidirectionality of influence, the literature will likely continue to be interpreted from the causal perspective of parent influences on children's development (See

Anderson, Lytton, and Romney, 1986; Conger, Friedberg, and Conger, 1987; and Mink and Nihira, 1986 for further discussions of this issue). Clearly, more work is needed to investigate this complex issue.

A STUDY OF DISCIPLINARY STRATEGIES AND PLAYGROUND COMPETENCE

Whether or not parents consistently use power assertive or inductive disciplinary strategies, past research suggests that the predominant disciplinary strategy has the most influence on child competence with peers. Findings from research by Hoffman (1963) demonstrated that mothers' use of induction was positively related to children's prosocial behavior toward peers only if the mothers were low in the use of power assertion. However, in families where the mothers were high in power assertion, reasoning was negatively related with children's prosocial behavior toward peers. Hoffman theorized that children may be provoked to rebel against the parent regardless of other disciplinary strategies used if the parents frequently used power assertive strategies (cf. Maccoby and Martin, 1983; Putallaz and Heflin, 1990).

In accordance with the notion that the predominant style of discipline would have the most influence on children's behavior with peers, we set out to further explore relations among both maternal and paternal inductive and power-assertive disciplinary strategies, children's playground behavior, and status with peers (see Hart, et al., 1992a). Other work is also currently being devoted to investigating social cognitions discussed earlier that may mediate relations between parental discipline and children's playground behavior (Hart et al., 1992b). Few studies that have included aspects of induction or power assertion have explored corresponding child behavior in naturalistic settings such as the playground.

Since the relevant literature and methodological details associated with this study have already been reported in Hart et al. (1992a), our purpose here is only to present a brief overview of the aims, methodology, and results of the study. We will also present new data on relations between parental discipline and children's nonsocial/withdrawn behavior that were not included in the published report.

Aims

Several aims were pursued in this investigation. Much of the past research in this area has only focused on the effects of maternal discipline or only on either power assertive or inductive aspects of discipline. Therefore, our first aim was to delineate maternal and paternal disciplinary roles (both power assertive and inductive) and to investigate their individual and interactive relations with observed child behavior and peer status. Based on literature reviewed by Hart et al. (1992a), we anticipated that preschoolers of more inductive and less power assertive mothers and fathers would display more prosocial behavior and less antisocial and disruptive playground behavior and be more accepted and less rejected by peers. In accordance with Rubin et al. (1990), we also hypothesized that children of more power assertive parents would be prone to exhibit more withdrawn and/or nonsocial behavior with peers. We further expected that these findings would hold true when maternal discipline was controlled for paternal discipline and vice versa. However, we hypothesized that relative to fathers, mothers would carry a greater weight of influence with regard to child behavior and peer status.

A second aim of our study was to see if past research findings on preschoolers' playground behavior and peer status could be replicated. Specifically, we anticipated that preschoolers who engaged in more prosocial (i.e., cooperative play, social conversation) and less antisocial (aggression, arguing) and disruptive (rough and tumble play) playground behavior would be more accepted and less rejected by peers. We further expected that withdrawn and aimless playground behavior would be linked to negative peer reputations (cf. Chapters 5 and 9, this volume). We also examined the interactive roles that preschoolers' sex and age might play in relations among parental discipline, behavior, and peer status. A final aim of our study was to determine whether these behavioral orientations served as mediating mechanisms between self-reported disciplinary styles and preschooler's peer status.

Methodology

Subjects for this study were 106 preschool-age children attending 1 of 5 preschool programs (age range = 40–71 months;

median age = 54 months) in a moderate-sized southern community. Children (53 boys and 53 girls) and parents (both mothers and fathers) were predominantly white (96%) and were from middle to upper middle-class backgrounds. To assess whether mothers and fathers were prone to use inductive or power assertive disciplinary strategies, mothers and fathers of preschool-age children were interviewed separately in individual tape recorded home interviews and were asked to respond to seven hypothetical situations similar to those used in past research describing disciplinary contexts. After the audiotapes were transcribed, the data were reliably coded using an extensive hierarchical coding scheme designed to capture varying shades or degrees of the power assertion–induction dichotomy.

Children were also observed on the playground using a scan sampling procedure over a 4–6-week period, resulting in 85 2-second scans per child. Children's peer interactive behavior was coded into the following categories: (a) cooperative play—nondisruptive mutual activity with others; (b) social conversation—face–to–face talk; (c) arguing—hostile talk; (d) aggression—physical harm intended hostile acts; and (d) rough play—boisterous, quasiagonistic activity. Nonsocial/withdrawn behavior was coded into: (a) solitary play—alone and occupied with a nondisruptive task; (b) parallel play—play activity near but not with others; (c) unoccupied behavior—alone and off-task; and (d) onlooking behavior—watching others but not interacting. Behaviors oriented toward or interacting with the teacher were coded as "teacher orientation." Sociometric testing was conducted using standard picture board nomination techniques. Procedures outlined by Coie, Dodge, and Coppotelli (1982) were then used to create a measure of social preference.

Results Involving Peer-Interactive Playground Behavior, Discipline, and Peer Preference

Using multivariate analysis of variance (MANOVA) procedures (see Hart et al., 1992a, for details), results indicated that preschoolers of inductive mothers and fathers engaged in less rough play than did children of power assertive mothers and fathers. In addition, preschoolers of inductive mothers were more accepted by peers than were preschoolers of power assertive mothers. In contrast, paternal discipline was not significantly related to peer preference nor to any of the other behaviors. Additional findings suggest that prosocial (social conversation and cooperative play) and disruptive (rough play) behaviors mediated relations between maternal discipline and peer preference.

We also found that age and gender characteristics of the child interacted with aspects of parental discipline and peer relations during the preschool years. Older preschoolers and daughters of inductive mothers engaged in more prosocial behavior than did other children of the same age and gender who had power asser-tive mothers. No significant interactive effects of maternal and paternal discipline emerged in the analyses.

Other findings suggested that preschoolers' age and gender may also work in combination with interactive behavior to en-hance or diminish peer preference during the preschool years. Older preschoolers who displayed more antisocial (arguing + ag-gression) and disruptive playground behavior (rough play) were less preferred by playmates. Similarly, older female preschoolers who engaged in more prosocial behavior were more preferred. However, no significant effects were found with younger pre-schoolers, or younger females. Implications of all these findings are discussed by Hart et al. (1992a).

Results Involving Nonsocial/Withdrawn Playground Behavior

Findings regarding nonsocial/withdrawn playground behavior were obtained in the analyses and were not reported in the Hart et al. (1992a) paper due to space limitations. However, some interesting findings did emerge that we would like to briefly present here.

Because substantial correlations were found between scores of onlooking and unoccupied behaviors, a composite score was created by summing the scores contained in these two categories and referred to as withdrawn behavior. Nonsocial behavior with peers (e.g., solitary play, parallel play, and teacher orientation) were retained as separate scores in subsequent analyses.

Discipline and nonsocial/withdrawn behavior/peer prefer-ence. Findings from MANOVAS conducted in a similar manner to those in Hart et al. (1992a) indicated no significant multivari-ate main effects of maternal discipline, paternal discipline, sex, and age on preschoolers' nonsocial/withdrawn playground behavior. However, a significant interaction of maternal discipline with sex emerged from the analysis $F(4,94) = 2.67$, $p < .05$.[1] A significant three-way interaction involving paternal discipline, sex, and age was also found $F(4,94) = 2.32$, $p < .05$. No other interactions involving maternal discipline, paternal discipline, sex, or age were significant.

Subsequent univariate analyses revealed significant interactions of maternal discipline with sex for solitary play, parallel play, and withdrawn behavior but not for teacher orientation Fs $(1,97) = 4.38, 4.21, 3.82$, $p < .05$. Univariate analyses also found a significant interaction of paternal discipline with sex and age for withdrawn behavior $F(1,97) = 7.80$, $p < .001$, but not for solitary play, parallel play, or teacher orientation. An analysis of simple effects indicated that females of power assertive mothers engaged in more solitary play and withdrawn behavior than did females of inductive mothers [$M = 13.68$ ($SD = 10.36$) and 10.68 ($SD = 6.57$); 19.23 ($SD = 8.74$) and 16.71 ($SD = 6.08$), respectively] but there was no significant effect of maternal discipline for sons in this regard [$M = 9.98$ ($SD = 5.43$) and 12.52 ($SD = 9.08$); 14.19 ($SD = 3.97$) and 16.48 ($SD = 6.54$), respectively]. In addition, males of power assertive mothers exhibited more parallel play than did males of inductive mothers [$M = 15.41$ ($SD = 5.90$) and 10.92 ($SD = 6.33$)], but there was no significant effect of maternal discipline for females in this regard ($M = 15.41$ ($SD = 6.35$) and 10.93 ($SD = 8.19$)].

Simple effects analyses also revealed that older males of power assertive fathers engaged in more withdrawn behavior than did older males of inductive fathers [$M = 18.21$ ($SD = 4.30$) and 12.75 ($SD = 6.51$)]. However, no significant effects were obtained for younger males, younger females, or for older females in this regard.

Nonsocial/withdrawn behavior and peer preference. Next, separate analyses of variance (ANOVAs) were conducted to explore all main effects and interactions involving age, sex, and nonsocial/withdrawn behavioral orientations on peer preference. No significant main effects were obtained. However, analyses yielded significant interactions of sex with solitary play and sex with teacher orientation Fs $(1,97) = 7.69$ and 4.08, $p < .001$ and $.05$, respectively. A significant three-way interaction of withdrawn behavior with age and sex was also significant Fs $(1,97) = 8.15$,

$p < .001$. No significant effects emerged involving parallel play. Because children's peer preference and behaviors were both measured on a continuous scale, the significant two-way interactions indicated that the linear relationship between peer preference and solitary play and between peer preference and teacher orientation was different for males than for females (see Hart et al., 1992, for procedural explanation). In the case of the three-way interaction involving withdrawn behavior, this linear relationship was different for both younger and older males and females. Partial regression coefficients calculated for the two sex groupings for solitary play and teacher orientation revealed a highly significant negative relationship between peer preference and solitary play for females ($b = -.060$, $p < .001$) but not for males ($b = .01$, n.s.) and a significant negative relationship between peer preference and teacher orientation for males ($b = -.085$, $p < .05$) but not for females ($b = .012$, n.s.). For withdrawn behavior, separate partial regression coefficients for each of the four sex and age combinations revealed a highly significant negative relationship between peer preference and withdrawn behavior for older males ($b = -.070$, $p < .001$). The relationship between peer preference and withdrawn behavior was not significant for younger males, younger females, or older females (b's $= .03$, $-.03$, $.01$, n.s., respectively).

Mediational paths involving nonsocial/withdrawn behavior. Finally, using procedures described in Hart et al. (1992a) mediational paths involving maternal and paternal discipline, nonsocial/withdrawn behaviors, and peer preference were also explored. Unlike mediational paths involving maternal discipline and interactive behavior reported in Hart et al. (1992a), results of mediational analyses using nonsocial/withdrawn behaviors were inconclusive.

Summary: Parenting and Child Behavior/Peer Preference

In summary, analyses for peer interactive (Hart et al., 1992a) and nonsocial/withdrawn behavior indicated that maternal induction (as contrasted with power assertion) was linked to greater acceptance by peers and to more prosocial behavior, particularly for girls and for older preschoolers (cf. Hart et al., 1992a). In contrast, maternal power assertion (as contrasted with induction) was related to less acceptance by peers and to more disruptive behavior. In addition, maternal power assertion was linked to more solitary play and withdrawn behavior for girls and to more parallel play for boys. Inductive discipline by fathers was only related to fewer instances of rough play for both boys and girls and to lower levels of withdrawn behavior for older boys.

Gender and age qualifications. These findings indicated that girls' prosocial behavior, solitary play, and withdrawn behavior was more strongly linked to maternal discipline than were these same behaviors of boys. Similarly, withdrawn behavior in older boys was linked to paternal rather than maternal power assertion. These findings provided partial support for our sex role orientation hypothesis (described in Hart et al., 1992a) by indicating that power assertive discipline is more related to less competent playground behavior for children of same sex parents. This appears to be particularly true for withdrawn behavior since power assertive mothers were linked to daughters and power assertive fathers were linked to older sons in this regard (cf. Rubin et al., 1990). However, nonsupportive findings also indicated that any sex role orientation may not apply to all types of behavior. For instance, findings for boy's parallel play crossed gender lines and appeared to be related to maternal rather than to paternal power assertion. Likewise, *both* maternal and paternal power assertion were linked to playground disruptive behavior for *both* boys and girls.

Findings also partially supported our view that developmental patterns of emerging behavioral orientations may interact with aspects of parenting by becoming more stable as children mature (see Hart et al., 1992a). This seems to hold true for prosocial behavior since maternal induction was linked to this behavior more for older than for younger children.

Summary: Child Behavior and Peer Preference

Age and gender were also found to work in combination with both interactive and nonsocial/withdrawn behavioral orientations and peer status. Older preschoolers who engaged in more prosocial and less antisocial or disruptive behavior were more preferred by peers. Boys who interacted more with the teacher were less preferred. In addition, older boys who engaged in withdrawn behavior and girls who displayed more solitary play were also less preferred.

Age qualifications. Many of the age qualifications indicating that older rather than younger preschoolers' peer status would be related to behavior was anticipated (see Hart et al., 1992a). Although findings may be due, in part, to sociometric measurement limitations with younger preschoolers (Hart et al., 1992a), they can also be explained by past research indicating that the connection between peer status and social skills may be in the process of emerging across the preschool years due to dynamic changes in interpersonal-interactive capabilities (cf. Ramsey, 1990; Johnson, Christie, and Yawkey, 1987). For instance, many studies have shown that cooperative acts, person-oriented verbal aggression, and rough play increase significantly while nonsocial/ withdrawn behavior decreases from the early to the late preschool years (see Hart et al., 1992a; Hartup, 1983; Ramsey, 1990; Rubin, Fein, and Vandenberg, 1983; Parke and Slaby, 1983, for reviews).

Data from our sample regarding age differences in playground behavior paralleled many of these earlier findings. Additional analyses (t tests) indicated that older preschoolers as compared with younger preschoolers displayed significantly more social conversation ($M = 9.62$ and 6.61), cooperative play ($M = 11.10$ and 7.33), arguing ($M = 3.01$ and 1.49), rough play ($M = 6.40$ and 3.98) and significantly less solitary play ($M = 9,87$ and 12.96), and withdrawn behavior ($M = 15.68$ and 17.97). Due to emerging patterns of increasing interactive and decreasing nonsocial/withdrawn behavior that likely become more stable across the preschool years, it was not surprising that older preschoolers, as opposed to younger preschoolers, were more likely to view prosocial behavior more positively with regard to their playmate preferences. Likewise, antisocial/disruptive play was viewed more negatively in this regard.

Gender qualifications. Sex differences in preschooler's peer status as a function of behavior (sometimes in combination with age differences) also should not be surprising in light of past research (e.g., Chapter 6, this volume). Prior studies have demonstrated that boys are more physically active than girls on the playground (see Grusec and Lytton, 1988, for a review). This physical activity likely increases with age and is probably viewed as more normal by peers as boy's large motor skills continue to develop across the preschool years. Therefore, our data, not surprisingly, showed that older boys, in particular, who engaged in more withdrawn nonphysical activities were not looked upon favorably by peers. Likewise, boys who spent inordinate amounts of time with the teacher were less preferred by peers, indicating that such behavior may be more acceptable to peers for girls than for boys (cf. Coie et al., 1990).

Findings regarding prosocial and solitary play for females also should not be surprising, despite the fact that significant relations between solitary play and peer status have not been consistently found in other studies nor have sex differences always been explored in this regard (e.g., Ladd, 1983; Ladd, Price, and Hart, 1988, 1990; Chapter 9, this volume; Rubin, 1982). Past research findings have indicated that girls, as compared with boys, are more likely to seek proximity to others and emphasize interpersonal relations and prosocial behavior with peers (Grusec and Lytton, 1988). Thus, it was not surprising that higher levels of prosocial behavior and lower levels of solitary play were linked to greater peer acceptance for girls more so than for boys.

In summary of the findings involving linkages between behavior and peer status, results showing linkages between playground interactive behaviors and peer status and relations between nonsocial/withdrawn behavior and peer status were in accordance with past research (e.g., Ladd, Price, and Hart, 1988; 1990; Ladd and Price, 1987; Chapter 5, this volume) but were further defined by age and/or sex differences. Findings for withdrawn and nonsocial behavior were also in accordance with the suggestion of Rubin et al. (1990, 1991) that children who remain behaviorally inhibited relative to their peers will become increasingly salient to their age-mates. Their deviance from age-appropriate social and emotional norms do indeed appear to result in the establishment of negative peer reputations, although findings with preschoolers appear to be qualified by the sex of the child.

Summary: Interactive Relations and Mediational Linkages

What about interactive relations and mediational linkages involving both maternal and paternal discipline and child playground competence with peers? Although 65% of the mothers and fathers in the sample reported using similar disciplinary strategies, when their styles differed, each parent was equally likely to be power assertive or inductive (see Hart et al., 1992).

Results of further analyses indicated no significant relations with behavior when the mother favored an inductive style, but the father was more power assertive or vice versa. However as anticipated (cf. Hart et al., 1992a), relative to fathers, more consistent patterns of findings involving relations among maternal discipline, child behavior, and peer status suggested that mothers may carry the weight of influence with their children in this regard. This is not surprising in light of recent findings indicating that mothers discipline their children six times more often than fathers (Hart, Myers, and DeWolf, in preparation) and that fathers are peripheral to young children's intellectual and psychosocial functioning (Hawkins and Eggebeen, 1991).[2] Moreover, findings from our analyses reported in Hart et al., (1992) suggested that maternal discipline may be indirectly linked to peer status through child disruptive and prosocial behavioral mechanisms (cf. Putallaz and Heflin, 1990). These findings were in accordance with our earlier remarks suggesting that maternal induction facilitates a more prosocial orientation with peers that, in turn, contributes to a positive reputation in the peer group.

However, statistical mediational linkages involving withdrawn and nonsocial aspects of behavior as well as paternal discipline were not found. For instance, even though maternal power assertion was linked to girls' solitary play that, in turn, was linked to less acceptance by peers, no mediational linkages were found. Likewise, significant linkages involving paternal power assertion, older boys' withdrawn behavior, and subsequent peer status were not found to be mediational in nature. In fact, no mediational linkages were found for fathers (perhaps due to the primacy effect of mothers) nor were any linkages found involving antisocial behavior (see Hart et al., 1992a, for further discussion).

One cautious interpretation of these mediational findings is that it may be the more outgoing, highly visible interactive prosocial and disruptive behaviors rather than nonsocial/withdrawn behaviors that are the most salient to peers when judging the social reputations of others. It was also these interactive rather than nonsocial/withdrawn behaviors that were most consistently linked to parental discipline across age and sex groupings (cf. Hart et al., 1992). As Ladd and Price (Chapter 5, this volume) suggest, nonsocial behavior may limit preschooler's interactions with peers and, thus, minimize peers' opportunities to adequately evaluate them as potential playmates. Inadequate or inconsistent judgments by peers at this age may suppress our ability to reliably detect potential mediating roles that withdrawn and nonsocial behavior may play between parenting and peer status from a statistical standpoint.

Although sociometric category placements appear to be somewhat problematic with preschoolers (cf. Vaughn and Mize, 1991), another possibility could be that sociometric subgroupings may be more precise than a measure of peer preference in detecting the mediational effects of this type of behavior, particularly the withdrawn-rejected and withdrawn-neglected subgroups (Crick, 1991). That is not to say, however, that nonsocial/withdrawn behaviors in this study were not linked to peer preference in meaningful ways (see above). Other possibilities for the lack of mediational linkages in this type of research are offered by Burleson, Delia, and Applegate (1992).

OVERALL SUMMARY AND FUTURE DIRECTIONS

Overall, findings from our study were supportive of the literature reviewed earlier indicating that there are meaningful pathways linking parental disciplinary strategies to children's playground behavior and peer status. Our data suggests that this is particularly true for interactive playground behavior. Children appear to glean behavioral information from parents in disciplinary contexts that translate into behavioral orientations that are enacted with peers. In support of Putallaz and Heflin (1990), some of these behavioral orientations appear to provide mediational linkages between maternal discipline and peer status.

Moreover, findings involving relations among parental discipline and child behavior and child behavior and peer status were generally supportive of past research where child behavioral data was collected in settings other than playgrounds. Induction was linked to prosocial behavior and power assertion was linked to disruptive and withdrawn behaviors. However, the fact that power assertion was related to playground disruptive behavior rather than to aggression as in past research may indicate that different types of agonistic behavior associated with power assertion may be more prominently displayed on the playground than in other settings. More research is needed to address this possibility.

Significant relations involving disciplinary strategies from our investigation, however, should be cautiously interpreted until future replicative work is conducted using validating measures of discipline (e.g., observations) to assure the validity of the disciplinary constructs that were used. Although Kochanska, Kuczynski, and Radke-Yarrow (1989) found good correspondence between self-reported and observed child-rearing practices, there is still uncertainty as to whether parents' responses to hypothetical situations reflect their actual behaviors (e.g., Dishion, 1990; Endsley and Brody, 1981; Holden and Edwards, 1989; Rubin and Mills, 1992). Likewise, there is no assurance that observed parental behavior in contrived analogue situations accurately reflects real-life parental responses. The features of contrived situations are usually confined to looking at a narrow range of behavior that may not be representative of or generalizable to real-life settings. Similarly, there is uncertainly as to whether parents will respond normally to their children in naturalistic settings when researchers are observing them (e.g., observer effects). Notwithstanding these difficulties, future studies should rely on construct validational designs that would take the limitations of both observational and interview approaches into account across varying socioeconomic status groupings.

With regard to the power assertive discipline construct, more research is needed to assess why some children may respond to power assertion with withdrawal from peers and others with aggression. As Maccoby and Martin (1983:44) have noted, "Whereas the parents of aggressive children tend to be authoritarian, children of authoritarian parents may or may not be aggressive, and so far the aspects of family interaction that are important in determining whether a child of authoritarian parents will be subdued or 'out of control' have not been satisfactorily identified" (See Barber, Olsen, and Shagle, in press, for further discussion of this issue). On the other hand, withdrawn or aggressive child characteristics may elicit power assertive responses from parents. Recent research findings have indicated that, under certain socioecological setting conditions, parents may respond to the child's withdrawal or aggression with power assertive strategies (Rubin et al., 1989, 1990, 1991). Again, this returns us to the direction of effect issue discussed earlier where further research and clarification is needed.

As far as inductive discipline is concerned, more work is needed to assess social cognitions that may be enhanced by this disciplinary strategy that contributes to prosocial behaviors, which, in turn, may be linked to positive reputations with peers (cf. Hart, et al., 1992b). As has been demonstrated in this chapter, much has already been done in this regard exploring linkages involving power assertion, social cognitions, and antisocial behavior (e.g., Dishion, 1990; Dodge et al., 1990, Weiss et al., 1992). Also, what types of child social cognitions are associated with parenting styles that are related to social withdrawal (cf. Rubin et al., 1990)? This is also a fruitful area for inquiry.

The current findings also point to a need for more careful investigation of relations between solitary behaviors and peer status (cf. Rubin et al., 1991). As Coie et al. (1990) suggest, some types of solitary behaviors may or may not be linked to peer status depending on appropriateness to the social context. Our findings further suggest that age and gender of the child may be relevant to preschoolers in this regard. This may have implications for further research. For instance, future studies should further delineate relations between nonsocial/withdrawn playground behavior and peer status while taking into account age and gender differences in multiple aspects of solitary behavior that have been linked to peer status in past research (e.g., parallel-constructive, solitary-dramatic, solitary-functional play—Rubin, 1982). Further defining parallel play, for example, may yield significant findings that corroborate past research (Rubin, 1982), particularly in light of the fact that no significant relations were found between peer status and the global parallel play category used in our investigation (cf. Chapter 5, this volume).

Although by no means comprehensive as to directions for future work, it is our hope that this final section and the overall chapter will stimulate thinking about ways of further exploring linkages between parental discipline and/or other aspects of parenting and child playground competence with peers. Understanding such linkages will greatly enhance our ability to derive intervention programs that will help parents and children experience more optimal associations with each other and child associations with peers.

NOTES

1. This finding should be cautiously regarded because it dropped out in additional analyses where paternal discipline was not included

and the sample size was increased for mothers participating in the study (see Hart, DeWolf, and Burts, 1992).

2. More recent findings, however, suggest that when looking at more global patterns of child-rearing, paternal child-rearing styles are related to both older children's prosocial behavior and peer status in ways that are similar to mothers (Deković and Janssens, 1992).

REFERENCES

Anderson, K. E., Lytton, H., and Romney, D. M. (1986). Mothers' interactions with normal and conduct-disordered boys; Who affects whom? *Developmental Psychology, 22,* 604–609.

Applegate, J. L., Burke, J. A., Burleson, B. R., and Delia, J. G. (1992). Reflection-enhancing parenting as an antecedent to children's social-cognitive and communicative development. In J. Goodrow, A. McGillicuddy-Delisi, and I. E. Siegel (Eds.), *Parental belief systems: The psychological consequences for children* (Vol. 2). Hillsdale, NJ: Erlbaum.

Applegate, J. L., Burke, J. A., Burleson, B. R., Delia, J. G., and Kline, S. L. (1985). Reflection-enhancing parental communication. In I. E. Siegel (Ed.), *Parental belief systems* (pp. 107–142). Hillsdale, NJ: Erlbaum.

Applegate, J. L., and Delia, J. G. (1980). Person-centered speech, psychological development and the contexts of language usage. In R. St. Clair and H. Giles (Eds.), *The social and psychological contexts of language* (pp. 245–282). Hillsdale, NJ: Prentice-Hall.

Bandura, A. (1986). *Social foundation of thought and action: A social cognitive theory.* Englewood Cliffs, NJ: Prentice-Hall.

Barber, B. K., Olsen, J. E., and Shagle, S. C. (in press). Associations between parental psychological and behavioral control and youth internalized and externalized behaviors. *Child Development.*

Barocas, R., Seifer, R., Sameroff, A. J., Andrews, T. A., Croft, R. T., and Ostrow, E. (1991). Social and interpersonal determinants of developmental risk. *Developmental Psychology, 27,* 479–488.

Baumrind, D. (1967). Child care practices anteceding three patterns of preschool behavior. *Genetic Psychology Monographs, 75,* 43–88.

———. (1971). Current patterns of parental authority. *Developmental Psychology Monograph, 4,* (1, Pt. 2).

————. (1973). The development of instrumental competence through socialization. In A. D. Pick (Ed.), *Minnesota symposia on child psychology* (Vol. 7, pp. 3–46). Minneapolis: University of Minnesota Press.

Bearison, D. J., and Cassel, T. Z. (1975). Cognitive decentration and social codes: Communicative effectiveness in young children from different family contexts. *Developmental Psychology, 11*, 29–36.

Becker, W. C. (1964). Consequences of different kinds of parental discipline. In M. L. Hoffman and L. W. Hoffman (Eds.), *Review of developmental research* (Vol. 1, pp. 169–208). New York: Russell Sage Foundation.

Becker, W. C., Peterson, D. R., Luria, Z., Shoemaker, D. J., and Hellmer, L. A. (1962). Relations of factors derived from parent-interview ratings to behavior problems of five-year-olds. *Child Development, 33*, 509–535.

Bell, R. Q., and Chapman, M. (1986). Child effects in studies using experimental or brief longitudinal approaches to socialization. *Developmental Psychology, 22*, 595–603.

Belsky, J. (1984). The determinants of parenting: A process model. *Child Development, 55*, 83–96.

Belsky, J., Steinberg, L., and Draper, P. (1991). Further reflections of an evolutionary theory of socialization. *Child Development, 62*, 682–685.

Bhavnagri, N. P., and Parke, R. D. (1991). Parents as direct facilitators of children's peer relationships: Effects of age of child and sex of parent. *Journal of Social and Personal Relationships, 8*, 423–440.

Bigelow, B. J. (1977). Children's friendship expectations: A cognitive-developmental study. *Child Development, 48*, 246–253.

Bigelow, B. J., and LaGaipa, J. J. (1975). Children's written descriptions of friendship: A multidimensional analysis. *Developmental Psychology, 11*, 857–858.

Biller, H. B. (1981). The father and sex role development. In M. E. Lamb (Ed.), *The role of the father in child development* (pp. 319–358). New York: John Wiley and Sons.

Brody, G. H., and Shaffer, D. R. (1982). Contributions of parents and peers to children's moral socialization. *Developmental Review, 2*, 31–75.

Burleson, B. R. (1983). Interactional antecedents of social reasoning development: Interpreting the effects of parent discipline on children. In D. Zarefsky, M. O. Sillars, and J. R. Rhodes (Eds.), *Argument in transition: Proceedings of the third summer conference on argumentation* (pp. 597–610). Annandale, VA: Speech Communication Association.

Burleson, B. R., Delia, J. G., and Applegate, J. L. (1992). Effects of maternal communications and children's social-cognitive and communication skills on children's acceptance by the peer group. *Family Relations, 41,* 264–272.

Cassidy, J., Parke, R. D., Butkovsky, L., and Braungart, J. M. (1992). Family-peer connections: The roles of emotional expressiveness within the family and children's understanding of emotions. *Child Development, 63,* 603–618.

Cochran, M. M., and Brassard, J. A. (1979). Child development and personal social networks. *Child Development, 50,* 601–616.

Cohn, D. A., Patterson, N. A., and Christopoulos, C. (1991). The family and children's peer relations. *Journal of Social and Personal Relationships, 8,* 315–346.

Coie, J. D., Dodge, K. A., and Coppotelli, H. (1982). Dimensions and types of social status: A cross-age perspective. *Developmental Psychology, 18,* 557–570.

Coie, J. D., Dodge, K. A., and Kupersmidt, J. B. (1990). Peer group behavior and social status. In S. R. Asher and J. D. Coie (Eds.), *Peer rejection in childhood* (pp. 17–59). Cambridge: Cambridge University Press.

Conger, R. D., Friedberg, P. J., and Conger, K. J. (1987). *An exploratory study of child behavior as a deterrent to negative parenting.* Paper presented at the biennial meeting for the Society for Research in Child Development, Baltimore, MD.

Coopersmith, S. (1967). *The antecedents of self-esteem.* San Francisco: W. H. Freeman and Co.

Crick, N. R. (1991, April). Subgroups of neglected and rejected children. In J. T. Parkhurst and D. L. Rabiner (Chairs), *The behavioral characteristics and the subjective experience of aggressive and withdrawn/submissive rejected children.* Symposium conducted at the biennial meeting of the Society for Research in Child Development, Seattle.

Crnic, K. A., and Greenberg, M. T. (1990). Minor parenting stresses with young children. *Child Development, 61,* 1628–1637.

Damon, W. (1977). *The social world of the child.* San Francisco: Jossey-Bass.

Deković, M. and Janssens, J. A. M. (1992). Parents' child-rearing style and child's sociometric status. *Developmental Psychology, 28,* 925–932.

Dishion, T. J. (1990). The family ecology of boys' peer relations in middle childhood. *Child Development, 61,* 874–892.

Dix, T. (1991). The affective organization of parenting: Adaptive and maladaptive processes. *Psychological Bulletin, 110,* 3–25.

Dix, T., Ruble, D. N. and Zambarano, R. J. (1989). Mothers' implicit theories of discipline: Child effects, parent effects, and the attribution process. *Child Development, 60,* 1373–1391.

Dlugokinski, E. L., and Firestone, I. J. (1974). Other centeredness and susceptibility to charitable appeals: The effects of perceived discipline. *Developmental Psychology, 10,* 21–28.

Dodge, K. A. (1986). A social information processing model of social competence in children. In M. Perlmutter (Ed.), *Minnesota symposium on child psychology: Vol. 18* (pp. 77–125). Hillsdale, NJ: Erlbaum.

Dodge, K. A., Bates, J. E., and Pettit, G. S. (1990). Mechanisms in the cycle of violence. *Science, 250,* 1678–1683.

Eisenberg, N., Fabes, R. A., Schaller, M., Carlo, G., and Miller, P. A. (1991). The relations of parental characteristics and practices to children's vicarious emotional responding. *Child Development, 62,* 1393–1408.

Eisenberg, N. and Miller, P. A. (1990). The development of prosocial behavior versus nonprosocial behavior in children. In Lewis, M., and Miller, S. M. (Eds.). *Handbook of Developmental Psychopathology.* New York: Plenum Press.

Endsley, R. C., and Brody, G. H. (1981). Professional isolation of child and family specialists as revealed in a time series analysis of parent-child relations research methods. *Family Relations, 30,* 5–15.

Feshbach, N. D. (1974). The relationship of child-rearing factors to children's aggression, empathy, and related positive and negative social behaviors. In J. DeWit and W. W. Hartup (Eds.), *Determinants and origins of aggressive behaviors* (pp. 427–436). The Hague: Mouton.

Furman, W., and Bierman, K. L. (1983). Developmental changes in young children's conception of friendship. *Child Development, 54,* 549–556.

Gerris, J. R. M., and Janssens, M. A. M. (1987). *Parental discipline behaviors, subjective parental situations perceptions, and objective characteristics of discipline situations.* Paper presented at the biennial meeting of the Society for Research in Child Development, Baltimore, MD.

Glick, J. (1978). Cognition and social cognition: An introduction. In J. Glick and K. A. Clarke-Steward (Eds.), *The development of social understanding* (pp. 1–9). New York: Gardner Press.

Grusec, J. E., and Kuczynski, L. (1980). Direction of effect in socialization: A comparison the parent's versus the child's behavior as determinants of disciplinary techniques. *Child Development, 51,* 1–9.

Grusec, J. E., and Lytton, H. (1988). *Social development: History, theory, and research.* New York: Springer-Verlag.

Hart, C. H., DeWolf, D. M., Wozniak, P., and Burts, D. C. (1992a). Maternal and paternal disciplinary styles: Relations with preschoolers' playground behavioral orientations and peer status. *Child Development, 63,* 879–892.

Hart, C. H., DeWolf, D. M., and Burts, D. C. (1992b). Linkages among preschoolers' playground behavior, outcome expectations, and parental disciplinary strategies. *Early Education and Development, 3,* 265–283.

Hart, C. H., Ladd, G. W., and Burleson, B. R. (1990). Children's expectations of the outcomes of social strategies: Relations with sociometric status and maternal disciplinary styles. *Child Development, 61,* 127–137.

Hart, C. H., Myers, K. W., and DeWolf, D. M. Linkages between child misbehaviors and parental choice of disciplinary style. Manuscript in preparation.

Harter, S. (1982). A cognitive-developmental approach to children's understanding of affect and trait labels. In F. Serafica (Ed.), *Social cognitive development in context* (pp. 27–61). Guilford Press.

Hartup, W. W. (1983). Peer relations. In E. M. Hetherington (Ed.), P. H. Mussen (series Ed.), *Handbook of child psychology: Vol. 4. Socialization, personality, and social development* (pp. 103–198). New York: Wiley.

Hartup, W. W., Brady, J. E., and Newcomb, A. F. (1983). Social cognition and social interaction in childhood. In E. T. Higgins, D. N. Ruble, and W. W. Hartup (Eds.), *Social cognitive and social development: A sociocultural perspective* (pp. 82–109). New York: Cambridge University Press.

Hartup, W. W., and Moore, S. G. (1990). Early peer relations: Developmental significance and prognostic implications. *Early Childhood Research Quarterly, 65,* 1–18.

Hawkins, A. and Eggebeen, D. J. (1991). Are fathers fungible? Patterns of coresident adult men in maritally disrupted families and young children's well being. *Journal of Marriage and the Family, 53,* 958–972.

Hetherington, E. M., and Parke, R. D. (1979). *Child psychology: A contemporary viewpoint.* New York: McGraw-Hill.

Higgins, E. T. (1981). Role taking and social judgement: Alternative developmental perspectives and processes. In J. H. Flavel and L. Ross (Eds.), *Social cognitive development* (pp. 119–153). Cambridge: Cambridge University Press.

Hoffman, L. W. (1982). Work, family, and the socialization of the child. In R. D. Parke (Ed.), *Review of child development research* (Vol. 7, pp. 223–282). Chicago: University of Chicago Press.

Hoffman, M. L. (1963). Parent discipline and the child's consideration for others. *Child Development, 34,* 573–588.

———. (1970). Moral development. In P. H. Mussen (Ed.), *Carmichael's manual of child psychology* (Vol. 2). New York: Wiley.

———. (1975a). Altruistic behavior and the parent-child relationship. *Journal of Personality and Social Psychology, 31,* 937–943.

———. (1975b). Moral internalization, parental power, and the nature of parent-child interaction. *Developmental Psychology, 11,* 228–239.

———. (1984). Moral development. In M. L. Bornstein and M. E. Lamb (Eds.), *Developmental psychology, an advanced textbook* (pp. 278–324). Hillsdale, NJ: Erlbaum.

Hoffman, M. L. and Saltzstein, H. (1967). Parent discipline and the child's moral development. *Journal of Personality and Social Psychology, 5*, 45–57.

Holden, G. W., and Edwards, L. A. (1989). Parental attitudes toward childrearing: Instruments, issues, and implications. *Psychological Bulletin, 106*, 29–58.

Hymel, S., Wagner, E., and Butler, L. J. (1990). Reputational bias: View from the peer group. In S. R. Asher and J. D. Coie (Eds.), *Peer rejection in childhood*. New York: Cambridge.

Johnson, J. E., Christie, J. F., and Yawkey, T. D. (1987). *Play and early childhood development*. Glenview, IL: Scott, Foresman, and Company.

Jouriles, E. M., Murphy, C. M., Farris, A. M., Smith, D. A., Richters, J. E., and Waters, E. (1991). Marital adjustment, parental disagreements about child rearing, and behavior problems in boys: Increasing the specificity of the marital assessment. *Child Development, 62*, 1424–1433.

King, N. R. (1987). Elementary school play: Theory and Research. In J. H. Block and N. R. King (Eds.), *School play: A source book* (pp. 143–166). New York: Garland.

Kochanska, G. (1991). Socialization and temperament in the development of guilt and conscience. *Child Development, 62*, 1379–1392.

Kochanska, G., Kuczynski, L., and Radke-Yarrow, M. (1989). Correspondence between mothers' self-reported and observed child-rearing practices. *Child Development, 60*, 56–63.

Ladd, G. W. (1983). Social networks of popular, average, and rejected children in school settings. *Merrill-Palmer Quarterly, 29*, 283–307.

———. (1991). Family-peer relations during childhood: Pathways to competence and pathology? *Journal of Social and Personal Relationships, 8*, 307–314.

———. (1992). Themes and theories: Perspectives on processes in family-peer relationships. In R. D. Parke and G. W. Ladd (Eds.), *Family-peer relationships: Modes of linkage* (pp. 3–34). Hillsdale, NJ: Erlbaum.

Ladd, G. W., and Crick, N. R. (1989). Probing the psychological environment: Children's cognitions, perceptions, and feelings in the peer culture. In M. Maehr and C. Ames (Eds.), *Advances in motiva-*

tion and achievement: Motivation enhancing environments (Vol. 6, pp. 1–44). Greenwich, CT: JAI.

Ladd, G. W., and Hart, C. H. (1992). Creating informal play opportunities: Are parents' and preschoolers' initiations related to children's competence with peers? *Developmental Psychology, 28,* 1179–1187.

Ladd, G. W., Hart, C. H., Wadsworth, E. M., and Golter, B. S. (1988). Preschoolers' peer networks in nonschool settings: Relationship to family characteristics and school adjustment. In S. Salzinger, J. Antrobus, and M. Hammer (Eds.), *Social networks of children, adolescents, and college students.* (pp. 61–92). Hillsdale, NJ: Erlbaum.

Ladd, G. W., and Price, J. M. (1987). Predicting children's social and school adjustment following the transition from preschool to kindergarten. *Child Development, 58,* 1168–1189.

Ladd, G. W., Price, J. M., and Hart, C. H. (1988). Predicting preschoolers' peer status from their playground behaviors and peer contacts. *Child Development, 59,* 986–992.

———. (1990). Preschoolers' peer networks and behavioral orientations: Relationship to social and school adjustment. In S. R. Asher and J. D. Coie (Eds.), *Peer rejection in childhood* (pp. 90–118). New York: Cambridge.

Ladd, G. W., Profilet, S. M., and Hart, C. H. (1992). Parents' management of children's peer relations: Facilitating and supervising children's activities in the peer culture. In R. D. Parke and G. W. Ladd (Eds.), *Family-peer relationships: Modes of linkage* (pp. 215–254). Hillsdale, NJ: Erlbaum.

Lamborn, S. D., Mounts, N. S., Steinberg, L., and Dornbusch, S. M. (1991). Patterns of competence and adjustment among adolescents from authoritative, authoritarian, indulgent, and neglectful families. *Child Development, 62,* 1049–1065.

Loeb, R. C. (1975). Concomitants of boys' locus of control examined in parent-child interactions. *Developmental Psychology, 11,* 353–358.

Lytton, H. (1980). *Parent-child interaction.* New York: Plenum Press.

Maccoby, E. E., and Martin, J. A. (1983). Socialization in the context of the family: Parent-child interaction. In E. M. Hetherington (Ed.), P. H. Mussen (Series Ed.), *Handbook of Child Psychology: Vol. 4. Socialization, personality and social development* (pp. 1–102). New York: Wiley.

MacDonald, K. B. (1987). Parent-child physical play with rejected, neglected, and popular boys. *Developmental Psychology, 23*, 705–711.

MacDonald, K., and Parke, R. D. (1984). Bridging the gap: Parent-child play interaction and peer interactive competence. *Child Development, 55*, 1265–1277.

Mead, G. H. (1934). *Mind, self, and society.* Chicago: University of Chicago Press.

Mink, I. T., and Nihira, K. (1986). Family life styles and child behavior: A study of direction of effects. *Developmental Psychology, 22*, 610–616.

Mussen, P., Rutherford, E., Harris, S., and Keasey, C. B. (1970). Honesty and altruism among preadolescents. *Developmental Psychology, 3*, 169–194.

Parke, R. D., MacDonald, K. B., Beitel, A., and Bhavnagri, N. (1988). The role of the family in the development of peer relationships. In R. Peters and R. J. McMahon (Eds.), *Social learning systems approaches to marriage and the family* (pp. 17–44). New York: Bruner/Mazel.

Parke, R. D., and Slaby, R. G. (1983). The development of aggression. In E. M. Hetherington (Ed.), P. H. Mussen (Series Ed.), *Handbook of child psychology: Vol. 4. Socialization, personality, and social development* (pp. 547–641). New York: Wiley.

Patterson, G. R. (1982). *Coercive family process.* Eugene, OR: Castilia.

Patterson, G. R., Reid, J. R., and Dishion, T. J. (1992). *Antisocial boys.* Eugene, OR: Castalia.

Pettit, G. S., Dodge, K. A., and Brown, M. M. (1988). Early family experience, social problem solving patterns, and children's social competence. *Child Development, 59*, 107–120.

Pettit, G. S., Harrist, A. W., Bates, J. E., and Dodge, K. A. (1991). Family interactions, social cognition, and children's subsequent relations. *Journal of Social and Personal Relationships, 8*, 282–402.

Pettit, G. S. and Mize, J. (in press). Substance and style: Understanding the ways in which parents teach children about social relationships. In S. Duck (Ed.), *Understanding relationship processes. Vol. 2: Learning about relationships.* Newbury, Park, CA: Sage.

Piaget, J. (1926). *The language and thought of the child.* London: Routlege and Kegan Paul.

Putallaz, M. (1987). Maternal behavior and children's sociometric status. *Child Development, 58,* 324–340.

Putallaz, M., Costanzo, P. R., and Smith, R. B. (1991). Maternal recollections of childhood peer relationships: Implications for their children's social competence. *Journal of Social and Personal Relationships, 8,* 403–422.

Putallaz, M., and Heflin, A. H. (1990). Parent-child interaction. In S. R. Asher and J. D. Coie (Eds.), *Peer rejection in childhood* (pp. 189–216). New York: Cambridge University Press.

Ramsey, P. G. (1990, April). Changing levels of social participation in early childhood classrooms. In A. Taylor (Chair), *Social competence in the context of schooling.* Symposium conducted at the annual meeting of the American Educational Research Association, Boston.

Roberts, W. L. (1989). Parents' stressful life events and social networks: Relations with parenting and children's competence. *Canadian Journal of Behavioral Science, 21,* 132–146.

Rollins, B., and Thomas, D. (1974). A theory of parental power and child compliance. In R. Cromwell and D. Olson (Eds.), *Power of families* (pp. 38–60). New York: Wiley.

———. (1979). Parental support, power, and control techniques in the socialization of children. In W. R. Burr, R. Hill, F. I. Nye, and I. L. Reiss (Eds.), *Contemporary theories about the family Vol. 1* (pp. 317–364). New York: The Free Press.

Rubin, K. H. (1982). Nonsocial play in preschoolers: Necessarily evil? *Child Development, 53,* 651–657.

Rubin, K. H., Fein, G., and Vandenberg, B. (1983). Play. In E. M. Hetherington (Ed.), P. H. Mussen (Series Ed.), *Handbook of child psychology: Vol. 4. Socialization, personality, and social development* (pp. 103–198). New York: Wiley.

Rubin, K. H., Hymel, S., Mills, R. S. L., and Rose-Krasnor, L. (1991). Conceptualizing different developmental pathways to and from social isolation in childhood. In D. Cicchetti and S. Toth (Eds.), *Rochester symposium on developmental psychopathology: Vol. 2* (pp. 91–122). Hillsdale, NJ: Erlbaum.

Rubin, K. H., and Krasnor, L. R. (1986). Social-cognitive and social behavioral perspectives on problem solving. In M. Perlmutter (Ed.),

Cognitive perspectives on children's social and behavioral development: Vol. 18. The Minnesota symposia on child psychology (pp. 1–68). Hillsdale, NJ: Erlbaum.

Rubin, K. H., LeMare, L. J., and Lollis, S. (1990). Social withdrawal in childhood: Developmental pathways to peer rejection. In S. R. Asher and J. D. Coie (Eds.), *Peer rejection in childhood* (pp. 217–248). New York: Cambridge University Press.

Rubin, K. H., and Mills, R. S. L. (1992). Parents' thoughts about children's socially adaptive and maladaptive behaviors: stability, change, and individual differences. In J. Goodrow, A. McGillicuddy-Delisi and I. E. Siegel (Eds.), *Parental belief systems: The psychological consequences for children* Vol. 2). Hillsdale, NJ: Erlbaum.

Rubin, K. H., Mills, R. S. L., Rose-Krasnor, L. (1989). Maternal beliefs and children's competence. In B. Schneider, J. Nadel, G. Attili, R. Weissberg (Eds.), *Social competence in peers.* Amsterdam: Klewer Academic Publishers.

Rushton, J. P. (1980). *Altruism, socialization, and society.* Englewood Cliffs, NJ: Prentice Hall.

Saltzstein, H. (1976). Social influence and moral development, In T. Lickona (Ed.), *Moral development and behavior.* New York: Holt, Rinehart, and Winston.

Schank, R. C., and Abelson, R. (1977). *Scripts, plans, goals, and understanding.* Hillsdale, NJ: Erlbaum.

Sears, R. R., Maccoby, E. E., and Levin, H. (1957). *Patterns of child rearing.* Evanston, IL: Row, Peterson, and Company.

Sears, R. R., Whiting, J. W. M., Nowlis, V., and Sears, P. S. (1953). Some child-rearing antecedents of aggression and dependency in young children. *Genetic Psychology Monographs, 47,* 135–234.

Spivak, G., Platt, J. J., and Shure, M. B. (1976). *The problem solving approach to adjustment: A guide to research and intervention.* San Francisco: Jossey-Bass.

Straus, M. A. (1991). Discipline and deviance: Physical punishment of children and violence and other crime in adulthood. *Social Problems, 38* (2), 133–154.

Symonds, P. M. (1939). *The psychology of parent-child relationships.* New York: Appleton-Century-Crofts.

Trickett, P. K., and Kuczynski, L. (1986). Children's misbehaviors and parental disciplinary strategies in abusive and nonabusive families. *Developmental Psychology, 22,* 115–123.

Turiel, E. (1977). Distinct conceptual and developmental domains: Social convention and morality. In C. B. Keasey (Ed.), *Nebraska symposium on motivation, 1977: Social-cognitive development* (pp. 77–116). Lincoln: University of Nebraska Press.

———. (1983). *The development of social knowledge: Morality and convention.* Cambridge: Cambridge University Press.

Vaughn, B. E., and Mize, J. (1991, April). *Two methods of assessing sociometric status categories for preschool children: Cross-method congruence and temporal stability.* Paper presented at the biennial meeting of the Society for Research in Child Development, Seattle.

Vissing, V. M., Straus, M. A., Gelles, R. J., and Harrop J. W. (1991). Verbal Aggression by parents and psychosocial problems of children. *Child Abuse and Neglect, 15,* 223–238.

Weiss, B., Dodge, K. A., Bates, J. E., and Pettit, G. S. (1992). Some consequences of early harsh discipline: Child aggression and a maladaptive social information processing style. *Child Development, 63,* 1321–1335.

Zahn-Waxler, C., Radke-Yarrow, M., and King, R. A. (1979). Child rearing and children's prosocial initiations toward victims in distress. *Child Development, 50,* 319–330.

Part V

PLAYGROUND BEHAVIOR
AND
LITERACY DEVELOPMENT

11

BECKY L. REIMER

When the Playground Enters the Classroom

Within this chapter, the author historically describes her year-long ethnographic study of 5-year-olds, documents the separateness of child and adult worlds, and details her journey towards "insider" status. She also shares one theme from this study: How playground chase games between genders were transformed into classroom reading and writing activities.

HISTORY OF THE STUDY

In 1988, I undertook a mini-ethnographic study of one kindergarten class in an inner-city, western-state school. This study evolved from my year's prior curriculum work with the classroom teacher. She, with my assistance, redesigned her curriculum so her students would have more decision-making power in the course, content, and structure of the reading that occurred in the classroom. In the change process, peer-peer interactions became quite spontaneous and frequent during the kindergarten sessions. These peer interactions were obviously important to the students; although, at times, they seemed contradictory to the teacher's intentions. I specifically studied: (a) what occurred between and among peers in the schoolroom during reading and writing events; (b) why children chose to interact with other children; and (c) what children learned during interactions with peers.

Although the primary focus of the study was on classroom reading and writing events, I spent time on the playground with the children. As Erickson points out, "The analytic task is to follow lines of influence out the classroom door into the surrounding environments" (1986, p. 143). Many classroom peer interactions which were initially confusing to me and to the teacher were clarified after I understood the ways and whys of children's playground activities.

316

DIFFERENCES BETWEEN ADULTS AND CHILDREN

Doing research with children is not easy. For years, children have been described as unreliable research participants by adult researchers. Researchers have watched children, from afar, and have attempted to explain children's behaviors through adult conceptualized theories (Corsaro, 1985; Fine and Sandstrom, 1988; Tammivaara and Enright, 1986). Unfortunately, this research neglects a most basic difference between children and adults; that is, that children and adults live in different interpretive worlds (Cochran-Smith, 1984; Corsaro, 1983; Garvey, 1986; Roskos, 1988; Rowe, 1987). Children and adults are segregated not only by age but by roles and responsibilities in our society. As a result, what children and adults know and do are different and thus they bring different lenses of experience and meaning to situations (Tammivaara and Enright, 1986).

The Child's Social World

In this study, I was reminded often of the differences between the two worlds. The children would reframe their activities for the adult eyes or hide their activities from the adults. The adults would also misinterpret the children's activities as chaotic and meaningless or fail to see what was occurring.

Early in the research one of the 5-year-olds quickly demonstrated a very basic difference in assumptions between the adult's and the child's world. Seeking a method to help me memorize names and faces, I took polaroid pictures of each individual student. I wondered why the students persisted in having other students in their picture. A few days later, Ron, one of the 5-year-olds, pulled from his pants pocket a wad of 2 by 3 inch pieces of paper that looked like someone's note stationery. Hand-drawn and written on each sheet were stick figures and words. When asked where he got the idea for doing the drawings, he said "From you, Becky (the researcher). Your pictures." Ron carefully explained to me the purpose of each picture of student pairs, giving such reasons as they play together; they chase; they are monsters.

Ron and I both used the medium of pictures to represent our different worldviews. My world, as represented in my need for pictures of individual students was individual, static, and noninteractive. The 5-year-old's world, as displayed in Ron's partner pictures and the insistence by the other children for group pictures, was social, dynamic, and interactive. Ron's representation of his world and explanation of it was not an immature version of an adult's world; it was just different from the adult's. In this situation, it was I who was very slow to understand what Ron was trying to communicate with his pictures. In particular, the children in this site needed social interaction, chose dynamic, fluid activities, and recast the teacher's individually designed activities into their socially, interactive frames.

Different Interpretations

Adults and children in this site did interpret, use, and invent materials and/or activities in accordance to their worldviews. Brown-eyed Andrea represented this difference in her drawing from the last day of school (see Figure 11.1). Her teacher had asked her and her classmates to draw a final picture which I could put into a book about the year. She asked them to think about what they learned as a reader or writer and/or what they remembered about Becky (the researcher) being with them in their class. Andrea drew a picture of Becky (the researcher) and herself each with thought balloons. In Andrea's invented spelling, she wrote "Mi iDA" (my idea) for her own thought balloon with the sun inside and "BEkES iDA" (Becky's idea) for Becky's thought balloon with the rain inside. When I asked Andrea to tell me about the picture, Andrea responded with, "I have different thoughts from you. You thought it would be raining and I thought it would be sunny." Rosa, a tall and slender 5-year-old, had been eavesdropping on the conversation and added, "Yeh, Becky, you think about monster games different and we had to tell you about vampire girls. 'Member? You thought vampire girls were blood. 'Member'" Both girls were reporting on separate incidents they remembered in their interactions with me, incidents where I had asked for clarification of confusing student activities which could not be explained through my adult lens. It is easy for the adult to label children's play as chaotic and potentially harmful, but when this play is understood through the child's world, chaos becomes reinterpreted as an organized, structured, and symbolic system. The goal of the adult researcher is to somehow enter and explain that organized, structured, and symbolic play world of the child (Corsaro, 1983; Erickson, 1986).

Figure 11.1. Andrea's Representation of Different Worldviews

Status Difference

The adult does see less of the child's world because children often hide their world from the adult. Many unofficial literacy-related events occurred in the classroom that the teacher was not aware of and/or was offered explanations of such that would fit her adult world. At the writing center one day, the shortest and most frail looking 5-year-old, Greg was busy writing the names of some of the students in class. There was quite a lot of noise and activity at that center. What Greg was actually doing was writing names of the students and then crossing off names of those who could not be on his team during playground activities. Greg was using writing, inside the classroom, to prepare for play outside the classroom. When the teacher approached the writing center, Greg announced that he was writing a list of names of his friends to take home so his Daddy could see his friend's names. Greg had learned to recast his activity meant for his peer's eyes into an acceptable frame for the adult's eyes.

In this site, children also recast activities so that the adults might better understand the activity from the adult's perspective. During a journal writing activity, Adrian, a Tongan child who was more fluent in his native language than English, drew a complex picture of a machine with movable parts and explained it to the children sitting around him using such phrases as "This goes up. This goes down. See this flap. It heavy. It moves . . ." When the teacher came around to talk with Adrian about his picture, he began to use much simpler language forms and labeled the picture as a table. He, too, recast his activity for an adult frame by labeling his drawing with an object from the classroom.

NEGOTIATING A NONTRADITIONAL ADULT ROLE

Children can very easily spot an adult because adults are those people who direct children to sit in a certain place, to talk a certain amount of time, and to stop doing a certain behavior. Adults also initiate activities with children, are taller than children and ask questions in order to teach lessons to children during strange times and in strange places. Adults don't play children's games (Corsaro, 1983, 1985). The task of any researcher who seeks a child's worldview and explanation becomes one of counteracting the varied markers of "adultness." It is not an impossible task and can even be done by "tall" adults (Corsaro, 1985; Fine and Sandstrom, 1988; Rowe, 1987). Becoming an insider is the goal of all participant observation research and requires time and careful plotting.

Cautious but Curious: Reactive Field Entry

The students' acceptance of me into their play world and lives came gradually. I adapted Corsaro's reactive field entry method to my situation (1985). I did not actively seek out communication with the students nor direct any students. I reacted when students directed talk to me but did so in a cautious manner. Loitering was my major activity for the first few weeks. During this time of loitering, I paid careful attention to body gestures, movements, and talk of the students in an effort to learn those behaviors. I did not talk to the adults in the setting and consciously worked on my eye glances. Adults look to other adults in a setting quite often; conversation is invited in that manner. I carefully chose places to be where the students were and positioned myself in the middle of those places and not on the outskirts, like adults do. I noted all references to myself by the students and the teacher, gaining a glimpse of how the students were viewing me as a participant in their classroom. During the third week in the site, one of the students pointed to me, as I was standing in the hall outside of the classroom, and called me, "The Big Kid," signifying a role other than adult for me.

The time spent in reactive field entry allowed me to observe and pattern my responses after a child. Luis, a student, walked up to me requesting that I "See. See." something in his pocket. He pulled from his pocket some money. My time spent observing the children allowed me to think about responding from a child's rather than a teacher's perspective. With a child's mind, I pulled a quarter from my pocket and showed Luis, "See, I got some too." With an adult's mind, I might have asked the child where he got that money or requested that the child not bring money to school.

Overcoming the Researcher's Utility: Deferring to Other Children

The students explored what I might or might not be able to do for them. I did have skills and capabilities the students did not. During the second week on the playground, the 5-year-old children began to ask me to lift them onto the playground equipment or tie their shoes which utilized my height or acquired skills.

Within the classroom, students requested that I do their work for them: cut out their pictures, spell their names, write down their message, or read a book. A problem for all participant observers is how to blend in with the individuals in the scene and become an accepted member without using unnecessary gifts or doing special favors (Corsaro, 1985; Fine and Sandstrom, 1988; Spradley, 1980). This is most especially true in a classroom situation where a teacher expects students to do their own work and would not welcome a researcher doing a child's work. During reactive field entry, I had noticed how the children quickly rescued each other in varied situations in the classroom and on the playground. I had watched Rosa rescue Adrian during a writing time when the teacher was asking Adrian some questions about his picture. Rosa filled in all the verbal answers for Adrian. I myself had been rescued by a boy who clarified to a group of other boys in which chair I could sit. I adapted a rescuing strategy into a deferring strategy by allowing other children to answer solicitations for my help. During writing and reading times, when the children were to do their own work, I would, as I have noticed the other children do, defer a question asked of me onto another child.

Blonde-haired Tammy, sitting on my left at the writing table, turned to me and asked me, "How do you make 'N'?" I quickly and matter of factly turned to Sarah and asked, "How do you make 'N'?" Sarah leaned her body on the table in front of me and with crayon in hand wrote an 'N' on Tammy's paper.

Learning from the Children: The Researcher as Dumb

Allowing the children to rescue me became a helpful research strategy during the second stage of the research. I could invite rescuing by standing or sitting still and looking to the other students. Eventually, one of the other students would answer for me or help me do some task.

Being rescued allowed me to participate in the children's activities but did not facilitate my understanding of the meaning of the activities from the children's perspectives. Because children are very adept at responding to nonverbal cues, I began to use nonverbal means to communicate my confusion about events. I would shrug my shoulders, lower my eyebrows, display a questioning face, and throw up my arms in frustration during activities with the children. Amazingly, many of the children would stop and carefully demonstrate as well as verbally explain what was occurring or about to occur.

> I had just walked out to the playground. Rosa grabbed my hand and said, "Come play kissin' girl. Come on." She tugged at my arm and I ran with her to the brick wall opposite the door from which I had just exited. We stood there for about a minute, a few more girls ran to us and placed their hands on the brick wall beside us. Suddenly, all of the girls screamed, jumped and ran away. Rosa dropped my arm after tugging on it. I didn't know what we were doing and I was quite confused. As I turned around, Scott was standing about five feet in front of me, perched on his toes, as though he were about to run. I furrowed my eyebrows and shrugged my shoulders.
>
> I honestly didn't know what was happening.
>
> Scott moved closer to me and disgustedly said, "I'm gonna fly to them," as he pointed to the girls who had run from this place and were now perched on the dome climbing apparatus. I questioned back, "You're gonna fly to them?"
>
> "Yeh, didn't you see me?" he stated incredulously while taking a semi-squatting stance, raising and flapping his arms in the air.
>
> "No, I didn't see you."
>
> "Run, Becky. I'm gonna fly to you." He prompted me into action. I had obviously missed a very important nonverbal cue in this chase game and he graciously took the time to explain to me what I had missed.

During this phase of acceptance, the students began to tease me using varied physical and verbal means such as patting me on the head, hiding my camera and calling me a boy, each accompanied by snickers and coyish looks.

I would reveal my adult interpretation of the event to the children and the children would respond to my idea, oftentimes laughter accompanied their explanations.

Joint Acceptance: Reciprocal Questioning

I was gradually able to ask questions in the course of the activities, moving to verbal means to indicate confusions. The children would quickly offer helps and answers although, limited by my adult lens, I did not readily understand their response at times. As I asked questions of the children, the children also asked me questions of interest rather than utility. In a final interview, Ron asked me about my prior mental condition.

"Becky, were you retarded or somethin' before?" Ron asked of me during my end of the year formal interview with him. I had just asked him if he had any questions he would like to ask of me after I had barraged him with many. He turned his head towards mine, cocked it to the left and matter of factly asked of my prior mental condition. Surprised, I blinked my eyes and chuckled.

"Why no, I don't think I was retarded. Why do you ask, Ron?" I responded.

"Why didn't you know about kindergarten before? Did you forget about kindergarten before?" He clarified for me the intent behind his original question. He, like his other classmates, was surprised that an adult would participate in his kindergarten world. Other students had asked similar questions of me: "Did you forget what you were at 5? Did you forget to go to kindergarten? Did they have kindergarten when you were 5? Were you ever 5 before?" They, like Ron, wondered why a big person like myself would spend time in their kindergarten class being a student with them.

The students would, at times, direct my behavior before they would answer my questions. They would direct me to enter into their play space from a different pretend door than the one I was entering. They would tell me to ask them that question later or would announce to me that they were not going to answer my questions for the day. They would excuse my improper behaviors and help me cover up my adult mistakes as Jeremy did in the following example:

Rosa and I went to Mrs. Spring's area, better known as the Testing Area. I wanted to ask Rosa some questions and thought the nice, quiet, empty Testing Corner would be ideal. Mrs. Spring, the teacher's aide, used it to do her weekly skill testing of each student. As I sat down in that area with Rosa, snickers erupted from Jeremy who had been sitting at a far table in the room. He was running towards us, pointing to me and saying to the other students in the room, "Look. Look. Look at Becky." He put his hand over his mouth to hide his snickering. Laughter erupted from the other students in the room. Jeremy quickly rescued me. He picked up the yardstick which was resting against the bookcase at one end of the Testing Area, placed it in the entry way to the Testing Area and moved it up and down two times as though it were a gate. "There." he said. "It's o.k. now, Becky."

Jeremy had managed to change the context from a Testing Area to a place where I could be with other students. It was a simple but important symbolic distinction to the students.

DISCOVERING THEMES: SEEING CHASE GAMES IN THE CLASSROOM

The researcher, in ethnographic inquiry, is the major instrument for data collection. She not only needs to be very aware and conscious of her status, role and bias in the study, she also needs to carefully record events from the site and begin to process this data in ways that promote theory generation (Goetz and LeCompte, 1984; Spradley, 1980).

In this particular study, I supplemented my biweekly field notes with informal interviews, audio and videotapes of selected events, and photographs and copies of writings and drawings from the students. Data analysis was ongoing and based on constant comparative processes as advocated by Glaser and Strauss (1967), explained by Spradley (1980), and further interpreted by Lincoln and Guba (1985) and Erickson (1986). This process involved searching for descriptive and explanatory categories, integrating categories and their properties, and constructing theory in the sense-making of the data. (See Table 11.1 Hypotheses Tracings for Assertion 1)

In the process of comparing categories and domains of behaviors exhibited by the children, I became aware of the similarities of play in the classroom and on the playground. I was able to explain the covert reading and writing activities through the mechanisms and purposes of playground play.

Chase Games on the Playground: Signifying Gender Allegiance and Identity

Within the first three minutes on the playground during the first day of school, two boys announced to two girls approaching them, "Girls can't come here. You girls, you can't come

Table 11.1.   Hypotheses Tracings and Plausibility of Such

General Assertion 1: Gender is an Organizing Principle for Inter-action on the Playground and in the Classroom

---

Subassertion 1: A Need to Control Social Interactions

FN 9/14	Mats and Partnership
FN 10/5	"B" Entrapment Game
FN 10/21	Now You are Safe
FN 10/27	Let's Make a Hut
IC & MR 1/6	Bryan and Ron
IC & MR 1/11	Rosa and Andrea
IC & MR 12/7	Ron
IC & MR 6/1	The whole class viewed portions of videotapes
SD	Photographs

Subassertion 2: Marking Territories: Separating Genders

FN 8/28	No Girls Allowed
FN 10/21	Now You Are Safe
FN 9/12	You Can't Sit There, You're a Girl!
FN 3/14	I Want a Dolly!
FN & MR 4/4	You're a Girl!
IC & MR 1/6	Bryan and Ron
IC & MR 1/11	Rosa and Andrea
IC & MR 6/1	The whole class and teachers viewed portions of the videotapes
IC 7/15	Colleen Cox, the teacher
SD	Photographs

Subassertion 3: Entrapment Games: Limiting Social Interactions and Insuring Friendships

FN 9/14	Mats and Partnerships
FN 10/4	"B" Entrapment Game
FN 10/21	Chalk Boxes on the Playground
FN 10/21	Making a Track So No "B"s Get On It
FN 10/26	Roping Out Interactions
FN 10/27	You Can't Come In
FN	You're a Spider
FN	Be Our Dog

Continued

Table 11.1. *Continued*

IC & MR 12/7	Ron
IC & MR 1/4	Angela and Amber
IC & MR 1/6	Bryan and Ron
SD	Photographs

Subassertion 4: Chase Games: Interacting Within and Together Across Genders

FN 10/6	Tara Has a Boyfriend
FN 10/6	Good Guys and Bad Guys
FN 10/26	Are You a Good Guy or a Bad Guy
FN 11/3	Chase Games with Reading Mats
FN & MR 2/2	Amber, Amber, Luis Love You
FN 3/16	Hey, Becky, You Be the LookOut
FN 3/21	Becky Is a Vampire Girl
IC 10/6	Jessica
IC 10/26	Mike
IC & MR 1/6	Bryan and Ron
IC & MR 1/11	Rosa and Andrea
IC 2/2	Scott—I'm Gonna Fly to Them
IC & MR 6/8	The Whole Class—I Shared a Film Clip from My Set of Videotapes
IC 6/8	Ron
SD 3/21	Xeroxed Drawings/Writing by Children Regarding What They Did Outside During Recess

Subassertion 5: Changing Social Orders and Results

FN 2/2	I'm Knuckle Head
FN 2/3	Teams on the Playground
FN 2/24	We're On the Girl's Team
FN & MR 3/21	If I "X" You Out, You're Not On My Team!
FN & MR 4/6	How Come You Didn't Pick Me?
FN & MR 4/12	You Were Mean to Anita!
FN & MR 5/17	Pick a Girl Now!
IC 2/3	Brandon, Bryan, Rosa, and Tiffany
IC 3/21	Ron
IC 7/15	Colleen Cox, the teacher

FN Field Notes
MR Machine Recording (audiotapes and/or videotapes)
IC Interview Comment (informal and formal)
SD Site Documents (usually photographs and/or xeroxed copies of documents)

here." Even though other children would often offer rebuttals to these girl/boy division statements, most of what occurred in the children's play and in unofficial schoolroom interactions was driven by a view of the world as a social one split along gender lines. On the playground, the children used chase games to separate genders while at the same time to allow genders to interact. These games moved indoors allowing the children to signify gender allegiance and identity through reading and writing events.

Boys and girls had different roles in chase games on the playground. The growls from the boys and the accompanying flight and screaming from the girls were no accident. Boys could be "good guys" or "bad guys." Girls only seemed to be good guys. I was often asked whether I was playing a "bad guy" or a "good guy" role on the playground. "Bad guys" took many different forms: monsters, TV cartoon bad guys, robbers, pirates, bats, and dinosaurs. The job of the bad guy was to chase the girls or other bad guys. The good guys of male gender had the job of protecting girls. A boy could invite a chase game with a girl by announcing his bad guy role and making gestural stances and noises to represent his role. Girls could also invite a chase game by stopping for a few seconds, catching the glance of a bad guy, and then running fast to another part of the playground while screaming.

During the course of the year, the routines and roles involved in chase games did change. The changes were necessary transformations in purposes of play. Children wanted to meet new friends, play new games, discover the other gender, and apply new social learnings. The girls did transform their routines and roles in chase games during the year. Initially they developed the label of "kissin' girl" which they announced as their invitation to chase a boy. Girls could also announce their love or their friend's love for a boy and the boy would consent to be chased. "Vampire girls," the next convention introduced, allowed the girls to chase each other. Chase games were the most frequently occurring activity on the playground. When asked by their teacher to draw what they did on the playground one day in April, most of the children represented some form of chase involvement. Over one-half of the texts (11) represented some form of chase game. The remaining seven of the texts represented jumping rope (5) and "being friends" (2). Because the children coauthored a picture together, only 18 texts were produced among the 28 children. (See Figure 11.2 for a representative sample of their texts.)

Chase Games in the Classroom

Chase games occurred during "reading time." A child could grab someone's reading mat. The owner of the mat would chase the taker. A child could grab a book from a stack inside a structure and a chase would ensue. A child could grab a book from the tips of the fingers of another child, and again chase would begin. Grabbing a highly valued book from the bookcase would definitely invite a chase game.

Although chase games were greatly discouraged by the classroom teacher, they occurred during writing time also. Quickly grabbing a pencil from the pencil can, running to get the first seat at a table, grabbing someone's pencil and/or journal, and declaring a writing race were some of the overt manifestations of chase games within the classroom writing events. The children discovered other ways for genders to interact and signify themselves during the course of reading and/or writing events in the classroom. Some of these became covert activities, part of the underlife of these kindergarten students (Brooke, 1987).

In the following narrative, three children enact a chase game in the classroom writing center. Angela and Amber are great friends. These two girls do everything together that the teacher allows. Angela is a curly-haired blond who loves to wear frilly dresses while Amber wears her long, straight hair in a ponytail and prefers wearing jeans and t-shirt-like blouses. Bryan is a most respected peer in his group of 5-year-olds. He wears nicely pressed jeans, nicely pressed button-down shirts with collars and always seems to have the right answer when the teacher asks questions. In this narrative these three children bring a chase game from the playground into a writing event, transforming the physical running, screaming, and chasing activity from the playground into a covert verbal and written one. Numbers inserted indicate important points which will be explained later.

> Amber, Angela, and Bryan were at the writing center. The three were busy stapling blank books together from the half-sheets of white paper. There was some conversation about how many books each was going to make and to whom each would

Figure 11.2.   Playground Play Themes: A Representative Sample

write. All three decided collectively to write notes to the teacher in the teacher's journal first. After writing something to the teacher, Angela put the teachers journal away and picked up a single sheet of paper. She busily wrote on three pages of her book, walling her paper off from Bryan's eyes with her upper arm. He began to trace over the jack-o-lantern border on this paper.

He announced to the two girls, "I bringed my back pack today."

Angela queried, "Why?"

"Because I want to so I don't have to carry it home, all my papers."

Angela whined back, "Gee, you're no fair!"

Angela turned to Amber, "Amber, I might write to you. I have to write with some names on it. I need crayons." She left the table to find the bucket of crayons. Both Bryan and Amber quickly looked at Angela's composition. When Angela returned, both persons were busily engaged in their own writing.

Angela sat down, looked at her paper and then glanced at Bryan, "Don't write on my paper, Bryan."(1) She stood up from her chair and walked over to the cubby area pretending to place the paper in several different spots but finally placing it in Bryan's cubby. Angela returned to the writing table and announced, "I'm back, Amber."

Bryan leaned over to Amber and whispered something in her ear while Angela busily wrote on another page in her book. Angela announced, "Nope, it's not for me. It is for my sister. Her name is Mandy."(2) Angela looked to Amber for confirmation of her statement and said, "This one is mine, huh?" Angela pointed to the page she was currently writing.

Amber, instead of confirming Angela's statements, pointed to Angela's paper. "Here Bryan. Here's you." She pointed out Bryan's scrawled name on Angela's paper.

Angela quickly put her index finger to her mouth and reprimanded Amber, "SHHHHHHHHHHHH YOU DON'T TELL HIM!!!" and then tried to reaffirm her original statement, "I always write notes to Amber, huh?"(3)

Amber shook her head and said, "Yeh."

Angela reaffirmed again, "But it is specially for you, this is" as she pointed to the page in her book, looking at Amber's eyes.

Amber countered, "But you sometimes write to Bryan."

Angela leaned over to Amber and began to whisper in her ear. Angela sat back in her chair and began to write on her paper, "This is for Brandon, huh?" she said aloud for all but directed it at Amber. Amber didn't respond and Angela again pumped for a response, "Huh!"

Amber, startled by Angela's last "Huh," looked at Angela. "Oh, Oh, in our class! Yeh!"

Bryan, who was carefully watching this transaction between Amber and Angela, stood up from his seat and declared, "I'm gonna go tell Brandon." As he turned his body away from the table, he glanced back for Angela's reaction.

"NOOOOOO! It's for you. IT'S FOR YOOOOOOOOUUU! IT'S FOR YOU!" She bellowed(5).

"I peeked at it!" Bryan revealed.

Angela quickly folded her note and ran over to Bryan's cubby, placing the note inside. She returned to the writing table and began to write another note.

Angela's bellowing had drawn the physical attention of Bryan's mother to the writing table. She was the parent assistant for the day. When she arrived at the writing center, Amber announced, "I'm gonna write a letter for the teacher."

The parent looked surprised, "You are?" and watched Amber continue to write over numbers on the ditto calendar sheet she had previously pulled from the stack of papers. The parent also looked at what Bryan was composing and then left the center.

Bryan began to slide from his chair and did a crab-like walk over to the cubbies, pretending to sneak without being seen. I took advantage of his departure to interview Angela.

As she completed her fourth stack of stapled papers, each sporting many various sized and styles of Bryan's name, I asked her what she was doing.

"I'm writin' his name on it." she quickly replied.

I queried, "Why?"

"I want to give him a lot," she replied.

I queried again.

"Cause he's cute." She returned to the writing before her, indicating to me that I needed to stop asking questions. She wrote three more sets of her name and Bryan's name.

In the meantime, Bryan was still writing his first note: Bryan Green, to Carol Green, Love Bryan.

Angela was working on another note. I asked "What is this?" as I pointed to the note. On the note she had written Angela, Bryan and NoIES.

She answered, "It's for Bryan."

I again queried, "What does this say?" as I pointed to the NoIES.

She ran her finger under this collection of letters from right
to left. "Do you love me? I'm gonna give it to Bryanie honey!"
She folded up the note and put it in his cubby.

This was a 10-minute episode at the writing center. Angela's
surprising statement to Bryan not to write on her paper when in
fact he had not written anything in (1) was not a reprimand but a
bid for a chase game. It is only by looking at the whole interaction
the reader may come to understand the statement as a bid for
chase. Angela continued to tease Bryan into a chase game in (2)
by denying that her writing was for him when he could plainly
see that it was. She expected her other female compatriot to
confirm and play by girls' rules but her friend was not clear
about what to do in the situation and was reprimanded by Angela
in (3). Angela eventually whispered the behavior she expected of
Amber so that Amber could appropriately play in this game of
boy/girl chase in (4). Bryan called Angela's bluff in (5) and confirmed for himself that the chase game invitation was for him at
which point he reciprocated by going to his cubby, grabbing the
note left by Angela and replacing the note in Angela's box. The
unofficial writing served as a forum for gender interaction and
confirmation. In this example we see how one girl instructed the
other girl in appropriate role-playing during a written chase game,
thereby maintaining each gender's respective role within the interaction.

These children fulfilled their roles as students. Bryan produced a piece of writing that made both his mother and teacher
happy: a loving, caring note to his sister, Carol. Amber and Angela both announced their allegiance to the teacher by declaring
their writing to be for the teacher. At the same time, they signified
and reaffirmed their gender roles as valued in their playground
play with peers.

When The Chase Games Stop: Mixed Gender Teams

For this class of kindergarten children, chase games were the
primary playground activity for the school year. Chase games
helped the children play between the genders and afforded
mechanisms for social interaction. In late February, the three
high status males, or those boys who were the most frequent
chase game partners for the year and labeled the most frequently by the class members as preferred playmates, intro-

duced the concept of teams to the playground and established "bosses" for each team. Of course, the high status males were the "bosses." On those two playground days, little activity occurred. The two teams were in the far corner of the playground, blasting off to some far distant planet. The "bosses" alternated turns at being a lookout, commander of the ship, and chaser of the "bad guys" who were in the opposite corner of the playground. The "bad guys" were three boys who had verbally and loudly declared they could not ever play with girls. Their daycare schoolteacher had threatened the boys with sitting in the corner and writing "I will not play with girls" if they played with girls.

No longer were girls territorially bound away from boys and vice versa but they were actually included on the same teams. The only role left for the boys seemed to be one of protection. Unfortunately, while the three boys were off protecting the girls from the "bad guys," the girls and the remaining boys had nothing to do but wait. They too left the area only in time for recess to end. This team idea on the playground looked like wonderful, cooperative play among the genders. It certainly decreased the amount of activity that occurred on the playground that day, but the activity increased indoors later.

What follows is an interaction among five students at the Writing Center which occurred immediately after the team play on the playground. This interaction was quite atypical for this group of students at the writing table. I had not heard such a continuous round of bantering talk, never heard Bryan shift into this style of language, and had not seen this particular group of children only do the writing at the writing table as a task for the teacher rather than as a task for themselves. They did the minimal in terms of writing for the day, using their writing to screen from the teacher the real activity at that center.

Mike, Bryan, Louis, Rosa, and Amber attempt to engage each other in verbal or written chase games. Parenthetical remarks are inserted into this narrative to assist the reader in identifying markers of the chase games.

> Mike grabbed a sheet of paper and began to put marker to the sheet. He looked up at Rosa across the table from him and said to her with a grin on his face, "I'm gonna write your name!" He began to look at her picture with the attached name card

she had brought to the writing table from the bulletin board. (Mike makes a verbal bid for a chase game with Rosa.)

Rosa looked up at him and stared. Amber had her hand on Rosa's picture/name card and was attempting to copy it. Mike grabbed for the name and Rosa quickly sputtered to Amber, "No, no, no don't let him!" (Rosa rejected his bid for a chase game.)

Mike recoiled into his seat and responded, "I know your name still. I can write that," and he began instead to write his name.

As this interaction was drawing to a close, Bryan caught Amber's eyes and teasingly announced, "Amber, Amber, Louis loves you." (Bryan verbally bid for a chase game with Amber.)

Amber turned to Rosa, refusing to catch Bryan's glance. "Tell him to shut up." (Amber refused Bryan's bid.)

Mike tried again to taunt but this time Amber. "Amber, I'm writin' your name." He began to copy her name from her name card. As he completed the first two letters he teased, "I wrote your name. I wrote your name." (Mike verbally bid for a chase game with Amber.)

Amber turned her back to Mike and looked at Rosa. "So, I don't care!" (Amber rejects Mike's bid.)

From this point, the girls copied each other's name and the boys their names, each respective person spelling their name for the other respective members of their gender. Bryan colored a sheet of thin tissue-like paper he picked from the pile of writing paper. At one end he colored a purple circle mouth and placed two large purple eyes above the mouth. This was not his usual standard of drawing or writing. When one of the boys looked at what he did, Bryan spontaneously responded to the boy's glance.

"I'm making some Mr. Knothead."

There was some interaction among the boys and among the girls, each continuing in their copying of names while Bryan worked on his Mr. Knothead. Bryan began a monologue of sort while he watched carefully for his coparticipants' reaction.

"Go to bed and read a sock," he began. The other boys and Rosa began to laugh.

He continued, "Eat a brick and go fart on Ted. Eat a fart." He whispered his verbage. (Bryan tried to gain the attention of his peers, especially the girls via verbal name calling and silly rhymes.)

Rosa intruded with a statement to Louis. "All the girls in this class love you Louis." As she said this, she reached over with her pencil and touched Louis on the chest with the eraser end. (On several occasions, Rosa tried to engage Louis in a verbal chase game but he diverted her bids with name calling and other male-related talk. Louis is one of the boys who said he does not ever play with girls. He does, though, on occasion engage in a chase game on the playground.)

He looked up, shrugged his shoulders, and grinned, "Hey me? Knuckle head!"

Brian took up the dialogue from Louis and began again, "Hey, knuckle fart." The others at the table laughed. He continued, "Hold your cock Wilson's." Laughter again from the four.

Rosa intruded again. "Everyone in the whole school loves you Louis."

Louis grimaced back at Rosa and shook his head no.

She countered, "So. You love to chase girls!"

He quickly responded, "I love to chase girls but I don't love girls."

Rosa cocked her head to the left and said tauntingly from the right corner of her mouth, "All the girls love you!"

"No they don't!" he denied her claim and added, "I'm embarrassed when I fart in front of a class."

Mike concurred, "Me too!"

Bryan added his commentary, "When I fart in front of a girl!"

In the meantime, Ron walked up to the writing table chewing on some candy. Louis engaged in a dialogue with Ron about the source of the candy and left the table. Others left, except for Bryan and Rosa.

Bryan began again on his monologue. "Nobody loves me. Nobody in the whole world loves me."

Rosa countered his statements, "I like you."

"No you don't, you hate me."

The teacher entered the scene in order to mark the children off for the writing center's activity for the day and to interview the children about what they had accomplished. Bryan showed his item to her. He had cut the original strip of tissue paper into five pieces and taped the pieces onto another sheet of paper to make a body structure (head, two arms, upper body and lower body) and had written *gost* (ghost) on the top next to his name. When the teacher left the area, Bryan caught Rosa's eye and said to her, "Watch this. I'll rip my own creation." And he ripped his paper. Rosa said nothing in reply to Bryan.

Rosa reached for a book from the stack on the bookcase behind Bryan and began to flip through the pages. "I can tell you which one is you, that one is you," she announced to Bryan as she held an open page of the book up to Bryan's eyes.

Bryan immediately, got his own book, opened it to a page and retorted to Rosa. "That's you," he said to Rosa as he pointed to a picture in the book. "Now, you kiss me." As he said this, he put the book in front of his lips and made a kissing motion with his lips. This pattern of finding pictures in the books and saying the pictures were the other person continued for some time until Rosa decided to leave the writing center. (Bryan instructed Rosa in a "kissin' girl" chase game using the medium of magazine pictures.)

At the end of the day, the teacher commented, "Boy, I have to get control of my class back." She made a similar comment the following day and found herself frustrated and policing more during the course of those days. The change in social organization on the playground loudly rippled into the classroom and felt, to the teacher, as uncontrolled, unproductive chaos.

In the beginning of this narrative, Mike and Bryan, two of the three boys, made verbal and written bids for a chase game from the two girls, Amber and Rosa. Bryan was one of the bosses from the team play on the playground. Both Amber and Rosa rejected their bids and each gender group returned to do written activities within their respective gender group. Rosa then verbally bid for a chase game from Louis, meanwhile Bryan tried to catch the attention of the girls via verbal name calling and silly rhymes. Louis left the center. He apparently was not interested in the chase game and was a "bad guy" on the playground for the day. All leave the writing center except Bryan and Rosa. Bryan, using pictures in magazines, invited Rosa for a "kissin' girl" chase game and Rosa complied.

In this episode, Bryan tried to renegotiate some standing with the girls again. Bryan was always involved in multiple chase games and monster or army games during any recess time. He never lacked playmates on the playground. His high status and his gender were constantly validated everyday on the playground and in the schoolroom until playground teams were invented. Bryan was trying to reestablish his male gender identity via the male-related talk and verbal bids for chase. The playground monster and kissin' girl chase games transformed into verbal games in the writing center for the day.

During the course of the next 2 weeks, the children continued to work on this new social organization problem. They would remark during the course of finding seats at a table: "Who's team are you on? I'm not sittin' beside you, you're on the girls team. Are you on my team? We're friends, huh? We're on the same team." What started as a mixed gender concept had turned into a gender separation concept again. Teams were labeled as to girl or boy although girls could be on the boy's team and boys on the girls' team.

The children had transformed the new social organization back into something where boys could chase girls and vice versa but yet teams could be declared. A child's team allegiance, as discussed and bantered about inside and outside the classroom, could and would determine who he might sit by, who might sit by him, who might choose him, and who he might choose during classroom activities. If a child were angry with a friend because the friend didn't share the jump rope or broke a friend's trust in some way, team allegiance could be blamed and used as an excuse as does occur in the following example.

> It was Message Board writing and reading time. The teacher wrote a message to the class on the chalkboard. The children took turns pointing to words they knew in the message before and after choral reading it as a class. Carlos had just been given the pointing stick. He stood up from his place in the group, walked to the board with stick in hand and pointed out the words, and, and, and, good afternoon. As is the routine, when the person has finished pointing out words, he/she then turns around and gives the stick to someone else. Carlos turned around, looked at all the hands waving in the air with accompanying, "me, me pick me."
>
> Ron yelled, "Hey Carlos, pick me." Carlos handed the stick to Bryan instead and then sat down in the group again. He was only three children away from Ron. Ron leaded over to Carlos while Bryan was pointing out the words he could read.
>
> "How come you always choose Bryan?" Ron asked of Carlos.
>
> Carlos justified, "That's cause you're always on the girl's team."
>
> Louis, sitting in front of Ron and eavesdropping on this conversation corroborated Carlos's justification. He shook his head yes and said, "Uh huh. Uh huh. Yes, I saw you," while he looked at Ron.

Ron did play on the girl's team. He also played on the boy's team. So did Carlos and Bryan. It was easy for Carlos to justify his not picking Ron on the basis of his association with the girl's team.

The idea of gender representation and separation continued during the whole school year. By the end of the year, signing in via name writing became a gender-related event. The children came up with the convention of the boys signing in on one side of the paper and the girls on the other side. Teacher choosing children to participate in various activities was met with cautions and warnings about gender balance from the children: "Now pick a girl. Hey you picked too many boys." The children would also explain the teacher's choice of certain children for participation on the basis of gender: "You won't let me do that because I'm a boy, right? You only let girls," when, in fact, the teacher selection had more to do with wanting to involve a particular child in an activity rather than to balance the gender's involvement. The children used a gender lens, in this site, from which they would interpret and act upon their environment.

SUMMARY

The structure and organization of playground play of the 5-year-olds in this one site did transform some of the reading and writing events within the classroom setting. The most popular playground activity, chase games, was an avenue for gender separation and interaction. The children transformed these games from a physical outdoor chase activity to a verbal activity in reading and writing events. The children used this cognitive lens of gender to manipulate and interpret other classroom events during the remainder of the year. They found it easy to blame the other gender or one's participation with the other gender for broken friendships, seemingly unfair opportunities, and coincidental happenings.

Implications and/or Questions

As with all studies of single sites, generalizations to other sites are limited. What follows are some of the implications and/or questions that evolved from this study.

1. The research community needs to find avenues which will allow it to glimpse, if even briefly, the world lens of the child when the goal of research with young children is to

come to some better understanding of the ways and whys of children (Schwartzman, 1978). By understanding the child's world from the child's perspective, the research community could help practitioners and other researchers make more informed, child-relevant decisions regarding intervention with children and perhaps provide more comfortable entries for children into the adult world.

The teacher, in this study, was able to use the information gained about the child's world to more effectively intervene on the playground and the classroom. Very early in the study, after the researcher had pieced together some structural information about the chase games on the playground and the ways in which the children were using chalk and other tools to mark off "safety areas" where chase was not allowed, the teacher then used chalk to draw large safety areas on the playground asphalt when she began to feel the tone of the play change and felt the play to be potentially harmful. She carried those events into the classroom and invited discussion regarding rights and responsibilities of the children in play.

2. In other sites, researchers have documented the playground chase game phenomena among elementary-aged children as ways for genders to crossover (Thorne, 1986; Borman, 1979). As opposed to the boys apart from girls notion of gender, chase games allow students to develop relationships between the sexes. These researchers have also shown that chase games develop into sophisticated rituals with sexual overtones in older students. Do covert chase games exist in reading/writing events in older students? What occurs during these covert chase games? How does the need to establish gender roles and boundaries impinge upon what is learned from another author's text? How do covert chase games reify sex segregation inside schools and complicate the implementation of Title IX?

3. Since the children orchestrated reading and writing events into social ones, should or could teachers help them add other roles to the events that go beyond the gender chase game? Is it productive for us to do so? What should we do with the current gender-based interaction that occurs?

Can we help students to "go beyond" their current understanding of the opposite gender and/or perhaps help them
find ways to "listen" to each other apart from a chase
format?

4. Several correlational studies have shown differences
among girls and boys in reading preferences and capabilities. This study has begun to unpack these variables by
describing how gender roles do impinge on the children's
interactions with written texts and their preferences for
such. Further long-term ethnographic studies of this
nature are needed to continue unpacking the causal
linkages between variables of gender difference in reading
preferences as well as reading inabilities (Erickson, 1986;
Smith, 1987).

5. Within every classroom there will be official and unofficial
occurrences. Why did covert reading and writing activities
occur alongside overt teacher-valued activities in this
classroom? Even though this teacher sanctioned several
peer-evolved reading and writing activities and brought
them up for discussion in the large group situation, these
children still created and maintained peer-based activities.
These covert and off-task activities were not really subver-
sive to the task but instead were important to the development of gender role. Knowing the functions of the unofficial literacy events in the classroom may assist teachers
and researchers in understanding children's responses
and interpretations of literacy instruction and interactions
(Paris and Wixson, 1987).

REFERENCES

Borman, K. M. (1979). Children's interactions on the playground. *Theory Into Practice, 18,* 251–257.

Brooke, R. (1987). Underlife and writing instruction. *College Composition and Communication, 38*(2), 141–153.

Cazden, C. (1986). Classroom discourse. In M. Wittrock (Ed.), *Handbook of research on teaching.* New York: Macmillan.

Cochran-Smith, M. (1984). *The making of a reader.* Norwood, NJ: Ablex.

Corsaro, W. (1983). Entering the child's world: Research strategies for field entry and data collection in a preschool setting. In J. Green and C. Wallat (Eds.), *Ethnography and language in educational settings.* Norwood, NJ: Ablex.

————. (1985). *Friendship and peer culture in early years.* Norwood, NJ: Ablex.

Erickson, F. (1986). Qualitative methods in research on teaching. In M. Wittrock (Ed.), *Handbook of research on teaching.* NY: Macmillan.

Fine, G., and Sandstrom, K. (1988). *Knowing children: Participant observation with minors.* Newbury Park, CA: Sage Publications.

Forman, B. and Cazden, C. (1985). Exploring Vygotskian perspectives in education: The cognitive value of peer interaction. In J. Wertsch (Ed.), *Culture, communication, and cognition.* Cambridge: Cambridge University Press.

Garvey, C. (1986). Peer relations and growth of communication. In E. Mueller and C. Cooper (Eds.), *Process and outcome in peer relationships.* New York: Academic Press.

Glaser, B., and Strauss, A. (1967). *The discovery of grounded theory.* Chicago: Aldine.

Goetz, J., and LeCompte, M. (1984). *Ethnography and qualitative design in educational research.* New York: Academic Press.

Lincoln, Y., and Guba, E. (1985). *Naturalistic inquiry.* London: Sage Publications.

Paris, S., and Wixson, K. (1987). The development of literacy: Access, acquisition and instruction. In D. Bloome (Ed.), *Literacy and schooling.* Norwood, NJ: Ablex.

Roskos, K. (1988). Literacy at work in play. *The Reading Teacher,* 41(6), 562–566.

Rowe, D. (1987). *Literacy in the child's world.* Unpublished doctoral dissertation, Indiana University, Bloomington, IN.

Schwartzman, H. (1978). *Transformations: The anthropology of children's play.* New York: Plenum Press.

Smith, D. (1987). Illiteracy as a social fault. In D. Bloome (Ed.), *Literacy and schooling.* Norwood, NJ: Ablex.

Spradley, J. (1980). *Participant observation.* NY: Holt, Rinehart, and Winston.

Tammivaara, J., and Enright, D. S. (1986). On eliciting information: Dialogues with child informants. *Anthropology and Education Quarterly, 17,* 218–238.

Thorne, B. (1986). Girls and boys together. . . but mostly apart. Gender arrangements in elementary schools. In W. Hartup and Z. Rubin (Eds.), *Relationships and development.* Hillsdale, NJ: Lawrence Erlbaum Associates.

12

KATHRYN M. BORMAN, CHESTER H. LAINE,
AND DENIS S. LOWE

The Role of Soccer in a Narrative Context*

The connections among written communication, gender, and sport are not widely understood. Although investigators have undertaken studies of linkages between writing and gender (e.g., Lynch and Strauss-Noll, 1987; Lakoff, 1977; Flynn, 1988), or sport and gender (e.g., Borman and Kurdek, 1987a, 1987b), no studies to our knowledge have attempted to link all three. The game of soccer provides an exceptional opportunity to explore these linkages. It is a popular playground sport that involves strategy, cooperation, and competition among peers. Since few have studied ways that children transfer such features of this and other organized games into literacy events, the study presented later in this chapter was undertaken to examine these connections as they are evident among adolescent varsity soccer players.

In order to set a context for the study, the first section of the chapter focuses on age-related patterns in the developmental course of play at games (sports). The focus will be on middle childhood and adolescence with an emphasis on gender differences in motivational factors that contribute to sports participation. The second section focuses on possible reasons why there are gender defined motivational factors that contribute to participation in sports. The third section is devoted to exploring ways that written communication can provide greater insight into these motivational factors that underlie gender differences in sport participation. The final section of this chapter is devoted to our study exploring school and gender differences in written explanations of soccer by adolescent soccer players.

*The authors would like to acknowledge the helpful suggestions of Craig Hart, Sally Kilgore and Don Rubin on earlier drafts of the chapter.

Developmental Variations in Play at Games with an Emphasis on Gender

Middle Childhood. In considering the developmental course of play at games, Lever's early (1978) analysis of the complexity of fifth graders' play activities led Borman and Kurdek (1987a) to speculate that the playground activities of younger (Grade 2) children would likely be less complex along a number of dimensions than those observed for older (Grade 5) children. Specifically, following Lever's (1978) findings, complexity in terms of dimensions of role differentiation, play interdependence, explicitness of goals, and the number and specificity of rules was expected to vary. Indeed, Rubin, Fein, and Vandenberg (1983) and others have noted that children's rule-governed play increases beyond the preschool period. Thus, the Borman and Kurdek (1987a) research with elementary school children was designed as a 2-year study of 25 second graders and 24 fifth graders whose playground activities during school recess were observed at two intervals.

Researchers engaged in the Borman and Kurdek (1987a) study of elementary school-age children catalogued children's playground activities at both time 1 and time 2 one year later. They assessed grade and gender differences as well as the one year stability of both the frequency and complexity of these activities, and separately correlated boy's and girl's game complexity with logical reasoning, interpersonal understanding, and understanding game rules. Measures for the latter three characteristics included the Ravens Colored Progressive Matrices (Ravens, 1965) for logical reasoning, two sound filmstrips developed by Selman (1980) to tap dimensions of interpersonal understanding, and a videotaped portrayal of two playground games developed by the authors to assess children's understanding of game rules.

Results of this study indicated both grade and gender differences in the complexity of children's activities. Generally, older children participated in more complex activities than younger children and boys participated in more complex activities than girls. The complexity of children's games and activities increased over the 1-year period, especially for boys. Moreover, the correlates of game complexity differed for boys and girls. For boys, game complexity was negatively related to interpersonal understanding and positively related to understanding game rules, suggesting the *instrumental* importance of play activities for boys. In contrast, for girls, game complexity was positively related to interpersonal understanding suggesting a link to an interpersonal *relationship* focus during their playground activities. Thus, although age differences in complexity of play activities are well established, these findings indicate that gender differences among children of the same age with respect to motivational factors involving instrumental and relationship domains are also important to consider in future research.

Adolescence. Beyond correlates of game complexity, by the time children reach junior and senior high school, connections between play at games, academic achievement, and adult work roles begin to formulate and strengthen. In their review of literature related to high school play, Kleiber and Roberts (1987) identify a number of studies that show a strong positive association between participation in interscholastic athletics and enhanced academic orientation. Academic orientation in this area of research refers to levels of performance as measured by grade point average (GPA), academic aspirations, usually summarized as plans to attend college, and actual educational attainment in terms of number of years of schooling completed.

An illustrative example of the link between achievement and sport is research conducted by Hanks (1979). Findings indicated that by virtue of increased contact with achievement-oriented peers as well as with teachers and coaches, black and white male and female athletes come to value academic achievement and success in school. The conclusion of Hank's research and those of other similar studies was that the encouragement and attention athletes receive from a number of sources strengthens an overall achievement orientation among high school athletes. However, these sources of influence were mediated by the characteristics of the high school attended by athletes. Specifically, when students attended high schools emphasizing academic achievement, participation on varsity athletic teams did not necessarily lead to enhanced academic performance by athletes. In contrast, student athletes attending less academically oriented schools fared better academically. It would appear then that exposure to achievement-oriented peers and adults in less academically oriented high schools may have greater impact on the academic achievement of student athletes than does such exposure in high achievement-oriented high schools (cf., Shavi and Featherman, 1988; Kilgore, 1991). Part of this may be due to the fact that, in less achievement-oriented schools, athletes can set themselves apart from others by excelling academically. Such opportunity for setting oneself apart academically may not be as readily available in settings where an achievement orientation is more the norm. Thus, athletes may tend toward excelling athletically rather than academically in such situations.

Of interest also are findings from a recent study by Borman and Kurdek (1987b) in which linkages were found between boys' overall motivation to play soccer and their valuing of academics, getting into a good college or university, and preparing for a future occupation. These findings were somewhat analogous to our previously cited work in which school-age boys focused on the instrumental importance of play activities. As with school-age girls, such findings were not present for adolescent girls. Rather, their involvement with soccer was, in fact, related to valuing having lots of friends. As with younger children, these findings highlight adolescent girl's emphasis on interpersonal relations over instrumental gains in play activities.

Regardless of gender differences in motivation for participation in sports, these findings are also in line with Kleiber and Roberts' (1987) argument that for adolescents play becomes bifurcated with adolescents either pursuing games and organized sports in their most "oversocialized and professionalized forms" (p. 197) or in pursuing activities that are more antisocial and deviant. The latter could include acts of vandalism, sexual behaviors, and racist invectives that Fine (1988) has called "dirty play." Thus, it appears that adolescents with an orientation to organized play as found in sports may be following more normative paths to adulthood in terms of instrumental achievement orientation, occupational preparation, and interpersonal-relationship preparation than are their more deviant peers. In light of previously cited work regarding the effect of school structures, this may be more the case for adolescents in less academically oriented schools.

In summary, past research indicates that sports are linked to an instrumental motivation for boys and to a relationship motivation for girls. During the elementary school years, this is reflected in an emphasis on rule understanding for boys and in an interpersonal understanding for girls. During adolescence, participation in sports is linked to achievement and school success for both males and females. However, relative gender group differences regarding instrumental and relationship orientations have also been found in this age group. Whereas boys tend to connect sports participation more with instrumental indices including academic valuing and occupational preparation, girls tend to equate such participation with a greater emphasis on fostering interpersonal relations.

Gender Defined Motivational Factors in Sport Participation

Why are there different motivational factors in sport participation for boys and girls? Shedding light on this question, 25 years after Title IX, Borman and Kurdek (1987b) found a linkage between both soccer motivation and knowledge of the sport and high personal distress in girls as indicated by responses to items on the Interpersonal Reactivity Index, a 28-item measure developed by Davis (1981). It is interesting to note that these findings were obtained despite that fact that approximately half the girls participating in this study were members of a team that had traditionally been competitive at regional and state levels among girls' high school soccer teams in the state. For boys, however, high soccer motivation and knowledge tended to be related to low personal distress, suggesting the compatibility between participation in varsity athletics and personal well being. Thus, it would appear that the more competitive nature of the game may be what draws boys to sports. However, other factors seem to be more important for girls.

Perhaps the better match between boys' involvement in sports and their personal well being (relative to girls) can be explained, in part, by gender differences in motivational aspects of sport participation that are linked to relationship and instrumental motivational factors that boys and girls bring to the game. In considering the persistence of gender-typed socialization contexts throughout development, it is not surprising to observe that there are a number of divergent outcomes for boys and girls along a range of social dimensions including personality differences, contrasting social preferences, and differential problem-solving techniques (Eccles and Hoffman, 1983).

A number of researchers whose work examines personality variables note that throughout the life course, boys are more likely than girls to take an active, engaged, and independent approach to problem solving (Block, 1983). They also take a more instrumental stance, viewing group activities among their same-sex peers as opportunities for developing shared interests and abilities rather than for developing interpersonal relationships. With regard to self concept, they view themselves as powerful, ambitious, energetic, and having control over the environment (Block, 1983). Such characteristics are particularly well suited to the highly competitive nature of sports or team interactions.

Girls, on the other hand, are more prone to be less competitive and more often seek relationships that provide intimacy, solidarity, and nurturance. They also tend to be more tentative and interdependent (Block, 1983). These characteristics are reflected in their involvement in activities that are more prosocial and cooperative. With respect to self concept, girls tend to describe themselves as generous, sensitive, nurturing, considerate, and concerned for others, characteristics that are less conducive to highly competitive interactions with peers (Block, 1983). It appears that these different patterns persist into adulthood, allowing us to speculate that activities carried out in the name of play or sport have very real and deep connections to adult work life (Borman and Frankel, 1984; Borman and Kurdek, 1984).

In sum, different motivational factors in sport participation may be due, in part, to gender-defined personality characteristics. For boys, the competitive nature of sports may be conducive to filling instrumentally oriented needs. For girls, interpersonal rather than competitive needs may provide the motivational basis for sports participation.

Written Communication, Sport, and Gender-Related Issues

Much of the research literature reviewed to this point has uncovered gender-specific instrumental and relationship indices that are related to sport participation by using structured measures that have not allowed for free expression in a written communication format. Would open-ended written language provide greater insight into gender-typed perceptions of sport participation? We believe that it would. A spontaneous elicitation written format would allow more flexibility in determining what children naturally come up with on their own without being bound by structural limitations of measurement tools. Although gender-delineated relationship and instrumental patterns found earlier with regard to sports participation would likely be similar in both structured and spontaneous elicitation formats, we anticipated that written open-ended communication would more richly describe children's perceptions of reality.

Indeed, several lines of research focusing on written explanations of how to play a game from a developmental perspective have illustrated the potential richness of information that can be derived from such an approach. Kroll (1986), for example, using a method developed by Flavell (1968), asked students in grades 5, 7, 11, and in their first year of college to explain how to play a novel board game. Students' written explanations were subsequently scored to provide information on three variables: the adequacy of information provided; the presence of orienting details; and the extent to which students adopted a formal, abstract, or hypothetical approach as opposed to a more subjective orientation to the task. Interestingly, while Kroll's younger subjects provided both fewer informative details and less orienting information, only the college students provided explanations cast in the hypothetical mode, and only slightly more than half of them did so. Gender differences were not noted.

Although their examination of gender differences in writing did not attempt to link sport to the equation, the research of Lynch and Strauss-Noll (1987) is, nonetheless, instructive here. Following the ground-breaking work of Lakoff (1977), Lynch and Strauss-Noll asserted that language influences the way that people perceive reality; it reflects their values and assumptions, including the way that they regard the roles of males and females: "Women, like other subordinate groups, use language patterns which differ from these of the dominant group" (p. 90). In order to determine whether the descriptive writing of college freshmen displayed systematically different gender-related patterns of exposition, the authors analyzed in-class written assignments of 65 students.

Students were asked to provide written description of gender-typed objects, a common three-quarter inch metal household washer (male) and a 2-inch square of mauve velour fabric (female). Their analysis revealed, contrary to expectations, that male and female students uniformly wrote descriptive accounts of both objects that did not vary greatly in length. In other words, males and females used approximately the same number of words in describing both objects. Other findings, however, were related to gender. For example, men used a more technical vocabulary in describing the washer while women made more precise discriminations in naming colors describing the cloth.

Gender differences in pursuing leisure activities including sport have been widely documented. Among adolescents, boys spend about twice as much time as girls per week involved in sports and games (Czikszentmihalyi and Larson, 1984). Even when girls participate in varsity athletic competition, it is likely that such participation is not so central or so positively related to their noninterpersonal identities as it may be for boys. In the study of high school varsity soccer players mentioned previously, Borman and Kurdek (1987b) noted striking differences between male and female high school athletes in motivation to play soccer. As previously mentioned, for boys, motivation to play soccer was related to academic goals and values and future college and occupational role aspirations while for girls the motivation to play soccer was related to highly interpersonal goals and values such as getting along with teachers and coaches and having friends.

It was hoped that more detailed information concerning such gender-defined instrumental and relationship-oriented motivations and perceptions with regard to sports could be gathered through open-ended written communicative responses. An attempt at this was undertaken here.

Purpose of the Study

In considering the connections among written communication, gender, and sport for the study reported in this chapter, the authors determined to focus on several aspects of varsity players' written explanations of how to play soccer. The major purpose was to investigate gender differences in players' abilities to reflect their knowledge of the game in written explanations that incorporated information about *rules*, the *object* of the game, the various *positions* players take during the game, and *strategies* players employ to play the game.

In view of girls' more strongly interpersonal orientation and boys' more instrumental orientation, we hypothesized that girls would be more likely than boys to provide more elaborate explanations. These more intricate explanations reflected information that a novice soccer player would need to know (Kroll, 1986). In general, we hypothesized that the girls would be more aware of the needs of the novice soccer player and would provide more information than the boys. We anticipated that the girls would be more attentive to their novice audience and would describe the rules in greater detail, orient the reader with clearer statements of the object of the game, delineate the various positions more carefully, and better relate the numerous strategies that are used by soccer players.

A second purpose for the study was to explore the relationships between gender and the particular kinds of elements that players emphasized in their explanations of how to play the game. In particular, we were interested in the extent to which girls and boys emphasized cooperation and teamwork on the one hand and underscored competition and aggressiveness on the other. We also looked at the writers' mention of personal benefit and in particular, the degree to which the writer mentioned personal satisfaction and related outcomes other than winning. The degree to which cooperation, skill and endurance, and competition were emphasized were thus of interest to us. Determining the number of feminine and masculine pronouns used by the writers allowed us to investigate whether students viewed soccer as a masculine or feminine sport. Specifically, in explaining the game to someone else, were these young men and women more likely to refer to the players as women or men or to use gender neutral terms? Given our earlier findings, we expected differences to emerge along gender lines (Borman and Kurdek, 1987b).

In light of findings presented earlier suggesting school structural influences, a third purpose was to examine relationships among a range of outcome variables and a player's enrollment in an urban academic as opposed to a suburban athletic high school. Due to a greater academic orientation, we hypothesized that students attending the urban academic high school would be more likely to elaborate statements about rules, positions, and strategies. We also anticipated that they would write longer essays overall than their suburban athletic high school counterparts. However, in contrast to studies presented earlier, no attempt was made in this investigation to assess the academic achievement of players attending these two types of schools.

METHOD

Subjects

Participants were 67 students from two high schools. Students from one high school (20 males, 15 females) had a long history of prior involvement with soccer through experience in club-sponsored athletics; in fact, the suburban township in which they lived was referred to as "soccer country." The girls' team had been state champions in 1982 and 1983, and was ranked first in the metropolitan area during the year of the study (1984). Students from the other high school (16 males, 14 females) participated on teams with erratic records. The girls had a losing season (4–6–2) during the year of the study; the boys performed relatively well (9–5–1) and advanced in sectional play, although they eventually lost at the regional level. The school at which these students were enrolled is considered the elite academic public high school in the city and is attended by children from socially diverse but relatively wealthy families.

Subjects were freshmen (11.8%), sophomores (26.5%), juniors (41.2%), and seniors (19.1%). Mean age was 16.41 years (SD=0.98). Socioeconomic status was assessed by prestige scores from the Duncan Socioeconomic Index, which were assigned to fathers' and mothers' occupations. Mean scores were 60.47 and 46.15, respectively, placing this sample in the upper middle-class range.

Measures

Participants were asked to describe soccer to someone who was unfamiliar with the game (Borman and Kurdek, 1987b). Our focus was the athletes' knowledge of soccer as articulated in their essays. The two major independent variables of interest to the research reported here are gender and school. It should be noted that results obtained in the earlier related study (Borman and Kurdek, 1987a) yielded no statistically significant differences for the variables of interest for age, grade, or school. Gender differences, however, *were* consistently observed in all analyses. Thus, in this chapter, analysis will focus on gender differences in soccer knowledge as they emerged in a fine-grained content analysis of all players' essays.

Subjects at each school completed all measures together in a single session supervised by the first author. Subjects were given as much time as they needed to complete all measures. Each session was held after school and lasted approximately an hour and a half. The first author also attended several games during the season, observing play from the stands and from the bench alongside the players. Observations were made following administration of the measures designed to tap demographic background information, motivation to play soccer, school climate, empathy, occupational interest, and parental child-rearing practices. Students also provided information regarding gender, age, grade, and parents' occupation.

Writing Prompt: Knowledge of Soccer

All of the writers were asked to explain the game. Because they were explaining the same game, systematic comparisons among the explanations were possible. Also, because the students in the urban academic high school and in the suburban high school had long histories of prior involvement with soccer through school and club-sponsored athletics as mentioned previously, we were assured that they understood the game that they were explaining.

Subjects were instructed to: "Assume you have been approached by someone who has never played soccer before. This person is about your age and the same gender as you. What would you say to this person about how to play the game?" This prompt was meant to elicit players' knowledge of rules, the object of the game, and the various positions involved in soccer.

Content Analyses

Rubrics, or scoring guides, were developed for each of the textual variables. The rubrics for each of the variables appear in the appendix (see Appendix 12.A). The 67 pieces of writing, written by student varsity soccer players in grades 9 through 12, were then grouped together and scored for all analyses in one intermittent week-long rating session. The raters were two experienced high school English teachers pursuing graduate programs in education. Eleven textual analyses were completed on the pieces of writing to address these question.

- How much information does the writer provide regarding the codified rules and regulations of the game?
- Does the writer orient the reader by explaining the object of the game?
- Does the writer list the various positions that players might play?
- Does the writer include notions of teamwork and cooperations in his or her explanation of the game?
- Does the writer include notions of competition in his or her explanation of the game?
- To what extent does the writer emphasize the personal benefits of playing soccer?
- To what extent does the writer emphasize endurance or physical condition in his or her explanation of the game?
- Does the writer provide the reader with tips, hints, tactics, or strategies for playing soccer?
- To what degree does the writer adopt an abstract or formal approach when explaining the game?
- How many words does the writer use to explain the game?
- How many feminine and masculine pronouns were used to explain the game?

Despite the overlapping nature of the rubrics, we believe that distinctive aspects of writing are reflected in each of the measures used in this study. These differences, as well as the commonalities among the measures, will be examined below in our analysis and discussion of results.

Each essay was coded by two different raters for each analysis. The two raters independently scored all pieces of writing. Both raters were blind to the purposes of the study. The percentage of exact agreement among the raters was computed for all of the analyses. The level of agreement between the two raters' scores was between 91% and 100%.

Although other statistical analyses for determining interrater reliability were available, we chose to use the percentage of exact agreement because it is frequently used in studies of this type, and is easily understood by readers.

RESULTS

In the following section we examined the findings of a series of chi-square analyses and the related content analyses of student's writing. Chi-square was selected as a procedure because of its ability to capture nonlinear effects. Because we expected both school-related and gender-related differences, analyses were carried out separately for these two sets of independent variables.

Chi-Square Analysis

To determine the extent to which these textual features were related to the gender of the writer, a series of chi-square analyses were undertaken. The textual variables were: *rules of the game, object of the game, list of positions, explanatory approach, personal benefits, strategies, cooperation, competition,* and *number of words.*

The data reported in Table 12.1 suggested a relationship between the gender of the writer and types of explanations (explanatory approach only). These results illustrated the greater tendency of boys to use objective rather than other types of explanations. Girls more often used mixed or hypothetical modes. No relationship was demonstrated between the gender of the writer and the remaining textual variables.

Our review of the literature and the data collected in the earlier study suggested a number of additional hypotheses. Although girls emphasized cooperation and teamwork to a greater degree than the boys, these differences were not significant. One girl explained that "being able to cooperate with team members is essential." Another stated that "watching a good team play makes it all worthwhile." Other girls emphasized that they viewed

Table 12.1. Percentages of Respondents Mentioning Types of Explanations, By Gender

Types of Explanations	Male (N = 40)	Female (N = 27)
Objective	58%	22%
Mixed	17	30
Hypothetical	10	33
No Explanation	15	14

Chi-Square = 10.21, $p < .05$

soccer as a "team sport." One argued that "in soccer a player isn't an individual but is a component of the whole unit." "No one person can win or lose the game," stated another.

Some writers drew the attention of their readers to the competitive aspects of the game: "You must be aggressive," said one young writer. Another explained that "soccer is a highly aggressive game and not for the feeble of body or mind." Warlike images were used by some writers. "One team attacks and overwhelms the other," explained one writer. "The object is to attack the opposing team's goal." The notions of the competitive aspects of the game appeared in the essays; however, we found no statistically significant gender effects in the use of such imagery.

We anticipated that the girls, being more alert to the needs of their novice readers, would assume less prior knowledge and list more of the rules of soccer than the boys. Girls *did* provide more rules in their explanations than boys; however, differences were not significant. Some writers did emphasize the personal benefits of soccer, benefits other than winning. For example, one athlete said, "playing soccer can be fun." Another argued, "I want the person, no matter how well they play, to have fun." However, we found no significant gender differences.

Likewise, boys did not emphasize the physical conditioning and endurance needed to play soccer to a significantly greater degree than the girls. Both boys and girls were among those that mentioned the physical aspects of the game. "Soccer takes a player of great shape and endurance," reasoned one writer. Another stated that "soccer is a game that requires much skill, speed, agility, and stamina."

Other related findings indicating gender differences were noted. In sum, whereas girls were more likely to utilize writing strategies that reflected an orientation to the novice in their explanations, boys were more likely to take a less formal approach than the girls. The boys were more likely than the girls to refer to the participants in the game as "you." The girls were more likely to refer to the participants as "one player." For example, one boy explained, "you move the ball down the field and a player on the other team tries to keep you from getting it closer to his goal." This writer's explanation implies that the reader (addressed as "you") is directly involved as a participant in the game. Girls in our sample tended to take a more formal approach in their explanations. For example, one girl wrote, "one player dribbles the ball down the field while the players on the other team try to keep him from getting the ball close to their goal." Although the information is almost identical, this writer avoids addressing the reader as "you" and instead refers to how any two individuals (referred to as "one player" and "a player on the other team") can play the game. Six boys and four girls did not explain the game at all; they talked about explaining it, but they never discussed participants or participation in the game.

Twenty-three of the 40 boys (58%) used a less formal approach in their explanation of soccer; an additional 17% used some elements of a more formal approach. Girls, on the other hand, avoided addressing the reader as "you." The girls, in general, assumed a more abstract and formal orientation than the boys. Although 6 of the 27 girls (22%) used a less formal approach to explain soccer to a novice friend, 17 (63%) used some aspects (mixed and hypothetical explanations) of a more formal approach in their explanations.

None of our subjects implied that they were playing soccer with the reader (e.g., I kick the ball down the field and *you* try to keep me from getting it closer to my goal.) This more abstract orientation had been evident in Kroll's (1986) study.

School-related hypotheses were also examined. Students in the urban academic high school listed more rules (see Table 12.2), listed positions more frequently (see Table 12.3), and wrote longer essays (see Table 12.4) than the students in the other setting. These results were congruent with our conjecture that students in the urban academic high school would, in fact, be more elaborate in their explanations of how to play the game.

Analysis of Variance

Given the fact that both school and gender relationships existed for those factors related to what could be viewed as the writer's sensitivity to the novice, it was important to determine the degree to which these effects were independent and/or whether school-gender interaction effects existed. The authors examined these issues by constructing a scale indicative of the degree to which an essay was oriented toward a novice. It was assumed that a more elaborated account would provide more information to a novice player and that explaining the object of

Table 12.2.   Percentages of Respondents Mentioning Rules, By School

Rules	Academic High School (N = 28)	Athletic High School (N = 39)
No Rules	32%	80%
1–2 Rules	21	5
3–4 Rules	7	10
5 or more Rules	39	5

Chi-Square = 19.72, *p* < .01

Table 12.3.   Percentages of Respondents Mentioning Positions By School

Aspect of the Game	Academic High (N = 28)	Athletic High (N = 39)
No Positions	50%	92%
Some Positions	50	8

Chi-Square = 13.25, *p* < .001

Table 12.4.   Percentages of Respondents Writing Shorter vs. Longer Essays in T-Units—By School

Number of T-Units		Academic High (N = 28)	Athletic High (N = 39)
Shorter Essays	1.	0%	8%
	2.	0	18
	3.	3.6	20.5
	4.	11	8
	5.	14	10
	6.	4	8
Longer Essays	7.	7	13
	8.	25	10
	9.	11	3
	10.	0	3
	11.	9	0
	12.	7	0
	13.	7	0
	14.	4	0

Chi Square = 26.46, *p* < .05

the game would better orient the novice. Standard scores were calculated for each player separately on the *Number of Words, Rules of Game,* and *Object of the Game* variables. Summed standardized scores of these variables were used as an indicator of the degree to which a subject was oriented toward the novice in writing his or her essay. An analysis of variance allowed the authors to evaluate the effects of gender and school as well as the possibility of interaction in students' writing.

Results indicated that there were significant main effects of gender and school on orientation to a novice. Students attending the academic urban high school wrote longer essays (i.e., used more words, and also, more frequently explained the rules and object of the game of soccer) than did there suburban athletic high school counterparts $F(1,63) = 15.89$, $p < .001$. Gender-related differences were also evident in the number of words present and the explanatory approach concerning the rules and object of the game taken by the writer, with girls being more oriented toward the novice when compared to boys $F(1,63) = 11.97$, $p < .001$. No school by gender interactive effects emerged in the analysis.

CONCLUSIONS

In presenting some concluding observations, we are mindful that the current data analysis, particularly the chi-square analysis, did not yield persuasive or definitive findings for all the eleven questions of interest. Nonetheless, we believe that the questions themselves and the textual analysis of the students' writing present useful and strategic approaches to understanding connections among writing, gender, sport, and school-related characteristics.

In sum, boys were less likely to use a formal approach in their explanations than girls. However, girls were found to be more oriented toward the novice, thus focusing on meeting interpersonal needs. In addition, nonsignificant trends indicated that girls in the study had tendencies to emphasize teamwork and cooperation more than boys.

Upon reflection, girls' more formal approach may be linked to their consideration of the task in a more literal fashion than may be the case for boys. Girls are more likely than boys to "play by the rules in school," cooperate with teachers and coaches, and generally take on the role of good citizens (Block, 1983). Moreover, results in an earlier related study (Borman and Kurdek, 1987b) indicated that girls, regardless of their high school affiliation, valued relationships with their teachers and coaches more than they valued the competitive element of playing varsity soccer. The reverse was true for boys. In a developmental frame, these findings suggest the consistent instrumental value of play at games for boys from middle childhood onward. However, it may be the case that "oversocialized" play most dramatically effects high school girls, orienting them more strongly than boys to "acceptable, rule-governed" behavior on and off the playing fields. This may play a role in the fostering of interpersonal relationships as reflected in their being more tuned into helping the novice understand the rules and object of the game and focusing on teamwork and cooperation in the execution of the game.

With regard to school effects, players from the academic high school wrote longer essays, listed more rules, mentioned more positions (wing, goalie, forward, etc.), and provided more detailed written explanations of the game to a novice. As interesting as what urban academic students mentioned more than their suburban high school counterparts is what they did not focus on. Although elements of game play related to cooperation and competition were present, these components were less emphasized than more concrete elements, namely rules governing the game and roles taken by specific players. This emphasis makes sense given the nature of the task, namely to explain how to play the game to a novice.

Student achievement in subjects and areas such as writing and verbal expression typically taught and routinely tested in schools are affected by a number of school-related characteristics. Specifically, the amount of classroom instruction, the level of instruction (academic vs. gender education vs. vocational training), the characteristics of peers, the quality of the teaching environment, and the social learning environment (Shavi and Featherman, 1988; Dar and Resh, 1986) have a substantial impact on student performance on a range of psychometric measures. These effects are pronounced during adolescence and are particularly strong for adolescents enrolled in highly academically oriented courses as was the case for students attending the college prep urban high school in this study.

Future work on linkages among sport, gender, writing, and emphasis on academic achievement in the school should be aimed at providing an understanding on how these relationships change or remain constant. For example, it would be useful to know if patterns of orientation to a novice player noted here persist for older athletes attending college and participating on intercollegiate teams.

In conclusion, gender was the foremost variable of interest in our analysis of written accounts of soccer knowledge. Results presented in this chapter indicate that written explanations of how to play the same highly competitive interscholastic varsity sport are differently constructed for girls and boys who play on high school varsity soccer teams. Other results indicate that high school characteristics, particularly structural features such as an emphasis in the curriculum on academic achievement, also affects students' orientation to sport. Thus, future work exploring linkages between written communication, gender, and participation in sports should take such school features into account. Hopefully, this investigation will provide the foundation for continued work in this area.

APPENDIX 12.A

Trait: Rules of Game

How much information does the writer provide regarding the codified rules and regulations of the game? These are the rules that might appear in an official's rule book rather than a player's strategies for winning the game.

1. A *one* paper provides no information about the rules of the game. None of the essential rules are mentioned.
2. A *two* paper provides a minimal amount of information about the rules of the game. At least one essential rule is mentioned.
3. A *three* paper provides a moderate number of pieces of information about the game. At least three essential rules are mentioned.
4. A *four* paper provides an extensive amount of information about the rules of the game. At least five essential rules are mentioned.

Examples of Essential Rules:

• rules governing the type and size of ball
• rules governing kick offs
• rules protecting players from tripping, striking, obstructing, etc.
• rules governing the number of players on the field for each team
• rules related to the role of the goalie
• rules describing the parts of the body that can or cannot be used to hit the ball
• rules to protect the goalie
• rules governing what to do when the ball goes out of play
• rules applying to various out-of-play situations
• rules about time divisions during the game
• rules about how points are scored
• rules about the goal and scoring
• rules on equipment and uniforms
• rules governing penalty kicks
• rules governing the field of play (size, lines, etc.)

Example: "Just remember, no hands and kick the ball. That is all it takes to start out and have fun."
"There are two teams."
"The object is to get the ball in the goal."

Note: Do not count the same rule twice
The rule must be stated or explained explicitly; mentioning types or categories of rules is not explaining a rule.
An inaccurate rule counts as a rule.

Trait: Object of the Game

The beginning of an explanation often serves the function of setting the stage for an elaboration of specific rules of play, orienting the reader to the general purpose of the game. To assess the extent to which the writer includes such orienting information, determine whether the writer's explanation provides an explicit statement of the object of the game of soccer.

1. A *one* paper provides no statement of the object of the game.
2. A *two* paper provides an explicit statement of the object of the game.

Examples: "The object of the game is to score a goal."
"The players try to kick the ball into the goal."
"The object is to attack the opposing team's goal."

Trait: List of the Positions

Another way to orient the reader to the general purpose of the game is to list the various positions that the players might play during the game.

1. A *one* paper does not list any of the positions on a soccer team.
2. A *two* paper lists some of the major positions on a soccer team.

Note: The positions on a soccer team include: wing, forward, goalie, fullbacks, halfbacks, etc.

Trait: Explanatory Approach

This analysis focuses on the degree to which the writer adopts an abstract and formal approach when explaining the game of soccer. A writer's approach is identified both by examining the formality of the pronouns used to refer to the participants in the game (e.g., "you" versus "one player") and by considering the extent to which an explanation implies that the writer and the reader are both involved in the game.

How does the writer refer to the individuals who play the game? The writer could approach the explanation in one of several ways.

1. In a *one* paper, the writer uses a *subjective* approach. The writer's explanation implies that he or she will be involved in playing the game with the reader (e.g., *I* kick the ball down the field and *you* try to keep me from getting it closer to my goal.) The use of "I" must be in reference to the participant or player rather than in reference to the speaker, writer, or explainer.
2. In a *two* paper, the writer uses an *objective* approach. The writer's explanation implies that the reader (addressed as "you") and some other player (not the writer) are playing the game (e.g.,

"*You* move the ball down the field and *a player on the other team* tries to keep *you* from getting it closer to *their* goal.) An objective approach employs a more abstract orientation than a subjective approach, because the writer ceases to consider herself or himself a potential participant in the game.

3. In a *three* paper the writer mixes or combines elements of the objective and the hypothetical approach. Sometimes the writer's explanation implies that the reader (addressed as "you") and some other player (not the writer) are playing the game. At other times the writer avoids addressing the reader as "you" and instead refers to how any two individuals (typically referred to as "one player" and "a player on the other team") can play the game.

4. In a *four* paper the writer uses a *hypothetical* approach. The writer avoids addressing the reader as "you" and instead refers to how any two individuals (typically referred to as "one player" and "a player on the other team") can play the game (e.g., "*One player* dribbles the ball down the field while *the players on the other team* try to keep *him* from getting the ball close to *their* goal.") A hypothetical approach entails a more abstract and formal orientation than the objective approach, because the writer begins to use the language of a set of official rules.

5. In a *five* paper the writer never refers to the individuals who play the game. The writer talks about what he or she might discuss but never actually explains the game. The writer does not discuss the participants or participation in the game.

Trait: Personal Benefit or Self-Enhancement

Does the writer mention something, other than winning, as a personal benefit of playing or watching soccer?

1. A *one* paper does not mention a personal benefit, other than winning, as an outcome of the game.
2. A *two* paper mentions a personal benefit, other than winning, as an outcome of the game.
3. A *three* paper emphasizes personal benefits, other than winning, as an outcome of the game.

Examples:

- "I would like the person, whether they played good or bad, to have fun and like playing soccer."
- "Watching a good team play together makes it all worthwhile."
- "Soccer is a great game that, although it takes a lot of skill and endurance to be good, can be extremely fun and very exciting to a person just starting out."

- "I would tell the person how much fun the game is and how widely soccer is played throughout the nations."
- "It is very fun if you like games where a strategy is necessary and keeping in shape."
- "Always try to be the best you can be, as a teammate, an individual and a player."
- "Teammates are friends who are allowed to criticize and most of all congratulate you."
- "No one is singly noticed if they make a mistake and it is a great deal of fun."
- "It is a very fun game that everyone enjoys."
- "This is a great sport and very exciting."
- "Once these skills have been mastered, the game becomes easy and lots of fun."
- "Have a good time and stay in shape."

Trait: Strategies

Does the writer provide his or her reader with tips, hints, tactics, or strategies or playing soccer? These may be personal or team strategies.

1. A *one* paper does not mention strategies.
2. A *two* paper refers to strategies.
3. A *three* paper makes extensive references to strategies.

Examples: "Don't be fancy."
   "Don't take unnecessary risks"
   "Boy, pay attention and be alert to what ever happens on the field."

Trait: Cooperation or Teamwork

To what extent does the writer include notions of teamwork and cooperation in his or her explanation of the game?

1. A *one* paper provides no indication of the role of cooperation or teamwork in the playing of soccer.
2. A *two* paper provides some indication of role of cooperation or teamwork in the playing of soccer.

Examples: "Being able to cooperate with team members is essential."
   "Watching a good team play makes it all worthwhile."
   "Soccer is a team sport."
   "In soccer a player isn't an individual but is a component of the whole unit."
   "No one person can win or lose the game."

Trait: Competition

To what extent does the writer include notions of competition in his or her explanation of the game?

1. A *one* paper provides no indication of the role of competition in the playing of soccer.
2. A *two* paper provides some indication of the role of competition in the playing of soccer.

Examples: "You must be aggressive."
"Soccer is a highly aggressive game and not for the feeble of body or mind."
"One team attacks and overwhelms the other."
"The object is to attack the opposing team's goal."

Trait: Physical Condition or Endurance

To what extent does the writer emphasize endurance or physical condition in his or her explanation of the game?

1. A *one* paper does not mention physical condition or endurance.
2. A *two* paper mentions physical condition or endurance.
3. A *three* paper emphasizes physical condition or endurance.

Example: "Soccer takes a player of great shape and endurance."
"Soccer is a game that requires much skill, speed, agility and stamina."

Procedures for Counting Words

These procedures are based on a training guide provided for the National Assessment of Educational Progress (1980). In scoring the essays, students' writing has to be marked and segmented. Blue pencil is used for this purpose, to allow essays to be photocopied without showing the markings.

Word Counts

Each word in the essay is counted, including the title. Contractions are counted as two words. Acronyms are counted as many words as they are intended to represent. For example, CIA is counted as representing three words.

REFERENCES

Applebee, A. N., Langer, J. A., and Mullis, V. S. (1986). The writing report card: Writing achievement in American schools. Princeton, NJ: Educational Testing Service.

Block, J. (1983). Differential premises arising from differential socialization of the sexes: Some conjectures. *Child Development, 54,* 1335–1354.

Borman, K. M., and Frankel, J. (1984). Gender inequities in Childhood social life and adult work life. In Borman, K. M., Quarm, D. and Gideonse S. (Eds.), *Women in the Workplace: Effects on Families.* Norwood, NJ: Ablex.

Borman, K. M., and Kurdek, L. A. (1987a). Grade and gender difference in and the stability and correlates of the structural complexity of children's playground games. *International Journal of Behavioral Development, 10* (2), 241–51.

———. (1987b). Gender differences associated with playing high school soccer. *Journal of Youth and Adolescence, 16,* 379–400.

———. (1984, September). Children's game complexity as a predictor of later perceived self competence and occupational interest. Paper presented at the meeting of the American Sociological Association, San Antonio, TX.

Czikszentmihalyi, M., and Larson, R. (1984). *Being Adolescent.* New York: Basic Books.

Dar, Y., and Resh, N. (1986). *Classroom Composition and Pupil Achievement: A Study of the Effect of Ability-Based Classes.* New York: Gordon and Breach.

Davis, M. H. (1981). The young person's job search: Insight from a study. *Journal of Counseling Psychology, 28,* 321–33.

Eccles, J. S., and Hoffman, L. W. (1983). Sex roles, socialization, and occupational behavior. In H. W. Stevenson, and A. E. Siegal (Eds.), *Child Development Research and Social Policy.* Chicago, IL: Chicago Press.

Fine, G. A. (1988). Good children and dirty play. *The Journal of the Association of Play and Culture, 1* (1), 43–56.

Flavell, J. H. (1968). *The Development of Role Taking and Communication Skills in Children.* New York: Wiley.

Flynn, E. (1988). Composing as a Woman. *College Composition and Communication, 39,* 423–435.

Greenberg, K. L., Wiener, H. S., and Donovan, R. A. (Eds). (1986). *Writing assignment: Issues and strategies.* New York: Longman.

Hanks, M. (1979). Race, sexual status, and athletics in the process of educational achievement. *Social Science Quarterly, 60* (3), 482–496.

Hunt, K. W. (1965). Grammatical structures written at three grade levels. Champaign, IL: National Council of Teachers of English.

Kilgore, S. B. (1991). The Organizational context of tracking in schools. *American Sociological Review, 56,* 189–203.

Kleiber, P. A., and Roberts, G. C. (1987). High School Play. In J. H. Block and N. D. King (Eds.), *School Play: A Source Book.* New York: Garland.

Kroll, B. M. (1986). Explaining how to play a game: The development of informative writing skills. *Written Communication, 3,* 195–218.

Lakoff, R. (1977). Women's Language. *Language and Style, 10,* 222–247.

Lever, J. (1978). Sex differences in the complexity of children's play. *American Sociological Review, 43,* 471–82.

Lynch, C., and Strauss-Noll, M. (1987). Mauve washers: Sex differences in freshman writing. *English Journal, 76,* 90–94.

Mullis, I. V. S., and Mellon, J. C. (1980). *Guidelines for describing three aspects of writing: Syntax, cohesion and mechanics.* Denver, CO: National Assessment of Educational Progress.

Ravens, J. C. (1965). *Guide to Using the Coloured Progressive Matrices.* London: Lewis.

Rowan, K. E. (1988). A contemporary theory of explanatory writing. *Written Communication, 5,* 23–56.

Rubin, K. H., Fein, G., and Vandenberg, B. (1983). Play. In P. H. Mussen (Ed.), *Handbook of Child Psychology. Vol. 4: Socialization, Personality, and Social Development.* New York: Wiley.

Selman, R. L. (1980). *The Growth of Interpersonal Understanding.* New York: Academic Press.

Shavi, Y. G., and Featherman, P. L. (1988). Schooling, teaching and teenage intelligence. *Sociology of Education, 61,* 42–51.

Soccer Association for Youth. (1987). *S.A.Y. Soccer.* Cincinnati, OH: Soccer Association for Youth.

13

CRAIG H. HART, LEA MCGEE, AND SUE HERNANDEZ ———

Themes in the Peer Relations Literature:
Correspondence to Playground Interactions
Portrayed in Children's Literature

During the past decade we have witnessed a proliferation of research focusing on peer relationships in childhood. Despite recent research interest in this aspect of children's development, little is known about ways that children's peer relations are portrayed by authors of storybooks that children are exposed to during their childhood years. Moreover, few if any writers have explored whether children's stories involving peer relations correspond to major themes that are found in the peer relations literature. Likewise, little is known about ways that children's literature may point to new ideas and fresh perspectives for researchers studying peer relations.

In this chapter we examine both the peer relations research and children's literature. We first examine the themes that emerge from research and then ask whether these same themes are reflected in children's literature. Because the focus of this book is on the nature of children's friendships and peer relations on playgrounds, we limit our examination of children's literature to books where children interact on playgrounds, in parks, or at accepted neighborhood play spaces (such as streets or vacant lots). We begin the chapter by reviewing research on children's peer acceptance and friendships. Most of this review will be restricted to peer relations in the preschool and grade school years. In the second portion of the chapter we turn our attention to peer relations in playground settings in children's literature. In the final part of the chapter, we will briefly explore ways that children's literature can be used as an intervention tool to facilitate social skills training. It is our hope that this chapter will stimulate thought about ways that children's literature can be used to teach young children about peer relations. Moreover, the themes derived from the research literature should provide authors with new ideas for writing stories, which highlight peer relations in playground settings.

RESEARCH LITERATURE REVIEW

The majority of research on children's peer relations has centered around investigating correlates of acceptance in the peer group (e.g., popularity) and friendship formation and maintenance (Hartup, 1983; Ladd, 1989). Many have argued that acceptance and friendship are conceptually and empirically distinct constructs based on social skills that are partly non-overlapping (e.g., Berndt, 1984; Furman and Robbins, 1985; Parker and Gottman, 1989). Parker and Asher (1987) suggest that certain skills may facilitate the formation of close emotional ties to one or a few age-mates (i.e., having friends) despite the inability to get along well in a larger group of peers (i.e., peer acceptance). Conversely, skills used in becoming accepted by peers may not necessarily contribute to forming and maintaining close friendships. Group acceptance and friendship also do not appear to have the same function in children's lives. Whereas group acceptance provides a sense of inclusion in children's lives, friendship serves to provide intimacy, affection, enhancement of worth, and reliable alliance (Furman and Robbins, 1985).

Most of the major themes in the peer acceptance literature revolve around children's behavior (e.g., prosocial behavior, disruptive behavior, aggression, play styles, and group entry styles), social cognition (e.g., strategies, goals, social problem solving, intention cue detection/decision making, attributions), affect (e.g., loneliness, self-efficacy), and nonbehavioral characteristics (e.g., physical attractiveness, handicaps, birth order, social class, the child's name). Themes in the friendship literature include friendship formation processes and skills (e.g., exchanging information, managing conflict, establishing a common ground, communication clarity, self-disclosure), friendship selection (proximity, age, and similarity), friendship interactions and maintenance (e.g., time spent with friends, cooperation, competition and conflict among friends), and functions of friends (e.g., transmitting social norms and knowledge, nurturance, intimacy, protection). Before moving onto children's literature, an overview of these general themes is in order.

PEER ACCEPTANCE

Identification and categorization of children with successes and difficulties in their peer relations has been largely based on sociometric data (e.g., Coie, Dodge, and Coppotelli, 1982; Newcomb and Bukowski, 1983). Such research has been fostered by accumulating evidence indicating that problematic peer relations in childhood constitute a risk factor for later academic and socioemotional adjustment difficulties (e.g., Kupersmidt, Coie, and Dodge, 1990; Parker and Asher, 1987). Using peer rating and nomination methodologies, researchers have been able to make distinctions between different groups of children. In general, popular children are those who receive many positive and few negative nomination on measures in which peers are asked to identify three classmates with whom they like or don't like to play. Average children typically include those who receive numbers of positive and negative nominations. Neglected children are those who receive few positive or negative nominations. Rejected children receive few positive and many negative nominations from peers. Finally, controversial children receive many negative as well as positive nominations from peers.

Many studies have indicated that rejected children are significantly less well liked than other groups. Whereas average children are less well liked than popular children, neglected children do not differ significantly from average or popular groups in overall acceptance (e.g., French and Waas, 1985; Rubin, Hymel, LeMare, and Rowden, 1989). Since all studies of peer acceptance do not necessarily use this classification scheme, research shedding light on antecedents and correlates of peer status will be presented in terms of more or less popular and rejected. For purposes of elaborating themes, finer distinctions will be made when deemed necessary.

Children's Behavior

Prosocial behavior, aggression, and disruptive behavior. Numerous studies have shown that unpopular children use prosocial, relationship-enhancing behaviors less frequently than do their more popular counterparts in peer group situations. For instance, popularity among preschool children is associated with friendly approaches to peers (Marshall and McCandless, 1957), nurturance giving (Moore and Updegraff, 1964), positive peer contacts including cooperation and social conversation with individual peers (Ladd and Price, 1987), and giving social reinforcement (Hartup, Glazer and Charlesworth, 1967). Whereas peer popularity in samples of grade school children have also been reported to be predicted by the same types of behaviors (e.g., Bonney, 1943; Campbell and Yarrow, 1961; Coie and Kupersmidt, 1983; Dodge, 1983), low status children of both age groups appear to be less adept at enacting these behaviors in peer group situations (e.g., Gottman, Gonso, and Rasmussen, 1975; Hartup et al., 1967; Ladd, Price, and Hart, 1988; Masters and Furman, 1981; Moore, 1967).

The use of aggressive and disruptive behaviors have also been found to distinguish preschool (e.g., Dunnington, 1957; Hartup et al., 1967; McGuire, 1973; Masters and Furman, 1981; Moore, 1967; Vaughn and Waters, 1981), grade school (e.g., Dodge, 1983; Dodge, Coie, Pettit, and Price, 1990; Gottman et al., 1975; Ladd, 1983), and adolescent children (Lesser, 1959) who differ in peer status (see Coie, Dodge, and Kupersmidt, 1990, for a review). For instance, rejection by peers is positively related to aggression, rough play (in preschool samples only), and arguing behavior (see Chapter 10, this volume; Ladd et al., 1988; Ladd and Price, 1987). Moreover, several investigations suggest that such antisocial/disruptive behavior is the cause rather than the consequence of peer rejection (e.g., Coie and Kupersmidt, 1983; Dodge, 1983; Ladd, Price, and Hart, 1988; Chapter 5, this volume). Similar types of aggressive and/or disruptive behavior have been connected with object-possession and peer group entry disputes in the peer conflict literature (Shantz, 1987). Although not rejected, it should also be noted that the controversial group of children is characterized as being both highly aggressive as well as highly prosocial (see Newcomb and Bukowski, 1983; Coie and Dodge, 1988). They also tend to be viewed as good at sports (Price, 1989).

Are all rejected children aggressive and disruptive? There is evidence indicating that there are two (and possibly four) subgroups of rejected children, those who are aggressive towards peers and those who tend to withdraw from interactions (Asher and Williams, 1987; Cillessen, van Ijzendoorn, van Lieshout, and Hartup 1992)[1]. Recent findings suggest that rejected-aggressive children are seen by peers and/or teachers as being more immature, mean, easy to anger, bossy, bothersome, and strange or difficult to understand (Crick and Dodge, 1989; Crick, 1991). These children have also been described as being aggressive, impulsive, disruptive, dishonest, hypersensitive, and noncooperative (Cillessen et al., 1992). Although aggressive-rejected children have been found to be more extremely rejected, children classified as withdrawn-rejected tend to be viewed by others as being highly submissive (i.e., likely to give in easily), withdrawn (e.g., more likely to play alone), aversive (e.g., immature, strange, bothersome), and moderately aggressive (Crick, 1991). Coie et al. (1990) have suggested that as some children become aware that they are disliked and unwanted by peer group members, withdrawn behavior may occur (see also Coie and Dodge, 1988). For others aggressive behavior may often be an antecedent to rejection (see Coie and Kupersmidt, 1983); Chapter 5, this volume).

Readers should be cautioned that withdrawn-rejected children should not be confused with neglected children, since not all neglected children appear to exhibit shy or withdrawn behavior (see Coie et al. 1990; Rubin et al. 1989; Rubin, LeMare, and Lollis, 1990). In fact, using measures of teacher and peer perceptions, Crick (1991) recently found two subgroups of neglected children in a large sample of school-age children (neglected-withdrawn and neglected-nonwithdrawn). Neglected-withdrawn children were portrayed as being submissive, quiet, and fairly nice. Due to these characteristics, such children probably do not receive much attention from teachers or peers. More specifically, as with rejected-withdrawn children, neglected-withdrawn children were perceived by others as being highly submissive and withdrawn. However, they were also viewed as being significantly more prosocial (e.g., cooperative, helpful), and less aversive and aggressive (not mean or bossy, doesn't get mad easily) than rejected-withdrawn children.

Neglected-nonwithdrawn children, in comparison with neglected-withdrawn children, were viewed as being less submissive and withdrawn, but more mature and better liked by peers. They were also perceived as being less prosocial and more likely to get angry and blame peers in aversive situations. These children represented more than 80% of the neglected group in the sample. Since prior work indicates that the neglected status is relatively unstable over time (Coie and Dodge, 1983), perhaps it is this larger neglected group that is better able to change their status in new groups with relative ease. This may be more difficult for children in the smaller withdrawn-rejected group due to their withdrawn and submissive nature. Although available evidence clearly suggests that children in the aggressive-rejected subgroup are at risk for later disorders (e.g., criminality, school withdrawal), it may be that the withdrawn-neglected and rejected groups are more prone to internalizing disorders (e.g., anxiety, depression, loneliness) and victimization problems (see Chapter 4, this volume) that could contribute to later emotional/personality disorders as well (see Hartup and Moore, 1990; Kupersmidt, et al., 1990; Rubin, LeMare, and Lollis, 1990; Rubin, Hymel, Mills, and Rose-Krasnor, 1990). More research is needed to clarify these issues.

Play styles. Another theme that emerges in the peer acceptance behavior literature concerns play styles that popular and unpopular children use. Research by Ladd and his colleagues (Ladd, 1983; Ladd et al., 1988; Ladd and Price, 1987) demonstrated that more popular grade-school (i.e., popular and average) engaged in significantly more cooperative play and less onlooker behavior on the playground than did their rejected counterparts (Ladd, 1983). In contrast, rejected children spent significantly more time in unoccupied behaviors and rejected girls engaged in more parallel play. For preschool children, cooperative play on the playground also forecasted gains in peer acceptance (Ladd and Price, 1987); Ladd et al., 1988).

Further evidence of relations between play styles and children's peer acceptance is derived from research by Rubin and his colleagues (Rubin, 1982; Rubin and Daniels-Beirness, 1983; Rubin, Daniels-Beirness, and Hayvren, 1982). Findings from their work suggest that negative relations exist between immature or high-activity types of solitary play activity (termed dramatic play and solitary functional play) and children's acceptance by peers (Rubin, 1982; Rubin and Daniels-Beirness, 1983). Negatively toned interactions and participation in rough and tumble play were also negatively correlated with peer acceptance for preschool age children (See also Chapter 10, this volume; Ladd, Price, and Hart, 1988; Ladd and Price, 1987). Despite the fact that rough and tumble play is not always consistently defined across studies (Boulton and Smith, 1989), research with preschool and school-age children has indicated that both rejected and popular children engage in this type of play, which is not always disruptive (Hart, DeWolf, Wozniak, and Burts, 1992a; Smith, 1989). Rough and tumble play leads to games with rules for popular children and to aggression for rejected children (Dodge, Coie, Pettit, and Price, 1990; Pellegrini, 1988). For preschoolers, more research is needed to explore linkages between rough and tumble play and other play behaviors, particularly since they engage more in sociodramatic play than in games with rules (Johnson, Christie, and Yawkey, 1987; Rubin, Fein, and Vandenberg, 1983).

With regard to peer acceptance, Rubin and colleagues found that more popular preschoolers were more likely to participate in group dramatic play and games with rules, receive social overtures from others, and have higher levels of social interaction with peers (e.g., Rubin et al., 1982). Peer popularity at this age was also found to be positively related to more constructive forms of noninteractive but parallel play (i.e., engaging in similar activities in the proximity of peers—see Rubin, 1982). Moreover, similar patterns of findings emerged when peer status in first grade was predicted by many of these same behaviors that were observed in kindergarten (Rubin and Daniels-Beirness, 1983).

Group entry styles. Research conducted over the past decade also suggests that popular children have greater tendencies to behave in ways that are relevant to ongoing interactions in the peer group (e.g., Dodge, Schlundt, Schocken, and Delugach, 1983; Howes, 1987; Putallaz, 1983; Putallaz and Gottman, 1981). In these studies, unpopular children employed more self-oriented disruptive entry strategies (e.g., disagreeing, asking informational questions, saying something about themselves, and stating their feelings and opinions). In contrast, popular children tended to avoid interrupting the group's activity by employing low-risk tactics such as waiting and hovering and then moving toward higher-risk tactics such as mimicking the peer group and making group-oriented statements (see Dodge et al., 1983).

Which of these strategies are most successful? Silently approaching the group and hovering, then copying group members' behavior appears to be a successful sequence of moves. For preschoolers, Corsaro (1979) found that such a two-step sequence led to successful entry 88.5% of the time. Sixty-nine percent of 7- to 8-year-old boys successfully entered the group using this approach in the Dodge et al. (1983) study. It should also be noted that children were not very likely to be successful in entering if they only waited and hovered at the edge of the group, being ignored 80–90% of the time (Corsaro, 1979; Dodge et al., 1983).

More recently, Putallaz and Wasserman (1989) found that first graders as compared with fifth graders joined smaller groups, attempted entry proportionately more, and were involved in less sustained interactions. In addition, individual children were easier to approach because acceptance was high. However, small groups of two or three were approached with greater caution with triads being the most difficult to enter. Entering groups of four became easier again for most children.

Somewhat related are other investigations indicating that unpopular children may be poorer communicators in such situations (e.g., Gottman et al., 1975; Hazen and Black, 1989; Rubin, 1972). Moreover, withdrawn children (both neglected and rejected) appear to have the most difficulty in peer group entry situations due to less confidence that peers will grant admission and lower feelings of efficacy for enacting relevant strategies when compared with children in other status group (Crick, 1991; Crick and Dodge, 1989). Rejected-withdrawn children are also less likely than other children to expect that peer group members would like them. This view does not appear to be held by rejected-aggressive children (Crick, 1991).

Social Cognition

Goals, strategies, and consequences. Results of several studies provide evidence that popular and unpopular children differ in their knowledge of appropriate goal orientations and strategies that are used to enact them in peer group situations (e.g., Asher and Renshaw, 1981; Gottman et al. 1975; Ladd and Oden, 1979). As an illustrative example, Renshaw and Asher (1983) proposed that in a game playing situation, children must coordinate the goal of winning with the goal of maintaining the relationship with the partner. Pursuing this line of thinking, Taylor and Gabriel (1989) found that whereas higher status children varied their performance goal (e.g., winning the game) and relationship goal (e.g., helping) enactments in a computer simulated board game in response to changing game conditions, rejected boys enacted performance oriented goals to the exclusion of relationship oriented goal enactments under the same conditions. The findings suggest that rejected boys may lack adaptive goal coordination strategies (see Rabiner and Gordon, 1992).

Along a similar vein, Rubin and Krasnor (1986) suggest that rejected children use less adaptive strategies because they do not consider the appropriate consequences for their actions. Indeed, several studies suggest that aggressive and rejected children are more likely to think that unfriendly strategies (e.g., commanding a peer) would be instrumentally successful (e.g., would succeed in getting what they wanted) than do their more popular peers (see Crick and Ladd, 1990; Hart, DeWolf and Burts, 1992b; Hart, Ladd, and Burleson, 1990; Perry, Perry, and Rasmussen, 1986). Furthermore, Hart et al. (1990, 1992b) found that more prosocial and popular children perceived friendly strategies (e.g., making a polite request) as leading to both self-oriented gains (getting something that was wanted) and enhanced relationships with peers in hypothetical conflict situations.

Attention cue detection/decision making. As Ladd and Asher (1985) suggest, the work of Dodge and his colleagues (Dodge, 1980; Dodge and Frame, 1982; Dodge, Murphy, and Buchsbaum, 1984; Dodge and Newman, 1981) may also be interpreted in a goals framework. This line of research suggests that aggressive children have tendencies to construe a peer's intentions as hostile when no harm was intended in situations where the intentions behind the peer's actions are unclear. Moreover, aggressive children act upon this interpretation by employing aggressive or retaliatory behaviors. Dodge and Coie (1987) reported that this is true only for reactive aggression (e.g., the child striking back after being provoked) and not proactive aggression (e.g., the child using physical force to dominate others). It has been proposed that biases in social information processing in these situations may lead to self-protective and aggressive goals rather than to goals that would be relationship enhancing (see Ladd and Asher, 1985).

Social problem solving. How do these social cognitive processes illustrated above work together in promoting peer competence? Recently, several theorists have described how those processes might interact and have formulated general models of social problem solving based on social information processing approaches (see Rubin and Krasnor, 1986; Dodge, 1986). For instance, Krasnor and Rubin (1983) tested a model in which the relative importance of goals, strategies, and outcomes in social problem solving were assessed. Similarly, Dodge (1986) proposed a model based on findings indicating that children pass through several stages in the processing of information in order to respond competently in social problem solving situations. These stages include encoding social cues (e.g., attention, sensation, and perception of relevant cues), forming representations of these cues (e.g., integrating the cues with past experience and interpreting the cue based on prior knowledge), accessing one or more possible behavioral responses to the cues, evaluating possible consequences of each available response, and selecting an optimal response. It has been suggested that progression through these stages occurs very rapidly and perhaps unconsciously since children use rules, heuristics, and characteristic patterns in processing and responding (Dodge, 1985).

As a final note, one of the reoccurring findings in the social problem solving literature is that more popular children generate significantly more alternative solutions in social problem solving situations when compared with less popular or socially maladjusted peers (e.g., Shure and Spivack, 1978; Pettit, Dodge, and Brown, 1988). Such findings suggest that more socially competent children are adept at quickly thinking through a range of possible solutions/strategies before enacting a relevant response. Qualitatively, recent research also indicates that aggressive-rejected boys, in particular, have tendencies to generate more conflict escalating solutions that ignore the needs and feelings of others when compared with children in other status groups (Rabiner, Lenhart, and Lochman, 1990; Rabiner, Gordon, Klumb, and Thompson, 1991).

Affect

Loneliness and children's confidence. Children's loneliness has also been a topic of concern for researchers exploring processes underlying competence with peers. The evidence to date indicates that older rejected grade-school children feel the most lonely when compared with popular, average, neglected, and controversial children (see Asher, Hymel, and Renshaw, 1984; Asher and Wheeler, 1985). Similar findings have also been recently obtained with a sample of kindergarten and first-grade children (Cassidy and Asher, 1992). Moreover, loneliness was found to be significantly related to disruptiveness, aggressiveness, and shyness, and negatively correlated with prosocial behavior (see also Asher, Parkhurst, Hymel, and Williams, 1990).

For low-accepted children, the level of loneliness appears to decline when these children have reciprocal best friendship with other classmates (Parker and Asher, 1990). For children in general, recent findings involving kindergarten-age children further support that close friendships during school entrance facilitate positive school adjustment and achievement over the course of the school year (Ladd, 1990).

Children's confidence in social situations has also been an emerging theme in the peer relations literature. For instance, Goetz and Dweck (1980) conducted research exploring children's attributions about their own failure in social situations based on a "learned helplessness" paradigm. Children who were less accepted by their peers were more likely than popular children to attribute rejection to their own personal incompetence. These children also showed greater deterioration in their strategies for beginning a relationship than children who attributed rejection to other factors (e.g., traits of the rejector). Along a similar line, Wheeler and Ladd (1982) found relations between sociometric status and grade school children's perceptions of their abilities to be persuasive in conflict and nonconflict situations. In addition, children in this study reported feeling less efficacious in conflict rather than nonconflict situations. Although not conclusive, recent findings also indicate that withdrawn-rejected children experience negative self-perceptions, whereas aggressive-rejected children may distortedly view themselves more positively on a variety of dimensions (Boivin and Begin, 1989; Crick, 1991; Quiggle, Garber, Panak, and Dodge, 1992). Additional research suggests that popular children underestimate their competence with peers while average children are more accurate in their assessments (MacDonald, 1991). Neglected children appear to report the lowest perceived competence with peers (Patterson, Kupersmidt, and Griesler, 1990). Whatever rejected children's perceptions of their own abilities are, it appears that rejected children can make better impressions on peers when they are given information that leads them to expect interpersonal success with peers (Rabiner and Coie, 1989).

Nonbehavioral Characteristics

Several nonbehavioral characteristics are also related to peer acceptance. For instance, physical attractiveness discriminates more and less popular children in a variety of ways based on age, sex, body build, facial attractiveness, degree of acquaintance, etc. (see Hartup, 1983). In general, perceived physical attractiveness is positively related to peer acceptance. In preschoolers, Vaughn and Langlois (1983) found that this relationship appears to be stronger for girls than for boys. Moreover, findings suggest that physical attractiveness may influence sociometric outcomes in ways that are not necessarily related to social competence (Vaughn and Langlois, 1983).

What are some other nonbehavioral characteristics that distinguish popular and unpopular children? In an extensive review of this literature, Hartup (1983) explores nonbehavioral correlates of peer acceptance. For example, social class is related to peer acceptance with children of higher socioeconomic backgrounds having tendencies to be more popular with peers and respond to hypothetical social problem solving situations with less aggressive and more prosocial strategies. Moreover, in preschool children, aggression appears to be negatively related to peer status only in higher socioeconomic status groupings (see Ramsey, 1988).

Results of several studies reviewed by Hartup (1983) also suggest that later born children are more accepted by their peers than middle-born or first-born children. A child's name also appears to be related to peer acceptance. Children with offbeat names have tendencies to be less popular in the peer group. Finally, learning-disabled children, educable mentally retarded children, handicapped children, and "hyperactive" children all appear to have poorer peer relations than other children and, unfortunately, are more rejected by peers in regular classroom situations.

FRIENDSHIP

Friendship Formation Processes and Skills

Research by Gottman (1983) suggests that children who hit it off in their first meeting interact in a "connected" manner by exchanging information successfully (e.g., asking and answering questions in a relevant manner), managing conflict (e.g., giving reasons for disagreeing, being polite, and complying to weak demands of the other), and establishing a common ground (e.g., finding something to do together and exploring similarities and differences). Over time, these processes as well as communication clarity and self-disclosure become important factors in friendship formation (see Hetherington and Parke, 1986, p. 551).

Other research along this line indicates that younger elementary school children suggest that strangers would become friends if they did something special for one another or did something together (Smollar and Youniss, 1982). In contrast, older children emphasized the discovery of common interests and getting to know one another. Whereas not becoming friends was associated with negative interaction ("We fight") for younger children, older children focused on the discovery that two individuals have different personalities. Additional findings suggest that children disclose personal information more to friends than nonfriends and that this capacity is acquired with age (Rotenberg and Sliz, 1988).

Friendship Selection

What are factors that influence the selection of friends? Epstein (1989) suggests three. They are proximity, age, and similarity. First, home, community, and school establish the boundaries that place children in proximity to each other. For older children, neighborhoods still define the boundaries for children's choices of friends at school. Several studies involving grade school children indicate that the majority of friends versus students and other classmates live much closer to each other (Seagoe, 1933; Fine, 1980; Coates, 1985). However, for preschoolers, there appears to be little overlap between peers (not necessarily friends) found in nonschool networks (e.g., neighborhood) and those also present in preschool classrooms (Ladd, Hart, Wadsworth, and Golter, 1988). Research with preschoolers also suggests that approximately one-half to two-thirds of parents initiate to a greater or lesser degree their children's contacts with peers (see Ladd and Golter, 1988; Ladd and Hart, 1992) indicating that parents may play a role in friendship formation. Proximity may also play a role in this regard. Additional findings suggest that younger preschoolers of parents who initiate peer contacts (mainly mothers), have a higher proportion of network members residing in town than out of town relative to older preschoolers (see Ladd, Hart, Wadsworth, and Golter, 1988).

Proximity and peer contact are also dependent upon neighborhood housing arrangements (e.g., apartment versus single-family houses or rural community widely spaced farms), parental patterns of work, and school environment factors (see Epstein, 1989; Ladd, Profilet, and Hart, 1992). For instance, Ladd, Hart, Wadsworth, and Golter (1988), reported that children of both parents who worked full-time had larger peer networks, a greater number of playgroups, and engaged in more peer contacts in network members' homes. Within schools, Epstein (1989) also suggests that architectural features of the school and play yard, the amount of available equipment requiring sharing or creating crowding, demographic factors such as SES, sex, age, and race, and the number of extracurricular activities all work together to enhance or limit proximal features of children's friendship selection and interaction patterns. These environmental factors also emphasize age and other similarity/dissimilarity features of children that influence friendship selection patterns.

The majority of research findings also indicate that many children's friendships are mixed-age in nature (within a few years). Mixed-age friends appear to be the norm across age groupings in both school and neighborhood settings with levels of skill, similarity of interests, and social status being more important factors in friendship selection than age (Epstein, 1989). However, more research is needed to understand the dynamics of same-age, near-age, and mixed-age friendship relations.

Finally, similarity of character and personal characteristics influence friendship selection. Interestingly, very young children make friends with apparently little thought given to similarities and differences. However, from kindergarten on, children become increasingly aware of and are more prone to nurture friendships with others who have similar qualities, ideas, preferences, goals, and values (see Epstein, 1989).

Friendship Interactions and Maintenance

Once friendships are formulated, what is the nature of these relationships and how are they maintained? How do interactions with friends differ from those with nonfriends? Hartup (1989) suggests that for younger children, friendship relationships are characterized by participation in common pursuits (e.g., playing together). Older children characterize these relationships in terms of mutual understanding, loyalty, and self-disclosure (e.g., sharing similar and different ideas, secrets, etc.). Other factors besides age that come into play include time spent with friends, cooperation, competition, and conflict.

Time spent with friends. A fairly extensive body of literature indicates that preschool-age children spend more time with those they designate as friends than with other children (see Hartup, 1989). These friends are identified in a variety of ways. For instance, Hinde, Titmus, Easton, and Tamplin (1985) specified strong associates as those children with whom the subject spends 30% or more of their time. Other studies rely on sociometric interviews (e.g., asking children who they like to play with most outdoors, etc.) and then verifying these procedures with observation of who children actually play with the most (e.g., Biehler, 1954; Hagman, 1933; Marshall and McCandless, 1957). Friendships are also confirmed in some studies by teacher and parent nominations (Hartup, Laursen, Stewart, and Eastenson, 1988; Vespo, 1987). Although less well-documented in the research literature, schoolchildren also spend much more time with friends than nonfriends (see Hartup, 1989).

Cooperation. Children who are friends are also more likely to cooperate together (see Hartup, 1989). For instance, Newcomb, Brady, and Hartup (1979) found that interactions of friends versus nonfriends vary according to friendship status in a block-building task. Friends smiled and laughed more with each other, paid closer attention to equity rules, were more interactive, and directed their conversations more toward getting the task done than toward each other as individuals. Based on a review of this literature, Hartup (1989) concludes that cooperation is not only an outcome of children's friendships, but is also a condition that contributes to their maintenance as well.

Competition and conflict. Although the research on competition and friendship is sketchy, it appears that nursery school children behave more competitively with nonfriends than friends (Matsumoto, Haan, Yabrove, Theodorou, and Carney, 1986). Despite the fact that children generally believe that friends should not compete with one another, studies with older children suggest that boys may be especially competitive with friends, as long as it does not violate the terms of their relationship (see Berndt, 1985; Hartup, 1989).

Conflict is also a part of friendship (Hartup, 1989; Shantz and Hobart, 1989). In recapping the theoretical positions of Sullivan and Piaget, Youniss (1980) describes cooperation among friends as arising, in part, out of interpersonal conflicts as children learn to deal with differences in opinion by using the procedures of compromise, argument, negotiation, debate, and discussion. The research literature to date suggests that children do engage in more conflict with friends than with neutral associates. (e.g., Green, 1933; Hinde et al., 1985; Hartup et al., 1988). However, this appears due to the fact that children spend more time with friends (Hartup and Laursen, 1989).

Qualitatively, conflicts with friends differ from those with neutral associates and are contextually determined (see Chapter 3, this volume). For instance, Hartup et al. (1988) found that preschool children's conflicts with friends and nonfriends did not differ in content (i.e., possession of objects vs. behavioral issues). However, friends used negotiation and disengagement more than nonfriends in conflict resolution. Resolution strategies favoring more equitable than inequitable outcome, relative to winner and loser outcomes, were also more common between friends than nonfriends. In addition, conflicts involving friends were rated as less intense. Following conflict resolution, friends were more likely to continue in social interaction and stay in physical proximity when compared with neutral associates.

As a final note, more recent findings suggest that when conflict resolution alternatives are few and when interaction must continue, friends feel "freer" to disagree and do so more intensely (Hartup and Laursen, 1989). However, open confrontations with friends are still avoided less with friends than nonfriends. Alternatively, when resolution alternatives are many, friends tend to soften conflicts with each other in terms of frequency, affective intensity, and outcome equitability. It should be noted that when conflicts involve the violation of trust (e.g., lying to a friend for social gain, failure to provide emotional comfort), friends across grade-school age groupings report feelings of being let down (Kahn and Turiel, 1988).

Function of Friends

As Parker and Gottman (1989) point out, many authors have speculated on the functions of friendships in childhood. Some of these include play, teaching, nurturance (emotional security and support), intimacy, protection, and caregiving (cf. Lewis and Feiring, 1989). Other functions that friends perform include, but are not limited to, the enhancement of self-worth, providing reliable alliance and companionship, serving as a staging area for behavior, providing a cultural institution for the transmission of knowledge and social norms, serving as a context for the display of appropriate self-images, acting as prototypes for later relationships, and serving as a context for growth in the development of social skills (Fine, 1981; Furman and Buhrmester, 1985; Furman and Robbins, 1985; Hartup and Sancilio, 1986; Sullivan, 1953).

However, what specific functions appear to characterize developmental aspects of friendship? Using detailed observational data of different age children who were friends and who were becoming friends, Parker and Gottman (1989) developed a model describing children's friendship functions in early and middle childhood (as well as in adolescence).

Their observations suggest that friendship interaction in early childhood revolves around level of enjoyment, entertainment, and satisfaction experienced in their play. Friends aim for attaining the highest level of stimulation and excitement in their play interactions. Much of this is reflected in the high level of fantasy play that is evident during the early childhood years. Children create drama (e.g., involving lost-found or danger-rescue themes), ensuring that it ends in some satisfying, nonthreatening way. Friends tend to endlessly repeat the drama, with only slight variation in successive play episodes. Over the course of these coordinated play activities, Parker and Gottman suggest that children learn not only how to manage their emotions, but also how to manage conflicts, maintain clear communication, take on the perspectives of others, and negotiate and renegotiate themes, props, roles, acts, and settings.

Middle childhood friendship interactions are characterized to an extensive degree by gossip (Parker and Gottman, 1989). Disparaging gossip makes up the majority of conversations among middle childhood friends. Parker and Gottman also note that other social processes such as humor, self-disclosure (particularly regarding others' embarrassing moments), information exchange, and exploration of similarities also occur almost exclusively in the context of gossip. The object of friend's gossip are frequently movies, sports, and rock stars. Children of this age have a strong desire for belonging and social acceptance. For this reason, gossip serves to reaffirm membership with friends of same-sex peer social groups and reveals attitudes, behaviors, and beliefs that provide the basis for inclusion or exclusion in these groups. Through gossip, children find that they can safely sample peer attitudes without having to make their own views explicit first. Compared with the high emotional displays of early childhood friendships, children in middle childhood try to project an impression of reason and rationality in their interactions with friends in order to appear "cool" and always under emotional control. Emotionality and sentimentality is to be avoided since children tend to believe displays of such feelings will lead to their rejection. For instance, as Parker and Gottman note, boys and girls of this age would prefer to die than admit affection.

PEER RELATIONS ON PLAYGROUNDS IN CHILDREN'S LITERATURE

Children's literature frequently explores themes of friendship and the nature of interactions with others, especially with friends. However, the number of books that explore the nature of friendships and peer relations specifically as they occur in playground settings is small. That is, there are hundreds of children's books dealing with themes related to friendship, but only a handful that deal with this theme in a playground setting. In reality, it is in this type of setting that children have more spontaneous opportunities to select and interact with playmates in the relative absence of adult guided activities (see Chapter 1 and Chapter 14, this volume). In addition to setting constraints, books we found were limited in the representation of different ethnic groups and in males and females being equally represented in equivalent types of roles. Despite these limitations, the books discussed in this chapter represent examples of the books that we could locate having both themes related to friendship and peer relations events occurring in playground settings.

Books dealing with friendship and peer relations in playground settings can be characterized in roughly two groups. The first group of books consists of literature called sports stories. These stories are about children on a sports team. Many, although not all, of the events in these stories occur on a playground—usually at a playing field or ballpark. However, not all sports stories explore friendship themes. For example, some books such as *Supercharged Infield* (Christopher, 1985) focus on adventure and mystery.

Sports books often stress themes of personal perseverance in the face of difficulties (e.g., practicing makes one better even if it does not make one a star), team cooperation and spirit, and the nature of competition. Other themes include playing one's best for friends on the team and for personal satisfaction and gaining satisfaction from mastering a difficult-to-learn skill. They explore what happens when a player does not play well and is singled out for ridicule by other players.

The second group of books consists of stories where some events occur on a playground (or at a camp, picnic ground, park, or play space in a neighborhood). These events may include a game such as baseball, kickball, or stickball, but the sport is not the unifying topic of the story. These stories often have school-age characters where several events occur at school including on the school playground. These stories may have many or a few events that occur in the playground setting. Themes of friendship in these stories are more varied. They may deal with finding a new friend, breaking up with a best friend, or overcoming the ridicule of a bully.

In this portion of the chapter, we discuss books that reflect the findings of peer relations research. We first describe books that highlight peer acceptance research, and then we describe books that highlight friendship research.

PEER ACCEPTANCE IN CHILDREN'S LITERATURE

Children who feel lonely, incompetent, and unworthy as well as children who are friendly and well-liked are familiar characters in children's literature. The bully—the character who is pushy, bossy, aggressive, and abusive—is also a familiar face in children's literature.

Nothing's Fair in Fifth Grade (DeClements, 1981) includes an example of both a more popular and a rejected child. Elsie, a dramatically overweight fifth grader, is a new girl in class. She has no friends and makes no attempts to interact with others. While the other children play games or talk together on the playground, Elsie stands against the wall. Many of the children dislike her (she steals their lunch money to buy candy) and make fun of her. Diane, one of the more popular children, is one of

Elsie's tormentors. As soon as she sees Elsie, she comments, "Ugh . . . I hope she isn't going to be in this room." (p. 4).

Jennifer, the main character and Diane's friend, begins to see what life must be like for Elsie. She offers to be Elsie's friend. Elsie does not believe that Jennifer is sincere in her offer of friendship. She says, "Why do you want a fat slob who sits and stuffs her face?" (p. 52). Jennifer continues to insist she'll be Elsie's friend. She tells Elsie that she just never thought about her having feelings. Jennifer is realistic about her offer of friendship. She knows that the other kids don't like Elsie. She worries that the other kids will desert her and leave her with Elsie as her only friend. Despite these concerns, Jennifer walks home with Elsie, gets Elsie to tutor her in math, and sticks up for her when the other kids taunt her. Jennifer's other friends gradually see the positive side of Elsie, and Elsie's circle of friends begins to grow. Eventually Elsie becomes an accepted member of the fifth grade.

This story illustrates many of the findings of research on peer acceptance. Jennifer, the more popular child, illustrates the use of prosocial behavior: She makes friendly approaches and gives support to Elsie. She also illustrates the use of decision-making and social problem-solving skills: She is perceptive of Elsie's feelings and tries several strategies both to win Elsie's friendship and to gain acceptance for Elsie among the other children.

Elsie, the rejected child, illustrates withdrawn social behavior and ineffective play and group entry styles: She spends much of her time initially watching other children making no attempts to enter in play. She illustrates loneliness and other nonbehavior characteristics of less popular children: She reacts negatively to Jennifer's first attempts at friendship. She attributes her loneliness to her perceived unappealing physical appearance.

The findings of peer acceptance research are reflected in several other children's books as well. In some books the prosocial behaviors associated with more popular children are found in a supporting character, the main character's best friend. These best-friend supporting characters help the main character deal with losing a game, not measuring up, or taking the abuse of a bully. They are nurturing, supportive, and cooperative. For example, Mark Branden in *Big Play and the Small League* (Jackson, 1968) needs to make good at the final tryout for Small League. On the way to the tryouts, Johnny, Mark's best friend, remarks, "Look, Mark, every coach of the Small League will be there. They'll be bidding like crazy for guys. You're a cinch to knock 'em dead" (p. 10). Initially Mark fails to make the league, but later he makes the team when two players drop out.

In *The Diamond Champs* (Christopher, 1977) Kim Rollins, a new player to baseball, regrets his decision to join a new, special team. However, his friend urges him to stay with it. With the encouragement of his friends, the mysterious coach, and his family, Kim becomes a credible player through hard work and perseverance.

In some books, examples of aggressive behaviors and ineffective use of attention cues are found in the bully. Bullies are easily recognized. They are bossy, threatening, belittling, and aggressive. For example, Josh Morris in *Roots in the Outfield* (Zirpoli, 1988) has a problem, Nick Cutter. Nick is on his baseball team and in his class at school. He makes fun of Josh's lack of athletic ability taunting him with the nickname Root, short for Rooted to the ground. Nick and his friends make Josh's life miserable. They chant "Boot the Root" when Josh misses a play and their team loses a game. Finally, Nick issues an ultimatum to the coach, "I'll only play on September second on one condition. Morris doesn't play in the game" (p. 28). The whole team agrees by chanting, "Boot the Root. Boot the Root." Josh ends up meeting a famous baseball player who has disappeared during a losing streak. He and the player practice and both gain new confidence and skill.

Bullies often misinterpret social cues; they interpret neutral activities as threatening. For example, Peter in *Veronica Gantz* (Sachs, 1968) wants Veronica to be the catcher, not the pitcher. Veronica, the bully of the neighborhood, insists on being the pitcher. Peter tries to convince her. He says, "You're a good pitcher . . . but I think you'd make a better catcher. . . . You're a good catcher. I've been studying the way you play" (p. 89). Veronica misses the compliment. She quits and plays on the other, losing, team.

Several books illustrate children's entry into group play. For example, Freddy in *Who Will Be My Friends?* (Hoff, 1960) moves to a new house. He goes to the playground where some boys are playing ball. They ignore Freddy. He begins throwing and catching his ball himself. The boys observe how well he can handle the ball and invite him to play. Mark, in *Boy at Bat* (Renick, 1961) gets a new baseball glove. He hopes now that the big boys will let him play. He takes his glove and ball and sits near first base. He begins throwing and catching his ball. When Gordon gets mad and goes home, Mark gets his chance to play.

Dealing with competition, learning to balance goals and consequences, is another theme explored in children's literature. In *Battle Day at Camp Delmont* (Weiss, 1988) Maude and Sally, best friends, end up on opposing teams. Maude remains so friendly to Sally that her teammates complain, "Which side are you on?" (unpaged). Her teammates claim they're Maude's friends, too, and urge her to do her job as a teammate. Maude and Sally face each other on the tennis court in the battle day finals. Maude realizes that Sally is playing her best so she does too. Maude wins the game, and her team wins the battle. Sally understands, and they stay best friends.

Benjy in *Benjy and the Power of Zingies* (Van Leeuwen, 1982) illustrates the zany ways characters go about social problem solving. Benjy has trouble with several of his classmates, but his main problem is Alex. Alex makes fun of Benjy's kicking, calls Benjy "Squirt," and lets his dog destroy Benjy's dinosaur picture. Benjy imagines several ways to deal with Alex such as getting a shark for a pet and letting it bite Alex, banging Alex's and Brian's heads together, and letting Alex get eaten by a dinosaur. Finally, Benjy decides to punch Alex in the nose and carefully plots how to do it. First, he eats lots and lots of Zingies, the breakfast of champions, to build up his body. He practices with a punching bag. When these ideas backfire, Benjy bribes Matthew to punch Alex. Matthew lets him have it on the playground.

Some books explore special problems, including those experienced by learning disabled, physically unattractive, or foreign-born children. Children who are perceived as different often have difficulty gaining the acceptance of others. For instance, Shirley Temple Wong in *In the Year of the Boar and Jackie Robinson* (Lord, 1984), a recent immigrant from China, longs for her classmates to accept her as a friend. Applebaum in *Wrongway Applebaum* (Lewis, 1984) has a difficult time learning to read and spell. He can't remember rules or things other people think are important. He, too, has no friends. Eventually these children gain the acceptance of others as they make special efforts to let others know them and to learn about their peers.

Table 13.1 presents a reference list of other children's books that include children's interactions with their peers on playground settings. This list includes descriptions of themes from peer acceptance research that are reflected in each book.

Table 13.1.   Peer Acceptance in Children's Literature

Title	Recommended Grade	Annotations on Peer Acceptance
Beim, J. (1952). *The Smallest Boy in the Class.* New York: Morrow.	P-1	Aggression, disruptive of group, goal of personal satisfaction over group, relationship oriented, disruptive behavior related to lack of confidence, views self positively when aggressive
Berenstain, S., and Berenstain, J. (1988). *The Berenstain Bears and the Double Dare.* New York: Random House.	2-4	Bullying, self-defense and peer-defense, fear of being rejected if not compliant with group's negative demands, renewed confidence in belief system
Burchardt, N. (1966). *Project Cat.* New York: Scholastic.	2-4	Bossy, goal of personal attention vs. group project, a peer's intentions construed as hostile when no harm intended, employing aggressive retaliatory behavior.
Christopher, M. (1974). *Jinx Glove.* Boston: Little, Brown, and Co.	2-4	Cooperative play, coordination of the goal to win and the goal to maintain relationships, group goal more important than personal participation, feelings of rejection due to poor performance, loss of self-confidence, renewed self-confidence.
Giff, P. (1984). *The Beast in Ms. Rooney's Room.* New York: Dell.	2-4	Assertion, lying to achieve group acceptance, lack of confidence related to lack of academic ability, group rejection due to school failure
Waber, B. (1969). *Lovable Lyle.* Boston: Houghton Mifflin.	2-4	Friendly, cooperative, helpful, negative comments, anxious to please, a peer's intentions construed as hostile when no harm intended, aggressive retaliatory behavior, aggressiveness related to jealousy, depression related to rejection

FRIENDSHIP IN CHILDREN'S LITERATURE

Many children's stories explore friendship. They show the joys of making a new friend and the anguish when best friends part. *Ellen Tebbits* (Cleary, 1951) tells the story of two girls who become best friends.

Since Nancy Jane has moved away from next door, Ellen does not have a best friend, although she has lots of friends at school. She also has a terrible secret—her mother makes her wear woolen underwear, the high-necked kind that buttons down the front. Ellen's problem arises in ballet class. She has to roll down the top of the underwear so it doesn't show under her ballet costumes. But the top bunches up and worse—the bottom beings to fall down. Ellen keeps hitching up her underwear. The teacher's son, Otis, interrupts the class by imitating Ellen—leaping and hitching, leaping and hitching.

Austine, a new girl in town comes to the rescue. She leaps into Otis and gets the teacher to send him away. Then Ellen discovers another secret. Austine wears woolen underwear, too. Austine and Ellen discover they only live two blocks apart, they both love to cook, and they both are glad they found someone else who has to wear woolen underwear. Austine tells Ellen how lonely she's been and invites Ellen over to bake brownies.

Austine and Ellen become the best of friends. When Ellen gets dirty bringing a beet to school, Austine helps her clean up and lends her a sweater. When Ellen brags she can ride horses when she really can't, Austine keeps her secret. Again and again Ellen thinks how lucky she is to have such a loyal girl for her best friend. But one day Ellen slaps Austine over a fight about Ellen's beautiful new dress. Austine's new dress has no sash, and she repeatedly pulls on Ellen's. Even though Ellen feels bad about the slap, she thinks Austine should apologize first. But Austine ignores Ellen and plays with other friends. Weeks pass, and the girls do not speak.

Finally one day they are sent outside to clap the erasers clean. Ellen gets so mad at Austine and their fight that she pulls on Austine's sash. She pulls so hard it accidentally rips off Austine's dress. Ellen apologizes and invites Austine to slap her. She ends up apologizing for the first slap. Austine confesses how mad and awful she has felt, too. She reveals how jealous she was of Ellen's new dress with the beautiful sash. Each claims the fight was her fault and they become best friends once again.

This story illustrates many of the findings of research on friendship. Ellen and Austine form a friendship when Austine does something special for Ellen: gets rid of the pest, Otis. They disclose personal information: They both have to wear woolen underwear. They discover common interests: They both love cooking and have woolen underwear. Ellen and Austine illustrate perfect choices for friends: They live in close proximity and are in the same class in school. They maintain their friendship through loyalty and cooperation: Austine helps Ellen and keeps her secrets. However, they also have conflicts: They fight, separate, and make up. Their friendship serves many purposes: the enjoyment of sharing activities, the satisfaction of disclosing personal information, and the joy of belonging.

The findings of friendship research are reflected in several other children's books. Inappropriate ways to go about forming new friendships are explored in *Say Hello, Vanessa* (Sharmat, 1979). Vanessa is too shy to talk to other children or even answer the teacher's questions. Her mother convinces her to find someone else who is alone and say hello. Vanessa says hello too softly, then too loudly. Finally she speaks up in class and Moose makes friends with her. She learns to say hello to everyone she meets. Queenie in *The Berenstain Bears and the In-Crowd* (Berenstain and Berenstain, 1989) discovers that belittling others, offering bribes, and wearing sharp clothes are not the way to make friends. Emmie in *Leo, Zack, and Emmie* (Ehrlich, 1981) tries to make a friend by doing everything better than everyone else and drawing attention to herself. She grabs the ball and runs away with it.

Several books reveal how friendships are maintained and strengthened. In some stories best friends break up or a best friend makes a new friend. Zack, Leo's best friend, feels left out when Leo and Emmie spend all the time together making a giant plant as a class report (Ehrlich, 1981). Leo and Emmie decide to try to talk to Zack. They play with him and offer to show him how to make a giant plant. Zack learns that Emmy and Leo can be his best friends.

Table 13.2 presents a reference list of several other children's books that explore the theme of friendship and include playground settings. This list includes descriptions of themes from friendship research that are reflected in each book. It should be noted that we were able to locate many more children's books that were centered around themes of friendship as compared with themes of peer acceptance (see Tables 13.1 and 13.2).

Table 13.2.   Friendship Formation and Maintenance in Children's Literature

Title	Recommended Grade	Annotations on Friendship Formation
Beim, J. (1952). *Kid Brother.* New York: William Morrow.	P–1	Establishing common interests, same age, same neighborhood, spending time together, sharing plans
Beim, J. (1945). *Two is a Team.* New York: Harcourt, Brace, and World.	P–1	Establishing common interests, managing conflict, same age, same neighborhood, spending time together, cooperation, conflict, competition
Beim, J. (1952). *The Smallest Boy in the Class.* New York: Morrow.	P–1	Establishing common interests, same class, same interests, cooperation, nurturing, protecting
Berenstain, S., and Berenstain, J. (1986). *The Berenstain Bears and the Trouble with Friends.* New York: Random House.	P–1	Establishing common interests, managing conflict, same age, same size, same neighborhood, same interests, spending time together, cooperation, laughing, smiling, conflict, resolution of conflict, renewing friendship
Blegvad, L. (1985). *Anna Banana and Me.* New York: Atheneum.	P–1	Establishing common interests, communication, same neighborhood, spending time together, cooperation, competition and conflict, sharing secrets and intimacy
Bonsall, C. (1963). *The Case of the Hungry Stranger.* New York: Harper and Row.	P–1	Exchanging information, communication clarity, same neighborhood, same interests, spending time together, cooperation, competition and conflict, transmitting social norms, intimacy, protection
Cohen, M. (1967). *Will I Have a Friend?* Eau Claire, WI: E. M. Hale	P–1	Sharing thoughts, establishing common interests, same age, same interests

Continued

Table 13.2. *Continued*

Title	Recommended Grade	Annotations on Friendship Formation
Hillert, M. (1978). *Play Ball.* Chicago: Follett.	P–1	Managing conflict, establishing common ground, communication, same neighborhood, cooperation, conflict
Hoban, R. (1969), *Best Friends for Frances.* New York: Harper and Row.	P–1	Communication, same neighborhood, cooperation, enjoyment, entertainment, satisfaction
Kessler, L. (1983). *The Big Mile Race.* New York: Greenwillow.	P–1	Loyalty, competition and conflict, entertainment
Simon, N. (1958). *My Beach House.* Philadelphia: Lippencott.	P–1	Friendly and polite, establishing common ground, cooperative play
Steiner, C. (1962). *Jack is Glad.* New York: Knopf.	P–1	Negative interaction, establishing comon ground, conflict, helping
Viorst, J. (1979). *Rosie and Michael.* New York: Atheneum.	P–1	Conflict, cooperation, loyalty, nurturing, protecting
Wells, R. (1981). *Timothy Goes to School.* New York: Dial.	P–1	Establishing common ground, similar problems, communication, same age, spending time together, laughing and smiling
Blume, J. (1972). *Tales of a Fourth Grade Nothing.* New York: Dial.	2–4	Establishing common ground, similarities, spending time together, cooperation
Burchardt, N. (1966). *Project Cat.* New York: Scholastic.	2–4	Communication clarity, cooperation, conflict, renewing friendship, protecting
Christopher, M. (1974). *Jinx Glove.* Boston: Little, Brown.	2–4	Friendly gestures, conflict, cooperation, nurturing, intimacy
Giff, P. (1987). *The Mystery of the Blue Ring.* New York: Dell.	2–4	Exchanging information, conflict, intimacy, loyalty, protection

Continued

Table 13.2.   *Continued*

Title	Recommended Grade	Annotations on Friendship Formation
Giff, P. (1987). *Powder Puff Puzzle.* New York: Dell.	2–4	Communication, cooperation, conflict, nurturing, problem solving
Giff, P. (1988). *Ronald Morgan at Bat.* New York: Viking Kestrel.	2–4	Confidence in friend's ability, nurturing, intimacy
Hutchins, H. (1983). *The Three and Many Wishes of Jason Reid.* New York: Viking Kestrel.	2–4	Exchanging information, conflict, cooperation, nurturing, protecting, intimacy
Kellogg, S. (1986). *Best Friends.* New York: Dial.	2–4	Same neighborhood, same age, same class in school, same soccer team, similar likes and dislikes, spending time together, fantasizing, lonely when apart, jealousy when friend is on vacation, conflict, renewing friendship, cooperation, protecting, nurturing
Kessler, L. (1965). *Here Comes the Strikeout.* New York: Harper and Row.	2–4	Common interests, helping, teaching, nurturing
Lovelace, M. (1940). *Betsy-Tacy.* New York: Thomas Y. Crowell.	2–4	Chasing, aggressive inquiry, invitation to a party, same age, same class in school, spending time together, cooperation, planning activities, sharing, nurturing, intimacy, transmitting social norms
Marshall, J. (1972). *George and Martha.* Boston: Houghton Mifflin.	2–4	Same neighborhood, similar interests, spending time together, honesty, consideration of feelings, respecting privacy, transmitting social norms, nurturing, protecting, listening, cheering up

Continued

Table 13.2. *Continued*

Title	Recommended Grade	Annotations on Friendship Formation
McCall, E. (1961). *The Buttons and the Little League.* Chicago: Benefic Press.	2–4	Exchanging information, cooperation, nurturing
Schulz, C. (1974). *A Charlie Brown Thanksgiving.* New York: Random House.	2–4	Disclosing personal information, exchanging information, politeness, managing conflict, same neighborhood, cooperation, conflict, nurturing
Schulz, C. (1976). *It's the Easter Beagle, Charlie Brown.* New York: Random House.	2–4	Exchanging information, self-disclosure, same neighborhood, similar interests, conflict, cooperation, spending time together, apologizing, resolution, transmitting knowledge, nurturing, protecting
Schulz, C. (1974). *It's Arbor Day, Charlie Brown.* New York: Random House.	2–4	Self-disclosure, same neighborhood, similar interests, spending time together, cooperation, conflict, competition, nurturing, protecting, instilling confidence
Sharmat, M. (1970). *Gladys Told Me to Meet Her Here.* New York: Harper and Row.	2–4	Managing conflict, establishing common ground, communication, spending time together, cooperation, conflict, protecting, helping, nurturing, intimacy, loyalty
Stolz, M. (1960). *A Dog on Barkham Street.* New York: Harper and Row.	2–4	Same neighborhood, same age, similar interests, spending time together, working on group projects, commiserating, protecting, social problem solving

Continued

Table 13.2.   *Continued*

Title	Recommended Grade	Annotations on Friendship Formation
Waber, B. (1969). *Lovable Lyle.* Boston: Houghton Mifflin.	2–4	Negative interaction, same neighborhood, same friends, cooperation, smiling, laughing, resolution of conflicts, protecting nurturing
Adler, D. (1985). *Jeffrey's Ghost and the Fifth Grade Dragon.* New York: Henry Holt.	5–8	Spending time together, communication, cooperation, loyalty, protecting, self-disclosure
Avi. (1984). *S. O. R. Losers.* New York: Bradbury.	5–8	Spending time together, communication, laughing, smiling, conflict, cooperation, protecting, nurturing, problem solving
Blume, J. (1980). *Superfudge.* New York: Dell.	5–8	Establishing common ground, same neighborhood, communication, resolution, laughing, cooperation, intimacy
Cone, M. (1982). *Mishmash and the Big Fat Problem.* Boston: Houghton Mifflin.	5–8	Spending time together, helping, conflict, cooperation, problem solving, intimacy, nurturing
DeClements, B. (1981). *Nothing's Fair in the Fifth Grade.* New York: Scholastic.	5–8	Problem solving, competition, conflict, intimacy, nurturing, adventure, sharing information, protecting, helping
Girion, B. (1979). *Misty and Me.* New York: Scholastic.	5–8	Establishing common ground, competition and conflict, helping, intimacy, transmitting social norms
Hurwitz, J. (1984). *The Hot and Cold Summer.* New York: William Morrow.	5–8	Establishing common ground, exchanging information, inviting, requesting information, helping, bragging, similar age, same neighborhood, cooperation, spending time together, problem solving, bossing, conflict, jealousy, intimacy, nurturing

Continued

Table 13.2. *Continued*

Title	Recommended Grade	Annotations on Friendship Formation
Paterson, K. (1977). *Bridge to Terabithia.* New York: Thomas Y. Crowell.	5–8	Establishing common ground, communication clarity, self-disclosure, living in the same area, same age, similar interests, spending time together, fantasizing together, nurturing, intimacy
Walker, H. (1960). *Meg and the Treasure Nobody Saw.* Racine, WI: Golden Press.	5–8	Self-disclosure, exchanging information, problem solving, protecting, intimacy, helping
Wallace, B. (1980). *A Dog Called Kitty.* New York: Archway.	5–8	Self-disclosure, protecting, nurturing, understanding, problem solving

APPLICATIONS FOR INTERVENTION

As was mentioned at the beginning of this chapter, research findings suggest that children who have problematic peer relations are at risk for a variety of problems throughout their lives. How can children's literature that promotes strategies for obtaining peer acceptance and friendship be used to help children overcome social skill deficits? As Zaragoza, Vaughn, and McIntosh (1991) point out, most social skill intervention programs consist of several aspects of a cognitive behavioral model. These aspects generally include coaching, modeling, rehearsal, feedback, and reinforcement. More specifically, Ladd and Mize (1983) recommend that in social skills training, the first training step should consist of direct instruction. Such instruction should provide children with information about a performance standard with which children can identify. This step is then followed by subsequent rehearsal and feedback training variables (see also Ladd, 1985; Mize and Ladd, 1990; Ramsey, 1991).

It is in the direct instructional phase that children's literature would be most relevant. This phase can be achieved through modeled instruction and/or verbal instruction regarding acceptable social behavior and performance. While videotapes, role enactments, and discussion have been used in many social skills intervention programs, few, if any have used children's storybooks in the first step of the intervention process (cf. Conger and Keane, 1981; Zaragoza et al., 1991). We believe that storybooks would be particularly useful in social skills training because children readily identify with characters that are presented in a narrative format. Moreover, modeled storybook behavior occurring in spontaneous play contexts with peers such as on the playground should be more relevant to children's naturalistic social lives than would situations portrayed in the context of adult-directed activities.

Indeed, recent research suggests that children's books that address children's social cognitions and behavior in a narrative context can be a useful intervention tool. Bhavnagri and Samuels (1990) selected children's books that portrayed preschoolers' understanding and behavior regarding peer relationship skills documented in the empirical research literature. After these stories were read to the experimental group, preschoolers in this group discussed effective strategies for enhancing peer relationships. This was then followed by children practicing specific social skills in activities that further supported peer related concepts that had been presented in the book. Results of the study indicated that the experimental group, as compared with the control group, made significant gains in thinking of effective strategies for solving peer related hypothetical problems as measured by a social knowledge interview developed by Asher, Renshaw, and Geraci (1980).

Among many possibilities for future study, research along this line could be used to assess the utility of using storybooks in peer leadership training on conflict resolution. Based on skills derived from storybook information, children could not only practice conflict resolution strategies in playground environments, but could be taught to assist in monitoring each others' behavior in cooperative intervention activities such as those described by Price and Dodge (1989) and Furman and Gavin (1989). Beyond research, teachers and school counselors have access to a wide variety of children's literature. Many of these storybooks could also be used in creative classroom interventions designed to help children who are lacking in social skills.

CONCLUSION

During the last decade many researchers have explored children's friendships and relations with their peers. This theme has long been an important part of another body of literature—children's literature. Authors, just as researchers, seek to reveal and to contribute to our understanding of children. The best of children's literature is not didactic. It does not seek to teach or preach, but rather to "open individuals and their society for our observation and our understanding" (Lukens, 1986, p. 4). The literature we have described in this chapter not only reveals human nature, but also reinforces the findings of peer relations research. It does it in humorous, touching, and memorable ways. There is much in children's literature that can enrich their understanding of interactions with others and with friends. We can only hope that more authors will use playground settings in their stories, and that more creative ways will be found to use storybooks in social skills intervention programs.

NOTE

1. Recent findings suggest that there are two additional rejected subtypes that do not appear to differ much from sociometrically average children (see Cillessen et al., 1992 and Bierman, Smoot, Aumiller, 1993).

REFERENCES
(Research Literature Review)

Asher, S. R., Hymel, S., and Renshaw, P. D. (1984). Loneliness in children. *Child Development, 55,* 1456–1464.

Asher, S. R., Parkhurst, J. T., Hymel, S., Williams, G. A. (1990). Peer rejection and loneliness in childhood. In S. R. Asher and J. D. Coie (Eds.), *Peer rejection in childhood* (pp. 253–273). New York: Cambridge University Press.

Asher, S. R., and Renshaw, P. D. (1981). Children without friends: Social knowledge and social skill training. In S. R. Asher and J. M. Gottman (Eds.), *The development of children's friendships* (pp. 273–296). Cambridge: Cambridge University Press.

Asher, S. R., Renshaw, P. D., and Geraci, R. L. (1980). Children's friendships and social competence. *International Journal of Psycholinguistics, 10,* 27–39.

Asher, S. R., and Wheeler, V. A. (1985). Children's loneliness: A comparison of rejected and neglected peer status. *Journal of Consulting and Clinical Psychology, 53,* 500–505.

Asher, S. R., and Williams, G. A. (1987, April). New approaches to identifying rejected children at school. Paper presented in G. W. Ladd (Chair), *Identification and treatment of socially rejected children in school settings,* at the American Educational Research Association, Washington, DC.

Berndt, T. J. (1984). Sociometric, social-cognitive, and behavioral measures for the study of friendship and popularity. In T. Field, J. L. Roopnarine, and M. Segal (Eds.), *Friendships in normal and handicapped children* (pp. 31–52). Norwood, NJ: Ablex.

————. (1985). Prosocial behavior between friends in middle childhood and early adolescence. *Journal of Early Adolescence, 5,* 307–318.

Bhavnagri, N. P., and Samuels, B. (1990). *Preschool children's social cognitions of peer relationships through children's literature.* Paper presented at the Fifth Annual Southwest Social Science Conference, Houston, TX.

Biehler, R. F. (1954). Companion choice behavior in the kindergarten. *Child Development, 25,* 45–50.

Bierman, K. L., Smoot, D. L., and Aumiller, K. (1993). Characteristics of aggressive-rejected, aggressive (non-rejected), and rejected (non-aggressive) boys. *Child Development, 64,* 139–151.

Boivin, M., and Begin, G. (1989). Peer status and self-perception among early elementary school children: The case of the rejected children. *Child Development, 60,* 591–596.

Bonney, M. (1943). Personality traits of socially successful and socially unsuccessful children. *Journal of Educational Psychology, 34,* 449–472.

Boulton, M. J., and Smith, P. K. (1989). Issues in the study of children's rough-and-tumble play. In M. N. Bloch and A. D. Pellegrini (Eds.), *The ecological context of children's play* (pp. 57–83). Norwood, NJ: Ablex.

Campbell, J. D., and Yarrow, M. R. (1961). Perceptual and behavioral correlates of social effectiveness. *Sociometry, 24,* 1–20.

Cassidy, J., and Asher, S. R. (1992). *Loneliness and peer relations in young children. Child Development, 63,* 350–365.

Cillessen, A. H. N., van Ijzendoorn, H. W., van Lieshout, C. F. M. and Hartup, W. W. (1992). Heterogeneity among peer-rejected boys; subtypes and stabilities. *Child Development, 63*, 893–905.

Coates, D. L. (1985). Relationships between self concept measures and social network characteristics for black adolescents. *Journal of Early Adolescence, 5*, 319–338.

Coie, J. D., and Dodge, K. A. (1983). Continuities and changes in children's social status: A five-year longitudinal study. *Merrill-Palmer Quarterly, 29*, 261–282.

Coie, J. D., and Dodge, K. A. (1988). Multiple sources of data on social behavior and social status in the school: A cross-age comparison. *Child Development, 59*, 815–829.

Coie, J. D., Dodge, K. A., and Coppotelli, H. (1982). Dimensions and types of social status: A cross-age perspective. *Developmental Psychology, 18*, 557–570.

Coie, J. D., Dodge, K. A., and Kupersmidt, J. (1990). Peer group behavior and social status. In S. R. Asher and J. D. Coie (Eds.), *Peer rejection in childhood* (pp. 17–59). New York: Cambridge University Press.

Coie, J. D., and Kupersmidt, J. (1983). A behavioral analysis of emerging social status in boys' groups. *Child Development, 54*, 1400–1416.

Conger, J. C., and Keane, S. P. (1981). Social skills intervention in the treatment of isolated or withdrawn children. *Psychological Bulletin, 90*, 478–495.

Corsaro, W. A. (1979). "We're friends, right?": Children's use of access rituals in a nursery school. *Language in Society, 8*, 315–336.

Crick, N. R. (1991, April). Subgroups of neglected and rejected children. Paper presented in J. T. Parkhurst and D. L. Rabiner (chairs), *The behavioral characteristics and the subjective experience of aggressive and withdrawn/submissive rejected children*, at the meeting of the Society for Research in Child Development, Seattle, WA.

Crick, N. R., and Dodge, K. A. (1989, March). *Rejected children's expectations and perceptions of peer interaction.* Paper presented at the annual meeting of the American Educational Research Association, San Francisco.

Crick, N. R., and Ladd, G. W. (1990). Children's perceptions of the oucomes of social strategies: Do the ends justify being mean? *Developmental Psychology, 26,* 612–620.

Dodge, K. A. (1980). Social cognition and children's aggressive behavior. *Child Development, 51,* 162–170.

———. (1983). Behavioral antecedents of peer social rejection and isolation. *Child Development, 54,* 1386–1399.

———. (1985). Facets of social interaction and the assessment of social competence in children. In B. H. Schneider, K. H. Rubin, and J. E. Ledingham (Eds.), *Children's peer relations: Issues in assessment and intervention* (pp. 3–22). New York: Springer-Verlag.

———. (1986). A social information processing model of social competence in children. In M. Perlmutter (Ed.), *Minnesota symposium on child psychology: Vol. 18* (pp. 77–125). Hillsdale, NJ: Erlbaum.

Dodge, K. A., and Coie, J. D. (1987). Social information processing factors in reactive and proactive aggression in children's peer groups. *Journal of Personality and Social Psychology, 53,* 1146–1158.

Dodge, K. A., Coie, J. D., Pettit, G. S., and Price, J. M. (1990). Peer status and aggression in boys' groups: Developmental and contextual analyses. *Child Development, 61,* 1289–1309.

Dodge, K. A., and Frame, C. L. (1982). Social cognitive biases and deficits in aggressive boys. *Child Development, 53,* 620–635.

Dodge, K. A., Murphy, R. R., and Buchsbaum, H. (1984). The assessment of intention-cue detection skills in children: Implications for developmental psychopathology. *Child Development, 55,* 163–173.

Dodge, K. A., and Newman, J. P. (1981). Biased decision-making processes in aggressive boys. *Journal of Abnormal Psychology, 90,* 375–379.

Dodge, K. A., Schlundt, D. C., Schocken, I., and Delugach, J. D. (1983). Social competence and children's sociometric status: The role of peer group entry strategies. *Merrill-Palmer Quarterly, 29*(3), 309–336.

Dunnington, M. J. (1957). Behavioral differences of sociometric status groups in a nursery school. *Child Development, 28,* 103–111.

Epstein, J. L. (1989). The selection of friends: Changes across the grades and in different school environments. In T. J. Berndt and G. W. Ladd (Eds.), *Peer relationships in child development* (pp. 158–187). New York: John Wiley and Sons.

Fine, G. A. (1980). The natural history of preadolescent male friendship groups. In H. C. Foot, A. J. Chapman, and J. R. Smith (Eds.), *Friendship and social relations in children* (pp. 293–320). New York: Wiley.

———. (1981). Friends, impression management, and preadolescent behavior. In S. R. Asher and J. M. Gottman (Eds.), *The development of children's friendships* (pp. 29–52). New York: Cambridge University Press.

French, D. C., and Waas, G. (1985). Behavior problems of peer-neglected and peer-rejected elementary-age children: Parent and teacher perspectives. *Child Development, 56,* 246–252.

Furman, W., and Buhrmester, D. (1985). Children's perceptions of the personal relationships in their social networks. *Developmental Psychology, 21,* 1016–1024.

Furman, W., and Gavin, L. A. (1989). Peers' influence on adjustment and development: A view from the intervention literature. In T. J. Berndt and G. W. Ladd (Eds.), *Peer relationships in child development.* New York: Wiley.

Furman, W., and Robbins, P. (1985). What's the point? Issues in the selection of treatment objectives. In B. H. Schneider, K. H. Rubin, and J. E. Ledingham (Eds.), *Children's peer relations: Issues in assessment and intervention* (pp. 41–54). New York: Springer-Verlag.

Goetz, T. E., and Dweck, C. S. (1980). Learned helplessness in social situations. *Journal of Personality and Social Psychology, 39,* 246–255.

Gottman, J. M. (1983). How children become friends. *Monographs of the Society for Research in Child Development, 48*(3, Serial No. 201).

Gottman, J. M., Gonso, J., and Rasmussen, B. (1975). Social interaction, social competence, and friendship in children. *Child Development, 46,* 709–718.

Green, E. H. (1933). Friendships and quarrels among preschool children. *Child Development, 4,* 237–252.

Hagman, E. P. (1933). The companionships of preschool children. *University of Iowa Studies in Child Welfare, 4,* 1–69.

Hart, C. H., DeWolf, D. M., Wozniak, P., and Burts, D. C. (1992a). Maternal and paternal disciplinary styles: Relations with preschoolers' playground behavioral orientations and peer status. *Child Development, 63,* 879–892.

Hart, C. H., DeWolf, D. M., and Burts, D. C. (1992b). Linkages among preschoolers' playground behavior, outcome expectations, and parental disciplinary strategies. *Early Education and Development, 3,* 265–283.

Hart, C. H., Ladd, G. W., and Burleson, B. R. (1990). Children's expectations of the outcomes of social strategies: Relations with sociometric status and maternal disciplinary styles. *Child Development, 61,* 127–137.

Hartup, W. W. (1983). Peer relations. In E. M. Hetherington (Ed.), P. H. Mussen (Series Ed.), *Handbook of child psychology: Vol. 4, Socialization, personality and social development,* 4th ed. (pp. 1–101). New York: Wiley.

———. (1989). Behavioral manifestations of children's friendships. In T. J. Berndt and G. W. Ladd (Eds.), *Peer relationships in child development* (pp. 46–70). New York: John Wiley and Sons.

Hartup, W. W., Glazer, J. A., and Charlesworth, R. (1967). Peer reinforcement and sociometric status. *Child Development, 38,* 1017–1024.

Hartup, W. W., and Laursen B. (1989, April). *Contextual constraints and children's friendship relations.* Paper presented at the biennial meetings of the Society for Research in Child Development, Kansas City, MO.

Hartup, W. W., Laursen, B., Stewart, M. I., and Eastenson, A. (1988). Conflict and the friendship relations of young children. *Child Development, 59,* 1590–1600.

Hartup, W. W., and Moore, S. G. (1990). Early peer relations: Developmental significance and prognostic implications. *Early Childhood Research Quarterly, 5,* 1–17.

Hartup, W. W., and Sancilio, M. F. (1986). Children's friendships. In E. Schopler and G. B. Mesibov (Eds.), *Social behavior in autism* (pp. 61–80). New York: Plenum.

Hazen, N. L., and Black, B. (1989). Preschool peer communication skills: The role of social status and interaction context. *Child Development, 60*, 867–876.

Hetherington, E. M., and Parke, R. D. (Eds.). (1986). *Child psychology: A contemporary viewpoint* (3rd ed.). New York: McGraw-Hill.

Hinde, R. A., Titmus, G., Easton, D., and Tamplin, A. (1985). Incidence of "friendship" and behavior with strong associates versus non-associates in preschoolers. *Child Development, 56*, 234–245.

Howes, C. (1987). Peer interaction of young children. *Monographs of the Society for Research in Child Development, 53*(1, Serial No. 217).

Johnson, J. E., Christie, J. F., and Yawkey, T. D. (1987). *Play and early childhood development.* Glenview, IL: Scott Foresman and Company.

Kahn, P. H., & Turiel, E. (1988). Children's conceptions of trust in the context of social expectations. *Merrill-Palmer Quarterly, 34*, 403–419.

Krasnor, L. R., and Rubin, K. H. (1983). Preschool social problem solving: Attempts and outcomes in naturalistic interaction. *Child Development, 54*, 1545–1558.

Kupersmidt, J. B., Coie, J. D., and Dodge, K. A. (1990). The role of peer relationships in the development of disorder. In S. R. Asher and J. D. Coie (Eds.), *Peer rejection in childhood* (pp. 274–308). New York: Cambridge University Press.

Ladd, G. W. (1983). Social networks of popular, average, and rejected children in school settings. *Merrill-Palmer Quarterly, 29*, 283–308.

———. (1985). Documenting the effects of social skills training with children: Process and outcome assessment. In B. Schneider, K. Rubin, and J. Ledingham (Eds.), *Children's peer relations: Issues in assessment and intervention.* New York: Springer-Verlag.

———. (1989). Toward a further understanding of peer relationships and their contributions to child development. In T. J. Berndt and G. W. Ladd (Eds.), *Peer relationships in child development* (pp. 1–12). New York: John Wiley and Sons.

———. (1990). Having friends, making friends, keeping friends, and being liked by peers in the classroom: Predictors of children's early school adjustment? *Child Development, 61*, 1081–1100.

Ladd, G. W., and Asher, S. R. (1985). Social skill training and children's peer relations. In L. L'Abate and M. Milan (Eds.), *Handbook of social skills training and research* (pp. 219–244). New York: Wiley.

Ladd, G. W., and Golter, B. S. (1988). Parents' management of preschooler's peer relations: It is related to children's social competence? *Developmental Psychology, 24,* 109–117.

Ladd, G. W., and Hart, C. H. (1992). Creating informal play opportunities: Are parents' and preschoolers' initiations related to children's competence with peers? *Developmental Psychology, 28,* 1179–1187.

Ladd, G. W., Hart, C. H., Wadsworth, E. M., and Golter, B. S. (1988). Preschoolers' peer networks in nonschool settings: Relationship to family characteristics and school adjustment. In S. Salzinger, J. Antrobus, and M. Hammer (Eds.), *Social networks of children, adolescents, and college students* (pp. 61–92). Hillsdale, NJ: Lawrence Erlbaum Associates.

Ladd, G. W., and Mize, J. M. (1983). A cognitive-social learning model of social skill training. *Psychological Review, 90,* 127–197.

Ladd, G. W., and Oden, S. (1979). The relationship between peer acceptance and children's ideas about helpfulness. *Child Development, 50,* 402–408.

Ladd, G. W., and Price, J. M. (1987). Predicting children's social and school adjustment following the transition from preschool to kindergarten. *Child Development, 58,* 1168–1189.

Ladd, G. W., Price, J. M., and Hart, C. H. (1988). Predicting preschoolers' peer status from their playground behaviors. *Child Development, 59,* 986–992.

Ladd, G. W., Profilet, S., and Hart, C. H. (1992). Parents' management of children's peer relations: Facilitating and supervising children's activities in the peer culture. In R. D. Parke and G. W. Ladd (Eds.), *Family-peer relationships: Modes of linkage.* Hillsdale, NJ: Erlbaum.

Lesser, G. S. (1959). The relationships between various forms of aggression and popularity among lower-class children. *Journal of Educational Psychology, 50,* 20–25.

Lewis, M., and Feiring, C. (1989). Early predictors of childhood friendship. In T. J. Berndt and G. W. Ladd (Eds.), *Peer relationships in child development* (pp. 246–273). New York: John Wiley and Sons.

Lukens, R. (1986). *A Critical Handbook of Children's Literature.* Glenview, IL: Scott, Foresmann.

MacDonald, C. D. (1991, April). *Children's awareness of their popularity and social acceptability.* Poster presented at the biennial meeting of the society for Research in Child Development, Seattle, WA.

Marshall, H. R., and McCandless, B. R. (1957). A study in prediction of social behavior of preschool children. *Child Development, 28,* 149–159.

Masters, J. C., and Furman, W. (1981). Popularity, individual friendship selection and specific peer interaction among children. *Dvelopmental psychology, 17*(3), 344–350.

Matsumoto, D., Haan, N., Yabrove, G., Theodorou, P., and Carney, C. C. (1986). Preschoolers' moral actions and emotions in prisoner's dilemma. *Developmental Psychology, 22,* 663–670.

McGuire, J. M. (1973). Aggression and sociometric status with preschool children. *Sociometry, 36,* 542–549.

Mize, J., and Ladd, G. W. (1990). Toward the development of successful social skills training for preschool children. In S. R. Asher and J. D. Coie (Eds.), *Peer rejection in childhood.* New York: Cambridge University Press.

Moore, S. (1967). Correlates of peer acceptance in nursery school children. In W. W. Hartup and N. L. Smothergill (Eds.), *The young child.* Washington, DC: NAEYC.

Moore, S. G., and Updegraff, R. (1964). Sociometric status of preschool children as related to age, sex, nurturance-giving, and dependence. *Child Development, 35,* 519–524.

Newcomb, A. F., Brady, J. E., and Hartup, W. W. (1979). Friendship and incentive condition as determinants of children's task-oriented social behavior. *Child Development, 50,* 878–881.

Newcomb, A. F., and Bukowski, W. M. (1983). Social impact and social preference as determinants of children's peer group status. *Developmental Psychology, 19,* 856–867.

Parker, J. G., and Asher, S. R. (1990, April). *Friendship adjustment, group acceptance, and feelings of loneliness and social dissatisfaction in childhood.* Paper presented at the annual meeting of the American Educational Research Association, Boston, MA.

————. (1987). Peer relations and later personal adjustment: Are low-accepted children "at risk"? *Psychological Bulletin, 102,* 357–389.

Parker, J. G., and Gottman, J. M. (1989). Social and emotional development in a relational context: Friendship interaction from early childhood to adolescence. In T. J. Berndt and G. W. Ladd (Eds.), *Peer relationships in child development* (pp. 95–132). New York: John Wiley and Sons.

Patterson, C. J., Kupersmidt, J. B., and Griesler, P. C. (1990). Children's perceptions of self and of relationships with others as a function of sociometric status. *Child Development, 61,* 1335–1359.

Pellegrini, A. D. (1988). Elementary school children's rough-and-tumble play and social competence. *Developmental Psychology, 24,* 802–806.

Perry, D. G., Perry, L. C., and Rasmussen, P. (1986). Cognitive social learning mediators of aggression. *Child Development, 57*(3), 700–711.

Pettit, G. S., Dodge, K. A., and Brown, M. M. (1988). Early family experience, social problem solving, and children's social competence. *Child Development, 59,* 107–120.

Price, J. M. (1989, April). *A behavioral analysis of socially controversial boys in small peer groups.* Paper presented at the biennial meeting of the Society for Research in Child Development, Kansas City, MO.

Price, J. M., and Dodge, K. A. (1989). Peers' contributions to children's social maladjustment: Description and intervention. In T. J. Berndt and G. W. Ladd (Eds.), *Peer relationships in child development.* New York: Wiley.

Putallaz, M. (1983). Predicting children's sociometric status from their behavior. *Child Development, 54,* 1417–1426.

Putallaz, M., and Gottman, J. M. (1981). An interactional model of children's entry into peer groups. *Child Development, 52,* 986–994.

Putallaz, M., and Wasserman, A. (1989). Children's naturalistic entry behavior and sociometric status: A developmental perspective. *Developmental Psychology, 25,* 297–305.

Quiggle, N. L., Garber, J., Panak, W. F., and Dodge, K. A. Social information processing in aggressive and depressed children. *Child Development, 63,* 1305–1320.

Rabiner, D., and Coie, J. (1989). Effect of expectancy inductions on rejected children's acceptance by unfamiliar peers. *Developmental Psychology, 25,* 450–457.

Rabiner, D. L. and Gordon, L. V. (1992). The coordination of conflicting social goals: Differences between rejected and nonrejected boys. *Child Development, 63,* 1344–1350.

Rabiner, D. L., Gordon, L., Klumb, D., and Thompson, L. (1991, April). *Social problem solving deficiencies in rejected children: Motivational factors and skill deficits.* Paper presented at the biennial meeting of the Society for Research in Child Development, Seattle, WA.

Rabiner, D. L., Lenhart, L., and Lochman, J. E. (1990). Automatic versus reflective social problem solving in relation to children's sociometric status. *Developmental Psychology, 26,* 1010–1016.

Ramsey, P. G. (1988). Social skills and peer status: A comparison of two socioeconomic groups. *Merrill-Palmer Quarterly, 34,* 185–202.

Ramsey, P. G. (1991). *Making friends in school: Promoting peer relationships in early childhood.* New York: Teachers College Press.

Renshaw, P. D., and Asher, S. R. (1983). Children's goals and strategies for social interaction. *Merrill-Palmer Quarterly, 29,* 353–374.

Rotenberg, K. J., and Sliz, D. (1988). Children's restrictive disclosure to friends. *Merrill-Palmer Quarterly, 34,* 203–215.

Rubin, K. H. (1972). Relationship between egocentric communication and popularity among peers. *Developmental Psychology, 7,* 364.

———. (1982). Non-social play in preschoolers: Necessarily evil? *Child Development, 53,* 651–657.

Rubin, K. H., and Daniels-Beirness, T. (1983). Concurrent and predictive correlates of sociometric status in kindergarten and grade one children. *Merrill-Palmer Quarterly, 29,* 337–351.

Rubin, K. H., Daniels-Beirness, T., and Hayvren, M. (1982). Social and social-cognitive correlates of sociometric status in preschool and kindergarten children. *Canadian Journal of Behavioral Science, 14*(4), 338–349.

Rubin, K. H., Fein, G., and Vandenberg, B. (1983). Play. In E. M. Hetherington (Ed.), P. H. Mussen (Series Ed.), *Handbook of child psychology: Vol. 4. Socialization, personality, and social development* (pp. 693–774). New York: Wiley.

Rubin, K. H., Hymel, S., LeMare, L., and Rowden, L. (1989). Children experiencing social difficulties: Sociometric neglect reconsidered. *Canadian Journal of Behavioral Science, 21*, 95–111.

Rubin, K. H. Hymel, S., Mills, R. S. L., and Rose-Krasner, L. (1990). Conceptualizing different developmental pathways to and from social isolation in childhood. In D. Cicchetti and S. Goth (Eds.), *Rochester symposium on developmental psychopathology, Vol. 2* (pp. 91–122). Hillsdale, NJ: Erlbaum.

Rubin, K. H., and Krasnor, L. R. (1986). Social-cognitive and social behavioral perspectives on problem solving. In M. Perlmutter (Ed.), *The Minnesota symposia on child psychology* (Vol. 18, pp. 1–68). Hillsdale, NJ: Lawrence Erlbaum Associates.

Rubin, K. H., LeMare, L. J., and Lollis, S. (1990). Social withdrawal in childhood: Developmental pathways to peer rejection. In S. R. Asher and J. D. Coie (Eds.), *Peer rejection in childhood* (pp. 217–252). New York: Cambridge University Press.

Seagoe, M. V. (1933). Factors influencing the selection of associates. *Journal of Educational Research, 27*, 32–40.

Shantz, C. U., and Hobart, C. J. (1989). Social conflict and development: Peers and siblings. In T. J. Berndt and G. W. Ladd (Eds.), *Peer relationships in child development* (pp. 71–94). New York: John Wiley and Sons.

Shantz, C. U. (1987) Conflict between children. *Child Development 58*, 283–305.

Shure, M. B., and Spivack, G. (1978). *Problem solving techniques in childrearing.* San Francisco: Jossey-Bass.

Smith, P. K. (1989). The role of rough-and-tumble play in the development of social competence: Theoretical perspectives and empirical evidence. In B. Schneider, G. Attil, J. Nadel, and R. Weissberg (Eds.), *Social competence in developmental pespectives.* (pp. 239–255). Hingham, MA: Kluwer Academic Publishers Group.

Smollar, J., and Youniss, J. (1982). Social development through friendship. In K. H. Rubin and H. S. Ross (Eds.), *Peer relationships and social skills in childhood* (pp. 278–298). New York: Springer-Verlag.

Sullivan, H. S. (1953). *The interpersonal theory of psychiatry.* New York: Norton.

Taylor, A. R., and Gabriel, S. (1989, April). *Cooperative vs. competitive game-playing strategies of peer accepted and peer rejected children in a goal conflict situation.* Paper presented at the biennial meeting of the Society for Research in Child Development, Kansas City, MO.

Vaughn, B. E., and Langlois, J. J. (1983). Physical attractiveness as a correlate of peer status and social competence in preschool children. *Developmental Psychology, 19,* 561–567.

Vaughn, B. E., and Waters, E. (1981). Attention structure, sociometric status, and dominance: Interrelations, behavioral correlates, and relationships to social competence. *Developmental Psychology, 17*(3), 275–288.

Vespo, J. E. (1987). *Best friends and associates: The core elements of social organization in preschool classes.* Unpublished manuscript, State University of New York, Stony Brook.

Wheeler, V. A., and Ladd, G. W. (1982). Assessment of children's self efficacy for social interactions with peers. *Developmental Psychology, 18,* 795–805.

Youniss, J. (1980). *Parents and peers in social development: A Piaget-Sullivan perspective.* Chicago: University of Chicago Press.

Zaragoza, N., Vaughn, S., and McIntosh, R. (1991). Social skills interventions and children with behavior problems: A review. *Behavioral Disorders, 16,* 260–275.

CHILDREN'S BOOK REFERENCES

Berenstain, S., and Berenstain, J. (1989). *The Berenstain Bears and the In-Crowd.* New York: Random House.

Cleary, B. (1951). *Ellen Tebbits.* New York: Dell.

Christopher, M. (1977). *The Diamond Champs.* Boston: Little, Brown.

———. (1985). *Supercharged Infield.* Boston: Little, Brown.

DeClements, B. (1981). *Nothing's Fair in Fifth Grade.* New York: Scholastic.

Ehrlich, A. (1981). *Leo, Zack, and Emmie.* New York: Dial.

Hoff, S. (1960). *Who Will Be My Friends?* Pleasantville, NY: Reader's Digest Services.

Jackson, C. (1968). *Big Play in the Small League.* New York: Hastings House.

Lewis, M. (1984). *Wrongway Applebaum.* New York: Coward-McCann.

Lord, B. (1984). *In the Year of the Boar and Jackie Robinson.* New York: Harper and Row.

Renick, M. (1961). *Boy at Bat.* New York: Charles Scribner's Sons.

Sachs, M. (1968). *Veronica Ganz.* New York: Dell.

Sharmat, M. (1979). *Say Hello, Vanessa.* New York: Scholastic.

Van Leeuwen, J. (1982). *Benjy and the Power of Zingies.* New York: Dial.

Weiss, N. (1988). *Battle Day at Camp Delmont.* New York: Puffin Books.

Zirpoli, J. (1988). *Roots in the Outfield.* Boston: Houghton Mifflin.

CONCLUSION

CRAIG H. HART

Children on Playgrounds:
Applying Current Knowledge to
Future Practice and Inquiry

In 1987, Anthony Pellegrini published an article titled, "Children on Playgrounds: 'A Review of What's Out There.'" In the article, he stated that "we know very little about what children do on the playground and know even less about the ways in which these behaviors relate to their learning and development." In many ways, this statement is still true. We hope this volume has filled some of the gaps regarding the developmental significance of playground activities and has opened the door to further insight and inquiry into this relatively unexplored context of human development. The purpose of this concluding chapter is to gauge our progress by (a) providing a few thoughts as to how knowledge presented in this book might be applied, (b) pulling together what we have learned from these chapters, and (c) pointing to new directions for future work in this area.

APPLICATIONS

How can the research literature presented in this volume be applied to real-life situations? Upon reflection, it appears that this question can best be answered by individual readers depending on their needs. For instance, those designing playgrounds should find the research-based recommendations provided by Hartle and Johnson (Chapter 2) to be most useful in constructing safe and developmentally appropriate outdoor play environments. Those who struggle with conflict and bullying problems on playgrounds should also find insights that will help in solving the problems of these situations. As an example, information derived from research presented by Hartup and Laursen (Chapter 3) should help practitioners understand how varying group arrangements facilitate or diminish conflicts. Armed with this knowledge, adjustments could be made to mitigate conflict-enhancing situations. In addition, the specific practical guidelines presented by Olweus (Chapter 4) for how to help bullies and their victims would be of considerable value to those who work with them.

Practitioners should also benefit from answers to many questions that were provided in this volume. Some of these questions include those that were raised in the introductory chapter and additional ones that follow: What is normative playground behavior? How do children select their own play groups in outdoor play settings? How are children's playground behavior and play patterns that are observed on a day-to-day basis linked to acceptance or rejection by peers? Does aggressive behavior in outdoor play settings have different developmental significance for boys than for girls? How are parenting styles and other familial background factors related to children's behavior in outdoor play settings? Can outdoor play activities enhance indoor classroom learning? How can varying playground types foster development in each of the major developmental domains? What types of storybooks would be useful in helping children understand and implement effective social interaction strategies? Answers to these and other questions found in this volume should be useful in making more informed decisions about ways to facilitate development in relatively unconstrained outdoor play settings.

KNOWLEDGE THAT WE HAVE GAINED

Beyond answers to questions that researchers and practitioners may have, what specific knowledge have we gained from this collection of papers? In addition to a theoretical and historical overview of play and playground features that enhance play potential, Hartle and Johnson (Chapter 2) have provided information concerning how varying outdoor play environments may enhance or diminish physical, social, and cognitive aspects of children's development. Educators and developmentalists should be able to apply this information from the first part of the volume when justifying the importance of outdoor play activities.

In the second part of the volume, Hartup and Laursen (Chapter 3) provided a scholarly and thorough review of the conflict literature. They postulated that disagreements on the playground are common occurrences that have developmental significance. Moreover, disagreements may be differentially manifested and resolved in varying interpersonal and activity contexts. In conjunction with a new contextual theory of children's conflicts that is presented in this chapter, Hartup and Laursen concluded that future research should include the investigation of conflict that occurs in the many contextual settings found on ordinary playgrounds.

Along a similar vein, Olweus (Chapter 4) discussed another form of conflict that often occurs on playgrounds by focusing on bullies and their victims. A wealth of information was provided to help us understand bullying behavior and characteristics of bullies, victims, and the like. More importantly, the successful intervention model and practical guidelines that are presented at the conclusion of the chapter should be most useful for helping bullies and their victims. Like Hartup and Laursen, Olweus's work points to a need for more research in this area that focuses exclusively on bully/victim problems in relatively unconstrained environments provided by many playground settings.

The third part of the volume provided readers with exposure to a wide variety of observational methodologies that can be used to answer research questions associated with activities on the playground that tend to be more child- rather than adult-directed. For instance, Asher and Gabriel (Chapter 7) discussed the strengths and limitations of various observational methodologies for studying children's conversations. They also presented an innovative audio-videotape methodology that can capture both verbal and nonverbal behavior in context.

The broader research potential of remote observational recording procedures was further illustrated by Serbin and colleagues (Chapter 6). Findings presented in their chapter showed that such observational methodologies were more useful than teacher and peer assessments for assessing problem behaviors, particularly in girls (see also Boulton and Smith, Chapter 8). They also demonstrated how normative playground activities and sex differences in behavior across seasons and recess time intervals can be documented using remote videotaping procedures. Various nonvideotaping, observational time sampling procedures were also illustrated in the chapters by Ladd and Price and Boulton and Smith (Chapter 8).

These chapters illustrating observational techniques also provided rich information about children's behavior and peer relations in playground settings. For instance, readers found that children's preferences for play companions and activities in playground settings tended to vary as a function of both race and sex (e.g., Boulton and Smith, Chapter 8). Also, the structure of child-selected peer contacts changed in ways that were predictive of peer status when observed over the course of a school year (Ladd and Price, Chapter 5). Similar to prior work conducted in other settings (see Asher and Coie, 1990), data presented by Ladd and Price (Chapter 5) further indicated that prosocial and cooperative playground behavior promoted acceptance by peers. In contrast, hostile playground behavior led to rejection by peers and appeared to be more of a cause than a consequence of peer rejection. Children who displayed aggressive and disruptive behavioral orientations appeared to develop negative reputations with playmates that persisted over time.

Additional aggressive behavioral data gathered by Serbin and colleagues (Chapter 6) suggested that in naturalistic playground settings, such behavior may have different developmental significance for boys and girls. Beyond aggression (particularly reactive aggression), Ladd and Price (Chapter 5) found that noninteraction with playmates in playground settings also tended to facilitate rejection by peers. Their findings further indicated that physical and interpersonal features of playgrounds may contribute to the quality of children's social interactions with peers.

A similar picture of playground interaction and peer relations emerged in chapters presented in the fourth part of the volume. However, the focus of these chapters was on exploring ways that behavioral patterns of interaction with peers on the playground and in other free play settings may be linked to familial variables. Pettit and Harrist (Chapter 9) presented observational data indicating that there may be linkages between family interactional styles that are lacking in interactional synchrony and in the use of social-contextual cues and social–cognitive and behavioral deficits displayed by children in free play contexts. For instance, children who were more aggressive and/or isolated from peers were more likely to have experienced coercive and intrusive (i.e., negatively synchronous and nonsynchronous) family interactions. In contrast, children who were more cooperative and prosocial had experienced sensitive and responsive (i.e., positively synchronous) family interactions.

Similarly, Hart, DeWolf, and Burts (Chapter 10) presented information regarding pathways through which parental disciplinary strategies may be related to child behavior and competence with peers. Data presented in their chapter indicated that whereas power assertive disciplinary styles were significantly related to both disruptive and socially withdrawn playground behaviors, inductive disciplinary strategies were linked to prosocial behavior with peers. However, mothers rather than fathers appeared to carry the weight of influence in this regard. Some forms of child behavior were also found to mediate the relationship between maternal discipline and children's acceptance by peers.

In the final section of the book, our attention shifted to exploring ways that playground activities and peer relations translate into literacy and social cognitive events. In many instances, we found that outdoor play activities enhanced classroom learning experiences. For instance, in her ethnographic study, Reimer (Chapter 11) demonstrated that 5-year-olds readily transformed outdoor playground activities into reading and writing events in the classroom. Gender-based outdoor play activities also appeared to create a cognitive lens through which indoor classroom events were manipulated and interpreted by children throughout the school year.

Borman, Laine, and Lowe (Chapter 12) reviewed literature and presented data suggesting that during the middle childhood and adolescent years participation in outdoor games (sports) is reflected in an instrumental orientation for boys and in a relationship orientation for girls. Boys tended to equate sports participation with rule understanding and academic valuing, while girls tended to emphasize the fostering of interpersonal relations through such activities.

Finally, Hart, McGee, and Hernandez (Chapter 13) showed that many of the salient themes in the peer relations research literature are reflected in children's literature that highlights playground interaction. The authors show how children's literature of this nature can be a useful intervention tool for researchers, teachers, and other practitioners who are interested in fostering children's interpersonal skills.

FUTURE DIRECTIONS

In addition to recommendations in individual chapters for future work and useful applications for child-sensitive teaching and intervention, it would also be useful to consider some of the issues that cut across chapters and point to new directions for studying and working with children on playgrounds. Although by no means comprehensive, the following areas were selected for consideration: methodology, contextual issues, and additional suggestions for future study. It is hoped that ideas presented in these three sections will provide a springboard from which readers can embark in creating new vistas for exploration by incorporating their own views of the contributions of the chapters in this volume.

Methodology

Since much of outdoor behavior consists of naturally occurring play with peers, the playground offers unique opportunities for the continued exploration of peer relations in relatively unconstrained, child-directed social environments. Many of our observational schemes for documenting playground interaction may need adjustment in light of more recent advances in our understanding of the developmental significance of certain behavioral activities. For instance, Bakeman and Brownlee (1980) suggested that one of Parten's dimensions of social play involving parallel interaction may actually be used as part of a larger strategy to enter the peer group. As is pointed out in several places in this volume, recent research findings indicate that children who silently approach the peer group, hover, and then mimick the group are more successful in gaining entry. Such a sequence of tactics could seemingly involve transitional, unoccupied, onlooker, and parallel behavioral movements toward ongoing peer group interactions.

However, many of these noninteractive behaviors, when observed in isolation, appear to be indicative of lesser competence (cf. Chapters 5 and 10, this volume). This may also be true when observed in sequence. For instance, Putallaz and Wasserman (1989) discovered in their study of naturalistic entry behavior on the playground that children who were less accepted by their peers were less likely to move beyond these types of tactics to more overt and effective entry bids. However, many observational coding schemes do not differentiate between adaptive behavioral sequences in the context of leading to a particular goal and consistent behavioral patterns that are indicative of maladjustment. Thus, precise judgments about behavior cannot be made (e.g., Chapter 10, this volume). Some of these problems might be resolved by applying a sequential analytic approach to data collected in the manner that Asher and Gabriel (Chapter 7, this volume) and Serbin and her colleagues (Chapter 6, this volume) have described (cf. Boulton and Smith, 1989). Moreover, as Pellegrini (1987) points out, many times in our observational models there is a mismatch between the coding scheme and the age of the child observed. Certainly more fine tuning is needed for combining more precise and workable observational methodologies with analytic strategies for observational data collected in playground settings.

Contextual Issues

What about the developmental significance of children's activities and behaviors in indoor versus outdoor play contexts? For years, it has been common practice for researchers to combine behavioral data gathered from both indoor and outdoor play settings for analyses (e.g., Vaughn and Waters, 1981; Hinde, Stevenson-Hinde, and Tamplin, 1985; Marshall and McCandless, 1957). However, would it be prudent in future work to avoid potential confounds by considering the contextual features of the environment in which the data are collected? In a somewhat related question, do playground studies either reviewed or presented in this volume offer new information or do they primarily confirm what is evident from classroom-based and laboratory research?

Although such issues concerning indoor and outdoor play were not directly explored in this volume, data gathered by Dodge, Coie, and Brakke (1982) on third- and fifth-grade boys suggests that it would be important to make contextual distinctions in some instances when conducting future research. Their work indicated that what is found in laboratory or classroom-based research versus on the playground may differ in some respects, particularly when studying the behavior of rejected children. Aggressive behavior between rejected children and other groups (popular, average, neglected) was found to be significantly more pronounced during playground interactions than during teacher-directed classroom activities. However, during classroom seat work observational periods, rejected children also made more prosocial approaches toward peers than did popular children but not on the playground. Such approaches at task-inappropriate times were rejected by peers and reprimanded by teachers at a high rate.

These findings led Dodge et al. to speculate that social cognitive deficits may account for the inept timing of such social approaches in classroom settings and their nonuse in outdoor settings. These investigators also found that more solitary activities and fewer prosocial and aggressive acts occurred in the classroom than on the playground. As suggested in the introductory chapter and as illustrated by the work of Dodge et al., context should be an important consideration in future work, particularly in light of additional evidence suggesting that children may have different motivations for the types of behavior that they engage in during adult-directed versus child-directed play (see Eisenberg, Lundy, Shell, and Roth, 1985).

Is it always the case that playgrounds are contexts where child-directed activities relatively free of constraints occur? Hartle and Johnson (Chapter 2, this volume) and Ladd and Price (Chapter 5, this volume) have pointed out that child-directed playground activities can be enhanced or constrained by many features including playground size and type, equipment, and number of children present. In addition, teacher/child ratios and the amount of teacher directiveness and involvement likely vary by participating children's ages and by playground type. Despite this, many would agree with King (1987) that outdoor environments are still more conducive to child-directed activities with less adult intervention than are indoor play environments. However, as Hartup and Laursen (Chapter 3) also point out, child-directed activities can also exist indoors during free play activities (open settings) when children have more freedom to select their companions and activities. Such "open" indoor settings are likely more pronounced in early rather than in later childhood settings. In contrast, child directiveness can also be mitigated in outdoor settings during organized games and activities (closed settings).

Thus, it would seem that the framework proposed by Hartup and Laursen involving "open" and "closed" settings will likely prove more useful than simply distinguishing between indoor and outdoor play settings in many aspects of future work. Similar frameworks have been useful in ecological studies of linkages between children's behavior and both indoor materials and activity settings (cf. Prescott, Jones, Kritchevsky, Milich, and Haselhoef, 1975; Phyfe-Perkins, 1980). As Pettit and Harrist noted in Chapter 9, no consistent differences were found in children's interactive and noninteractive behaviors in indoor and outdoor play environments when both settings were open (i.e., relatively unstructured and child-directed).

We should be cautious, however, in making generalizations that are too broad until more replicative and extended work is conducted in this regard. For instance, although many interactive and noninteractive behavior patterns may not differ significantly between open indoor and outdoor play settings, this may not be the case for cognitive dimensions of play (cf. Henniger, 1980; Piaget, 1962; Smilansky, 1968). There is some literature indicating that beyond issues of opened and closed settings, child age, gender, props, and equipment may facilitate and/or diminish certain types of play in different settings (cf. Chapter 2, this volume). Props and equipment found in outdoor play environments appeared to facilitate more fantasy play in boys and older children and most of the functional play observed in children overall (e.g., Henniger, 1980; Sanders and Harper, 1976). In contrast, the indoor play environment seemed to promote more constructive play for children overall and dramatic play for girls and younger children (see Henniger, 1980; Droege and Howes, 1991).

It is hoped that currently available information on contextual issues will assist practitioners in making applied curriculum decisions that will maximize developmental opportunities across both settings. It should also help researchers make informed decisions as to which behavioral variables should be controlled for in cross-contextual studies involving open and/or closed settings. This literature also points to a need for more exploration of sex and age differences in naturally occurring play across different settings. For instance, many of the conclusions that have been reached in this volume are based studies that focus on a narrow age range and may not apply to all stages of development. Additionally, given the fact that outdoor play experiences appear to enhance classroom academic tasks (e.g., Chapter 11, this volume), it would seem important that practitioners and researchers further consider ways that activities occurring in *both* settings facilitate development in each. Exploring developmental contributions of cognitive dimensions and/or the combined social and cognitive dimensions of play (e.g., Rubin, Maioni, and Hornung, 1976) across both contexts seems to be a logical next step in this regard.

Additional Suggestions for Future Studies

Much work remains to be done in many areas of playground research. For instance, as Pellegrini (1987) has suggested, still remaining are confounds inherent in much of the research that has explored the effects of playground design on playground behavior. The differences in child behavior across different studies may be as much a function of within-playground variation as across-playground variation (see Pellegrini, 1987, for a review).

Many of the themes in peer relations research literature that were covered in the Hart, McGee, and Hernandez chapter (Chapter 13) could also be further investigated in playground settings. For instance, with regard to children's play styles, more work is needed for understanding the developmental significance of rough and tumble play (cf. Smith, 1989). In light of research showing that there are corresponding increases between rough and tumble play and available square footage, the playground offers a unique setting for exploring this behavior (Smith and Connolly, 1976). Recent findings indicate that 10 to 11% of children's playground behavior is of this nature and varies according to location on the playground (Humphreys and Smith, 1984; Pellegrini, 1989). As several chapters in this volume have illustrated, the playground is indeed a rich and relatively unconstrained environment for exploring the developmental significance of this type of play behavior (e.g., Chapters 5, 6, 9, 10, and 13).

Several lines of inquiry could be either begun or continued in this regard. For instance, Boulton and Smith (1989) have recently suggested that much of the complex structure of rough and tumble play has yet to be explored (see also Koyama and Smith, 1991). As has been elaborated elsewhere, there is also a need to investigate the functions that rough and tumble play may serve at different ages (see Chapter 13, this volume; Hart, DeWolf, Wozniak, and Burts, 1992). Following the lead of Pellegrini (1991) in his study of rough and tumble play in popular boys, further investigations could also focus on ways that various gender and peer status groupings interact during bouts of rough and tumble play relative to other forms of social interaction.

Finally, most of the chapters in this volume have been concerned with children on playgrounds that are generally associated with schools and/or early childhood programs. What about other neighborhood or community-based outdoor recreational settings that provide children with less structured activities such as community pools, campsites, and parks? Do these settings foster development in similar ways that school-based outdoor play environments do? What happens to children if they are deprived of such outdoor play opportunities? What about children raised in rural areas that offer almost limitless outdoor play experiences? Bryant (1985) suggests that these other environments may indeed allow children a role in structuring their own activities in ways that may provide opportunities for developing self-mastery, control, and autonomy with respect to their self- and social development. Moreover, parents may also play a significant role in fostering development in these settings as well as in their own yards and neighborhood outdoor play spaces by the way that they assist in initiating and arranging informal play groups and monitor and supervise outdoor play activities and interactions (see Ladd and Hart, 1992; Ladd, Profilet, and Hart, 1992).

Indeed the possibilities for future inquiry appear to be almost limitless. It is hoped that our current understanding of how children's growth and development is enhanced in outdoor play settings will be enlarged upon over the years to come. Promoting such inquiry by raising issues and questions was the primary aim of this volume. Through further research, we should not only come to better know what children do on playgrounds but also understand ways that playground structure and activities relate to their learning and development. Application of such knowledge will go far in maximizing opportunities for children to develop to their full potential.

REFERENCES

Asher, S. R., and Coie, J. D. (1990). *Peer rejection in childhood*. New York: Cambridge.

Bakeman, R., and Brownlee, J. (1980). The strategic use of parallel play: A sequential analysis. *Child Development, 51*, 873–878.

Boulton, M. J., and Smith, P. K. (1989). Issues in the study of children's rough-and-tumble play. In M. N. Bloch and A. D. Pellegrini (Eds.), *The ecological context of children's play* (pp. 57–83). Norwood: Ablex Publishing Corporation.

Bryant, B. (1985). The neighborhood walk: Sources of support in middle childhood. *Monographs of the Society for Research in Child Development, 50* (3, Serial No. 210).

Dodge, K. A., Coie, J. D., and Brakke, N. P. (1982). Behavior patterns of socially neglected and rejected preadolescents: The role of social approach and aggression. *Journal of Abnormal Child Psychology, 10*, 389–409.

Droege, K. L., and Howes, C. (1991, April). *The effect of toy structure and center location on preschoolers' pretend play*. Paper presented at the biennial meeting of the Society for Research in Child Development, Seattle, WA.

Eisenberg, N., Lundy, T., Shell, R., and Roth, K. (1985). Children's justifications for their adult and peer-directed compliant (prosocial and nonsocial) behaviors. *Developmental Psychology, 21*, 325–331.

Hart, C. H., DeWolf, D. M., Wozniak, P., and Burts, D. C. (1992). Maternal and paternal disciplinary styles: Relations with preschoolers' playground behavioral orientations and peer status. *Child Development, 63*, 879–892.

Henninger, M. L. (1980). Free play behaviors of nursery school children in an indoor and outdoor environment. In P. Wilkinson (Ed.), *Environments of play* (pp. 100–118). New York: St. Martin's Press.

Hinde, R. A., Stevenson-Hinde, J., and Tamplin, A. (1985). Characteristics of 3- to 4-year-olds assessed at home and their interactions in preschool. *Developmental Psychology, 21*, 120–140.

Humphreys, A. P., and Smith, P. K. (1984). Rough-and-tumble in preschool and playground. In P. Smith (Ed.), *Play in animals and humans* (pp. 241–270). London: Blackwell.

King, N. R. (1987). Elementary school play: Theory and research. In J. H. Block and N. R. King (Eds.), *School play: A source book* (pp. 143–166). New York: Garland.

Koyama, T., and Smith, P. K. (1991). Showing-off behavior of nursery children. *Aggressive Behaviour, 17,* 1–10.

Ladd, G. W., and Hart, C. H. (1992). Creating informal play opportunities: Are parents' and preschoolers' initiations related to children's competence with peers? *Developmental Psychology, 28,* 1179–1187.

Ladd, G. W., Profilet, S. M., and Hart, C. H. (1992). Parents' management of children's peer relations: Facilitating and supervising children's activities in the peer culture. In R. D. Parke and G. W. Ladd (Eds.), *Family-peer relationships: Modes of linkage.* Hillsdale, NJ: Erlbaum.

Marshall, H. R., and McCandless, B. R. (1957). A study in prediction of social behavior of preschool children. *Child Development, 28,* 149–159.

Pellegrini, A. D. (1987). Children on playgrounds: A review of "What's out there." *Children's Environments Quarterly, 4,* 2–7.

––––––. (1989). Elementary school children's rough-and-tumble play. *Early Childhood Research Quarterly, 4,* 245–260.

––––––. (1991, April). *Popular boys' rough-and-tumble play, group composition, and social competence.* Paper presented at the biennial meeting of the Society for Research in Child Development, Seattle, WA.

Phyfe-Perkins, E. (1980). Children's behavior in preschool settings: A review of research concerning the influence of the physical environment. In L. C. Katz (Ed.), *Current Topics in Early Childhood Education (Vol. 3).* Norwood, NJ: Ablex.

Piaget, J. (1962). *Play, dreams, and imitation in childhood.* London: Heinemann.

Prescott, E., Jones, E., Kritchevsky, S., Milich, C., and Haselhoef, E. (1975). *Assessment of child rearing environments: An ecological approach,* Parts I and II. Pasadena, CA: Pacific Oaks.

Putallaz, M., and Wasserman, A. (1989). Children's naturalistic entry behavior and sociometric status: A developmental perspective. *Developmental Psychology, 25,* 297–305.

Rubin, K. H. Maioni, T. L., and Hornung, M. (1976). Free play behaviors in middle- and lower-class preschoolers: Parten and Piaget revisited. *Child Development, 47,* 414–419.

Sanders, K. M., and Harper, L. V. (1976). Free-play fantasy behavior in preschool children: Relations among gender, age, season, and location. *Child Development, 47,* 1182–1185.

Smilansky, S. (1968). *The effects of sociodramatic play on disadvantaged preschool children.* New York: Wiley.

Smith, P. K. (1989). The role of rough-and-tumble play in the development of social competence: Theoretical perspectives and empirical evidence. In B. Schneider, G. Attil, J. Nadel, and R. Weissberg (Eds.), *Social competence in developmental perspectives* (pp. 239–255). Norwell, MA: Kluwer Academic Publishers Group.

Smith, P. K., and Connolly, K. (1976). Social and aggressive behavior in preschool children as a function of crowding. *Social Science Information, 16,* 601–620.

Vaughn, B. E., and Waters, E. (1981). Attention structure, sociometric status, and dominance: Interrelations, behavioral correlates, and relationships to social competence. *Developmental Psychology, 17,* 275–288.

NAME INDEX

433

SUBJECT INDEX

445